INVICTA

REFERENCE COLLECTION

0753408147

BURNIE, D.

The Concise Animal   591.03

Encylopedia

THE CONCISE
ANIMAL
ENCYCLOPEDIA

KINGFISHER
Kingfisher Publications Plc
New Penderel House
283–288 High Holborn
London WC1V 7HZ
www.kingfisherpub.com

First published as The Kingfisher Illustrated Animal Encyclopedia by Kingfisher Publications Plc 2000

Reprinted in a revised format by Kingfisher Publications Plc 2003
2 4 6 8 10 9 7 5 3 1
1TR/0203/SF/*RD SOT(RNB)/157MA

A CIP catalogue record for this book is available from
the British Library.

ISBN 0 7534 0814 7

Printed in China

Cover design by Jo Brown

FOR BOOKWORK

Project editor	Louise Pritchard
Assistant editor	Annabel Blackledge
Art editor	Jill Plank
Assistant designer	Yolanda Belton
Picture researcher	Alan Plank

FOR KINGFISHER

Project editor	Katie Puckett
Managing editor	Miranda Smith
Art editor	Mike Davis
Artwork research	Christopher Cowlin
Artwork archivists	Wendy Allison, Steve Robinson
DTP co-ordinator	Nicky Studdart
Production controller	Jacquie Horner
Indexer	Sylvia Potter

THE CONCISE
ANIMAL
ENCYCLOPEDIA

WRITTEN BY DAVID BURNIE

KINGFISHER

CONTENTS

Bluebottle
(Calliphora vomitoria)

Red piranha
(Serrasalmus nattereri)

Oyster drill   Common
(Ocenbra   periwinkle
erinacea)   *(Littorina
                   littorea)*

Common frog   Fire salamander
(Rana temporaria) *(Salamandra salamandra)*

REPTILES

Eurasian robin
(*Erithacus rubecula*)

Common iguana
(*Iguana iguana*)

MAMMALS

BIRDS

Giraffe
(*Giraffa camelopardalis*)

INTRODUCTION

OUR PLANET IS HOME TO A VAST AND VARIED COLLECTION
OF ANIMALS. THEY LIVE EVERYWHERE, FROM THE TOPS OF
MOUNTAINS TO THE DEPTHS OF THE SEA, AND THEY HAVE
ALL DEVELOPED THEIR OWN METHODS OF SURVIVAL.

Animals are all around us, so it is easy to think that we know exactly what animals are. But the animal kingdom is amazingly varied. Some animals have fur or feathers, others have shells or scales, while many have no hard body parts at all. Animals often have eyes, ears and legs, but there are many creatures that survive perfectly well without them. Many small animals spend most of their lives fastened in one place, and some microscopic ones can even survive being dried out or frozen solid.

Despite their differences, all animals share two key features. Firstly, unlike the simplest living things which are made of only a single cell, animals' bodies are made of lots of cells. These cells work together, like a team, carrying out the different tasks necessary to stay alive. Secondly, unlike plants, animals need to eat. Food is their fuel, and many cannot survive for long if it starts to run out.

Animals are also the only living things that have muscles and nerves. This allows them to move parts of themselves, and also to sense their surroundings. Animals with complicated nervous systems, such as mammals and birds, react more quickly than any other living things. Using their well-developed brains, they can keep track of things happening around them, and make split-second decisions to catch food or avoid being eaten.

Shield bug
(Sehirus bicolor)

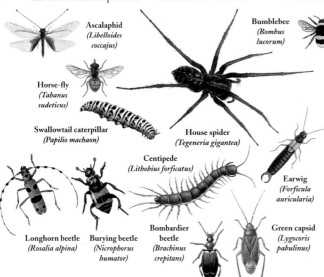

Ascalaphid
(Libelloides coccajus)

Horse-fly
(Tabanus sudeticus)

Swallowtail caterpillar
(Papilio machaon)

Centipede
(Lithobius forficatus)

Longhorn beetle
(Rosalia alpina)

Burying beetle
(Nicrophorus humator)

Bombardier beetle
(Brachinus crepitans)

House spider
(Tegeneria gigantea)

Bumblebee
(Bombus lucorum)

Earwig
(Forficula auricularia)

Green capsid
(Lygocoris pabulinus)

HOW MANY ANIMALS?

When scientists first started to classify animals (see pages 8-11), they thought that there might be several thousand different kinds on Earth. Since then, they have found that animal life is far richer than anyone had imagined. Already, more than two million types of animals have been discovered and classified. The true total will probably never be known, but some scientists think it could be 30 million, or even as high as one hundred million.

Mammals and birds make up only a small proportion of this huge figure. Although they are spread all over the globe and are often large and conspicuous, they are outnumbered many times by much smaller animals, such as insects, spiders and worms. One bucketful of garden soil can contain more than a million tiny roundworms and, throughout the world, the total number of these animals runs into thousands of billions. However, because animals like these are small and difficult to see, we hardly notice that they are there.

ABOVE *Chinchillas* (Chinchilla laniger) *live on rocky slopes on high mountains. Their thick fur helps to keep them warm in the harsh climate.*

FITTING IN

Most animals are extremely particular about where they live. For example, brine shrimps always live in salty lakes, while blue morpho butterflies live in tropical rainforests. Homes like these are called habitats, and they provide everything that an animal needs in order to survive.

Like animals themselves, habitats are amazingly varied. They include grasslands and forests, as well as deserts, mountains, caves, oceans and the deepest part of the seabed. Some animals even live inside others – a living habitat that provides shelter and food.

In each habitat, animals have features that are specially adapted to help them to survive. They may have strong legs for running or jumping, or poisonous stings for defending themselves or killing their prey. They also behave in a particular way that is suitable for living in that habitat.

All these features develop through evolution, which works through a process called natural selection. This ensures that parents with the features most useful for survival leave the most young. As a result, the useful features become more common, and each species slowly changes, or evolves, over time. Evolution started more than three-and-a-half million years ago, when life on Earth began, and it is still continuing today.

ANIMALS IN DANGER

During Earth's long history, evolution has produced many new kinds of animals. At the same time, many species have become extinct. In nature, extinction is usually a rare event, but in recent times it has become much more common.

Some of the world's largest and most impressive animals, such as the tiger, black rhino and giant panda, are now so rare that they are endangered. In just 10 or 20 years' time, the only place to see them may be in zoos. Many other animals will be in serious trouble if their numbers continue to fall.

Animals are in danger for many reasons, and most of these are to do with humans. People collect animals as pets, and hunt them for food and for 'fun'. They take over and destroy their habitats, leaving the animals with nowhere to live. We must look after the animals we have left, before it is too late.

ABOVE *Illegal hunting and a shrinking habitat has threatened the tiger* (Panthera tigris) *and the numbers left in the wild are diminishing rapidly.*
LEFT *Like many kinds of marsupial, the quokka* (Setonix brachyurus) *has been harmed by artificial changes to its habitat.*

CLASSIFICATION

TO STUDY LIVING THINGS, SCIENTISTS ORGANIZE, OR CLASSIFY, THEM INTO GROUPS. THE GROUPS WORK LIKE FOLDERS IN A GIGANTIC FILING SYSTEM. THEY SHOW HOW LIVING THINGS ARE RELATED BY EVOLUTION, AND WHERE THEY BELONG IN THE NATURAL WORLD.

On these two pages, you can see how scientists classify a single animal – the Eurasian green treefrog. The diagram below shows all the groups to which the frog belongs, starting with the largest and ending with the smallest. The largest groups that animals are divided into are called kingdoms, and the smallest are called species. Most biologists classify living things into five kingdoms, but classification can change as new discoveries are made.

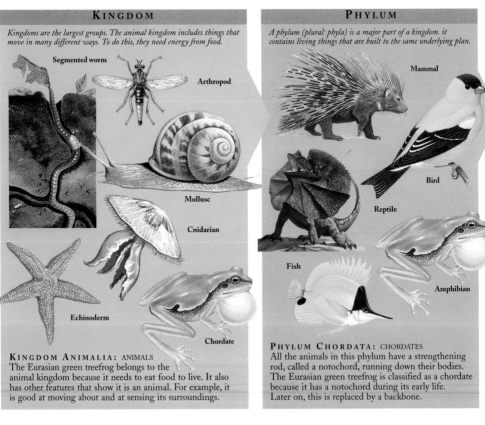

KINGDOM

Kingdoms are the largest groups. The animal kingdom includes things that move in many different ways. To do this, they need energy from food.

Segmented worm

Arthropod

Mollusc

Cnidarian

Echinoderm

Chordate

KINGDOM ANIMALIA: ANIMALS
The Eurasian green treefrog belongs to the animal kingdom because it needs to eat food to live. It also has other features that show it is an animal. For example, it is good at moving about and at sensing its surroundings.

PHYLUM

A phylum (plural: phyla) is a major part of a kingdom. it contains living things that are built to the same underlying plan.

Mammal

Bird

Reptile

Fish

Amphibian

PHYLUM CHORDATA: CHORDATES
All the animals in this phylum have a strengthening rod, called a notochord, running down their bodies. The Eurasian green treefrog is classified as a chordate because it has a notochord during its early life. Later on, this is replaced by a backbone.

KINGDOMS OF THE LIVING WORLD

MONERANS
Monerans include bacteria and other kinds of microscopic life. They are the smallest living things, and also the simplest and the toughest. Monerans were the first living things on Earth.

PROTISTS
Like monerans, protists have just a single cell, but they are larger and more complicated. This kingdom includes protozoans – tiny creatures that behave like animals – and also creatures that behave more like plants.

FUNGI
Fungi live on living things or their dead remains, and they grow tiny threads that spread through their food. Most fungi are microscopic, but some are easy to see because they grow mushrooms and toadstools when they reproduce.

PLANTS
Instead of eating food, plants live by capturing the energy in sunlight. They use this energy to build up the substances that they need. Unlike monerans and protists, they have lots of cells. Plants are essential for animal life because they provide them with food. If there were no plants, almost all the world's animals, including meat-eaters, would soon die out.

ANIMALS
The animal kingdom contains living things that have many cells and eat food. This kingdom is more varied than any of the other four, and it contains more species than all the others put together. Because animals do not need sunlight to survive, they can live in a great range of habitats, including caves, mountains and the ocean depths.

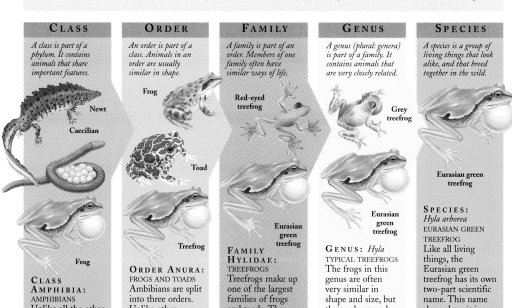

CLASS	ORDER	FAMILY	GENUS	SPECIES
A class is part of a phylum. It contains animals that share important features.	*An order is part of a class. Animals in an order are usually similar in shape.*	*A family is part of an order. Members of one family often have similar ways of life.*	*A genus (plural: genera) is part of a family. It contains animals that are very closely related.*	*A species is a group of living things that look alike, and that breed together in the wild.*

CLASS AMPHIBIA: AMPHIBIANS
Unlike all the other chordates, animals that are classified as amphibians spend their lives partly in water and partly on land, and they need to stay moist to survive. The Eurasian green treefrog is like this.

ORDER ANURA: FROGS AND TOADS
Ambibians are split into three orders. Unlike other amphibians, frogs and toads do not have tails, which makes them quite easy to identify. The Eurasian green treefrog is a typical member of this group, with long hind legs.

FAMILY HYLIDAE: TREEFROGS
Treefrogs make up one of the largest families of frogs and toads. The members of this family, including the Eurasian green treefrog, have flat toe-pads that help them to climb and to stick to leaves. They can be small, but the males often have loud calls.

GENUS: *Hyla* TYPICAL TREEFROGS
The frogs in this genus are often very similar in shape and size, but their colours and calls help in telling them apart. This genus contains about 250 species, which is about four-fifths of the total in the treefrog family. These frogs live in Europe, Asia and the Americas.

SPECIES: *Hyla arborea* EURASIAN GREEN TREEFROG
Like all living things, the Eurasian green treefrog has its own two-part scientific name. This name shows how it is classified, and which frogs are its closest relatives. Unlike common names, scientific names are written in Latin and can be understood by scientists all over the world.

THE ANIMAL KINGDOM

On these two pages you can see how all the animals in this book fit into the animal kingdom. Each 'folder' contains a distinct group of animals, and the folders are arranged to show which groups are most closely related. On this page you can find out about invertebrates, or animals that do not have backbones. On the opposite page are vertebrates and their relatives.

Subphylum

Class

Phylum

SIMPLE ANIMALS
(Several phyla)

Animals without heads or specialized sense organs, such as sponges, rotifers and moss animals, or bryozoans. Some are microscopic, others easily visible with the naked eye.

CNIDARIANS
(Phylum Cnidaria)

Animals with bag-like or bell-shaped bodies and mouths that are surrounded by stinging tentacles. They include jellyfish, sea anemones and corals, and most of them live in the sea.

FLATWORMS
(Phylum Platyhelminthes)

Animals with paper-thin, flat bodies with no legs. They move by sliding or swimming. Most flatworms live in water or damp places, but some live inside other animals.

ROUNDWORMS
(Phylum Nematoda)

Worms with cylindrical bodies covered by a hard outer 'skin'. Roundworms live in a huge variety of habitats, including soil and also inside a wide range of other living things.

SEGMENTED WORMS
(Phylum Annelida)

Worms whose bodies are divided up into rings, or segments. They include earthworms, and many other species that live in the soil, in fresh water or in the sea.

MOLLUSCS
(Phylum Mollusca)

Animals with soft bodies, often with a shell. They include snails, scallops and octopuses. Most live in water or damp places.

ECHINODERMS
(Phylum Echinodermata)

Sea animals whose bodies are often divided into five identical parts. They include starfish, sea urchins and sea cucumbers. They live in water, from the shallows to the greatest depths.

ARTHROPODS
(Phylum Arthropoda)

Animals that are covered by a body-case, or exoskeleton, and that have several pairs of rigid legs that bend at joints. Arthropods live in almost every habitat on Earth.

CRUSTACEANS
(Subphylum Crustacea)

Arthropods that have two pairs of feelers, or antennae. Crustaceans include crabs, lobsters, shrimps and woodlice. A few live on land, but most live in water.

CHELICERATES
(Subphylum Chelicerata)

Arthropods that have a body divided into two parts, and that feed with mouthparts called chelicerae. Unlike other arthropods, they do not have antennae.

ARACHNIDS
(Class Arachnida)

Animals that have four pairs of walking legs. Arachnids include spiders, scorpions, ticks and mites. Most of them live on land.

SEA SPIDERS
(Class Pycnogonida)

Animals with narrow bodies and slender legs that live in the sea. Like true spiders, they have small mouths, and usually four pairs of legs.

HORSESHOE CRABS
(Class Merostomata)

Sea animals with horseshoe-shaped bodies and long tails. They live in shallow coastal water, and often come ashore to lay their eggs.

UNIRAMIANS
(Subphylum Uniramia)

Arthropods that have a single pair of antennae, and pairs of unbranched legs. Most uniramians live on land, although some species live in fresh water.

CENTIPEDES AND MILLIPEDES
(Class Myriopoda)

Long-bodied arthropods that have hard exoskeletons and many pairs of legs. Centipedes have one pair of legs per body segment; millipedes have two pairs.

INSECTS
(Class Insecta)

Animals with three pairs of legs and often two pairs of wings. This gigantic class of animals contains more species than any other.

CHORDATES
(Phylum Chordata)

Animals that have a reinforcing rod called a notochord running down their bodies. The notochord works like an internal strut, anchoring muscles that make the body move. Like all the animals on the opposite page, the simplest chordates do not have backbones. However, most chordates do have a backbone, and it forms part of a complete internal skeleton.

SIMPLE CHORDATES
(Subphyla Urochordata and Cephalochordata)

Chordates that have a notochord, but not a backbone. They include lancelets, sea squirts and jelly-like animals that drift in the sea. They all live in water.

VERTEBRATES
(Subphylum Vertebrata)

Chordates with a backbone and a complete internal skeleton. Compared to most other animals, vertebrates are intelligent, with well-developed nervous systems and large brains.

JAWLESS FISH
(Class Agnatha)

Fish with eel-like bodies, jawless sucker-like mouths and scaleless skin. They include lampreys, which often feed on living fish, and hagfish, which eat dead remains. Unlike cartilaginous and bony fish, jawless fish do not have paired fins.

CARTILAGINOUS FISH
(Class Chondroichthyes)

Fish with skeletons that are made of cartilage instead of bone. They have rough skin and stiff fins. They include sharks, skates and rays. Most of them live in the sea.

BONY FISH
(Class Osteichthyes)

Fish that have bony skeletons, and skin that is usually covered by thin overlapping scales. Bony fish live in all kinds of watery places, from freshwater ponds to the deep sea, and they are the most numerous vertebrates on Earth. They usually lay eggs that are fertilized in the water.

AMPHIBIANS
(Class Amphibia)

Animals that live partly in water and partly on land, and that change shape as they grow up. Amphibians include frogs, toads, salamanders, newts and caecilians. As adults, they are all predators, hunting other animals for food.

REPTILES
(Class Reptilia)

Animals with scaly skin that live on land or in water. They include lizards, crocodiles and snakes. Most lay eggs, but some give birth to live young.

BIRDS
(Class Aves)

Warm-blooded animals that have wings, toothless beaks, and bodies covered with feathers. Most birds can fly, but several kinds are flightless. All birds lay eggs and many feed their young.

MAMMALS
(Class Mammalia)

Warm-blooded animals that have fur or hair, and that feed their young on milk. Most mammals develop inside their mothers' bodies or in a special pouch, but a tiny number hatch out from eggs. Most mammals have legs, but some have flippers or wings, allowing them to swim or fly.

SIMPLE ANIMALS

ANIMALS ARE MADE UP OF MANY CELLS AND THEY TAKE IN FOOD TO LIVE. THE WORLD'S FIRST ANIMALS EVOLVED FROM SINGLE-CELLED ORGANISMS CALLED PROTOZOANS ABOUT ONE BILLION YEARS AGO.

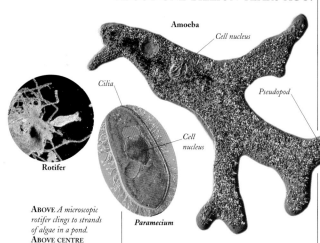

Amoeba

Cell nucleus

Cilia

Pseudopod

Cell nucleus

Rotifer

Paramecium

ABOVE *A microscopic rotifer clings to strands of algae in a pond.*
ABOVE CENTRE
A paramecium *has just one cell, which is controlled by its nucleus.*
ABOVE RIGHT *An amoeba's cell changes shape to move. It flows forwards, putting out lobes called pseudopods, or false feet.*

Many kinds of protozoan still exist today and almost all of them live in water. The simplest animals also dwell in water. Unlike protozoans, their bodies contain large numbers of cells. Many of them have complex body parts to help them to move and catch their food. Most simple animals can be seen only under a microscope but some, such as sponges, are large enough to see with the naked eye.

AMOEBA
Composed of only one cell, amoebas are protozoans with no fixed shape. Some build themselves tiny shells, but many have no hard parts at all and look like microscopic blobs of jelly. Amoebas move by making part of their cell flow in the direction they want to travel. The rest of the cell slowly follows. To feed, amoebas flow around other micro-organisms and then engulf them. To reproduce, they tear themselves in two.

SCIENTIFIC NAME	*Amoeba* and other genera
DISTRIBUTION	Worldwide
SIZE	Up to 0.7mm long

PARAMECIUM
This tiny, slipper-shaped protozoan is common in lakes, ponds and puddles. It moves constantly and speeds along by beating rows of microscopic hairs, called cilia, which work like miniature oars. *Paramecium* feeds on bacteria and other micro-organisms. It collects its food by sweeping it into a groove-shaped mouth.

SCIENTIFIC NAME	*Paramecium* species
DISTRIBUTION	Worldwide
SIZE	About 0.15mm long

TRICHOPLAX
This is probably the simplest animal in the world. It lives in sea water and looks like a tiny pancake composed of lots of cells. It creeps over rocks, digesting any algae that live on them. Although it is more complicated than a protozoan, *Trichoplax* does not have specialized organs. It was discovered in 1883 in an aquarium in Austria, and was originally thought to be an animal larva.

SCIENTIFIC NAME	*Trichoplax adhaerens*
DISTRIBUTION	Unknown
SIZE	About 3mm across

ROTIFER
Also known as wheel animals, rotifers are common in rivers, lakes, puddles and gutters. They are among the smallest animals that exist. Rotifers feed on protozoans and other tiny life-forms, which they catch by beating a crown of cilia to draw water into their mouths. In dry times, rotifers are dormant. Once in this state, they can stay inactive for many years.

SCIENTIFIC NAME	*Rotifera* and other genera
DISTRIBUTION	Worldwide
SIZE	About 0.25mm across

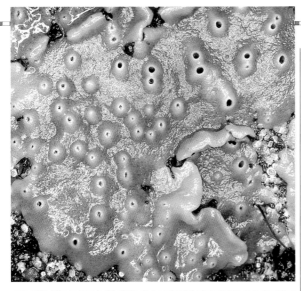

LEFT *The surface of a breadcrumb sponge looks like a volcano-studded landscape. Each of the 'volcanoes' pumps out water that the sponge has filtered for food.*

BREADCRUMB SPONGE

Most sponges have a skeleton made of tiny slivers of minerals and they grow into a great variety of shapes. The breadcrumb sponge is an encrusting species. This means that it forms in flat mats over rocks. It gets its name from its texture, because it crumbles into small pieces if touched. Like all sponges, it feeds by sucking in water through small openings on its surface. After filtering the water for food, it then pumps it back out of larger openings.

SCIENTIFIC NAME	*Halichondria panicea*
DISTRIBUTION	Atlantic Ocean, Mediterranean Sea, Pacific Ocean
SIZE	Up to 20cm across

WATER BEAR

These minute animals live mainly in puddles and small freshwater pools. They have a barrel-shaped body and clamber about on eight stubby legs, a bit like a bear. Water bears, also called tardigrades, feed on the juices of mosses and other plants, and sometimes on other animals. They need moisture to stay active, but they can curl up and hibernate for up to 25 years if their habitat dries out. A water bear in this drought-resistant state is called a tun.

Water bear under a microscope

SCIENTIFIC NAME	*Macrobiotus* and other genera
DISTRIBUTION	Worldwide
SIZE	Up to 1mm long

MOSS ANIMAL

Also known as bryozoans, moss animals are found in both fresh and salt water. They use tiny tentacles to collect particles of food. Instead of moving about, moss animals live in clusters of box-like cases. In some species, these cases form flat sheets that attach to shells and seaweeds. The cases of other varieties look like plant leaves spreading out in the water. These clusters are sometimes washed up on beaches after storms.

SCIENTIFIC NAME	*Membranipora* and other genera
DISTRIBUTION	Worldwide
SIZE	Typical cluster about 10cm high

Sponge

Jellyfish

Earthworm

Beetle

INVERTEBRATES

More than 97 per cent of the animal species on Earth are invertebrates. An invertebrate is any animal that does not have a backbone. Some are soft-bodied, but others are protected by a shell or body-case. Invertebrates were the first animals to appear on Earth and they live in all kinds of habitat, from caves and the deep-sea floor to the slopes of the highest mountains. Biologists classify invertebrates into about 30 major groups, or phyla. Four examples are shown here.

SPONGES
Unlike other invertebrates, sponges have a skeleton made of microscopic slivers of minerals.

CNIDARIANS
Jellyfish and other cnidarians have a body made of two layers of cells. All cnidarians live in water and many can sting.

SEGMENTED WORMS
Like many invertebrates, earthworms and their relatives have a body divided into repeated units, or segments.

ARTHROPODS
Insects, such as beetles, and other arthropods have an all-over body-case of hard plates that meet at flexible joints.

CNIDARIANS

THESE WATER-DWELLING ANIMALS HAVE
A HOLLOW OR BELL-SHAPED BODY AND A
MOUTH THAT IS RINGED BY TENTACLES. THEY
INCLUDE JELLYFISH, SEA ANEMONES AND
CORALS, AS WELL AS LESS FAMILIAR ANIMALS
SUCH AS SIPHONOPHORES AND SEA PENS.

Common jellyfish

There are about 10,000 species of cnidarian. A few are found in fresh water but most live in the sea. A cnidarian's tentacles are highly sensitive, and are armed with batteries of stinging cells called nematocysts. If the tentacles brush against something edible, microscopic poison-tipped threads explode out of the nematocysts and into the prey.

Sea pen

ABOVE *The exposed tip of a sea pen is crowded with stinging polyps along two sides of a central 'stem'.*
ABOVE RIGHT *A common jellyfish has four violet reproductive organs in the centre of its 'bell'.*
RIGHT *A Portuguese man-of-war preys on fish and other sea animals.*

Portuguese man-of-war

SEA PEN
The sea pen looks like an old-fashioned quill pen, which is how it gets its name. A sea pen consists of lots of separate animals, called polyps, that live in a group. The lower part of a sea pen is anchored in sand or mud. The upper part contains lots of feeding polyps, which use their tentacles to catch drifting food. Some sea pens are more than 1.5m high, but most are smaller than this.

SCIENTIFIC NAME	*Pennatula* and other genera
DISTRIBUTION	Worldwide
SIZE	Typical colony about 40cm high

PORTUGUESE MAN-OF-WAR
With its gas-filled float, the Portuguese man-of-war drifts great distances in the wind, like a miniature sailing ship. Although it looks like a jellyfish, it is actually a siphonophore – a floating collection of cnidarians living together permanently. One forms the float, while others sting, digest food or take part in reproduction. The man-of-war's poisonous tentacles trail beneath the float as it drifts along, and can be up to 20m in length. They have powerful stings that have been known to kill people who become tangled up in them.

SCIENTIFIC NAME	*Physalia physalis*
DISTRIBUTION	Warm seas worldwide
SIZE	Up to 30cm across

COMMON JELLYFISH
Like most jellyfish, this blue species pushes itself through the water by contracting its bell-shaped body. Sea water is sucked into the 'bell', then forced back out, propelling the jellyfish through the water. These jellyfish are weak swimmers and they often become stranded on beaches by the

LEFT Dwarfed by their much larger parent, young beadlet anemones stretch out their tentacles to feed. If they get too crowded, beadlet anemones sometimes fight. This helps them to space themselves out in their rocky home.

BY-THE-WIND SAILOR

Like the Portuguese man-of-war, this animal is blown along by the wind. It has short tentacles, a flat, air-filled float and a single upright 'sail'. By-the-wind sailors feed on small sea animals and often drift in swarms that can be more than 100km wide. In the tropics, they are often blown ashore during storms, and millions can sometimes be seen on a single beach.

SCIENTIFIC NAME *Vellela vellela*

DISTRIBUTION Warm seas worldwide

SIZE Up to 8cm across

By-the-wind sailor
floating on the water

SEA GOOSEBERRY

Although they are similar in appearance to jellyfish, sea gooseberries are not cnidarians. They belong to a group of animals called ctenophores. They have round, jelly-like bodies and two long, slender tentacles, which they trail in the water to catch food. Sea gooseberries move by beating tiny hairs, or cilia, arranged in comb-like rows along their bodies. If they are disturbed – for example by being touched or shaken – they produce flashes of light that can be seen several metres away. They live close to the surface, and are sometimes washed up on the shore.

SCIENTIFIC NAME *Pleurobrachia and other genera*

DISTRIBUTION Worldwide

SIZE Typical length 3cm, excluding tentacles

Sea gooseberry
flashing its light

TOP This surface view of a by-the-wind sailor shows its vertical sail and cluster of hanging tentacles.
ABOVE Sea gooseberries look beautiful underwater but, when they are hauled out, they become shapeless bits of jelly.

tide. The common jellyfish attacks small fish using stinging tentacles that trail from the edge of its 'bell'. It pulls the paralysed prey into its mouth using larger, frilly tentacles. The stings are painful, though not dangerous to humans.

SCIENTIFIC NAME *Aurelia aurita*

DISTRIBUTION Atlantic Ocean, Pacific Ocean, Indian Ocean, Mediterranean Sea

SIZE Up to 30cm across

AUSTRALIAN BOX JELLYFISH

This medium-sized jellyfish is so poisonous that swimmers can die within minutes of becoming entangled in its tentacles. It is transparent, which makes it difficult to see. Australian box jellyfish start life in shallow water, near to river mouths. During the rainy season, they are swept out along the coast, often past places where people swim. Box jellyfish get their name from the shape of their bodies, which are cubic rather than bell-shaped. When their tentacles are stretched, they can measure up to 2m in length.

SCIENTIFIC NAME *Chironex fleckeri*

DISTRIBUTION Indian Ocean, Pacific Ocean

SIZE Up to 25cm across

BEADLET ANEMONE

Many sea anemones look more like colourful plants than animals. Some anchor themselves in the sand but most, like the beadlet anemone, spend their lives fastened to something solid – usually rock. They use their stinging tentacles to catch small animals swimming nearby. The beadlet anemone lives on the part of the shore that is often exposed at low tides, but it is expert at surviving out of the water. When the tide goes out, it pulls in its tentacles and fills its body cavities with water. This stops it from drying out when it is exposed to the air.

SCIENTIFIC NAME *Actinia equina*

DISTRIBUTION Atlantic Ocean, Mediterranean Sea

SIZE Up to 7cm high

ABOVE *This staghorn coral* (Acropora nasuta) *forms a dense underwater 'forest' that shelters a wide variety of animals. Like the coral itself, many of these animals feed at night.*

STAGHORN CORAL

Corals consist of tiny, soft-bodied animals called polyps, which often live in large groups. In reef building species, such as staghorn corals, the polyps make hard, chalky cases to protect themselves, and these cases cement together to form a reef. New polyps can grow from buds, but corals also reproduce by shedding eggs into the sea. Coral polyps feed on drifting larvae and other tiny animals, which they catch with their stinging tentacles. They also get food from microscopic algae that live inside their cells. The shape of a coral colony depends on the way in which the polyps grow. In staghorn corals, the colony branches repeatedly, making it look like a stag's horns, or antlers, which is how the corals get their name. Staghorn corals are fragile and usually grow in sheltered parts of a reef.

SCIENTIFIC NAME	*Acropora* species
DISTRIBUTION	Tropical seas worldwide
SIZE	Up to 1m high

RED CORAL

Unlike most corals, which have brightly coloured polyps set in a chalky-white skeleton, red coral has white polyps set in a black, pink or red skeleton. It grows on the shady sea floor, in water up to 200m deep.

SCIENTIFIC NAME	*Corallium rubrum*
DISTRIBUTION	Mediterranean Sea
SIZE	Up to 50cm high

BRAIN CORAL

With its round, deeply grooved surface, this slow-growing coral looks like a giant brain. It is formed by rows of polyps, with their tentacles arranged along the sides of their rows and their mouths forming a groove along the bottom. The coral's domed shape makes it strong enough to withstand pounding waves.

SCIENTIFIC NAME	*Symphyllia* and other genera
DISTRIBUTION	Tropical seas worldwide
SIZE	Up to 2m across

MUSHROOM CORAL

This coral consists of a single polyp and lives in sandy places on the seabed. Its tentacles point upwards to catch small animals that come within reach. Adult mushroom corals can move and, if upturned in a storm, can right themselves.

SCIENTIFIC NAME	*Fungia* species
DISTRIBUTION	Indian Ocean, Pacific Ocean
SIZE	Up to 25cm across

Orange sea fan coral
(*Synchiropus splendidus*)

Tentacles extended

Tentacles withdrawn

CORAL REEFS

Golden tubastrea coral
(*Tubastrea aurea*)

Some corals can live in cool, dark water, but all reef-building species need water that is bright, warm and clean. As these corals grow and die, their hard cases build into a pile that eventually forms a reef. The world's largest reef is the Great Barrier Reef off the coast of Queensland in Australia. It is more than 2,000km long and is the largest object ever built by living things. Coral reefs support a wide variety of sea-life, including sponges and certain fish that are immune to the corals' stings. The reefs provide food and some protection from predators.

FLATWORMS AND ROUNDWORMS

Tail sections full of eggs

A WORM IS ANY LONG, SOFT-BODIED ANIMAL WITHOUT LEGS. MANY WORMS SPEND THEIR LIVES IN WATER OR IN SOIL, BUT OTHER SPECIES ARE PARASITES, WHICH MEANS THEY LIVE ON OR IN OTHER LIVING THINGS.

Tapeworm

Flatworms are the simplest worms. They have a flat body, which can be paper thin. This group includes parasitic tapeworms and flukes as well as free-living species. Roundworms, or nematodes, have a cylindrical body. Many of them are parasites and they live in a wide range of animal hosts.

DOG TAPEWORM
Tapeworms are highly specialized flatworms that live parasitically inside a variety of animals including human beings. The dog tapeworm has a small round head equipped with several rows of hooks. Its ribbon-shaped body is divided into as many as 150 sections, each one containing thousands of eggs. The tapeworm uses its hooks to fasten itself to the inside of a dog's intestines, and lives by absorbing some of the food that the dog eats. As the tapeworm feeds, sections near the end of its body break away, carrying their eggs with them. New sections form behind the worm's head. Dog tapeworm eggs hatch if they are eaten by flea larvae. If a dog eats an infected flea, it too becomes infected with tapeworms.

SCIENTIFIC NAME *Dipylidium caninum*
DISTRIBUTION Worldwide
SIZE Up to 50cm long

SHEEP LIVER FLUKE
A fluke is a small parasitic flatworm that feeds on the blood or body of its host. The sheep liver fluke attacks sheep and cattle and can also infect people, making them seriously ill. Sheep liver flukes spread when their eggs are eaten by a pond snail. The eggs hatch into larvae, which eventually leave the snail. If they are eaten by a sheep, they move to its liver where they grow into adult flukes. Humans can catch liver flukes by eating unwashed watercress or other plants that grow where pond snails live.

Sheep liver fluke

SCIENTIFIC NAME *Fasciola hepatica*
DISTRIBUTION Worldwide
SIZE About 2cm long

CAT ROUNDWORM
Roundworms are thread-like worms with a slender body and a pointed mouth. The largest parasitic species, which live in whales, are up to 9m long, but most are much smaller than this. The cat roundworm lives in the intestines of cats. It passes from one cat to another when its eggs are eaten – usually in contaminated soil. Like its close relative the dog roundworm, it can hatch inside humans. This is dangerous, so hygiene is important around pet cats and dogs.

SCIENTIFIC NAME *Toxocara cati*
DISTRIBUTION Worldwide
SIZE Up to 15cm long

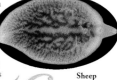

Roundworms

TOP *Tapeworms do not have eyes or mouths. They absorb all their food through their skin.*
CENTRE *Sheep liver flukes have a flattened body and a branching digestive system, which is clearly visible in their bodies.*
ABOVE *Adult cat roundworms live in a cat's intestines, but the young can live elsewhere in its body.*

SEGMENTED WORMS

WORMS WHOSE BODIES ARE DIVIDED UP
INTO RINGS OR SECTIONS ARE KNOWN AS
SEGMENTED WORMS, OR ANNELIDS. THEY
INCLUDE EARTHWORMS AND MANY SPECIES
THAT LIVE IN FRESH WATER OR IN THE SEA.

RIGHT
*These peacock
worms have
extended their
tentacles to collect
food from the water.*

S egmented worms usually have bristles along their
bodies, but some also have flaps that look like small
legs. They move by wriggling or by changing the
shape of their segments. There are at least 13,000 species
of segmented worm. Some rove about in search of food,
but many live in permanent tubes or burrows, collecting
anything edible that they find.

LEFT *Earthworms
have tiny bristles
along their bodies that
help them to push their
way through the soil.*

ABOVE *Sludge worms get
their bright red colour from
haemoglobin, a substance
that helps them to absorb
oxygen. Humans also have
haemoglobin in their blood.*

PALOLO WORM
The palolo worm lives in coral reefs, and spends
most of its life hidden in crevices. To reproduce,
it grows a special tail section packed with sperm
or eggs. On one night each year, the tail section
of all palolo worms breaks away and wriggles to
the surface of the water. At dawn, the sections
burst apart, the floating eggs are fertilized and
the worm's life-cycle starts anew.

SCIENTIFIC NAME	*Eunice viridis*
DISTRIBUTION	Pacific Ocean
SIZE	Up to 40cm long

SLUDGE WORM
These worms live in clusters on the bottom of
ponds and streams. They burrow into the mud
and live upside down, waving their bodies in the
water to collect oxygen. They are so efficient at
collecting oxygen that they can thrive in polluted
water, where oxygen levels are low.

SCIENTIFIC NAME	*Tubifex tubifex*
DISTRIBUTION	Europe, Asia, North America
SIZE	About 4cm long

COMMON EARTHWORM
Earthworms are some of the most useful animals
on Earth. As they tunnel into the ground, they
swallow particles of soil and digest any dead
remains that they contain. In damp weather, they
drag dead leaves underground and feed on them.
This way of feeding mixes up the soil, helping to
keep it fertile. Common earthworms are at their
most active in warm wet weather, when they
crawl to the surface to mate. Each worm has
both male and female reproductive organs.

SCIENTIFIC NAME	*Lumbricus terrestris*
DISTRIBUTION	Originally from Europe; introduced into many other parts of the world
SIZE	Up to 30cm long

MEDICINAL LEECH
Leeches are segmented worms that live in wet
places and often feed on blood. Their bodies are
flattened, with a sucker at each end, which they
use to move and to cling to animals while they
feed. A feeding leech produces a substance that
stops blood clotting. At one time, doctors used
medicinal leeches to 'bleed' patients regularly,
believing that blood loss could improve
people's health.

SCIENTIFIC NAME	*Hirudo medicinalis*
DISTRIBUTION	Europe
SIZE	Up to 15cm long

Leaf being dragged into the soil

Common earthworm in underground tunnel

Iridescent hairs

PEACOCK WORM

When it is feeding, this animal looks more like a flower than a worm. It lives underwater in a tube of mud and sand, which sticks up into the water from the seabed. To feed, it extends delicate tentacles from the top of the tube, trapping any edible particles that drift within its reach. If the peacock worm's feathery tentacles are touched, or if a shadow passes over it, it will instantly vanish into the safety of its tube.

SCIENTIFIC NAME *Sabella pavonina*

DISTRIBUTION Atlantic Ocean, Mediterranean Sea

SIZE Up to 25cm long, including tube

RAGWORM

These worms live in seashore mud. They wriggle along with the help of leg-like flaps, searching for shrimps and other small animals to eat. Unlike earthworms, ragworms have powerful jaws, and large ones can bite through human skin. Like lugworms, these animals are important for birds such as curlews, that have long beaks adapted for probing in the mud or sand for their food.

SCIENTIFIC NAME *Nereis diversicolor*

DISTRIBUTION Atlantic Ocean, Mediterranean Sea

SIZE Up to 12cm long

Ragworm

SEA MOUSE

Despite its name, this animal is not a mouse but a worm with an unusual appearance. Its body is covered with long bristles that look like golden-green fur and it has short stumpy flaps that work like feet. The sea mouse lives in shallow sea water, often quite close to the shore. It burrows its way through the sediment, feeding on small, soft-bodied animals, including other worms.

SCIENTIFIC NAME *Aphrodita aculeata*

DISTRIBUTION Atlantic Ocean, Mediterranean Sea

SIZE About 10cm long

LUGWORM

Like many other seashore worms, the lugworm lives in muddy sand. It builds a U-shaped burrow, strengthened with a lining of mucus, with two openings at the surface. The worm draws sand into the burrow through one opening. It digests any food in the sand, then ejects it through the other opening. At low tide, piles of mud show where these worms have been at work.

SCIENTIFIC NAME *Arenicola marina*

DISTRIBUTION Atlantic Ocean

SIZE Up to 20cm long

Lugworm

LEFT *Ragworms and lugworms both live on muddy shores, but only the lugworm burrows.* **BELOW** *The sea mouse lives on shores, near the low-tide mark.*

MOLLUSCS

AFTER ARTHROPODS (PAGES 32–89), MOLLUSCS MAKE UP THE SECOND LARGEST GROUP OF INVERTEBRATES, WITH MORE THAN 50,000 SPECIES. ALL MOLLUSCS HAVE A SOFT BODY AND MOST HAVE A CLOAK OF SKIN, CALLED A MANTLE, WHICH PRODUCES SUBSTANCES THAT FORM SHELL.

There are many varieties of mollusc. Some live on land, but the majority live in fresh water or in the sea. Molluscs include many small and slow-moving species, as well as the largest, fastest and most intelligent animals in the invertebrate world.

CHITONS AND TUSK SHELLS

These two small groups of molluscs contain animals that live in quite different ways. A chiton clings to rocks with a single sucker-shaped foot, and is the only mollusc with a shell made of eight separate plates. A tusk shell lives partly buried in the seabed, in deep and shallow water. Its pointed shell looks like a tiny elephant's tusk and has an opening at both ends. There are about 800 species of chiton and 350 species of tusk shell.

PURPLE OR GREEN CHITON

Even with colourful shell plates, this European chiton is well camouflaged for life on rocky shores. It moves slowly, grazing algae from the surface of rocks. The chiton's muscular sucker usually keeps it firmly in place but, if it does fall off a rock, it can curl up to protect itself.

SCIENTIFIC NAME	*Acanthochitona crinatus*
DISTRIBUTION	Atlantic Ocean, Mediterranean Sea
SIZE	Up to 1.3cm long

EUROPEAN TUSK SHELL

Tusk shells are the only molluscs that breathe through a hole in the rear end of their shells. The European tusk shell makes its home in deep water, so living animals are rarely seen, but empty tusk shells are often found washed up on the shore. The tusk shell anchors itself to the ocean floor with a single cone-shaped foot, which it can also use to pull itself into the sand to escape predators. Like other tusk shells, it feeds by probing the sand with 100 or more small tentacles. When a tentacle touches a particle of food, the animal uses it to pull the food towards its mouth.

SCIENTIFIC NAME	*Dentalium entalis*
DISTRIBUTION	Atlantic Ocean, Mediterranean Sea
SIZE	About 3cm long

ABOVE
This chiton is no larger than a fingernail, but some of its relatives are more than 30cm long.

SHELLS

Molluscs build their shells from the mineral calcium carbonate. The shell is laid down by the mantle and grows throughout its owner's life. Gastropods have a one-piece shell. As the animals grow, the shell extends, often forming a spiral shape around a central pillar. Bivalves (pages 26–29) have a two-part shell joined together by a hinge. In living molluscs, the outside of the shell is often covered by a thin, darker layer of material that stops acids in water from attacking the shell. In most species, the inside of the shell is smooth and shiny. It is made of a material called nacre, or mother-of-pearl.

Shell of a Roman snail
(Helix pomatia)

GASTROPODS

A gastropod is a mollusc with a single sucker-like foot and often a coiled or pointed shell. Four-fifths of the world's molluscs are gastropods. They feed on plants and animals using a mouthpart called a radula, which is packed with rows of tiny teeth. As the teeth at the front are worn away, newer ones take their place. Gastropods begin life as eggs. When land-dwellers hatch they look like small adults. Water-dwelling gastropods hatch as larvae and slowly change shape.

Thick coating of slime

Two pairs of tentacles

Garden snail on the move

GARDEN SNAIL

Across Europe, and in places where it has been introduced accidentally, this snail is a serious pest. At night, or after heavy rain, it rasps its way through soft-stemmed plants. During dry weather, it shuts itself up inside its shell, sealing off the opening with a 'door' made of dried mucus. Like most slugs and snails, garden snails have both male and female reproductive organs, so any two snails can mate. They lay clusters of milky-coloured eggs that are left to develop in the soil.

SCIENTIFIC NAME	Helix aspersa
DISTRIBUTION	Originally from Europe; introduced into many other parts of the world
SIZE	Body up to 8cm long

GREAT BLACK SLUG

Most slugs do not have shells. They move over the ground on a layer of slippery mucus, leaving a shiny trail. The great black slug has a varied diet, which includes rotting vegetation and the dead bodies of other slugs. It finds its food by touch and smell, using its sensitive tentacles.

SCIENTIFIC NAME	Arion ater
DISTRIBUTION	Europe
SIZE	Up to 15cm long

ABOVE *Like other land slugs, the great black slug has a breathing hole on its side, just behind its head.*
BELOW *Sliding on a layer of mucus, the banana slug can reach a top speed of about 0.006km/h.*

BANANA SLUG

This yellow or green slug is the largest land mollusc in North America. It lives in coniferous rainforests and other damp, shady places, where it feeds on fungi and decaying plants. Banana slugs lay about 100 eggs each year, and can live for five years.

SCIENTIFIC NAME	Ariolimax columbianus
DISTRIBUTION	Northwestern North America
SIZE	Up to 20cm long

GIANT AFRICAN SNAIL

This mollusc is the world's largest land-dwelling snail. It can weigh more than 800g and its shell may measure as much as 20cm long. The giant African snail has been introduced to other warm countries, sometimes as a source of food. It has now become one of Southeast Asia's most destructive agricultural pests.

SCIENTIFIC NAME	Achatina fulica
DISTRIBUTION	Originally from Africa; introduced into many other parts of the tropics
SIZE	Body up to 30cm long

Common
limpet
shell

Common
periwinkle
shell

COMMON LIMPET

Limpets live on exposed seashore rocks, where they are battered by the full force of the waves. Their shells are conical instead of coiled, which helps to make them extremely strong. When the tide is out, limpets clamp their shells tightly to the rock, but at high tide they loosen their grip and wander over the surface of the rock to feed. Using their microscopic teeth, they scrape away tiny seaweeds and other algae, roving up to 1m from their home. When the tide goes out, they return to the exact spot from which they set off.

SCIENTIFIC NAME   *Patella vulgata*

DISTRIBUTION   Atlantic Ocean, Mediterranean Sea

SIZE   Shell up to 6cm across

RED ABALONE

Abalones have a shell that coils in an unusual way. As the shell grows, it spirals outwards very quickly, so most of the shell consists of a single shallow turn. The shell has a series of holes that the animal uses for breathing, and the inside surface is covered in a layer of shimmering mother-of-pearl. The red abalone is one of the largest species. It was once an important source of food for native Americans living on the coast.

SCIENTIFIC NAME   *Haliotis rufescens*

DISTRIBUTION   Western coast of North America

SIZE   Shell up to 25cm long

COMMON PERIWINKLE

Periwinkles live on rocky shores where they feed on seaweeds and plant remains. At low tide, crowds of them shelter in rocky crevices. Like other water-dwelling gastropods, common winkles have a hard flap, called an operculum, at the back of their foot. When the winkle withdraws into its shell, the operculum fits over the entrance, sealing the creature inside.

SCIENTIFIC NAME   *Littorina littorea*

DISTRIBUTION   Atlantic Ocean, Mediterranean Sea

SIZE   Shell about 3cm high

COMMON WHELK

Whelks live on the seabed in water up to 100m deep and feed on the remains of dead animals. Common whelks lay large clusters of eggs, and their empty egg-cases are often washed up on the shore. Females can produce more than a million eggs, but only a few of them hatch. The rest are food for the developing young.

SCIENTIFIC NAME   *Buccinum undatum*

DISTRIBUTION   Atlantic Ocean

SIZE   Shell up to 12cm long

ABOVE *This abalone's head is hidden beneath the top edge of its shell.*
BELOW *Like many sea snails, the common whelk has a long tube, or siphon, through which it draws in water over its gills.*

Ridged shell

Operculum seals
the shell when the
whelk is inside

Siphon

Sensory tentacle

Sucker-like foot

SPIRE SHELL OR TOWER SHELL

This mollusc has a shell that turns much more tightly than most. This gives it a shape rather like a church spire, which is how it gets its name. It lives on the seabed, buried up to the tip of its shell in sand or mud. It feeds by filtering small particles of food from the water. Spire shells can be abundant, and when they die, their empty shells are often washed up on the shore. Different varieties live throughout the world's oceans, even in places where the water is very cold. *Turritella communis* lives as far north as Iceland, in the icy waters of the North Atlantic Ocean.

SCIENTIFIC NAME	*Turritella communis*
DISTRIBUTION	Atlantic Ocean, Mediterranean Sea
SIZE	Shell up to 6cm high

Oyster drill shell   Spire shell

OYSTER DRILL

Although this rough-shelled mollusc looks harmless, it is a patient and very efficient predator. It attacks oysters using its microscopic teeth to bore a small hole through their shells. This can take up to a week. After the oyster drill has broken through the tough shell of its victim, it feeds on the soft flesh inside. Oysters are not able to move so, once the oyster drill has started its deadly work, the oyster has no way of escaping or fighting back.

SCIENTIFIC NAME	*Ocenebra erinacea*
DISTRIBUTION	Atlantic Ocean, Mediterranean Sea
SIZE	Shell about 6cm high

VIOLET SEA SNAIL

This remarkable mollusc is one of the world's great oceanic travellers. It lives in the tropics and drifts far out to sea, suspended upside down beneath a mass of bubbles made of mucus. Violet sea snails feed on other drifting animals, such as the by-the-wind sailor (page 15). Their empty shells are often thrown up on beaches after they die but, because these are thin, they easily break.

SCIENTIFIC NAME	*Ianthina ianthina*
DISTRIBUTION	Warm seas worldwide
SIZE	Shell up to 2cm high

GREAT POND SNAIL

Most water-dwelling molluscs get oxygen from the water using organs called gills. The great pond snail is an exception because it has a lung and breathes air. Great pond snails feed on microscopic algae and animal remains, and are almost always found in still water. Like land snails, they have both male and female reproductive organs. Pond snails fasten their eggs to the leaves of underwater plants.

SCIENTIFIC NAME	*Lymnaea stagnalis*
DISTRIBUTION	Europe, Asia, North America
SIZE	Shell up to 5cm high

ABOVE *Pond snails are useful in aquariums. They scrape algae from the glass, helping to keep it clean.*

LEFT *The violet sea snail is practically unsinkable because the bubbles of its 'raft' harden soon after they form.*

QUEEN CONCH

When it is fully grown, a queen conch can weigh up to 2kg. Protected by its massively built shell, it lives on the seabed in shallow water where it feeds mainly on seaweeds. Like all conches, it has a hard plate that can seal it into its shell. It can also use this plate to lever itself across the ocean floor. Queen conches were once common, but their numbers have fallen because people have killed them to collect their shells.

SCIENTIFIC NAME	*Strombus gigas*
DISTRIBUTION	Caribbean Sea
SIZE	Up to 23cm long

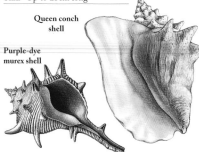

Queen conch
shell

Purple-dye
murex shell

PURPLE-DYE MUREX

There are many species of murex, some with spiny or branching shells. Most live close to the shore or on coral reefs, where they feed on animals, including other molluscs. The purple-dye murex gets its name from a purple dye that can be extracted from its body. During the days of the Roman Empire, the dye was used to stain clothes purple – a colour reserved for the emperor and other high-ranking officials.

SCIENTIFIC NAME	*Murex brandaris*
DISTRIBUTION	Mediterranean Sea
SIZE	Up to 7cm long

TIGER COWRIE

Cowries live mainly in tropical seas. Their shells have a long slit-shaped opening on the underside, and the upper surface is often shiny, with beautiful markings. The tiger cowrie is one of the largest species. Its milky-coloured shell is dappled with brown spots. People have collected cowrie shells for centuries and, in the past, have used some species as a form of money. A cowrie's shiny surface is not always visible on the live animal because it is often hidden by the mantle – the thin body layer that encloses the shell.

SCIENTIFIC NAME	*Cypraea tigris*
DISTRIBUTION	Indian Ocean, Pacific Ocean
SIZE	Up to 9cm long

TEXTILE CONE SHELL

Most gastropod molluscs are harmless, but cone shells are a deadly exception. They feed on fish and other animals, stabbing them with poisonous, harpoon-like mouthparts. A single, hollow tooth at the tip of the harpoon injects venom and is replaced each time it is used. There are more than 500 species of cone shell. Most live in coral reefs or in sand near the shore. The textile cone's venom is poisonous enough to kill anyone who touches it.

SCIENTIFIC NAME	*Conus textile*
DISTRIBUTION	Indian Ocean, Pacific Ocean
SIZE	Up to 9cm long

SEA SLUG

Slow-moving sea slugs are among the most colourful animals in the sea. They do not have shells, but their bright colours warn other animals that they are dangerous to attack. One reason for this is that they eat cnidarians (pages 14–16) and their skin stores stinging cells from their prey. If an animal tries to eat a sea slug, the stinging cells fire into its body. Sea slugs are most common in the tropics. *Chromodoris quadricolor* is common on Red Sea coral reefs, where many other eye-catching species are found.

SCIENTIFIC NAME	*Chromodoris quadricolor*
DISTRIBUTION	Red Sea, Indian Ocean
SIZE	About 5cm long

Sensory tentacles

Brightly coloured gills

ABOVE *Unlike land slugs, sea slugs do not have lungs. Instead, they breathe through tuft-like gills on their backs.*

BELOW *Sea hares often form lines to breed and each animal is fertilized by the one behind. The sea hare in front has laid a string of eggs on the rocky sea floor.*

Egg strings up to 20m long

SEA BUTTERFLY

These molluscs feed on algae or small animals. They live in the open ocean, and often form huge swarms close to the surface that can stretch for many kilometres. Like other gastropod molluscs, sea butterflies have a single foot, but the foot has two wing-like flaps that the animals beat to push themselves along. Some sea butterflies have a shell, but many do not. *Clione limacina* is one of the most common species. Its body is almost transparent, with a yellow tinge.

SCIENTIFIC NAME	*Clione limacina*
DISTRIBUTION	Arctic Sea, North Atlantic Ocean, northern Pacific Ocean
SIZE	Up to 2cm long

SEA HARE

The sea hare has a thin, fragile shell that is hidden away inside its humped body. It can move about in two different ways. It either creeps along using a muscular foot, or swims by moving the flaps that are normally folded over its back. The sea hare eats algae, and substances from its food give it its colour.

SCIENTIFIC NAME	*Aplysia punctata*
DISTRIBUTION	Atlantic Ocean
SIZE	Up to 14cm long

Narrow flaps of skin along the back

BIVALVES

There are about 15,000 species of bivalve, including mussels, oysters, clams and some animals that bore through wood or rock. Almost all live in water. Unlike gastropods, their shells are made up of two halves, called valves, hinged with an elastic ligament. Most bivalves have strong muscles that can tighten to lock their valves, securing them inside. Many spend their adult lives fixed in one place, and breed by releasing reproductive cells into the water. They use gills to breathe and to filter food from the water around them.

RIGHT This common mussel has opened its shell to feed. The mussel pumps water through two short, flattened siphons. One siphon sucks in the water and the other squirts it out.

COMMON MUSSEL

Like most bivalves, the common mussel starts life as a tiny larva drifting in the water. The larva eventually settles on a rock, where it slowly turns into an adult. Once it is on a solid surface, the mussel produces a sticky liquid that turns hard in water. This produces a collection of tough threads, called a byssus, which fixes the mussel in place. When the tide is high, mussels filter food from the surrounding water. At low tide, when they are exposed to the air, they keep their shells tightly shut. Mussels usually live on rocks in exposed places where the currents bring plenty of food their way.

SCIENTIFIC NAME	*Mytilus edulis*
DISTRIBUTION	Worldwide
SIZE	Up to 7.5cm long

FILTER FEEDING

Bivalves are not the only animals that live by filtering their food from the water. Other filter-feeding invertebrates include rotifers, sponges and many sea-dwelling worms. These animals all have body parts that work like sieves to collect small particles of food.

Blue whale *(Balaenoptera musculus)*

Some vertebrates also feed in a similar way. Instead of teeth, many whales have baleen, a substance with fringed edges. The baleen enables the whale to strain animals from the water. Flamingoes use their tongues to strain water through comb-like plates in their bills called lamellae.

Greater flamingo *(Phoenicopterus ruber)*

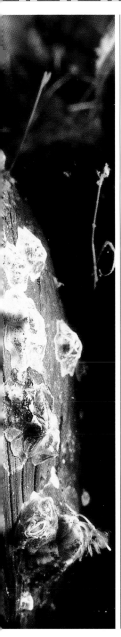

ZEBRA MUSSEL

This small, stripy mussel lives in rivers, lakes and canals, where it fastens itself to anything solid. At one time, zebra mussels were found only in Asia, but in the last 150 years they have spread westwards across Europe. In the 1980s, a ship accidentally carried zebra mussels to North America, where they have multiplied with amazing speed. Along the shores of the Great Lakes, these mussels have clogged up water treatment plants and power station pipes, and smothered and killed off water plants needed by other animals.

SCIENTIFIC NAME *Dreissena polymorpha*
DISTRIBUTION Asia, Europe, North America
SIZE About 4cm long

SWAN MUSSEL

This pale brown mussel lives in muddy rivers, partly buried in mud or silt. It feeds by sucking water in through a short, fleshy tube, or siphon.

Swan mussels on a riverbed

After filtering out any food, it pumps the water out through a second siphon. Swan mussel larvae do not drift in the water like the larvae of most mussel species. They fasten on to fish and feed on them for several weeks before dropping off to start their adult life on the riverbed.

SCIENTIFIC NAME *Anodonta cygnaea*
DISTRIBUTION Europe, Asia
SIZE Up to 23cm long

COMMON FAN MUSSEL

Muddy sands below the low-tide mark provide a home for the fan mussel. Instead of lying on its side, like most mussels, the fan mussel stands on the pointed end of its shell, where the hinge is. It anchors itself to stones and is partly buried in sand. The shell gapes open to let the mussel collect food particles from the water. Large species of fan mussel can be 45cm high.

SCIENTIFIC NAME *Pinna fragilis*
DISTRIBUTION Atlantic Ocean
SIZE Up to 30cm high

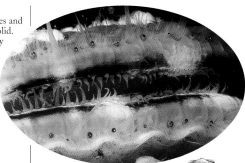

ABOVE *This edge-on view of a great scallop clearly shows the animal's tentacles and the numerous small eyes along its shell.*

Great scallop

GREAT SCALLOP

The great scallop is one of the few bivalves that can swim by opening and shutting its valves. If it is threatened, it makes an emergency escape by snapping its shell shut and squirting out a jet of water that makes it shoot backwards. It has a fringe of tentacles, and rows of more than one hundred tiny blue eyes along the edge of its shell.

SCIENTIFIC NAME *Pecten maximus*
DISTRIBUTION Atlantic Ocean, Mediterranean Sea
SIZE Up to 13cm long

EDIBLE OYSTER

This bivalve lives on the muddy shores of river estuaries. It has a rough, uneven shell with one flat valve and one curved valve. The flat valve faces upwards with the curved one fixed firmly to a rock or to another oyster.

Edible oyster shell

SCIENTIFIC NAME *Ostraea edulis*
DISTRIBUTION Atlantic Ocean, Mediterranean Sea
SIZE Up to 10cm long

HAMMER OYSTER

The T-shaped shell of this oyster makes it look like a hammer. The 'handle' is made of two valves that open when the oyster feeds. It lives in seabed sand in the tropics.

SCIENTIFIC NAME *Malleus malleus*
DISTRIBUTION Indian Ocean, Pacific Ocean
SIZE Up to 15cm long

COMMON COCKLE

Huge numbers of common cockles live along low-lying shores but, because they bury themselves in sand or mud, living animals are rarely seen. Their empty shells are often found on beaches where birds such as oystercatchers and seagulls have dropped them while feeding. Cockles feed by pumping water in and out through two frilly siphons. If a cockle is touched, it draws in its siphons and shuts its shell.

Frilly siphons used for feeding and breathing

Rounded, ridged shell

SCIENTIFIC NAME
Cerastoderma edule

DISTRIBUTION
Atlantic Ocean, Mediterranean Sea

SIZE About 4cm long

Shipworm's chalky case

TOP *The shell of a cockle can be white to mid-brown. It is deeply ridged with more than 20 ribs.*
ABOVE *When shipworms die, their chalky shells are left behind in the wood.*

HEART SHELL

This bivalve is unlike any other. Each of its valves has a coiled base that bulges outwards near the hinge. Together the valves give the animal a heart-like shape when seen from the side. Heart shells live in sand or mud in water at least 10m deep. Complete shells rarely turn up on the shore even when the animal is dead, because the two valves break apart so easily.

SCIENTIFIC NAME *Glossus humanus*
DISTRIBUTION Atlantic Ocean, Mediterranean Sea
SIZE About 9cm long

SOFT-SHELLED CLAM

This clam's shell has a soft, rubbery edge, which is actually part of the animal's body. Found in sand and mud, soft-shelled clams live up to 30cm beneath the surface. To breathe and feed, they use a pair of long siphons wrapped in a leathery sheath. One of the siphons sucks water into the clam's body. Once anything edible has been filtered out, the other pumps it back up to the surface of the sand. In North America, these clams are often dug up for food.

SCIENTIFIC NAME *Mya arenaria*
DISTRIBUTION Atlantic Ocean
SIZE Shell up to 10cm long

GIANT CLAM

The giant clam is the world's largest bivalve, with some specimens weighing as much as 300kg. More than 95 per cent of this weight is made up by the shell. These huge molluscs live in shallow water on coral reefs. Like many other bivalves, they filter food from the water around them using two siphons. Giant clams also feed in another way. Their fleshy, brightly coloured lips contain microscopic algae that make their own food using the energy in sunlight. A giant clam gets a share of this food and, in return, provides the algae with a safe place to live.

SCIENTIFIC NAME *Tridacna gigas*
DISTRIBUTION Indian Ocean, Pacific Ocean
SIZE Up to 1.1m across

SHIPWORM

With a long, fleshy body and only a tiny shell fixed to the end of it, this animal looks much more like a worm than a mollusc. The two halves of its shell have razor-sharp edges, which the shipworm uses to bore through submerged timber. As it burrows, it swallows and digests particles of wood, seriously weakening anything through which it bores. In the days when most ships were made of wood, constant repairs were needed to keep shipworms at bay.

SCIENTIFIC NAME *Teredo navalis*
DISTRIBUTION Worldwide
SIZE Up to 20cm long

Common piddock buried in rock

COMMON PIDDOCK

Piddocks live by filtering particles of food from sea water. They protect themselves by boring into rock, so that only the tips of their siphons are left outside in the water. As a piddock grows, it widens its burrow, but the entrance stays the same size. This means that the animal is trapped and it is almost impossible for a predator to extract it. These creatures often produce a green light. It is not known why they do this, since they spend their lives entombed in rock.

SCIENTIFIC NAME *Pholas dactylus*
DISTRIBUTION Atlantic Ocean, Mediterranean Sea
SIZE Shell up to 15cm long

Razor shell using its powerful foot to pull itself into the sand

ABOVE AND BELOW *Razor shells normally come to the surface of the sand only when the tide is in. There are several species of razor shell. Some are straight, while others are more curved.*

Large razor shell

Small razor shell (Ensis ensis)

LARGE RAZOR SHELL

Shaped like an old-fashioned razor, these bivalves have a long, narrow, square-ended shell. They live in sand near the low-tide mark, filtering food from the sea water above. Razor shells have a short foot that they can use to move about and to dig into the sand. The foot can grip the sand by contracting, pulling the shell downwards. When razor shells feed they are always alert for signs of danger. The slightest vibration makes them dig their way into the sand and they disappear with amazing speed.

SCIENTIFIC NAME *Ensis siliqua*

DISTRIBUTION Atlantic Ocean, Mediterranean Sea

SIZE Up to 15cm long

CEPHALOPODS

Octopuses, squid, cuttlefish and nautiluses are members of a group of molluscs called cephalopods. Cephalopods have a large head, well-developed eyes and a beak-like mouth ringed by sucker-tipped arms. They grab their prey with their arms and kill it with a poisonous bite. To move, cephalopods suck water into their mantle cavity – the space between the mantle and the body – and squirt it backwards, sending themselves speeding in the opposite direction, trailing their arms behind. There are about 650 species of cephalopod, all living in the sea.

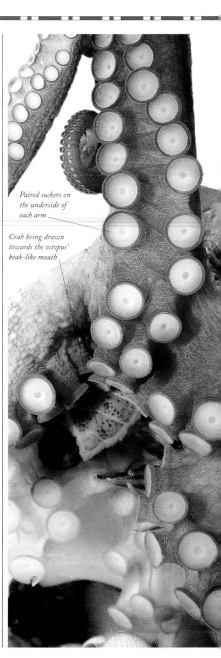

Paired suckers on the underside of each arm

Crab being drawn towards the octopus' beak-like mouth

ABOVE *A cuttlefish grabs a shrimp by shooting out a pair of extra-long tentacles.*

CUTTLEFISH

With their flattened bodies, cuttlefish are well suited to life on the seabed, where they hunt for other molluscs and small fish. They have a chalky internal shell called a cuttlebone. These cuttlebones are often washed up on the shore. Cuttlefish can change their colour to match their background and hide from predators. They do this by adjusting the size of pigment sacs in their skin.

SCIENTIFIC NAME	*Sepia officinalis*
DISTRIBUTION	Atlantic Ocean, Mediterranean Sea
SIZE	Up to 30cm long

COMMON SQUID

Squid have a streamlined shape for life in open water. They have a slender internal shell called a pen, which is covered by a muscular mantle. They use jet propulsion to move at speed, but can also swim slowly by rippling fin-like flaps on their sides. Like cuttlefish, squid have eight arms and two longer tentacles with a sucker-tipped pad at the end. They shoot out their tentacles to catch food. Common squid hunt in groups and rarely come near the shore.

SCIENTIFIC NAME	*Loligo vulgaris*
DISTRIBUTION	Atlantic Ocean
SIZE	Up to 50cm long

Common squid

Giant squid

ATLANTIC GIANT SQUID

The giant squid is the largest invertebrate in the world, weighing as much as two tonnes. It has the greatest eyes of any animal, up to 50cm in diameter, and its suckers can be more than 8cm across. It lives at great depths and feeds on fish, catching them in total darkness. No one has yet seen a giant squid in its natural habitat. Our knowledge of it comes mainly from dead or injured animals that have risen to the surface or have been washed ashore.

SCIENTIFIC NAME	*Architeuthis dux*
DISTRIBUTION	Atlantic Ocean
SIZE	Up to 16m long

CENTRE *The common squid feeds on fish and other animals.*
ABOVE *A giant squid could easily catch a diver in its tentacles.*

ABOVE AND LEFT *The common octopus does most of its hunting at night. During the day it hides in a lair among the rocks.*

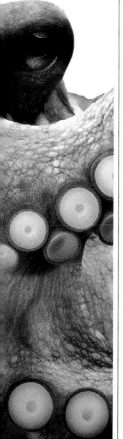

VAMPIRE SQUID

First seen in 1903, this jet-black animal is not a true squid, but the only known survivor of an ancient group of cephalopods that has otherwise become extinct. It has luminous eyes, and arms that work like the spokes of an umbrella, holding open a funnel that leads towards the animal's mouth. Vampire squid live in the darkness of the deep sea and no one has ever seen how they feed. Their eyes probably attract fish towards the funnel, and into the animal's mouth.

SCIENTIFIC NAME *Vampiroteuthis infernalis*

DISTRIBUTION Worldwide

SIZE Up to 30cm long

COMMON OCTOPUS

Unlike squid and cuttlefish, octopuses do not have a pair of long tentacles or an internal shell. The common octopus lives among rocks on the seabed. It is one of the world's most intelligent invertebrates and uses its eight arms to search for crabs and other small animals, reaching into crevices in the rocks to pull them out. The female common octopus is much smaller than the male. Octopuses breed by laying eggs, which the female guards in an underwater lair. It takes up to six weeks for her eggs to hatch and, throughout this time, the female has nothing to eat. Once hatching is complete, she dies.

SCIENTIFIC NAME *Octopus vulgaris*

DISTRIBUTION Atlantic Ocean, Mediterranean Sea, Caribbean Sea

SIZE Up to 90cm long

BLUE-RINGED OCTOPUS

This Australian octopus is the only cephalopod with a bite capable of killing humans. The bite itself is almost painless and it can take more than an hour for the poison to take effect. Fortunately, blue-ringed octopuses are not aggressive animals, so fatalities are rare. The species often lives near the shore, and is named after the bright blue rings that cover its body.

SCIENTIFIC NAME *Hapalochlaena maculosa*

DISTRIBUTION Coast of Australia

SIZE About 20cm long

ARGONAUT

This unusual octopus spends most of its life in open water. The female is up to 20 times larger than the male and she has a paper-thin spiral shell. Unlike with other molluscs, the argonaut's shell is not attached to its body – the female holds it in place with her arms. Female argonauts use their shell to protect their eggs and, once the eggs have hatched, it is often discarded.

SCIENTIFIC NAME *Argonauta argo*

DISTRIBUTION Warm seas worldwide

SIZE Females up to 20cm long, males from 1cm long

CHAMBERED NAUTILUS

Nautiluses are the only cephalopods that have a permanent external shell. Millions of years ago, they were among the most abundant invertebrates in the sea, but today only a handful of species still survive. A nautilus' shell contains a series of gas-filled chambers that work together as a float. The animal itself lives in the largest chamber, and is protected by a fleshy hood. It has as many as 90 arms, but they are short, and do not have suckers.

SCIENTIFIC NAME *Nautilus pompilius*

DISTRIBUTION Indian Ocean, Pacific Ocean

SIZE About 15cm across

LEFT *When feeding, the chambered nautilus holds its prey with its arms.*

ARACHNIDS

THERE ARE ABOUT 70,000 SPECIES OF ARACHNID, INCLUDING SPIDERS, SCORPIONS, MITES AND TICKS. AFTER INSECTS (PAGES 48–89), THEY MAKE UP THE SECOND LARGEST GROUP OF ARTHROPODS. MANY ARACHNIDS ARE PREDATORS AND HAVE A POISONOUS BITE.

Most arachnids live on land and hunt small animals. They have four pairs of legs and a body that is divided into two parts. Many arachnids have sharp fangs. They usually inject their prey with digestive juices. Once the juices have done their work, the arachnid sucks up its meal. Most arachnids lay eggs, but a few give birth to live young.

A daddy-long-legs spider showing how it gets its name

SPIDERS

These are the best-known arachnids because many of them live in our gardens or homes. All 35,000 species are carnivorous, which means that they eat other animals, and all of them kill their prey with poisonous fangs. Most spiders have four pairs of eyes, although they usually hunt by touch. They make silk, which they use to protect their eggs, to travel along and to trap their food.

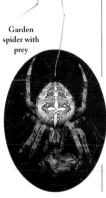

Garden spider with prey

DADDY-LONG-LEGS SPIDER
This slender spider is most often seen indoors, where it hangs upside down from its untidy web. If the web is touched, the spider vibrates up and down to fend off possible attack. Unlike some webs, the ones built by this spider are not sticky. If an insect lands on the web, the spider immobilizes it by quickly wrapping it up in silk. Daddy-long-legs spiders do not always wait for food to come their way. They sometimes wander onto other spiders' webs, stealing food and even eating the inhabitants.

SCIENTIFIC NAME	*Pholcus phalangioides*
DISTRIBUTION	Worldwide
SIZE	Legspan about 7cm

GARDEN SPIDER
The garden spider is an orb-weaver, a species that catches insects by building a round, sticky web. The spider spins its web at night and spends the day waiting on or near the web, ready to pounce on anything that gets caught. Each time something is trapped, the web may be damaged. Instead of carrying out repairs, garden spiders then often eat the web and make a completely new one to replace it.

SCIENTIFIC NAME	*Araneus diadematus*
DISTRIBUTION	Europe, Asia, North America
SIZE	Legspan up to 2cm

TRAPDOOR SPIDER
There are many species of trapdoor spider. They hide in underground burrows and ambush their victims from below. Their burrows are sealed with hinged doors made of silk and earth. To feed, they wait with the door slightly ajar, rushing out to grab any insects that wander nearby. They devour their victims underground.

SCIENTIFIC NAME	*Bothriocyrtum* and other genera
DISTRIBUTION	Worldwide
SIZE	Legspan up to 6cm

ABOVE *Bird-eating spiders and their relatives have jaws that bite downwards, impaling their victims against branches or the ground. This spider has caught a mouse and is about to start eating.*

BIRD-EATING SPIDER

Often called tarantulas, bird-eating spiders have bodies covered with dense hairs and are the largest spiders in the world. They live in tropical rainforests, where they spend the day in burrows and emerge at night to hunt. Although they have eight eyes, their eyesight is poor and they find their prey mainly by feeling for it with their feet. Bird-eating spiders really do eat small birds. They can drag young birds straight from their nests, or catch adult birds when they are roosting during the night. These spiders also feed on lizards, frogs, large insects and small mammals.

SCIENTIFIC NAME	*Theraphosa* species
DISTRIBUTION	Tropical South America
SIZE	Legspan up to 28cm

BLACK WIDOW SPIDER

Although this spider has tiny fangs, the female's bite can be deadly to humans. Fortunately, black widows are not aggressive, so few people are bitten. In the wild, black widows live under fallen branches and in other dry places, where they catch insects in untidy webs. Some live in gardens and near houses in towns.

SCIENTIFIC NAME	*Latrodectus mactans*
DISTRIBUTION	North America
SIZE	Legspan up to 2.5cm

SYDNEY FUNNEL-WEB SPIDER

This Australian spider is one of the most poisonous species in the world. It catches insects using silken trip-lines that it spreads out from the entrance of its burrow. The males sometimes bite people when they wander in search of a mate. Fortunately, an antivenin has been developed that counteracts the poison.

SCIENTIFIC NAME	*Atrax robustus*
DISTRIBUTION	Eastern Australia
SIZE	Legspan up to 5cm

Black widow spider

Sydney funnel-web spider

TOP *The female black widow spends most of its time motionless on its web.* ABOVE *Male Sydney funnel-web spiders do not hesitate to bite, using their large, powerful fangs.*

ARTHROPODS

Arthropods are animals that have an external body-case, or exoskeleton, and several pairs of legs. The exoskeleton is made from hard plates that meet at flexible joints. It forms all the outer parts of the body, including the jaws, claws, pincers, stings and wings. Exoskeletons protect arthropods from attack and also stop them from drying out. Arthropods are extremely successful, and they outnumber all the other animal species put together. They include arachnids, crustaceans, insects, centipedes and millipedes.

Scorpion

SCORPION
A scorpion's exoskeleton seals in moisture, acting like a waterproof suit of armour.

Crustacean

CRUSTACEAN
Crustaceans are the largest arthropods. They can grow larger than land-dwelling arthropods because the water helps to support their bodies.

Centipede

CENTIPEDE
In centipedes and millipedes it is easy to see the segments that divide an arthropod's body.

Insect

INSECT
Insects are the most numerous arthropods, and also the only ones that can fly. Most species have two pairs of wings.

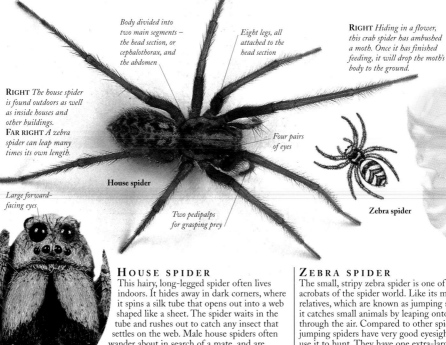

Body divided into two main segments – the head section, or cephalothorax, and the abdomen

Eight legs, all attached to the head section

RIGHT *Hiding in a flower, this crab spider has ambushed a moth. Once it has finished feeding, it will drop the moth's body to the ground.*

RIGHT *The house spider is found outdoors as well as inside houses and other buildings.*
FAR RIGHT *A zebra spider can leap many times its own length.*

Four pairs of eyes

House spider

Large forward-facing eyes

Two pedipalps for grasping prey

Zebra spider

Fang

Female carrying eggs

TOP AND ABOVE *The wolf spider has two large fangs which it uses to inject venom into its prey.*

HOUSE SPIDER

This hairy, long-legged spider often lives indoors. It hides away in dark corners, where it spins a silk tube that opens out into a web shaped like a sheet. The spider waits in the tube and rushes out to catch any insect that settles on the web. Male house spiders often wander about in search of a mate, and are sometimes seen at night, running across the floor. During their wanderings, they occasionally fall into baths and basins. The spiders cannot climb up the slippery sides, so they are unable to escape once they have fallen in.

SCIENTIFIC NAME	Tegeneria gigantea
DISTRIBUTION	Europe, North America, Australia
SIZE	Legspan up to 7cm

WOLF SPIDER

These large-bodied hunters rarely make webs. Instead, wolf spiders wander over the ground, often at night, using their large eyes to spot their prey. Like most spiders, wolf spiders wrap up their eggs in silk cocoons. The female fastens the cocoon to 'nozzles' on her abdomen that are called spinnerets and produce silk. This allows her to carry her eggs while she hunts. There are many species of wolf spider. *Lycosa narbonensis* used to be called the tarantula, but the name is now often used for bird-eating spiders (page 33).

SCIENTIFIC NAME	Lycosa narbonensis
DISTRIBUTION	Europe
SIZE	Legspan about 4cm

ZEBRA SPIDER

The small, stripy zebra spider is one of the acrobats of the spider world. Like its many relatives, which are known as jumping spiders, it catches small animals by leaping onto them through the air. Compared to other spiders, jumping spiders have very good eyesight and use it to hunt. They have one extra-large pair of eyes that helps them to judge distances before they leap. The zebra spider is often seen on sunny walls, even in the centre of towns. Other jumping spiders live in a variety of habitats, from hot, dry deserts to damp tropical rainforests.

SCIENTIFIC NAME	Salticus scenicus
DISTRIBUTION	Europe, North America
SIZE	Legspan up to 1cm

MONEY SPIDER

Often found in grassy fields, money spiders spin sheet-like webs to trap small insects near to the ground. They are probably the most numerous spiders on Earth. Although they are tiny and cannot travel far on their legs, they have an unusual way of spreading. On breezy days, they position themselves on the end of a long strand of silk. This blows about in the wind, carrying the spider off into the air. Traditionally, these spiders are supposed to bring good luck, which may explain how they got their name.

SCIENTIFIC NAME	Dismodicus and other genera
DISTRIBUTION	Mainly northern hemisphere
SIZE	Typical legspan 2mm

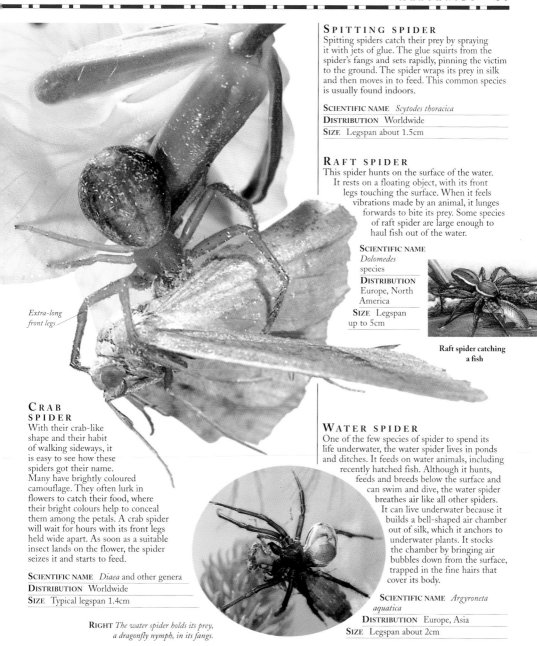

SPITTING SPIDER

Spitting spiders catch their prey by spraying it with jets of glue. The glue squirts from the spider's fangs and sets rapidly, pinning the victim to the ground. The spider wraps its prey in silk and then moves in to feed. This common species is usually found indoors.

SCIENTIFIC NAME *Scytodes thoracica*

DISTRIBUTION Worldwide

SIZE Legspan about 1.5cm

RAFT SPIDER

This spider hunts on the surface of the water. It rests on a floating object, with its front legs touching the surface. When it feels vibrations made by an animal, it lunges forwards to bite its prey. Some species of raft spider are large enough to haul fish out of the water.

SCIENTIFIC NAME *Dolomedes* species

DISTRIBUTION Europe, North America

SIZE Legspan up to 5cm

Raft spider catching a fish

CRAB SPIDER

With their crab-like shape and their habit of walking sideways, it is easy to see how these spiders got their name. Many have brightly coloured camouflage. They often lurk in flowers to catch their food, where their bright colours help to conceal them among the petals. A crab spider will wait for hours with its front legs held wide apart. As soon as a suitable insect lands on the flower, the spider seizes it and starts to feed.

SCIENTIFIC NAME *Diaea* and other genera

DISTRIBUTION Worldwide

SIZE Typical legspan 1.4cm

Extra-long front legs

WATER SPIDER

One of the few species of spider to spend its life underwater, the water spider lives in ponds and ditches. It feeds on water animals, including recently hatched fish. Although it hunts, feeds and breeds below the surface and can swim and dive, the water spider breathes air like all other spiders. It can live underwater because it builds a bell-shaped air chamber out of silk, which it anchors to underwater plants. It stocks the chamber by bringing air bubbles down from the surface, trapped in the fine hairs that cover its body.

SCIENTIFIC NAME *Argyroneta aquatica*

DISTRIBUTION Europe, Asia

SIZE Legspan about 2cm

RIGHT *The water spider holds its prey, a dragonfly nymph, in its fangs.*

SCORPIONS, TICKS AND MITES

As well as spiders, arachnids include several other groups of animals, ranging from giant scorpions to microscopic mites. These animals all have four pairs of legs, although some use the front pair as feelers instead of for walking. Arachnids include some hunters, but also animals that eat a variety of things, from plant and animal remains, to stored food, blood and even flakes of human skin.

SCORPION

Scorpions are the heavyweights of the arachnid world, with bodies as long as 23cm. They are armed with a pair of pincers and a long tail that carries a sting. They hunt small animals after dark, and usually catch their prey by using their pincers alone. A scorpion's sting is normally reserved for self-defence, and its effect varies from one species to another. The largest scorpions often have quite mild stings, but a few of the smallest ones are very dangerous. Scorpions are found in warm places throughout the world. Like other scorpians, the one shown on the right *(Urodacus novae-hollandiae)* carries its young on its back.

BELOW *This giant whip scorpion has swivelled its tail forwards, ready to spray acid over an enemy.*

SCIENTIFIC NAME	*Urodacus* and other genera
DISTRIBUTION	Warm places worldwide
SIZE	Typical length 7cm

GIANT WHIP SCORPION

This sinister-looking animal does not have a sting, but it does have strong pincers. It hunts for small insects after dark, using its whip-like front legs as feelers. If threatened, the whip scorpion can spray a jet of acidic liquid from the end of its body. The liquid smells like vinegar, which is why this animal is also known as a vinegarone.

Pincers for seizing prey

SCIENTIFIC NAME	*Mastigoproctus giganteus*
DISTRIBUTION	North America
SIZE	Up to 8cm long

Pseudoscorpion on a leaf

PSEUDOSCORPION

These scorpion-like animals are extremely common all around the world, though few people ever get to see one. This is not surprising because the largest are less than 8mm long. Pseudoscorpions, or false scorpions, live in soil, on rocks and among fallen leaves, where they feed on animals smaller than

BELOW *Scorpions have tiny eyes and they find their prey mainly by touch. Most of them hunt at night.*

Four pairs of walking legs

themselves. Pseudoscorpions do not have stings, but nip with their poisonous brown pincers. They often move around by clinging to spiders' legs.

SCIENTIFIC NAME	*Chelifer* and other genera
DISTRIBUTION	Worldwide
SIZE	Typical species about 2mm long

Female harvestman   **Male harvestman**

HARVESTMAN

Although harvestmen are frequently mistaken for spiders, they differ from them in several ways. They have an oval-shaped body which, unlike a spider's, is not divided into two parts. Their legs are extremely slender, they do not have fangs and they have just two eyes set in a turret on their back. Harvestmen feed on small animals, such as springtails, and on dead remains. Most of them hunt by day, and hide away by night.

SCIENTIFIC NAME	*Phalangium* and other genera
DISTRIBUTION	Worldwide
SIZE	Typical legspan 5cm

SEA SPIDERS AND HORSESHOE CRABS

Despite their names, sea spiders are not spiders and horseshoe crabs are not crabs. They belong to two separate groups of invertebrates that are related to arachnids. Like arachnids, they do not have 'feelers' (antennae) and their bodies are divided into two parts, although with sea spiders this is not always easy to see. There are at least 1,000 species of sea spider worldwide, but only four species of horseshoe crab off the eastern coasts of North America and Asia.

SEA SPIDER OR PYCNOGONID

Members of this group have between four and six pairs of spindly legs, a slender body and a tiny head. Many sea spiders live in deep water. They crawl over the seabed, clinging to anything within reach with their legs. Sea spiders eat small animals, such as bryozoans, harvesting them with their pincers. They pierce the prey with their jaws and then suck out the body fluids. Some sea spiders measure as much as 40cm across with their legs stretched out, but most are much smaller than this. They live throughout the world's oceans and can be brightly coloured.

SCIENTIFIC NAME	*Pycnogonum* and other genera
DISTRIBUTION	Worldwide
SIZE	Typical species about 2cm long

TICK

These flat-bodied parasites live by sucking blood. To find a host animal, a tick waits on grass or trees, sometimes for weeks or months. When a suitable animal walks past, it climbs aboard using its sharp claws and begins to feed. Its body swells up with blood and, when it is full, it drops off. Ticks attack many kinds of mammal, including humans. Some create problems for farmers because they feed on livestock.

SCIENTIFIC NAME	*Ixodes* and other genera
DISTRIBUTION	Worldwide
SIZE	Up to 1.5cm long after feeding

HOUSE DUST MITE

Mites are the smallest arachnids. Most are so tiny that they are invisible to the naked eye. Some live in water and some on animals. There is even a mite that lives on human eyelashes. Many mites clamber about in or on their food. The house dust mite lives in household dust and feeds on microscopic flakes of skin. It does no direct harm, but its droppings can be a problem because they can cause allergies such as asthma.

SCIENTIFIC NAME	*Dermatophagoides farinae*
DISTRIBUTION	Worldwide
SIZE	About 0.2mm long

HORSESHOE CRAB

With their domed body and spiny tail, horseshoe crabs look more like pieces of armour than living things. They live in shallow coastal sea water, where they burrow into the sand to eat worms and other animals. Horseshoe crabs have five pairs of legs and a small pair of pincers that they use to pick up their food. These are hidden by a shield called a carapace, and are only visible if the animal is turned upside down. Each year, female horseshoe crabs come ashore and lay their eggs near the high-tide line. The eggs hatch into larvae, which are washed out to sea with the tide.

SCIENTIFIC NAME	*Limulus polyphemus*
DISTRIBUTION	Atlantic coast of North America, Gulf of Mexico
SIZE	Up to 60cm long

ABOVE *A group of horseshoe crabs gather on a sandy beach to breed. While they are out of the water, many are attacked by birds.*

CRUSTACEANS

THESE CREATURES GET THEIR NAME FROM THEIR
EXOSKELETON, WHICH FORMS A CHALKY CRUST AROUND
THEIR BODY. LIKE OTHER ARTHROPODS, THEY HAVE TO
SHED THEIR EXOSKELETON AS THEY GROW, BECAUSE IT
DOES NOT GROW WITH THEM. MOST CRUSTACEANS HAVE
MANY PAIRS OF LEGS AND TWO PAIRS OF ANTENNAE.

This varied group of invertebrates contains about 38,000 species and includes animals as diverse as water fleas, barnacles, lobsters and woodlice. A few crustaceans live on land, but most live in either fresh water or in the sea. Crustaceans eat a range of things. Many sift their food from the water, while others hunt or scavenge for dead remains. Some are parasites, living on or inside other animals.

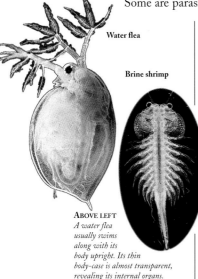

Water flea

Brine shrimp

ABOVE LEFT
*A water flea
usually swims
along with its
body upright. Its thin
body-case is almost transparent,
revealing its internal organs.*
ABOVE RIGHT *A brine shrimp uses
its legs to collect food from the water.*

WATER FLEA
Despite their name, water fleas are not true fleas, but tiny crustaceans that live in lakes and ponds. They have microscopic legs and large, feathery antennae. They swim jerkily through the water by flicking their antennae. Water fleas feed on bacteria and other minute life-forms. During the autumn, they scatter eggs, which settle in the mud and hatch the following spring. Water fleas' eggs are often carried to new areas on birds' feet. In warm weather, the adults multiply rapidly and many of them are eaten by fish.

SCIENTIFIC NAME	*Daphnia* species
DISTRIBUTION	Worldwide
SIZE	Up to 3mm long

BRINE SHRIMP
These small crustaceans live in salty lakes, which often dry out for long periods. To survive these droughts, brine shrimps lay tough eggs that can remain out of water for five years or more. Once wet, they hatch within a few hours.

SCIENTIFIC NAME	*Artemia* species
DISTRIBUTION	Worldwide
SIZE	About 1.5cm long

PLANKTON

Many crustaceans start life as microscopic larvae. They drift near the surface of the water with many other tiny life-forms. This teeming mass of life is called plankton. Many small crustaceans stay in the plankton all their lives, but others leave it as they grow, moving to different habitats, such as the shore.

Plankton also contains microscopic algae that absorb energy from sunlight. These grow and are eaten by tiny animals that, in turn, are eaten by larger animals. Eventually,

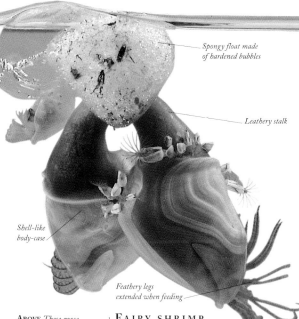

Spongy float made of hardened bubbles

Leathery stalk

Shell-like body-case

Feathery legs extended when feeding

ABOVE *These goose barnacles hang in the water from floats of gas-filled bubbles. Other species hang beneath floating wood.*

Plankton seen under a microscope

the energy from the sun is passed on to all the animals in the sea, from predators, such as sharks, to deep-sea sponges that filter the sea for food. Without plankton, most sea-life would not exist.

FAIRY SHRIMP
Specialists at living in temporary pools of water, fairy shrimps can be found in shallow ponds and puddles on muddy roads. Although their life-span is short, they breed quickly, often laying eggs when they are only two weeks old. Once their home has dried out the adults die, but their eggs survive to be spread far and wide by the wind. Fairy shrimps have few natural enemies, which helps them to survive.

SCIENTIFIC NAME	*Eubranchipus* and other genera
DISTRIBUTION	Worldwide
SIZE	Typical species 2.5cm long

TADPOLE SHRIMP
From a distance, this shrimp looks like a tadpole, with its large head and wriggling way of swimming. The front of its body is protected by a carapace and it has up to 70 pairs of legs. Tadpole shrimps live in puddles of water. In desert areas, they appear suddenly after storms, disappearing again during dry times, but leaving their eggs behind.

SCIENTIFIC NAME	*Triops* and other genera
DISTRIBUTION	Worldwide
SIZE	Typical species 4cm long

ROCK BARNACLE
Surrounded by what looks like a shell, barnacles used to be mistaken for molluscs. The shell is actually a specialized body-case with a volcano-like shape, and it is always fastened to something solid. Most barnacles fasten themselves to rocks, but some live on other animals, such as crabs or whales. They keep their cases closed at low tide to avoid dehydration. At high tide, barnacles extend their feathery legs from the top of the case and sieve particles of food from the water. There are many different species. *Balanus balanoides* is common along Atlantic shores.

SCIENTIFIC NAME	*Balanus balanoides*
DISTRIBUTION	Atlantic Ocean
SIZE	Up to 1cm wide

GOOSE BARNACLE
These barnacles have a long, leathery stalk and a case made of five shiny, white plates. They attach themselves to pieces of driftwood or to rafts of bubbles that they make themselves. Goose barnacles can drift thousands of kilometres across the oceans and are often thrown up on beaches after storms. Many centuries ago, they were thought to develop into geese, which is how they got their name.

SCIENTIFIC NAME	*Lepas fascicularis*
DISTRIBUTION	Worldwide
SIZE	Up to 6cm long

SEED SHRIMP OR OSTRACOD
When swimming, a seed shrimp looks like a tiny seed speeding through the water. Its body is enclosed by a hinged carapace, which the animal can shut to protect itself. It swims by flicking its antennae and can use its legs to crawl about in mud. Seed shrimps are found in ponds and lakes, where they feed mainly on algae.

SCIENTIFIC NAME	*Cypris* and other genera
DISTRIBUTION	Worldwide
SIZE	Typical species 2mm

Tadpole shrimp in a puddle

AMERICAN LOBSTER

Lobsters are the heaviest crustaceans. Some American lobsters can weigh 20kg but, because many are caught for food, few survive to grow to this size. Lobsters belong to a large group of crustaceans called decapods, all of which have ten legs. They are hunters and scavengers, using their powerful claws to crack open shells and to slice up the bodies of other animals, such as crabs, small fish and even other lobsters. They live on the seabed and in rocky crevices, and reproduce by laying thousands of eggs, which the female carries until they hatch.

SCIENTIFIC NAME	*Homarus americanus*
DISTRIBUTION	Atlantic coast of North America
SIZE	Up to 86cm long

ABOVE
The American lobster is the heaviest of all lobsters.
RIGHT *The bright colours of a cleaner shrimp help it to attract attention from fish that are in need of a clean.*

CARIBBEAN SPINY LOBSTER

Spiny lobsters have only small pincers, but are protected with sharp spines. They feed on worms and dead remains on the seabed. They usually move by walking, but they can swim backwards by flicking their tails. Caribbean lobsters spend the summer on reefs near the coast, but migrate to deeper water in the autumn. They travel in groups of 50 or more, scuttling along in a line.

SCIENTIFIC NAME	*Panulirus argus*
DISTRIBUTION	Caribbean Sea
SIZE	About 60cm long

CRAYFISH

These small relatives of the lobster live in lakes, rivers, streams and swamps. They hide away by day, usually in underwater holes, and emerge at night to hunt for snails, small fish and other water animals. Like lobsters, female crayfish carry their eggs around with them. When the eggs hatch, the young crayfish cling to their mother's body for several days until they are able to fend for themselves.

SCIENTIFIC NAME	*Astacus* and other genera
DISTRIBUTION	Europe
SIZE	About 10cm long

CLEANER SHRIMP

Brightly coloured cleaner shrimps feed by picking dead skin and parasites off the bodies of fish. This is a useful service to the fish, so cleaner shrimps get to clamber over their 'clients' without being chased away. *Lysmata grabhami* comes from the Caribbean, but other species are found throughout the tropics.

SCIENTIFIC NAME	*Lysmata grabhami*
DISTRIBUTION	Caribbean Sea
SIZE	About 5cm long

Spines protect the body

MANTIS SHRIMP

The front legs of the mantis shrimp work like the legs of a praying mantis (page 54). Each leg ends in a long claw with a set of six spines along one edge. The claw can snap back against the rest of the leg in a fraction of a second, stabbing and gripping at the same time. Mantis shrimps live on coral reefs and on the seabed in shallow water. They feed on worms, fish and other animals. Large species, like this one, can slice a fish in half, and could easily stab through a person's finger.

SCIENTIFIC NAME *Squilla empusa*
DISTRIBUTION Atlantic Ocean, Caribbean Sea
SIZE About 25cm long

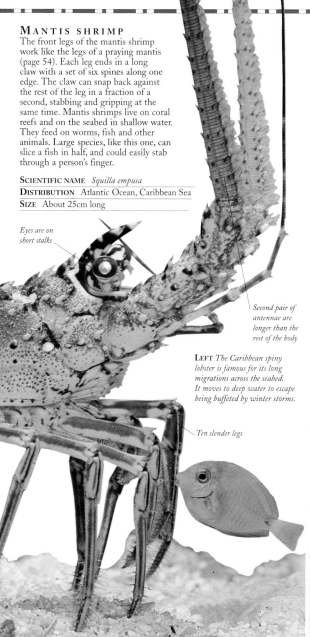

Eyes are on short stalks

Second pair of antennae are longer than the rest of the body

Ten slender legs

LEFT *The Caribbean spiny lobster is famous for its long migrations across the seabed. It moves to deep water to escape being buffeted by winter storms.*

RIGHT *Freshwater shrimps are sometimes found underground in streams that run through caves.*
BELOW *Sandhoppers are common along the high-tide mark.*

Freshwater shrimp

Sandhopper

FRESHWATER SHRIMP

Instead of swimming upright, freshwater shrimps often move along on one side, flicking and wriggling their way through shallow water. They can also jump. Freshwater shrimps are not true shrimps. They are amphipods, crustaceans with seven pairs of legs and a narrow body. Providing that they stay damp, they can survive out of water. Freshwater shrimps eat decaying leaves and the remains of small animals. They have long antennae that help them to find food.

SCIENTIFIC NAME *Gammarus* species
DISTRIBUTION Worldwide
SIZE About 2.5cm long

SANDHOPPER

There are many species of sandhopper. They are relatives of freshwater shrimps and live on the shore. The easiest way to see sandhoppers is to lift up a piece of seaweed. If any sandhoppers are feeding on it, they will jump away quickly. They jump by flicking their tails backwards against the ground, which throws them into the air.

SCIENTIFIC NAME *Orchestia* and other genera
DISTRIBUTION Worldwide
SIZE Up to 2cm long

KRILL

Found in the cold seas around Antarctica, these shrimp-like animals have a bright red body. They feed on planktonic algae, which they collect using legs covered with fine hairs. They live in vast swarms that are preyed on by fish, seabirds, seals and whales.

SCIENTIFIC NAME *Euphausia superba*
DISTRIBUTION Southern Ocean
SIZE About 6cm long

CRABS

Despite their different shape and way of moving, crabs are closely related to lobsters. A crab's body looks as if it has been stretched sideways and, in most species, the body is covered by a hard, chalky shell. There are more than 4,000 species of crab, including both the world's largest crustaceans and also some animals not much greater than a pea. Most crabs live in or close to water, although some return to the water only to breed. Crabs usually swim well, but many shore-dwelling species can also scuttle sideways away from danger at high speed.

Crab's underside is protected by its claws

RIGHT *When it holds its claws close to its body, the box crab is difficult to attack. This one is carrying a sea anemone for extra protection.*

Edible crab

Blue crab

TOP *Edible crabs are often caught for food by luring them into special pots.*
ABOVE *The blue crab has flattened back legs which it uses like a pair of paddles when it is swimming.*

EDIBLE CRAB
This crab has a heavy domed shell, or carapace, with a crimped edge that looks just like a pie-crust. As in other crabs, the carapace protects the animal's internal organs. The edible crab feeds on living animals and dead remains, using its powerful pincers to crack open shells. The adult crab lives in deep water, but its thick case makes it too heavy to swim. Instead, it sidles across the seabed, finding food mainly by touch and smell. Edible crabs lay up to three million eggs a year. Like most crabs, their larvae start life drifting in the plankton near the sea's surface.

SCIENTIFIC NAME *Cancer pagurus*

DISTRIBUTION European coasts, including the Mediterranean Sea

SIZE Up to 20cm across

SPONGE CRAB
A sponge crab camouflages itself by fastening living sponges to its back. The sponges continue to grow on the crab's back and the crab holds them in place using its two back legs. This works well until the sponge crab outgrows its shell and the time comes for it to moult. Just before it moults, the crab removes the sponges. Once its new shell has hardened, it puts the sponges back again, or replaces them with others.

SCIENTIFIC NAME *Dromia* and other genera

DISTRIBUTION Worldwide

SIZE Typical species 8cm across

BOX CRAB
This brightly coloured crab has pincers that fold away, giving its body a box-like shape. With its pincers stowed flat there is less chance that it might be injured by another animal. There are many species of box crab, and some carry sea anemones (page 15) on their shells. The sea anemones' stinging tentacles protect the crab from predators. The anemones benefit from this partnership as well, because they have more food to choose from when they are being carried about on the crab's back.

SCIENTIFIC NAME *Calappa granulata*

DISTRIBUTION Eastern Atlantic Ocean, Mediterranean Sea

SIZE Up to 11cm long

BLUE CRAB
Found in shallow waters close to the shore, blue crabs have a spiky edge to the front of their shell, and long spines that stick out on either side of their bodies. They walk along the seabed to find worms and other small animals, but they are also good swimmers. Like other swimming crabs they push themselves through the water with their back legs. Blue crabs are common and are often caught for food.

SCIENTIFIC NAME *Callinectes sapidus*

DISTRIBUTION Atlantic coast of North and South America, Caribbean Sea

SIZE Up to 23cm across

JAPANESE SPIDER CRAB

Spider crabs have a pear-shaped body and slender legs and pincers. The Japanese spider crab lives in water at least 30m deep and feeds mainly on molluscs. Its legspan can exceed 3m, making it both the world's largest crustacean and the world's largest arthropod. It moves by walking over the seabed, although its legs are so long that it has difficulty moving on land.

SCIENTIFIC NAME	*Macrocheira kaempferi*
DISTRIBUTION	Pacific coast of Japan
SIZE	Legspan up to 3.6m

DECORATOR CRAB

The decorator crab is a type of spider crab. Many spider crabs camouflage themselves by draping seaweeds and sponges over their bodies, and the decorator crab is an expert at this form of self-defence. It keeps still during the day, and is so well hidden that it is very difficult to spot it among weed-covered rocks. Like other camouflage-carrying spider crabs, it fastens its camouflage in place with the help of the hundreds of tiny hooks that cover its body.

SCIENTIFIC NAME	*Oregonia gracilis*
DISTRIBUTION	Pacific coast of North America
SIZE	Legspan up to 25cm

MASKED CRAB

This nocturnal animal has an oval body with a thin shell and a pair of long antennae. The shell has face-like markings, from which the masked crab gets its name. It spends the day buried in the sand, with only the tips of its antennae showing. On its inner edge, each antenna has a fringe of hairs that lock together to form a tube. The tube takes water to the buried crab so that it can breathe.

SCIENTIFIC NAME
Corystes cassivelaunus

DISTRIBUTION
Atlantic Ocean

SIZE Shell up to 4cm long

Tube formed by antennae

Male masked crab has claws twice as long as its body

ABOVE *Decorator crabs lose their camouflage when they moult, so they have to build up a new covering every time.*
RIGHT *Masked crabs live buried in sand in shallow water. At night, they clamber out onto the sand to feed.*

Only the front, protected part of the body sticks out from the shell

LEFT *A red hermit crab* (Dardanus megistos) *peers out from the shell that has become its home.*

HERMIT CRAB

Unlike most crabs, a hermit crab has a narrow body and a long, soft abdomen. Only the front part of the body is covered by a hard exoskeleton. To protect itself from attack, it backs into empty mollusc shells. Its abdomen is coiled to enable it to fit and its legs and claws are shaped so that it can block the entrance of the shell if anything tries to get in. As the crab gets larger, it periodically has to move home. It begins by carefully investigating empty shells with its claws and, if it finds a suitable one, quickly makes its move. For hermit crabs, finding a shell is a matter of life and death, and fights often break out among them when shells are in short supply.

SCIENTIFIC NAME	*Dardanus* and other genera
DISTRIBUTION	Worldwide
SIZE	Typical species 3cm across

MITTEN CRAB

Many crabs have hairy legs and some even have a hairy body. The hairs act as swimming aids or help to keep camouflage in place. The mitten crab has a tuft of hair behind each pincer, making it look as if it is wearing a pair of furry gloves or mittens. It lives in estuaries and in fresh water close to the coast.

SCIENTIFIC NAME	*Eriocheir sinensis*
DISTRIBUTION	Southern Asia, Europe
SIZE	About 10cm across

PEA CRAB

Instead of living out in the open, tiny pea crabs shelter inside the bodies or homes of other animals. They do little or no harm to their hosts, and survive on leftover scraps of food. Some pea crabs live inside worm burrows or on shrimps, but *Pinnotheres pisum* tucks itself away inside the shell of bivalve molluscs, such as mussels and oysters.

ABOVE *This pea crab lives inside the shell of a mussel. Adult pea crabs have to leave their hosts to breed.*

SCIENTIFIC NAME	*Pinnotheres pisum*
DISTRIBUTION	Atlantic Ocean, Mediterranean Sea
SIZE	Up to 1cm across

GHOST CRAB

These crabs live on sandy beaches in warm parts of the world. They spend the daytime hidden in burrows beneath the surface and emerge at night to pick over the sand for scraps of food. They feed on fruit and dead animals that are left when the tide goes out. Ghost crabs are very pale, which helps them to blend in against the sand. They are always on the lookout for danger. If anything comes too close, ghost crabs break into a high-speed run, shooting sideways across the sand and back into the safety of their burrow.

SCIENTIFIC NAME	*Ocypode* species
DISTRIBUTION	Tropical shores worldwide
SIZE	Typical species 5cm across

Huge legspan enables the crab to grasp the trunk of a coconut tree as it climbs

LAND CRAB

Adult land crabs spend their lives out of water, the females going back to it only to lay eggs. They survive by spending the day in burrows, feeding at night when there is less danger of drying out. Land crabs are found only in the tropics and subtropics, but they are sometimes so common that they pick over every square centimetre of the ground for food. Most feed on fallen leaves and fruit, but they are also attracted by dead fish and other animal remains.

SCIENTIFIC NAME	*Gecarcinus* and other genera
DISTRIBUTION	Warm coastal regions worldwide
SIZE	Typical species 10cm across

ROBBER CRAB

These are the largest and heaviest crustaceans that live on land. They weigh as much as 4kg and have massive strong claws. Despite their menacing appearance, robber crabs feed almost entirely on fruit, particularly young coconuts that have fallen before they are ripe. If they cannot find enough food on the ground, robber crabs will clamber up trees to eat. The males spend all their adult life on land, but females return to the sea to lay eggs.

SCIENTIFIC NAME	*Birgus latro*
DISTRIBUTION	Islands in the Indian and Pacific Oceans
SIZE	Legspan up to 1m

FIDDLER CRAB

Fiddler crabs live on muddy seashores, mainly in warm parts of the world. During high tide they hide away in burrows but, when the water drops, they crawl out on the mud to feed. Fiddlers eat tiny specks of food that are mixed up in the mud. They collect the mud with their pincers and then drop it in the form of pellets when they have eaten whatever it contains. Female fiddlers have two small pincers, but males have one small pincer and one giant one. The large pincer can be as heavy as the rest of the body put together. The males use their outsize pincers during their courtship displays, when they wave them at other fiddler crabs across the mud. This is to warn away rival males and to attract females to mate.

SCIENTIFIC NAME	*Uca* species
DISTRIBUTION	Worldwide in tropics and subtropics
SIZE	Typical width 2cm

Giant pincer of male fiddler crab

Female fiddler crab

ABOVE *Male and female fiddler crabs on the mud at low tide.*
BELOW *Two robber crabs tussle over a coconut washed up on the shore.*

Woodlice

WOODLOUSE

Apart from land crabs (page 45), woodlice are the only widespread crustaceans that have successfully taken up life on land. They can be found under logs and in damp crevices, where they feed on plant remains. Although woodlice do not live in water, they have gills and need to stay damp to breathe. If they find their way into a house, they often die of dehydration. Female woodlice lay eggs, which they keep in a pouch underneath their bodies. The eggs hatch as fully formed young that are soon able to take up life on their own.

SCIENTIFIC NAME	*Oniscus* and other genera
DISTRIBUTION	Worldwide
SIZE	Typical length 1.5cm

SEA SLATER

This animal looks like a large woodlouse, but it moves about much more quickly. It lives on rocks and piers near the high-tide mark. It scavenges for food washed in by the sea, using its long antennae to track down anything edible. The sea slater is nocturnal, sheltering in crevices during the day. Occasionally it does venture out in daylight. If it is caught out in the open, the sea slater will quickly dash for cover.

SCIENTIFIC NAME	*Ligia oceanica*
DISTRIBUTION	Worldwide
SIZE	Up to 2.5cm long

WATER SLATER

Compared to most water animals, water slaters are poor swimmers. They usually move by crawling about on their seven pairs of legs. They feed on fallen leaves and the dead remains of plants, and can survive in stagnant water that contains little oxygen. *Asellus aquaticus* lives in slow-flowing rivers, streams and ponds, but some of its relatives live in caves. These cave-dwellers are blind and colourless, unlike slaters that live above ground, which are a drab brown.

SCIENTIFIC NAME	*Asellus aquaticus*
DISTRIBUTION	Europe
SIZE	Up to 1.5cm long

RIGHT *The water slater absorbs oxygen through gills tucked away near the base of its legs.*

ABOVE *Sea slaters have large eyes at the side of their heads. Their bodies can change colour and are usually darker during the day than at night.*

SELF-DEFENCE

For wild animals, life is a dangerous business. Whenever they feed or move about, they run the risk of being attacked and eaten. They have to be experts in self-defence to survive this ever-present threat. The simplest method of self-defence is to make a fast escape. Crabs run for cover at high speed but, when cornered, they switch to another kind of self-defence, fighting back with their pincers. Many other animals behave in a similar way, defending themselves with weapons, such as sharp teeth, claws or stings.

Woodlice cannot move fast and they have no weapons. They rely on their unpleasant taste to deter predators. Many millipedes use a similar kind of self-defence. Some animals, such as poison-arrow frogs, taste bad and are also highly poisonous. If a woodlouse's chemical defences fail, it relies on its body-case, which acts like a suit of armour. Some woodlice can roll up into a ball if they are threatened. The same technique is used by other animals, including armadillos and pill millipedes.

Pill millipede in open and defence positions

CENTIPEDES AND MILLIPEDES

THESE LONG-BODIED ARTHROPODS HAVE MANY PAIRS OF LEGS.
CENTIPEDES ARE PREDATORS, AND KILL PREY WITH POISONOUS CLAWS
AT THE SIDES OF THEIR HEAD. MILLIPEDES EAT FRESH
AND DECAYING PLANTS AND HAVE SMALL JAWS.

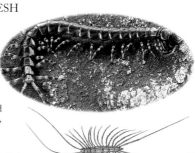

Centipedes and millipedes are closely related, but it is easy to tell them apart. Centipedes have a flat body with a single pair of legs on each segment. Millipedes have a cylindrical body and each of their body segments carries two pairs of legs. Centipedes can have up to 170 pairs of legs, while millipedes may have 375 pairs. There are about 2,800 species of centipede and 8,000 species of millipede. They are most common in warm countries.

GIANT CENTIPEDE

The name centipede means 100 feet – although some species have just 30. The giant centipede has boldly coloured legs, a sign that it is dangerous to touch. Its poisonous claws can kill small mammals and reptiles, and they are strong enough to pierce human skin with extremely painful results. Like other centipedes, this species spends the daytime in dark crevices and emerges to hunt at night. Centipedes reproduce by laying eggs, and many of them, including the giant centipede, are careful parents. The female lays eggs in an underground burrow and wraps herself around them. She licks them to keep them clean and guards them for several weeks until they hatch.

SCIENTIFIC NAME	*Scolopendra morsitans*
DISTRIBUTION	Warm places worldwide
SIZE	Up to 30cm long

LONG-LEGGED CENTIPEDE

This is the fastest centipede. It can sprint in short bursts at nearly 2km/h. The long-legged centipede often lives in houses, where it can be seen running across walls after its prey.

SCIENTIFIC NAME	*Scutigera coleoptrata*
DISTRIBUTION	Europe
SIZE	Up to 3cm long, excluding legs

GIANT MILLIPEDE

Giant millipedes live in the tropics, where there is a year-round supply of decaying leaves. They are largely harmless, although some species can squirt a poisonous spray if they are threatened. A millipede has a blunt head to help it to push through fallen leaves. Its body is reinforced with a chalky substance for extra strength.

SCIENTIFIC NAME	*Scaphistostreptus seychellarum*
DISTRIBUTION	Seychelles
SIZE	Up to 28cm long

PILL MILLIPEDE

With a maximum of 19 pairs of legs, pill millipedes are shorter than most of their relatives. They can roll up into a ball to avoid danger, just as many woodlice do. Pill millipedes live among fallen leaves, helping to break them down so their nutrients can be recycled.

SCIENTIFIC NAME	*Glomeris marginata*
DISTRIBUTION	Europe
SIZE	About 1.2cm long

TOP *The giant centipede has been accidentally introduced from Southeast Asia to many warm parts of the world, including the southern USA.*
ABOVE *The long-legged centipede hunts at night for small insects.*

INSECTS

INSECTS ARE AMONG THE MOST SUCCESSFUL ANIMALS ON EARTH. SO FAR, SCIENTISTS HAVE IDENTIFIED NEARLY ONE MILLION SPECIES. THEY RANGE FROM BEETLES LARGER THAN A HUMAN HAND TO FLIES SMALLER THAN THIS FULL STOP.

Curved antenna   *Tiny eye*

Three-pronged tail

TOP *This springtail (Tomocerus longicornis) is one of more than 1,500 species found throughout the world. Most springtails live in grass or leaf litter, but some float in clusters on pools and puddles.* **ABOVE** *Silverfish keep growing after they have reached maturity.*

Insects are arthropods with an external skeleton and jointed legs. An adult's body is divided into three parts – the head, the thorax and the abdomen. The head carries the eyes, antennae and several sets of mouthparts. Some insects crush or chew solid food, but most suck up liquids. The thorax usually carries three pairs of legs and one or two pairs of wings. The abdomen contains the insect's reproductive organs and most of its digestive system. Most insects start life as an egg. They hatch looking quite different from their parents and change shape as they mature. Many insects can fly, which makes them good at spreading from place to place. They live on land, in fresh water and in the air, but cannot survive in the sea.

WINGLESS INSECTS

These small, primitive animals live mainly among fallen leaves or in the soil. There are about 3,000 species worldwide, and they are found as far apart as the Amazon rainforest and Antarctica. Some species are numerous but, because they are mostly tiny and drab, few are ever noticed. As well as being wingless, these animals differ from most insects in other ways. They do not all have to mate to reproduce, and they alter in shape only slightly as they grow to adulthood.

SPRINGTAIL

Few people would recognize a springtail, but they are among the most common animals on Earth. In lush grassland, there can be more than 500 million in each hectare, feeding on plants and their decaying remains. Springtails get their name from a peg-like organ that is tucked under the rear of their bodies. If a springtail is disturbed, it suddenly releases the peg and flicks itself through the air. Most springtails do no harm, but some are serious farmland pests.

SCIENTIFIC NAME	*Tomocerus* and other genera
DISTRIBUTION	Worldwide
SIZE	Typical length 4mm

SILVERFISH

The silver scales that cover this creature's body give it its name. The silverfish often lives in houses, where it can be spotted scuttling away from the light when doors or drawers are opened. It feeds on starchy substances, such as paper, flour, breadcrumbs and some kinds of glue. Female silverfish lay pearly-white eggs in crevices and on floors. The young are white and turn silver as they get older.

SCIENTIFIC NAME	*Lepisma saccharina*
DISTRIBUTION	Worldwide
SIZE	About 1.5cm long

FIREBRAT

Although its body is brown, the firebrat is similar to the silverfish. It is found indoors, but chooses places that are hot and damp. It is common in bakeries, factories and heating ducts. The firebrat continues to moult throughout its life. Each time it moults, it is able to replace any legs that it may have lost in accidents.

SCIENTIFIC NAME	*Thermobia domestica*
DISTRIBUTION	Worldwide
SIZE	About 1.5cm long

LICE, THRIPS AND WEBSPINNERS

These unrelated groups of insects are all small and easily overlooked, but some can be serious pests. Thrips feed on plants and their decaying remains, and can cause widespread damage to crops. Webspinners eat plants or tiny animals. Lice live in two very different ways – booklice eat moulds or plants, but some lice are parasites that feed on blood, feathers or skin. These biting and sucking species cause discomfort to animals and people and spread disease. There are about 10,000 species of louse, webspinner and thrips and they are found all over the world.

HUMAN HEAD LOUSE

This parasitic insect lives in human hair, where it feeds by sucking blood. It is found only on the head, although its relatives – the body louse and the crab louse – live on other parts of the human body. Its short legs end in a single claw that can grip hairs so tightly that the insect is almost impossible to dislodge. It lays eggs that it fastens to hair. When the eggs are ready to hatch, the tops pop off and the young lice crawl out. Spread by physical contact, the head louse cannot fly. It can be killed with insecticidal shampoos.

SCIENTIFIC NAME *Pediculus humanus capitis*
DISTRIBUTION Worldwide
SIZE About 3mm long

BOOKLOUSE

If you see something move in an old book, it is probably a booklouse. These insects eat moulds that grow on paper and plants. Female booklice can often reproduce without having to mate. Most lay their eggs one by one in webs of silk.

SCIENTIFIC NAME *Liposcelis* and other genera
DISTRIBUTION Worldwide
SIZE Typical length 2mm

Long antenna

THRIPS OR THUNDERBUG

These tiny black insects fill the air on warm, stormy days. They often settle on clothes and skin. Thrips hibernate in crevices. Indoors, they squeeze into all kinds of objects, from clocks to computer keyboards, but rarely manage to escape.

SCIENTIFIC NAME *Thrips* and other genera
DISTRIBUTION Worldwide
SIZE Typical length 2mm

WEBSPINNER

Found among fallen leaves, webspinners live in a tangled network of silk tunnels. They produce the silk from glands on the tip of their front legs. They forage in and around their tunnels, and quickly disappear if disturbed.

SCIENTIFIC NAME *Embia* and other genera
DISTRIBUTION Worldwide
SIZE Typical length 1cm

Feathery wings

TOP *Booklice that live indoors, such as the common booklouse (*Liposcelis terricolis*), are almost all wingless.*
CENTRE *Thrips feed on plant juices. These are grain thrips (*Limothrips cerealium*) on a convolvulus flower.*
ABOVE *Like all thrips, onion thrips (*Thrips tabaci*) have piercing mouthparts.*

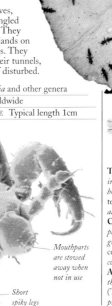

Abdomen swells up as the louse feeds

RIGHT *Head lice have a flattened body, a small head and very strong legs. Their colour varies, helping them to hide away in hair.*

Mouthparts are stowed away when not in use

Short spiky legs

DRAGONFLIES, MAYFLIES AND STONEFLIES

There are about 5,000 species of dragonfly, 2,000 species of mayfly and 1,600 species of stonefly. These insects are found throughout the world and they all start life as underwater nymphs. Nymphs look similar to their parents, though they do not have wings. Dragonfly nymphs are fierce predators and use a hinged mouthpart, called a mask, to attack small animals. Stonefly nymphs are also carnivorous, but mayfly nymphs eat microscopic plants. As adults, mayflies and most stoneflies eat nothing at all, but adult dragonflies are skilled hunters, catching other insects in mid-air.

Front and back wings similar in shape and size

Gauzy wings are outstretched when the dragonfly rests

Large thorax houses the dragonfly's wing muscles

GREEN DARNER

This North American dragonfly has a bright green, darning needle-shaped abdomen. It is one of the largest dragonfly species, and is commonly seen over ponds and slow-flowing streams. Darners hunt by sight, using their massive compound eyes to spot any movement that might be a meal. Their eyes are so huge that they meet in the middle of the head, giving them an all-round view of their surroundings. Green darner nymphs feed on tadpoles and small fish, and take two years to turn into adults.

SCIENTIFIC NAME	*Anax junius*
DISTRIBUTION	North America
SIZE	Up to 8cm long

BELOW *Dragonflies have the largest eyes in the insect world. In this species* (Hemianax papuensis) *from western Australia, they occupy most of the insect's head. Each eye is divided into about 25,000 compartments.*

EMPEROR DRAGONFLY

With a wingspan of nearly 14cm, this impressive insect is one of Europe's largest and fastest dragonflies. It is a 'hawker' dragonfly, which means that it spends most of its time on the wing, patrolling over water and marshland for food. Emperor dragonflies chase other dragonflies out of their feeding territories, and sometimes catch and eat smaller species. During their life underwater, emperor dragonfly nymphs are well camouflaged. This is essential for their survival because, if they are spotted by older nymphs, they are likely to be eaten.

SCIENTIFIC NAME	*Anax imperator*
DISTRIBUTION	Europe, Africa, Asia
SIZE	Up to 10.5cm long

BROAD-BODIED LIBELLULA

This thickset insect is a 'darter' dragonfly. Darters spend most of the time resting on a perch, darting into the air only when they spot likely prey. The broad-bodied libellula feeds over slow-flowing water and often perches on dead twigs. It holds its body horizontally with its wings swept forwards, ready to take off at a moment's notice. Both the male and female are brown in the first few days of life. After that however, the male's abdomen turns bright blue.

SCIENTIFIC NAME	*Libellula depressa*
DISTRIBUTION	Europe, central Asia
SIZE	Up to 7.5cm long

ABOVE *This emperor dragonfly's bright blue abdomen and clear wings show that it is a male. Dragonflies can beat their two pairs of wings independently, which allows them to hover, and move forwards and backwards.*

Four dark wing spots

Bright blue body of male

TOP *The four-spotted libellula* (Libellula quadrimaculata) *gets its name from the dark marks on its wings.*
ABOVE *The broad-bodied libellula takes one or two years to turn into an adult.*

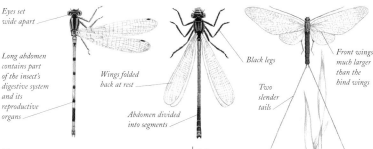

Eyes set
wide apart

Long abdomen
contains part
of the insect's
digestive system
and its
reproductive
organs

Wings folded
back at rest

Abdomen divided
into segments

Black legs

Two
slender
tails

Front wings
much larger
than the
hind wings

FAR LEFT *The common
blue damselfly is one of
the most widespread
damselflies in the world.*
CENTRE *The large red
damselfly (Pyrrhosoma
nymphula) is a European
species that often flies over
fields and meadows.*
LEFT *This species of mayfly
(Isonychia ignota) lives by
lakes and rivers in southern
and central Europe.*

COMMON BLUE DAMSELFLY

Damselflies are related to dragonflies. They are
smaller and thinner, often with wings that fold
over their backs when they rest. Damselflies look
delicate, but they are tougher than they seem.
The common blue damselfly can survive in the
Arctic tundra, where temperatures fall to -30°C.
Adult common blue damselflies feed on small
insects that they often pick off plants. They lay
their eggs in the stems of water plants, and their
nymphs usually live underwater for a year.

SCIENTIFIC NAME *Enallagma cyatherium*

DISTRIBUTION Europe, Asia, North America

SIZE Up to 4cm long

HELICOPTER DAMSELFLY

This rainforest damselfly has record-breaking
wings, which measure up to 19cm from tip to
tip. The damselfly hunts by flying slowly through
the forest in search of spiders. It hovers in front
of a spider's web like a helicopter, then makes a
lightning-fast lunge. It eats the spider's abdomen
but cuts off the head and legs, letting them fall
to the ground. Spiders do not seem to notice the
damselfly's approach, probably because its body
is slender and its wings transparent.

SCIENTIFIC NAME *Megaloprepus caeruleata*

DISTRIBUTION Central America, South America

SIZE Up to 12cm long

STONEFLY

The life of a stonefly begins in a cool stream or
lake, where it feeds on small animals and plants.
At between one and three years old, the nymph
clambers out of the water and turns into a dark
brown adult that lives for only about a month.
Stoneflies are not good fliers, and often scuttle
around on rocks at the water's edge.

SCIENTIFIC NAME *Perlodes* and other genera

DISTRIBUTION Worldwide

SIZE Typical length 3cm

MAYFLY

These insects have one of the strangest life-
cycles in the insect world. They spend up to
three years as underwater nymphs, feeding
on algae and tiny plants. Once they leave the
water and become winged adults, they have no
digestive system, so they cannot eat and often
die within hours. Adult mayflies appear in early
summer, when they flutter over rivers and lakes
in dense swarms. After mating, the females
scatter their eggs on water.

SCIENTIFIC NAME *Ephemera* and other genera

DISTRIBUTION Worldwide

SIZE Typical length 5cm, including tails

ABOVE *This is a European
species of stonefly
(Perlodes microcephala),
with two slender tails.*
BELOW *This adult stonefly
(Leuctra fusca) is resting
on a waterside flower.*

GRASSHOPPERS, KATYDIDS AND CRICKETS

There are at least 20,000 species of grasshopper, katydid and cricket and they are most common in warm parts of the world. They have powerful back legs that they often use to jump away from danger instead of flying. Many of these insects do not have wings, but those that do have two quite different pairs. The forewings are tough and leathery and they protect the delicate hindwings. Many crickets are hunters or scavengers, but most grasshoppers and katydids feed on plants. During the breeding season, all these insects communicate by sound. Each species has its own distinctive 'song', enabling males to attract the right mate. After mating, the females lay their eggs on plants or in the ground. The young, called hoppers, look like tiny versions of their parents, although they do not have fully formed wings.

Feet with hooked claws

Abdomen expands like a telescope for laying eggs in the ground

MEADOW GRASSHOPPER

This widespread insect lives in all kinds of rough grassland and its 'song' is one of the characteristic sounds of summer in the countries where it lives. As with most grasshoppers, the males do almost all the singing and they make their song by rubbing their back legs against their front wings. Each back leg has a line of tiny pegs on the side facing the grasshopper's body. When the legs move up and down, the pegs scrape against hard ridges on the wings and the result is a short burst of sound.

ABOVE *Meadow grasshoppers have very small hindwings and cannot fly.*

SCIENTIFIC NAME	*Chorthippus parallelus*
DISTRIBUTION	Europe
SIZE	Up to 2.4cm long

RIGHT *The great green bushcricket* (Tettigonia viridissima) *is a European relative of the northern katydid. It hunts other insects after dark using its outsize antennae to track them down.*

BELOW *This green katydid* (Horatosphaga leggei) *comes from Namibia in southwestern Africa. Many katydids are green, making them difficult to see among plants.*

Powerful back legs

Spiny forelegs grip prey

Slender hind legs

DESERT LOCUST

A locust is any kind of grasshopper that moves about in swarms, attacking and destroying crops. There are many species, but the desert locust is by far the most famous. These live like other grasshoppers but, in some weather conditions, they gather together. When their food runs out, they take off in a swarm that can contain 50 billion animals. This can do tremendous damage and, once the locusts settle on crops, little can be done to move them on.

SCIENTIFIC NAME	*Schistocerca migratoria*
DISTRIBUTION	Africa, Asia
SIZE	About 9cm long

NORTHERN KATYDID

Katydids are very narrow, and camouflaged to look like bright green leaves. They have very long antennae and their ears are on their front legs. They live in trees and bushes and their camouflage is so convincing that they are hard to spot until they move. Katydids feed mainly at night. This is also when they sing. Northern katydids have a two-part song that sounds just like 'katy-did, katy-did'. There are many other species of katydid, particularly in the tropics, and their calls can be very different.

SCIENTIFIC NAME	*Pterophylla camellifolia*
DISTRIBUTION	Eastern North America
SIZE	Up to 5.5cm long

LEFT *The desert locust is one of the most destructive insects in the world and has an appetite for all kinds of crops. It has long wings and is a good flier.*

CAMOUFLAGE

Grasshoppers, katydids and crickets have few defences against attack from other animals. To survive, many of them rely on being difficult for predators to see. This is called being camouflaged. Many insects use camouflage because they are small and easily disguised.

In the simplest kind of camouflage, an animal blends in with its background. Many grasshoppers are green or brown, which helps to hide them among leaves. Blending in is especially important in habitats where there are few places to hide from predators. In deserts, insects and lizards are camouflaged so that they blend in with stones. In polar regions, hares and foxes have a white coat and owls have white feathers to blend in with the snow. Some of these animals change colour with the seasons, so that they do not stand out when the snow melts in spring.

Another kind of camouflage, called mimicry, uses shape for disguise. For example, some caterpillars look like bird droppings, while many moths look just like twigs. By resembling things that are inedible, they stand a much better chance of being left alone by predators. Some animals boost their chances of survival by imitating other animals that are poisonous, or bite or sting. Even though they are harmless, predators think that they are dangerous and leave them alone.

RIGHT *This gum leaf grasshopper* (Goniaea australasiae) *from Australia is well camouflaged to hide on a eucalyptus leaf. Even its eyes are brown.*

TOP *Even though it lives underground, the mole cricket* (Gryllotalpa gryllotalpa) *can fly.*
CENTRE *The house cricket is also a good flier.*
ABOVE *The European field cricket* (Gryllus campestris) *cannot fly.*

HOUSE CRICKET

At one time, the chirping of house crickets was a common sound in many homes. Today, people are not so welcoming to these insects, but the house cricket is still widespread in homes and rubbish-dumps throughout the world. Crickets have short forewings, and hindwings that roll up. They sing mainly at night by lifting up their forewings and rubbing one against the other. Crickets eat a wide variety of food. The house cricket survives on all kinds of kitchen scraps, from breadcrumbs to old vegetables.

SCIENTIFIC NAME	*Acheta domestica*
DISTRIBUTION	Originally from Africa, Middle East; introduced worldwide
SIZE	About 2cm long

MOLE CRICKET

Unlike other crickets, mole crickets spend most of their life underground. They have small wings, a blunt, armoured head and powerful front legs that they use for tunnelling through the soil. Mole crickets eat plant roots, and can be a pest in some places. They are some of the noisiest insects in the world. During the breeding season, the males broadcast their song from a funnel-shaped chamber that acts as an amplifier. On a calm night, the song can be heard up to 1.5km away.

SCIENTIFIC NAME	*Gryllotalpa* species
DISTRIBUTION	Worldwide, particularly in warm regions
SIZE	Typical length 5cm

GIANT WETA

Weighing up to 80g – about three times as much as a mouse – this wingless cricket from New Zealand is one of the world's heaviest insects. Giant wetas spend the day hidden away and emerge at night to feed on leaves and seeds. Like many crickets, the female has a sword-shaped egg-laying tube, or ovipositor, that is easy to mistake for a dangerous sting. Wetas have existed in New Zealand for millions of years and, for most of that time, have had few natural enemies. Today, they are eaten by rats and other introduced mammals and are almost extinct.

SCIENTIFIC NAME	*Deinacrida heteracantha*
DISTRIBUTION	New Zealand
SIZE	Up to 8.5cm long

STICK INSECTS, MANTISES AND COCKROACHES

There are approximately 2,000 species of stick insect, 1,800 mantises and about 5,000 cockroaches. They all have wings but they often seem reluctant to use them. Stick insects and mantises spend most of their life on plants and are often superbly camouflaged. Cockroaches generally live on the ground. As well as living in different habitats, these insects eat different things. Stick insects are vegetarian, while mantises are stealthy hunters, stabbing other insects with their barbed front legs. Cockroaches are not fussy about what they eat. They nibble at anything edible that they can find. All these insects reproduce by laying eggs. Cockroaches lay theirs in a hard case that they sometimes carry around.

Praying mantis (Mantis religiosa) about to strike

BELOW *This American cockroach has recently shed its skin. It takes several hours for its new skin to harden.*
BOTTOM *Oriental cockroaches crowd together to nibble on a sandwich.*

STICK INSECT
Stick insects live in trees and bushes where they feed on leaves. Most species are green or brown and, although they can be more than 15cm long, they have such slender bodies that they are very difficult to spot. They move slowly, and normally feed at night. Some stick insects can fly, but their wings are almost invisible when they are folded. Female stick insects often reproduce without mating. They scatter their eggs as they feed, letting them fall to the ground. When the young hatch, they look like small wingless adults.

SCIENTIFIC NAME	*Carausius* and other genera
DISTRIBUTION	Worldwide
SIZE	Up to 30cm long

PRAYING MANTIS
A mantis holds its front legs together while waiting to attack, so that it looks as if it is praying. If an insect lands nearby, the mantis keeps watch by swivelling its head, then suddenly strikes. Its front legs snap around its victim and it starts to feed immediately, even though its prey may still be struggling to escape. Female mantises are larger than males, which can cause problems when they mate. The female may eat her partner, starting with the head. Except for flower mantises, which are brightly coloured with large petal-like flaps on their legs, most mantises are green or brown. They lay their eggs in foamy masses they that fasten to twigs. The foam soon hardens, protecting the eggs until they hatch.

SCIENTIFIC NAME	*Mantis* and other genera
DISTRIBUTION	Worldwide, usually in warm places
SIZE	Typical length 8cm

AMERICAN COCKROACH
Although it can fly, this unwelcome visitor to houses usually scuttles about on its long, bristly legs. It is one of the fastest runners in the insect world, dashing into crevices as soon as it is disturbed. American cockroaches are active at night and they eat leftover food, paper and even soap. Cockroaches rarely spread disease but they contaminate food and leave an unpleasant smell. In warm conditions, they breed rapidly.

SCIENTIFIC NAME	*Periplaneta americana*
DISTRIBUTION	Worldwide
SIZE	Up to 5cm long

ORIENTAL COCKROACH
This cockroach is a poor flier – the male has short wings and the female is wingless. It eats a wide range of food and leaves a particularly strong smell where it has been foraging.

SCIENTIFIC NAME	*Blatta orientalis*
DISTRIBUTION	Worldwide
SIZE	Up to 3.5cm long

TERMITES AND EARWIGS

There are about 1,900 species of termite and they are found only in warm parts of the world. Apart from ants, bees and wasps, termites are the only insects that live in permanent family groups. These groups are called colonies and they can be more than two million animals strong. In each colony, only the queen lays eggs. Other members of the colony, called workers and soldiers, maintain the nest, forage for food, look after the young and keep predators at bay. Termites are normally wingless but, during the breeding season, winged forms develop. These leave the nest to begin new colonies of their own. Some termites eat leaves and wood, but many use these to grow edible fungi that they cultivate underground. There are about 1,200 species of earwig, found throughout the world. They are not related to termites and do not live in colonies. They eat a wide variety of food and, like termites, are active mainly at night.

Feeding tunnels
inside the wood

Worker termite
with pale body

Soldier termite with
well-developed jaws

AFRICAN SAVANNA TERMITE
This termite builds giant nests up to 6m high. Workers make the nest by mixing soil particles with their saliva and then letting the mixture harden in the sun. The interior of the nest contains the colony's fungus 'gardens', together with chambers for the queen and the developing young. The queen is so large that she cannot leave her cell. She is tended by workers – they feed her and carry away her eggs. She can lay up to 30,000 eggs a day and may live for 25 years.

SCIENTIFIC NAME	*Macrotermes natalensis*
DISTRIBUTION	Tropical Africa
SIZE	Queen up to 14cm long; workers about 8mm long

COMPASS TERMITE
These Australian termites build nests in grassland and open woodland. Their nests are extremely narrow and the ridge at the top always points in a north–south direction. Compass termites build their nests in this way to control the temperature inside. At dawn and dusk, when the air is cool, the eastern or western face of the nest soaks up the warmth of the rising or setting sun. At midday, when the air is hot, the nest is edge-on to the sun, and because of this it does not absorb too much heat.

SCIENTIFIC NAME	*Amitermes meridionalis*
DISTRIBUTION	Australia
SIZE	Up to 8mm long

TREE TERMITE
Not all termites nest on the ground. Some species spend much of their life in trees, where they build football-shaped nests high above the ground. They often make these nests from chewed-up wood fibres. Tree termites live throughout the tropics. Like ground-dwelling termites, the soldiers protect the colony fiercely. The soldiers of the species *Nasutitermes arboreus* have a head like a nozzle and can squirt a toxic liquid at anything that attacks the nest.

SCIENTIFIC NAME	*Nasutitermes* and other genera
DISTRIBUTION	Worldwide
SIZE	Typical length 6mm

COMMON EARWIG
Despite their name, earwigs have no interest in climbing into human ears! Instead, they hide among flower petals and in dark crevices by day, emerging after dark to feed on plants and small animals. They have pincers at the end of their bodies that they sometimes use to catch their prey. Although the pincers look dangerous, they are far too weak to pierce human skin. Female earwigs are careful parents, guarding their eggs until they hatch.

SCIENTIFIC NAME	*Forficula auricularia*
DISTRIBUTION	Originally from Europe; introduced into North America, Australia, New Zealand
SIZE	Up to 1.5cm long

ABOVE *Termites feed after dark and shy away from daylight. Here, a piece of rotting wood has been broken open to show an Australian species of termite* (Mastotermes darwinensis) *feeding inside. While the soldiers stand guard, the workers run for cover.*
BELOW *Earwigs have wings but these are packed away under small wing covers and folded up many times.*

TRUE BUGS

There are at least 70,000 species of bug and they are found all over the world. The word 'bug' is often used to mean any kind of insect, but true bugs are insects of a particular kind. They have mouthparts shaped like a beak and they eat by piercing things and then sucking up liquid food. A bug's beak hinges where it joins its head and it can be stowed under the body when not in use. Many bugs live on plants and feed on sap. Others attack animals, feeding on blood and other fluids. Some bugs are wingless. Those that do have wings hold them in different ways. Some fold them flat on their backs like a pair of crossed hands, while others fit them together to make a shape like a roof. Bugs reproduce by laying eggs. The young look similar to their parents and change shape gradually as they mature.

ROSE APHID OR GREENFLY

Aphids are tiny sap-sucking bugs with a complicated life-cycle. They can reproduce with amazing speed because the females often do not need to mate. They give birth to live young and can do this several times a day. As a result, they are soon surrounded by their growing families, which cluster together as they feed. They can be found in almost any garden and they often attack crops, sometimes with serious results. The rose aphid is a common species that gardeners find particularly annoying. It appears on roses in spring, and damages leaves and buds.

SCIENTIFIC NAME	Macrosiphum rosae
DISTRIBUTION	Worldwide
SIZE	About 2mm long

TOP
These black bean aphids (Aphis fabae) *are crowded together on a broad bean plant. These aphids feed on many garden plants and spend the winter on shrubs.*
ABOVE *This orange-banded cicada* (Melampsalta melete) *is from Australia. There are more than 2,000 species of cicada, each with its own song.*

CICADA

These noisy insects live in trees and shrubs. The males call by clicking hard plates on their abdomen. Each plate pops in and out like the lid of a can, making a high-pitched screech. Cicadas live in warm places and they spend their early life underground.

SCIENTIFIC NAME	Tibicen and other genera
DISTRIBUTION	Worldwide
SIZE	Typical length 7.5cm, including wings

THORN TREEHOPPER

Many bugs are protected from attack because they taste or smell unpleasant, but the thorn treehopper has a different protection. Its thorax is covered by a large, bright green shield that spreads backwards over its wings. The shield has a sharp, upward-facing spine, making the insect look like a plant thorn. If a bird does try to eat the bug, the spine makes it difficult to swallow.

SCIENTIFIC NAME	Umbonia spinosa
DISTRIBUTION	South America
SIZE	About 1cm long

LANTERN BUG OR PEANUT BUG

This tropical bug has two pairs of moth-like wings and a head ending in a big bulbous 'nose'. The nose is the size and shape of a peanut and almost half as long as the body. Scientists do not know why lantern bugs have this. One suggestion is that it may put off predators, but there is no evidence that this is true.

SCIENTIFIC NAME	Lanternaria lanternaria
DISTRIBUTION	Central America, South America
SIZE	About 6cm long

ASSASSIN BUG

These bugs feed on other animals, either by killing them outright or by feeding on their blood. Most assassin bugs have a slender body and long legs and, although many species can fly, they often approach their victims on foot. In the tropics, assassin bugs sometimes live in houses. They hide away by day and come out after dark to suck blood from people while they sleep. *Rhodnius prolixus* is one of several assassin bugs that can spread dangerous diseases as it feeds.

SCIENTIFIC NAME	Rhodnius prolixus
DISTRIBUTION	South America
SIZE	About 1cm long

Pondskater catching prey

PONDSKATER

Pondskaters can walk on water because their legs are tipped with water-repelling hairs. They feed on other insects that have crash-landed on the water's surface. When the insects start to struggle, ripples spread out from them. The pondskaters feel the ripples and move in to feed.

SCIENTIFIC NAME	Gerris and other genera
DISTRIBUTION	Worldwide
SIZE	Typical length 1cm

BACKSWIMMER

These common freshwater bugs swim through water upside down. Their hind legs are long and flattened, and the insects use them like a pair of oars to push themselves along. Backswimmers are aggressive predators with a powerful bite. They feed on tadpoles and small fish and often live in garden ponds and cattle drinking-troughs. Backswimmers have to surface to breathe, but they trap a thin film of air around their bodies, which allows them to stay underwater for several minutes at a time. They are good fliers.

SCIENTIFIC NAME	*Notonecta* species
DISTRIBUTION	Worldwide
SIZE	About 1.5cm long

GIANT WATER BUG

This fearsome-looking insect is one of the largest water bugs in North America. It feeds on tadpoles, salamanders and small fish, and can stab its beak through human skin. An animal as large as this needs a good supply of oxygen. The giant water bug gets oxygen through a pair of telescopic breathing tubes that stick out from the end of its abdomen. It lays batches of about 100 eggs on underwater plants. The young are cannibalistic, which means that they eat each other, so only a few grow to adulthood.

SCIENTIFIC NAME	*Lethocerus americanus*
DISTRIBUTION	North America
SIZE	Up to 6cm long

ABOVE *A backswimmer* (Noctonecta glauca) *lurks at the surface of the water waiting for its prey. It is covered by a film of air.*
BELOW *The giant water bug clutches animals with its front legs, then stabs them with its mouthparts.*

LACEWINGS, CADDISFLIES AND FLEAS

There are about 5,000 species of both lacewing and caddisfly, and about 1,800 species of flea. Caddisflies are most common where there is cool flowing water, but lacewings and fleas are found everywhere. Adult lacewings and caddisflies all have long narrow wings but, apart from this, the two groups look different and live in different ways. They do have one important feature in common – they start life as grubs, or larvae, and change shape abruptly as they mature. This process is called 'complete metamorphosis'. Lacewings usually spend their whole life on land. Their wings are thin and transparent with a complicated network of veins. Caddisflies start life in fresh water. As adults they have wings covered in fine hairs. Fleas do not have wings. When they become adult they live on the skin of mammals and birds, where they feed by sucking blood.

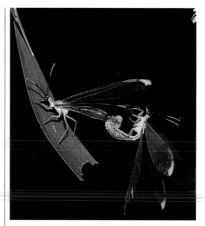

LACEWING

During early autumn, lacewings often come into houses in search of somewhere to hibernate. These insects are easily recognized by their lacy wings, but another striking feature is their eyes, which have a metallic golden sheen. The adults lay eggs on stalks of mucus that quickly dry out in the air. The stalks are long and slender, and probably help to keep the eggs out of the reach of hungry animals. Lacewing larvae have powerful jaws and often feed on aphids. Many camouflage themselves by wearing their victims' empty skin.

SCIENTIFIC NAME	*Chrysopa* and other genera
DISTRIBUTION	Worldwide
SIZE	About 1.8cm, including wings

Densely netted wings

ABOVE *This is an Australian ascaphalid (Nymphes melionides).* **LEFT** *This ascalaphid (Libelloides coccajus) lives in southern and central Europe.*

ASCALAPHID

With two pairs of long filmy wings, ascalaphids look similar to dragonflies and live in the same way, by hunting other insects on the wing. Unlike dragonflies, they have short abdomens and long antennae. Ascalaphids belong to the same group of insects as lacewings and spend all their life on land. Ascalaphid larvae look like ant-lions, but their bodies are flatter. They do not dig pits like ant-lions, instead they hide on the ground and under stones, grabbing any small insects that come within reach.

SCIENTIFIC NAME	*Libelloides* and other genera
DISTRIBUTION	Worldwide
SIZE	Typical length 5cm

Adult ant-lion
(Palpares libelluloides)

ANT-LION

In warm, dry parts of the world, sandy ground is often covered by small pits with sloping sides. Each one is made by an ant-lion for catching food. Ant-lions are insect larvae that grow up to look like lacewings. They have powerful jaws and lurk at the bottom of their pits with only their jaws exposed. If an ant walks near to the edge of the pit, the ant-lion flicks sand at it until the ant falls in. Then it sucks its prey dry, and throws the lifeless body back out of the pit.

SCIENTIFIC NAME	*Palpares* and other genera
DISTRIBUTION	Worldwide
SIZE	Typical adult about 10cm long, including wings; larva about 1.2cm long

MANTIS FLY

With its slender body and stabbing front legs, a mantis fly looks just like a small praying mantis (page 54). It is actually a relative of the lacewings, with similar delicate wings. Mantis flies use their front legs like praying mantises to catch prey, but they tackle much smaller insects. The European species *Mantispa styriaca* eats midges and other small flies, and its larvae feed on spiders' eggs.

SCIENTIFIC NAME	*Mantispa styriaca*
DISTRIBUTION	Europe
SIZE	About 1.8cm long, including wings

ABOVE
A green lacewing (Chrysopa septempunctata) *takes off from a flower bud using its wings like propellers.*

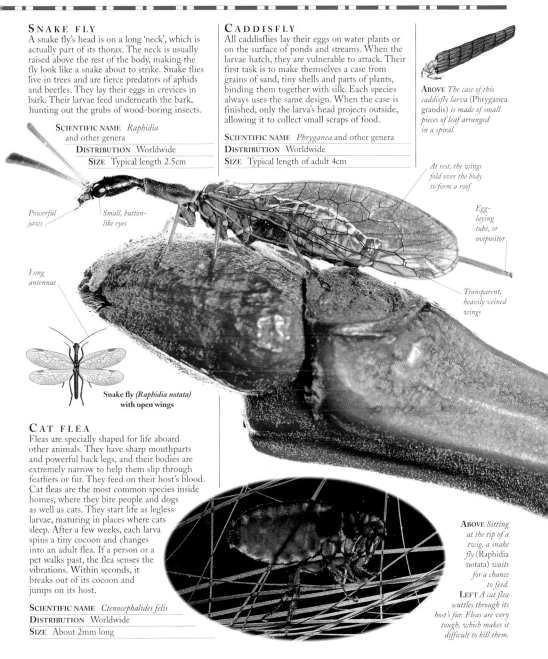

SNAKE FLY

A snake fly's head is on a long 'neck', which is actually part of its thorax. The neck is usually raised above the rest of the body, making the fly look like a snake about to strike. Snake flies live in trees and are fierce predators of aphids and beetles. They lay their eggs in crevices in bark. Their larvae feed underneath the bark, hunting out the grubs of wood-boring insects.

SCIENTIFIC NAME *Raphidia*
and other genera
DISTRIBUTION Worldwide
SIZE Typical length 2.5cm

CADDISFLY

All caddisflies lay their eggs on water plants or on the surface of ponds and streams. When the larvae hatch, they are vulnerable to attack. Their first task is to make themselves a case from grains of sand, tiny shells and parts of plants, binding them together with silk. Each species always uses the same design. When the case is finished, only the larva's head projects outside, allowing it to collect small scraps of food.

SCIENTIFIC NAME *Phryganea* and other genera
DISTRIBUTION Worldwide
SIZE Typical length of adult 4cm

ABOVE *The case of this caddisfly larva* (Phryganea grandis) *is made of small pieces of leaf arranged in a spiral.*

At rest, the wings fold over the body to form a roof

Egg-laying tube, or ovipositor

Powerful jaws

Small, button-like eyes

Long antennae

Transparent, heavily veined wings

Snake fly (Raphidia notata) with open wings

CAT FLEA

Fleas are specially shaped for life aboard other animals. They have sharp mouthparts and powerful back legs, and their bodies are extremely narrow to help them slip through feathers or fur. They feed on their host's blood. Cat fleas are the most common species inside homes, where they bite people and dogs as well as cats. They start life as legless larvae, maturing in places where cats sleep. After a few weeks, each larva spins a tiny cocoon and changes into an adult flea. If a person or a pet walks past, the flea senses the vibrations. Within seconds, it breaks out of its cocoon and jumps on its host.

SCIENTIFIC NAME *Ctenocephalides felis*
DISTRIBUTION Worldwide
SIZE About 2mm long

ABOVE *Sitting at the tip of a twig, a snake fly* (Raphidia notata) *waits for a chance to feed.*
LEFT *A cat flea scuttles through its host's fur. Fleas are very tough, which makes it difficult to kill them.*

BEETLES

With about 300,000 species, beetles make
up about one-third of all the insects that
scientists have identified. Found all over the world, they include
tropical heavyweights more than 12cm long, as well as tiny animals
only just visible to the naked eye. All beetles have hard forewings,
called elytra. When the elytra are closed, they fit together over the
abdomen, covering the hindwings like a case. The beetles can then crawl
about without damaging their hindwings, which they use to fly. Beetles
live on land and in fresh water, and they eat all kinds of food, from pollen
and leaves to wool and animal remains. They start life as larvae, or grubs,
with strong jaws and tiny legs or, in some cases, no legs at all. Many beetle
larvae are active hunters, but others tunnel their way through their food,
keeping safely out of sight. Once it is fully grown, a beetle larva turns into
a pupa and after weeks, or sometimes months, an adult beetle emerges.

*Streamlined body for
fast swimming*

*Large eyes
can see
underwater*

*Fringed
legs work
like paddles*

*Mouthparts
used for
tasting prey*

ABOVE *A green tiger beetle*
(Cicindela campestris) *makes
a meal of a caterpillar.*

*Antennae can detect animals
moving underwater*

*Front legs used for
grasping prey*

TIGER BEETLE

Tiger beetles rival cockroaches for the
title of the fastest-running insects
in the world. They spend most of
their lives on the ground, chasing
small insects in daylight and
snatching them up in their long,
powerful jaws. Their larvae dig
burrows in the ground. They use
their head to plug the burrow, then
ambush creatures that pass nearby.
Adult tiger beetles have very good
eyesight and most of them are good fliers.
Many species have bright metallic colours.

**Green tiger
beetle on the
ground**

SCIENTIFIC NAME	*Cicindela* and other genera
DISTRIBUTION	Worldwide
SIZE	Typical length 1.5cm

GREAT DIVING BEETLE

Although they are good fliers, diving beetles
spend almost all of their lives underwater.
They live in ponds and lakes, and breathe
air that they store under their elytra. This air
supply makes them very buoyant, and they
have to swim hard to stay submerged. Adult
diving beetles are ferocious predators, eating
tadpoles, and even small fish. When fully grown,
the larvae are even longer than the adults. They
are just as aggressive as their parents and catch
their prey with huge curved jaws. The great
diving beetle is one of the largest species –
many others are found throughout the world.

SCIENTIFIC NAME	*Dytiscus marginalis*
DISTRIBUTION	Europe, Asia, North America
SIZE	Up to 4cm long

ABOVE *A great diving
beetle recharges its air
reserves. It replaces the
bubble of air under its
elytra by breaking through
the surface of the water
with its abdomen.*

Air stored
beneath elytra

Whirligig beetle
(Gyrinus natator)
on water

Whirligig beetle
from above

Bombardier beetle
squirting vapour

Bombardier
beetle

Burying
beetle

Devil's
coach-
horse

ABOVE *The bombardier*
beetle, burying beetle and
devil's coach-horse spend
most of their life on the
ground. They can fly if
they have to.

BOMBARDIER BEETLE

The bombardier beetle has a unique and startling way of defending itself. If threatened, it squirts out an inflammable vapour that explodes as it sprays into the air. The explosion produces a sharp crack and a puff of smoke, and is often enough to deter the beetle's enemies. The vapour is made in the beetle's abdomen and streams out of a nozzle that can be pointed at the attacker.
Like other ground beetles, bombardiers and their larvae are carnivorous.

SCIENTIFIC NAME	*Brachinus crepitans*
DISTRIBUTION	Europe
SIZE	Up to 1cm long

BURYING BEETLE

Found all over the world, burying beetles are nature's undertakers. They have a good sense of smell, and use it to find the dead bodies of small birds and mammals after dark. When they discover a corpse, they dig away the soil beneath it until the body is buried. Once the remains are underground, the female makes a nest chamber near the body and lays her eggs on a ball of decaying flesh. She feeds the larvae for a few days after they hatch, but after this they feed on the corpse itself. Some burying beetles are black all over, others are black and red.

SCIENTIFIC NAME	*Nicrophorus* and other genera
DISTRIBUTION	Worldwide
SIZE	Typical length 3cm

DEVIL'S COACH-HORSE

With its long black body and powerful jaws, this nocturnal beetle has a menacing appearance. If anything does try to attack it, it opens its jaws and raises its abdomen like a sting. The devil's coach-horse belongs to a group of insects called rove beetles, which have short elytra but well-developed hindwings folded up many times.

There are many species of rove beetle but they are not often seen because they hide away by day. Most of them, including the devil's coach-horse, are carnivorous.

SCIENTIFIC NAME	*Staphylinus olens*
DISTRIBUTION	Europe
SIZE	About 2.5cm long

WHIRLIGIG BEETLE

These small oval beetles live on ponds and slow-flowing streams, where they speed about on the surface of the water. Their legs are short and covered with water-repellent hairs, which prevent them sinking through the surface. Whirligigs feed on small water animals and on insects that have fallen into the water. Their eyes are divided into two parts, so that they can see above and below the surface of the water at the same time.

SCIENTIFIC NAME	*Gyrinus* species
DISTRIBUTION	Worldwide
SIZE	Typical length 7mm

VIOLET GROUND BEETLE

Unlike tiger beetles, ground beetles hunt mainly at night and do not need to be brightly coloured. The violet ground beetle is a sombre purplish-blue colour, with an iridescent sheen. Ground beetles' legs are strong and powerful, enabling them to sprint after their prey. Their larvae are also efficient hunters. They actively search out caterpillars and other small insects, helping to destroy species that are garden pests. There are thousands of species of these useful insects – the violet ground beetle is common in gardens.

SCIENTIFIC NAME	*Carabus violaceus*
DISTRIBUTION	Europe
SIZE	Up to 3cm long

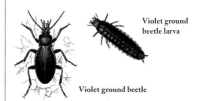

Violet ground
beetle larva

Violet ground beetle

DWARF BEETLE

As well as being the smallest beetles in the world, dwarf beetles are among the smallest of all insects. The smallest species *(Nanosella fungi)* looks like little more than a speck. These beetles feed on the decaying remains of plants and fungi. Their feathery hindwings fold when not in use.

SCIENTIFIC NAME	*Nanosella fungi*
DISTRIBUTION	Central America, South America
SIZE	About 0.25mm long

STAG BEETLE

Male stag beetles have outsize jaws shaped like a pair of antlers. During the breeding season they use their jaws to grapple with rival males, sometimes lifting them off their feet. The fights are not dangerous because the jaws cannot close fully. After the combat, the loser walks away. Adult stag beetles feed on tree sap, and their larvae grow up in decaying wood. There are nearly 1,000 species of stag beetle worldwide. Most are black or chestnut brown.

SCIENTIFIC NAME	*Lucanus* and other genera
DISTRIBUTION	Worldwide
SIZE	Males typically about 5cm long, including jaws; females smaller

DUNG BEETLE

As their name suggests, dung beetles eat animal dung. They also shape it into balls, rolling it away and burying it as food for their young. Their broad front legs and shovel-shaped heads are ideal tools for dealing with their food. Dung beetles are very useful animals because they get rid of dung and help to fertilize the soil. They are found in all warm parts of the world, but are particularly common in Africa. In the 1960s, thousands of African dung beetles were introduced into Australia to get rid of cattle dung.

SCIENTIFIC NAME	*Scarabaeus* and other genera
DISTRIBUTION	Worldwide
SIZE	Typical length 2.5cm

JAPANESE BEETLE

This small beetle feeds on leaves and fruit, and can seriously damage crops. Its larvae live underground, where they also cause damage when they feed. Originally from Japan, this beetle reached North America in 1916, stowing away inside a cargo of plants. It has now spread throughout the eastern USA. The Japanese beetle and its relatives often fly into brightly lit windows after dark.

SCIENTIFIC NAME	*Popilla japonica*
DISTRIBUTION	Japan, North America
SIZE	Up to 1.2cm long

Tough elytra

ABOVE *Despite its fearsome appearance, the male European stag beetle* (Lucanus cervus) *is a harmless vegetarian.*
BELOW *Stag beetles mate only after a lengthy courtship. The female lays her eggs in the rotting wood of old trees.*

Japanese beetle – a relative of the cockchafer

COCKCHAFER

This large beetle usually flies after dark, and sometimes causes alarm when it zooms noisily through open windows in spring. Despite its size, the cockchafer is harmless to people, though it can be a serious pest on farms and in gardens. Adult cockchafers feed on the leaves of trees but their larvae live underground, where they chew their way through roots and often attack cereals and other crops. They take up to four years to mature.

SCIENTIFIC NAME
Melolontha melolontha

DISTRIBUTION Europe

SIZE Up to 3cm long

Fan-shaped antennae

Hindwings unfolded, ready for flight

LEFT *Like all beetles, cockchafers flap only their hindwings when they fly. Their forewings stay still, sticking out at right angles to the body.*

HERCULES BEETLE

The male Hercules beetle is the world's longest beetle. Half its length is made up by a pair of gigantic 'horns'. The horns are arranged one above the other. The lower one is attached to the beetle's head and the upper one to its thorax. The horns are not used as weapons, but help the males to attract females. The females are much smaller than the males and have much shorter horns. Hercules beetles feed on fruit and are found only in the American tropics.

SCIENTIFIC NAME *Dynastes hercules*

DISTRIBUTION Central America, South America, Caribbean islands

SIZE Males up to 19cm long, including horns; females about 6cm long

Elytra lifted away from the body

Adult cockchafer

Cockchafer larva

GOLIATH BEETLE

This beetle is the heaviest insect alive today, weighing up to 100g. Despite its weight, it is a good flier. The Goliath beetle lives in tropical forests, where the adult eats flowers high above the ground. Its larvae develop in rotting wood.

SCIENTIFIC NAME *Goliathus giganteus*

DISTRIBUTION Central and western Africa

SIZE Up to 11cm long

CLICK BEETLE

These beetles have an unusual way of getting themselves out of danger. If click beetles are threatened, they drop to the ground on their back, with their legs held closely by their sides. Then, with a sudden click, they flick themselves into the air. Click beetles can do this because they have a special joint in their thorax. It is normally locked by a peg but, if the beetle arches its back, the joint suddenly bends, throwing the beetle skywards. Click beetles feed on plants. Their larvae – called wireworms – live underground and can cause a lot of damage to plants by eating their roots.

SCIENTIFIC NAME *Athous* and other genera

DISTRIBUTION Worldwide

SIZE Typical length 1.5cm

Click beetle larva

Male click beetle
(Athous haemorrhoidalis)

TOP *Cockchafer larvae have powerful jaws and well-developed legs. They curl up in the shape of a letter C.*
ABOVE *Click beetle larvae have a slender body and small legs, which is why they are called wireworms.*

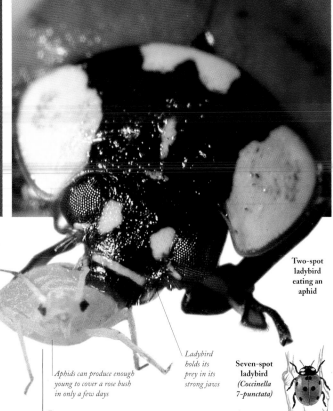

Two-spot
ladybird
eating an
aphid

G LOW - WORM

On warm summer nights, female glow-
worms climb up blades of grass and
produce a light to attract males
flying overhead. If anything disturbs
them, they switch off their light
immediately. They generate the
light in a special organ on the
underside of their abdomen.
The females look more like
woodlice than beetles, with
stubby legs and no wings.
Glow-worms eat small
snails. They paralyse
them with a digestive
fluid that turns the snail's body
to liquid, then suck up their meal.

SCIENTIFIC NAME	*Lampyris noctiluca*
DISTRIBUTION	Europe
SIZE	Up to 1.5cm long

F IREFLY

Fireflies are close relatives of glow-worms but,
unlike glow-worms, both males and females
produce a light as a way of finding a mate. Male
fireflies flash their light as they fly a few metres
above the ground. The females flash back from
the ground or from trees, guiding the males
towards them. Each species of firefly has its
own flashing sequence to find the right mate.

SCIENTIFIC NAME	*Photinus* and other genera
DISTRIBUTION	Worldwide
SIZE	Typical length 1.5cm

*Aphids can produce enough
young to cover a rose bush
in only a few days*

*Ladybird
holds its
prey in its
strong jaws*

Seven-spot
ladybird
*(Coccinella
7-punctata)*

L ADYBIRD

Few insects are as well known as ladybirds, or
as useful. These brightly coloured beetles spend
their life on plants. They feed on aphids and
other plant pests, which is why they are welcome
in gardens. Young ladybirds look quite unlike
their parents, with a narrow body and stubby
legs, but they usually eat the same kind of food.
During the autumn, ladybirds often gather
together to hibernate under loose bark or among
fallen leaves. Their bold colours warn birds and
other animals that they taste unpleasant. The
two-spot ladybird *(Adalia bipunctata)* is one of
the most common and widespread ladybirds.

SCIENTIFIC NAME	*Adalia* and other genera
DISTRIBUTION	Worldwide
SIZE	Typical length 5mm

TOP LEFT *Clinging to the
top of a blade of grass, a
female glow-worm waves
her luminous abdomen to
attract winged males.*
TOP RIGHT *Ladybirds can
eat up to 50 aphids a day.*
ABOVE *Many ladybirds
are named after their spots.
Some species have more
than 20 spots, which can
be difficult to count.*

MUSEUM BEETLE

This small insect belongs to a family of beetles that often damage fabrics, fur and stored food. It gets its name because it attacks stuffed animals, ruining many museum displays. The adult beetles, which are small and oval, do little harm. Most of the damage is done by their furry larvae, which are known as woolly bears. Museum beetles and their many relatives do not need to drink because they get all the water they need from their food. They can survive for years locked away in cupboards or cabinets, slowly eating their way through the contents.

SCIENTIFIC NAME	*Anthrenus museorum*
DISTRIBUTION	Worldwide
SIZE	About 4mm long

FURNITURE BEETLE

More commonly known as woodworm, this beetle bores its way through all kinds of dead wood. The larvae do most of the damage and, given enough time, they can reduce timber and furniture to dust. Adult furniture beetles tunnel their way out of the wood to breed, leaving circular holes that are a sure sign of woodworm damage. Like many other wood-boring beetles, these insects have a cylindrical body and a small head tucked away beneath the thorax. Because wood is not very nutritious, they can take a long time to reach maturity.

SCIENTIFIC NAME	*Anobium punctatum*
DISTRIBUTION	Worldwide
SIZE	About 4mm long

DEATHWATCH BEETLE

This small brown beetle feeds on wood, especially old trees and decaying trunks. If it gets inside a building, it can attack large timbers, sometimes causing them to collapse. Adult deathwatch beetles attract each other by tapping their jaws on the wood. This eerie sound would often be heard in the middle of the night, and was particularly noticeable while people sat silently watching over anyone who was seriously ill and likely to die.

SCIENTIFIC NAME	
Xestobium rufovillosum	
DISTRIBUTION	Worldwide
SIZE	About 7mm long

LONGHORN BEETLE

There are about 25,000 species of longhorn beetle. They are wood-boring insects that attack trees all over the world. They have long front legs and even longer antennae or 'horns', and many are beautifully coloured. The harlequin longhorn (*Acrocinus longimanus*) is one of the most spectacular of all. It has brilliant black, red and yellow markings and its antennae can be more than 12cm long – longer than the rest of its body. Harlequin longhorns live in tropical forests. They are active by day, but often crash into lights after dark.

SCIENTIFIC NAME	*Acrocinus* and other genera
DISTRIBUTION	Worldwide
SIZE	Up to 8cm long, excluding antennae

WASP BEETLE

This European longhorn beetle is vividly coloured yellow and black. Many people mistake it for a wasp – as do birds and other animals. They see its wasp-like colours, think it has a dangerous sting and leave it alone. The colours are only part of the beetle's strategy – it also moves in a jerky, wasp-like way.

SCIENTIFIC NAME	*Clytus arietis*
DISTRIBUTION	Europe
SIZE	Up to 1.8cm long

Furniture beetle

Deathwatch beetle

TOP *When furniture beetles become adults, they bite their way out of wood, making tiny round holes.*
ABOVE *Deathwatch beetles tap on wood during their breeding season in spring and early summer.*
BELOW *Wasp beetles are good fliers. This one is opening its brightly coloured forewings, ready to take off.*

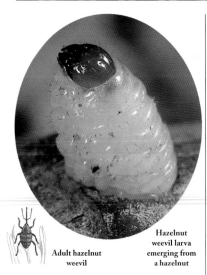

Adult hazelnut weevil

Hazelnut weevil larva emerging from a hazelnut

FLEA BEETLE
If a flea beetle is touched, it escapes by jumping like a flea. Flea beetles can do this because they have a small, light body and specially thickened hind legs. These tiny beetles nibble the surface of leaves and can be so numerous that they cause problems in gardens and on farms. Each kind of flea beetle has its own favourite plants. Some species feed on turnips, cabbages and cauliflowers. Other common species eat the leaves of potatoes, grapevines and beans.

SCIENTIFIC NAME	*Phyllotreta* and other genera
DISTRIBUTION	Worldwide
SIZE	Typical length 3mm

OIL BEETLE OR BLISTER BEETLE
These lumbering insects have a large abdomen and no hindwings. If they are touched, they can produce an oily liquid that blisters human skin. Adult oil beetles feed on plants, but their larvae are parasites of other insects. When the larvae hatch, they cling to other insects with their long legs and sharp claws and feed on the insects' eggs or young. Later, they become more like maggots, losing their legs before finally turning into adults. Some oil beetles attack bees, but many others target grasshoppers.

SCIENTIFIC NAME	*Meloe* and other genera
DISTRIBUTION	Worldwide
SIZE	Typical length 3cm

TORTOISE BEETLE
Tortoise beetles have a humped back formed by their thorax and elytra. The hump covers their legs and head, just like a tortoise's shell. These beetles feed on plants. They are often brightly coloured, sometimes with a metallic sheen. The green tortoise beetle *(Cassida viridis)* is brilliant green which makes it difficult to see on leaves.

SCIENTIFIC NAME	*Cassida* and other genera
DISTRIBUTION	Worldwide
SIZE	Typical length 1cm

COLORADO BEETLE
This beetle is one of the world's most damaging agricultural pests. Adult Colorado beetles and their larvae thrive on potato leaves and can soon reduce an entire field to little more than stalks. An inhabitant of North America, it originally fed on wild mountain plants. When potato farming spread across the continent in the mid-1800s, the beetle spread too. During the 1920s, it was accidentally introduced into Europe and it is still spreading in other parts of the world.

SCIENTIFIC NAME	*Leptinotarsa decemlineata*
DISTRIBUTION	North America, Europe; sporadically in other parts of the world
SIZE	Up to 1.2cm long

HAZELNUT WEEVIL
There are about 40,000 species of weevil, making them the largest and most successful family in the entire insect world. Most of them have a long, curving snout, with antennae halfway down and mouthparts at the end. The female hazelnut weevil uses its snout to gnaw holes in young hazelnuts. It lays an egg in each hole and the larva uses the nut as a home and as food. When the nut drops off the tree, the larva climbs out and turns into an adult in the soil.

SCIENTIFIC NAME	*Curculio nucum*
DISTRIBUTION	Europe
SIZE	Female about 7mm long, including snout; male slightly smaller

COTTON-BOLL WEEVIL
In the 1890s, the cotton-boll weevil spread to the USA from Mexico and it has been a problem there ever since. The adult weevils feed on the seedpods, or bolls, of cotton plants, and also lay their eggs inside them. Cotton bolls normally produce cotton fibres, but when they are attacked by weevils they fall off the plants, ruining much of the crop. Cotton-boll weevils breed quickly,

LEFT *A hazelnut weevil larva emerges from a nut, ready to turn into an adult.*
BELOW AND RIGHT *Green tortoise beetles keep their heads tucked under their 'shells'.*

ABOVE LEFT *The Colorado beetle has black stripes on its elytra.*
ABOVE RIGHT *Oil beetles cannot fly. This is a male beetle* (Meloe proscarabaeus); *females are slightly larger.*

Narrow gap between thorax and elytra

TOP AND ABOVE *Adult elm bark beetles emerge from trees in late spring and early summer. They spread a fungal disease through elm trees, preventing them from moving water from their roots to their leaves. The leaves turn yellow and fall early and, after a few years, the diseased trees die.*

Neck hinges where the head and thorax join

ABOVE *The giraffe beetle's neck is made up by a very long thorax and a stretched-out head.*

cramming up to ten generations into a single year. This makes it difficult to keep the numbers under control.

SCIENTIFIC NAME *Anthonomus grandis*
DISTRIBUTION North America, South America
SIZE Up to 7mm long

GIRAFFE BEETLE

This weevil has a hinged 'neck' that is more than twice as long as its body. Its antennae are just behind its mouthparts and look like whiskers at the end of its nose. The giraffe beetle lives on trees and its neck helps it to reach its food.

SCIENTIFIC NAME *Tribus attelabini*
DISTRIBUTION Madagascar
SIZE About 2.5cm long

ELM BARK BEETLE

Bark beetles live beneath tree bark, where they feed by tunnelling through the surface of the wood. As their larvae develop, they excavate a branching pattern of tunnels called a gallery, which is easy to see when dead bark falls away. When a larva turns into an adult, it stops feeding and tunnelling. The adult then chews its way through the bark and flies away to breed. As their name suggests, elm bark beetles attack elm trees. They do not kill elm trees themselves, but they spread Dutch elm disease as they feed. This disease originally came from Asia, but it has spread all over the northern hemisphere, killing millions of trees in Europe and North America.

SCIENTIFIC NAME *Scolytus scolytus*
DISTRIBUTION Europe, Asia, North America
SIZE About 5mm long

FLIES

Unlike most other insects, flies have just a single pair of wings. In the place of hindwings, they have small pin-shaped organs called halteres, which help them to balance during flight. Most flies are extremely nimble in the air. They can hover and land upside down, and they can dodge out of the way very quickly, which makes them difficult to catch. Adult flies almost always feed on fluids, including nectar and blood. Some have mouthparts that pierce and suck, but others have a pad that dissolves their food and soaks it up like a sponge. Fly larvae, or maggots, eat a wide range of different foods. Unlike adult flies, they do not have legs and often burrow through what they eat. Nearly 90,000 species of fly have been identified and they live all over the world. Many other insects, such as dragonflies (page 50) and butterflies (pages 72–79), have the word 'fly' in their name, but they do not belong to this group.

BITING MIDGE

Many small flies are known as midges. Some are quite harmless, but others have an extremely irritating bite that seems out of all proportion to their tiny size. Many of these biting midges belong to a family of insects that grow up in ditches and boggy ground. Like mosquitoes, the adult males are harmless, but the females need a meal of blood before they can lay their eggs. Biting midges are common in places where the ground is waterlogged. Some attack people, but many suck the blood of caterpillars and other insects.

SCIENTIFIC NAME	*Culicoides* and other genera
DISTRIBUTION	Mainly northern hemisphere
SIZE	Typical length 3mm

Midge

Mosquito

Bee fly

TOP *A male chironomid midge. This type of midge is harmless because neither the male nor female bites.*
CENTRE *Mosquitoes live wherever there are pools of water. This is the male of a European species (Culex pipiens).*
ABOVE *Unlike a real bee, the bee-fly has only one pair of wings.*

CRANE-FLY

Compared to other flies, crane-flies are large and clumsy, with a slow, haphazard way of flying. They have a slender body and wings, and are quite fragile. Their long legs break off easily, although losing one or two seems to do them little harm. Adult crane-flies do not eat, but their larvae, called leatherjackets, feed on rotting plants and roots. Leatherjackets live underground or in water and can be serious pests. There are many species of crane-fly. *Tipula maxima* is one of the largest, with a wingspan of about 6cm.

SCIENTIFIC NAME	*Tipula maxima*
DISTRIBUTION	Europe
SIZE	Up to 3cm long, excluding legs

MOSQUITO

There are more than 2,000 species of mosquito worldwide, and they live almost everywhere from the tropics to the Arctic. Male mosquitoes eat nectar from flowers, but the females have sharp mouthparts and feed by sucking blood. These small, biting flies often find their way indoors. Their bites are annoying because they itch, but they can also be dangerous because mosquitoes carry diseases. These are most common in the tropics and include yellow fever, dengue fever and malaria. Female mosquitoes lay their eggs on the surface of stagnant water. The eggs hatch into wriggling larvae that feed on tiny plants and animals. Once the larvae are fully grown, they change into comma-shaped pupae. These mature into adults that eventually fly away.

SCIENTIFIC NAME	*Culex* and other genera
DISTRIBUTION	Worldwide
SIZE	Typical length 1.2cm

**Black-fly
(*Simulium
equinum*)**

BLACK-FLY

Unlike mosquitoes and biting midges, these tiny flies grow up in running water. Their larvae are usually attached to water plants or to stones, and they collect food with two tufts of hairs. In early summer, adult black-flies float to the surface on bubbles of air. The males fly off to find plants and the females go in search of blood. In woods and wet places, swarms of female black-flies can make life uncomfortable for animals.

SCIENTIFIC NAME	*Simulium* and other genera
DISTRIBUTION	Worldwide
SIZE	Typical length 3mm

BEE-FLY

These furry flies look like bees but do not sting. Adult bee-flies feed at flowers. They grip the petals with their front legs, then hover while sucking nectar with their long mouthparts. Female bee-flies lay their eggs in or near the nests of solitary bees and wasps. Their larvae eat the food in the nest and also attack the grubs.

SCIENTIFIC NAME	*Bombylius* species
DISTRIBUTION	Worldwide
SIZE	Typical length 2.5cm

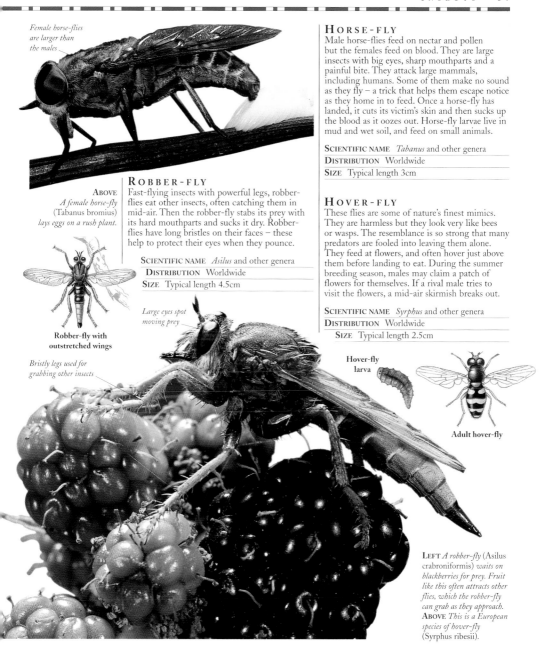

Female horse-flies are larger than the males

ABOVE
A female horse-fly (Tabanus bromius) lays eggs on a rush plant.

ROBBER-FLY

Fast-flying insects with powerful legs, robber-flies eat other insects, often catching them in mid-air. Then the robber-fly stabs its prey with its hard mouthparts and sucks it dry. Robber-flies have long bristles on their faces – these help to protect their eyes when they pounce.

SCIENTIFIC NAME	*Asilus* and other genera
DISTRIBUTION	Worldwide
SIZE	Typical length 4.5cm

Robber-fly with outstretched wings

Bristly legs used for grabbing other insects

Large eyes spot moving prey

HORSE-FLY

Male horse-flies feed on nectar and pollen but the females feed on blood. They are large insects with big eyes, sharp mouthparts and a painful bite. They attack large mammals, including humans. Some of them make no sound as they fly – a trick that helps them escape notice as they home in to feed. Once a horse-fly has landed, it cuts its victim's skin and then sucks up the blood as it oozes out. Horse-fly larvae live in mud and wet soil, and feed on small animals.

SCIENTIFIC NAME	*Tabanus* and other genera
DISTRIBUTION	Worldwide
SIZE	Typical length 3cm

HOVER-FLY

These flies are some of nature's finest mimics. They are harmless but they look very like bees or wasps. The resemblance is so strong that many predators are fooled into leaving them alone. They feed at flowers, and often hover just above them before landing to eat. During the summer breeding season, males may claim a patch of flowers for themselves. If a rival male tries to visit the flowers, a mid-air skirmish breaks out.

SCIENTIFIC NAME	*Syrphus* and other genera
DISTRIBUTION	Worldwide
SIZE	Typical length 2.5cm

Hover-fly larva

Adult hover-fly

LEFT *A robber-fly* (Asilus crabroniformis) *waits on blackberries for prey. Fruit like this often attracts other flies, which the robber-fly can grab as they approach.*
ABOVE *This is a European species of hover-fly* (Syrphus ribesii).

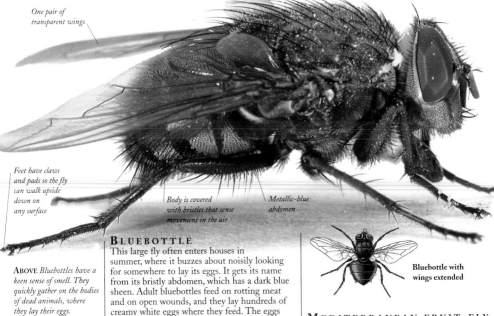

*One pair of
transparent wings*

*Feet have claws
and pads so the fly
can walk upside
down on
any surface*

*Body is covered
with bristles that sense
movement in the air*

*Metallic-blue
abdomen*

ABOVE *Bluebottles have a
keen sense of smell. They
quickly gather on the bodies
of dead animals, where
they lay their eggs.*

CENTRE AND ABOVE
*House-flies have large eyes
that take up most of their
head. Their mouthparts
fold up underneath their
head when not in use.*

BLUEBOTTLE

This large fly often enters houses in
summer, where it buzzes about noisily looking
for somewhere to lay its eggs. It gets its name
from its bristly abdomen, which has a dark blue
sheen. Adult bluebottles feed on rotting meat
and on open wounds, and they lay hundreds of
creamy white eggs where they feed. The eggs
produce wriggling larvae, or maggots, that
quickly burrow into the food. In hot weather,
the bluebottle's entire life-cycle takes just over
a month. Similar flies, called greenbottles,
live in much the same way.

SCIENTIFIC NAME	*Calliphora vomitoria*
DISTRIBUTION	Worldwide
SIZE	About 1.2cm long

HOUSE-FLY

This fly is probably one of the most
common insects on Earth. It has spread
with people across the planet and can be seen
in places as far apart as New Zealand and the
Arctic. Adult house-flies feed on anything sweet
or rotting, mopping it up with their spongy
mouthparts. As they feed, they often leave
patches of saliva that turn into 'fly-spots' when
they dry. Their larvae grow up in animal manure
and household waste, turning into adult flies
in as few as ten days if the weather is warm.
House-flies do not bite, but they are dangerous
because they spread many diseases as they feed.

SCIENTIFIC NAME	*Musca domestica*
DISTRIBUTION	Worldwide
SIZE	Up to 6mm long

**Bluebottle with
wings extended**

MEDITERRANEAN FRUIT-FLY

Originally from southern Europe, this small
fruit-eating fly is now a serious problem in
many warm parts of the world. It lays its eggs
on the skin of many kinds of fruit, including
oranges, peaches and cherries. The larvae feed
inside the fruit, often causing them to drop to
the ground. Like its 1,500 or more close
relatives, the 'medfly' has a short body,
colourful eyes and mottled wings.

SCIENTIFIC NAME	*Ceratitis capitata*
DISTRIBUTION	Warm places worldwide
SIZE	About 5mm long

VINEGAR-FLY

This tiny red-eyed fly is originally from Africa.
It breeds in rotting fruit, and is strongly attracted
by the smell of fruit and also by vinegar and
wine. It often flies around drinking glasses and
open bottles, sometimes falling in. Vinegar-flies
are important in science because they are easy to
raise in laboratories. They are used to investigate
the way in which characteristics are inherited.

SCIENTIFIC NAME	*Drosophila melanogaster*
DISTRIBUTION	Worldwide
SIZE	About 3mm long

BELOW *These Australian bush-flies have settled on a slice of cucumber to drink its moisture.*

Bush-flies suck up liquid through a spongy pad

AUSTRALIAN BUSH-FLY

A close relative of the house-fly, this insect lives in the Australian bush, where it can make outdoor life very uncomfortable during summer months. At this time of year, bush-flies buzz around the eyes and mouths of large animals, including humans. They land to drink their saliva and tears. These fluids contain water, and also dissolved substances that bush-flies can use as food. The females lay eggs in manure from all kinds of animals including emus, kangaroos and cattle. After hatching in the manure, the larvae complete their development in the soil.

SCIENTIFIC NAME *Musca vetustissima*

DISTRIBUTION Australia

SIZE About 8mm long

TSETSE-FLY

These blood-sucking insects from Africa attack wild mammals, farm livestock and people. They are dangerous because, when they bite, they can spread a disease called sleeping sickness. Adult tsetse-flies feed every few days. They track down their victims by sight, then pierce the skin using their sharp mouthparts. Female tsetse-flies give birth to fully formed larvae, one at a time. These burrow into the soil and immediately start to develop into adult flies. Tsetse-flies are difficult to control and, in some parts of Africa, sleeping sickness is a major problem.

SCIENTIFIC NAME *Glossina palpalis*

DISTRIBUTION Africa

SIZE About 1.2cm long

CARROT-FLY

An unwelcome visitor to gardens, this fly lays its eggs on carrots and related plants such as parsnips and celery. Its larvae eat their way through a carrot's root, making it stunted and deformed. Once the larvae are fully grown, they crawl out of the carrot and change into adults in the soil. Carrot-flies can produce two generations in a year, so the same crop can be attacked twice.

SCIENTIFIC NAME *Psila rosae*

DISTRIBUTION Worldwide

SIZE Up to 5mm long

SHEEP KED

This insect is a blood-sucking parasite that lives on sheep. It does not have wings, but it can scuttle about quickly on its strong, hooked legs. Sheep keds give birth to fully developed larvae. These immediately turn into pupae, producing adult keds about three weeks later.

SCIENTIFIC NAME *Melophagus ovinus*

DISTRIBUTION Worldwide

SIZE About 6mm long

RIGHT *An African tsetse-fly drinks a meal of human blood.*

BUTTERFLIES

There are more than 150,000 species of butterfly and moth (pages 80–83). Some of them are drab and inconspicuous, but many butterflies have large and brilliantly coloured wings. Unlike other insects, butterflies and moths are covered with tiny scales. The scales on their body often look like fur, but the ones on their wings are flat, and overlap like tiles on a roof. In many species, these scales reflect light in a particular way, making the wings shimmer. Adult butterflies and moths feed on nectar and other fluids, such as fruit and plant juices. They have long, tubular mouthparts for probing into flowers. Their larvae, called caterpillars, have biting jaws and feed mainly on plants. Butterflies are sun-loving insects and are most common in warm parts of the world.

TIGER SWALLOWTAIL

This insect belongs to a family of spectacular butterflies. It has a long 'tail' on each hindwing and is a strong flier. Tiger swallowtails feed from flowers and lay their eggs on trees. Their caterpillars are camouflaged to look like bird droppings when they are young. Later they turn green, with two yellow spots on their backs to scare away predators.

SCIENTIFIC NAME
Papilio glaucus
DISTRIBUTION
North America
SIZE Wingspan up to 16cm

Forewings are larger than hindwings

Antennae have a club-shaped tip

Mouthparts coiled up during flight

Six jointed legs

Common swallowtail

Common swallowtail
(*Papilo machaon*) caterpillar

LARGE SKIPPER

Skippers are small, fast-flying butterflies that dart from flower to flower. They often rest with their wings half-open, instead of folding them together like most butterflies. The large skipper is a common species that lays its eggs on grasses. Its caterpillars are bluish-green, which helps to camouflage them in the grass as they feed. The caterpillars hibernate through the winter and become adults the following spring.

SCIENTIFIC NAME *Ochlodes venatus*
DISTRIBUTION Europe, Asia
SIZE Wingspan up to 3.5cm

SMALL APOLLO

Compared to many butterflies, the small Apollo copes well with cold weather. It lives on flower-covered mountain slopes and in the tundra, a frozen, treeless area north of the Arctic Circle. Apollos fly slowly and close to the ground. The adults drink nectar from flowers, while the caterpillars eat the leaves of plants, such as stonecrops and saxifrages. Small Apollo caterpillars hibernate during the winter, which in the tundra can be more than six months long.

SCIENTIFIC NAME *Parnassius phoebus*
DISTRIBUTION Europe, northern Asia, North America
SIZE Wingspan up to 7.5cm

QUEEN ALEXANDRA'S BIRDWING

Birdwings are the biggest butterflies in the world, and the Queen Alexandra is the largest species of all. The males have metallic blue-green wings and a bright yellow body, but the females, which are larger, are black and brown. These giant insects live in dense tropical forest, where they feed on just one species of climbing vine. Because they fly high above the forest floor, they are rarely seen. Butterfly collectors once paid high prices for this species and as a result it became endangered. Today it is protected by law.

SCIENTIFIC NAME
Ornithoptera alexandrae
DISTRIBUTION Papua New Guinea
SIZE Wingspan up to 28cm

LEFT *This tiger swallowtail is landing on a cluster of lantana flowers. All species of swallowtail have large, boldly marked wings like these.*

Large white in flight

Antennae are used to detect scents in the air

Underside of orange tip's wings are mottled to camouflage it when resting with wings folded up

Small white

Small white caterpillar

ABOVE LEFT *The large white's* (Pieris brassicae) *markings are similar to those of the small white.*
LEFT *The small white lays its eggs among cabbage plants. It lays single eggs and its well-camouflaged caterpillars feed alone.*

SMALL WHITE

This insect may not be one of the world's most colourful butterflies, but it is one of the most successful. Its caterpillars feed on cabbage and related plants and have become a pest where these plants are cultivated. The small white originally came from Europe, but was introduced accidentally into North America in the 1860s, and into Australia in 1939. Today it is found on all continents except Antarctica. Small whites lay bright yellow eggs, but their caterpillars are pale green, helping them to stay hidden as they feed.

SCIENTIFIC NAME	*Pieris rapae*
DISTRIBUTION	Worldwide
SIZE	Wingspan up to 5cm

ORANGE TIP

This is a relative of the small white. The male butterfly has a bright orange tip to its front wings, but the female's wings are white and grey. Orange tips feed on relatives of the cabbage although, fortunately for gardeners, they do not attack cabbages themselves. As caterpillars, orange tips have a dangerous life. When they first hatch, they feed on each other, and the survivors then switch to a diet of plants.

SCIENTIFIC NAME	*Anthocharis cardamines*
DISTRIBUTION	Europe, Asia
SIZE	Wingspan up to 5cm

ABOVE *The orange tip has many relatives all over the world. Some also have orange wingtips, but others are red or crimson.*

METAMORPHOSIS

Many animals change shape as they mature. This process is called metamorphosis. It can happen gradually as an animal grows, or rapidly at a certain point in its early life. In the insect world, dragonflies, grasshoppers, cockroaches and bugs undergo 'incomplete metamorphosis'. This means that they change slightly every time they moult. Their wings do not fully develop until their final moult but, apart from this, they resemble their parents when they are young. Insects that develop in this way are called nymphs.

Butterflies, moths, and many other insects undergo 'complete metamorphosis'. They hatch from eggs as larvae, which include grubs, caterpillars and maggots. Instead of changing gradually, their bodies are dismantled and rebuilt during a resting stage called a pupa. Larvae also feature in the life-cycles of water animals, such as crustaceans, echinoderms and amphibians. By having a larval stage, these animals can use more than one kind of food, so improving their chances of survival.

ABOVE *It takes about four weeks for the monarch butterfly (page 78) to change from an egg into an adult butterfly. The caterpillar feeds and grows quickly before turning into a pupa, protected by a case called a chrysalis. Finally, the adult crawls out, dries off and flies away.*

ABOVE *The small copper is an energetic little butterfly, and can often be seen darting from flower to flower and chasing other butterflies in meadows and open spaces.*

LARGE BLUE

The large blue has an unusual life story. Like other blues, it produces caterpillars that look like small slugs. These start life by feeding on wild flowers but, within a few days, they are 'adopted' by ants, which take them into their underground nests. The ants are tricked by the shape and smell of the caterpillars into thinking that they are ant grubs. Once a large blue caterpillar is underground, it turns into a hungry predator, killing and eating ant grubs. After several months in the nest, it pupates, and the butterfly flies out of the ants' nest to begin its adult life. Despite its name, the large blue is not a large butterfly.

SCIENTIFIC NAME	*Maculinea arion*
DISTRIBUTION	Europe, northern Asia
SIZE	Wingspan up to 4cm

SMALL COPPER

The small copper is closely related to the large blue. They look different, but both species produce caterpillars that resemble small slugs. The small copper's caterpillars are green with white and red spots. Unlike the large blue caterpillars, they are vegetarians, feeding on dock leaves, sorrels and related plants. Small coppers breed very rapidly. If the summer is warm and dry, they can produce three generations in a single year. In exceptionally warm years, they sometimes manage to squeeze in a fourth.

SCIENTIFIC NAME	*Lycaena phleas*
DISTRIBUTION	Europe, Asia, North America
SIZE	Wingspan about 2.5cm

GREY HAIRSTREAK

When it is perched on a leaf, this small butterfly looks as if it has a head at each end of its body. There are brightly coloured spots near the tips of its hindwings that resemble eyes, and slender tails that look like antennae. This back-to-front look is shared by many other hairstreaks. It draws attention away from the butterfly's real head and probably helps it to survive attack from birds. The grey hairstreak's caterpillars eat a variety of plants, including cultivated beans.

SCIENTIFIC NAME	*Strymon melinus*
DISTRIBUTION	North America, Central America, South America
SIZE	Wingspan up to 3cm

EUROPEAN MAP BUTTERFLY

This butterfly gets its name from the intricate map-like markings on its wings, which are mainly brown and orange. It belongs to a large family of insects called the brush-footed butterflies, or nymphalids, which also includes emperors, admirals, fritillaries and monarchs. Nymphalids have six legs, but use only four of them for walking. The front pair are much shorter than the others and are held close to the butterfly's head. The European map butterfly's caterpillars are black or brown in colour, and are covered with long yellow and black spines to deter predators. They begin life in a group, feeding on nettles and similar plants, but gradually go their separate ways in search of food.

SCIENTIFIC NAME	
	Araschnia levana
DISTRIBUTION	Europe, parts of Asia
SIZE	Wingspan up to 3cm

Veins in butterflies' wings make them sturdy enough for flight

ABOVE *There are several types of map butterfly. The European map butterfly lays its eggs in tiny strings.*

Walking legs

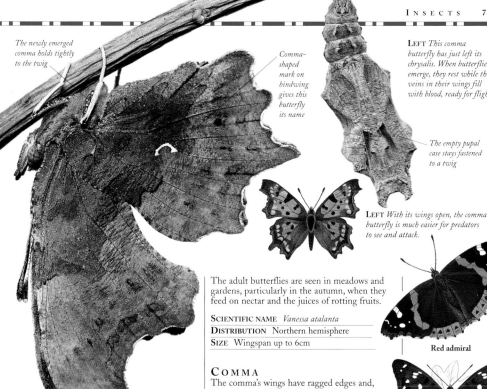

The newly emerged comma holds tightly to the twig

Comma-shaped mark on hindwing gives this butterfly its name

LEFT *This comma butterfly has just left its chrysalis. When butterflies emerge, they rest while the veins in their wings fill with blood, ready for flight.*

The empty pupal case stays fastened to a twig

LEFT *With its wings open, the comma butterfly is much easier for predators to see and attack.*

Red admiral

The adult butterflies are seen in meadows and gardens, particularly in the autumn, when they feed on nectar and the juices of rotting fruits.

SCIENTIFIC NAME	*Vanessa atalanta*
DISTRIBUTION	Northern hemisphere
SIZE	Wingspan up to 6cm

COMMA
The comma's wings have ragged edges and, when they are closed, the butterfly looks like a dead oak leaf. Commas lay their eggs on nettles and hop plants. The caterpillars have a white splash on their backs that makes them look like bird droppings. This disguise allows them to curl up on leaves and avoid being attacked.

SCIENTIFIC NAME	*Polygonia c-album*
DISTRIBUTION	Europe, northern Africa, Asia
SIZE	Wingspan up to 6cm

SILVER-WASHED FRITILLARY
Fritillaries are butterflies with wings covered with angular black marks. The silver-washed fritillary is a woodland species. Its caterpillars start life hidden in crevices in the bark of oak trees, later moving to the woodland floor and feeding on violets. Male silver-washed fritillaries have scented scales on their forewings. During courtship, as the male and female flutter around each other, the scales burst open, encouraging the female to mate.

SCIENTIFIC NAME	*Argynnis paphia*
DISTRIBUTION	Europe, northern Africa, Asia
SIZE	Wingspan up to 7cm

Purple emperor

Silver-washed fritillary

ABOVE *Like the map and comma butterflies, the red admiral, purple emperor and silver-washed fritillary belong to the nymphalid family.*

PURPLE EMPEROR
This beautifully coloured insect is a nymphalid and has only two pairs of walking legs. The purple emperor spends its time soaring high up in woodlands. The males often battle with each other above the trees. Their caterpillars feed on the leaves of sallow trees and have a pair of horns on the front of their head to ward off attack.

SCIENTIFIC NAME	*Apatura iris*
DISTRIBUTION	Europe, Asia
SIZE	Wingspan up to 7.5cm

RED ADMIRAL
This butterfly's name comes from the 'admirable' black, white and red colours on its wings. Red admirals lay their eggs in clusters on the underside of stinging nettles and related plants. Their caterpillars are black with brown and yellow spines. They feed on the nettle leaves, and protect themselves by chewing through the leaves and folding them over to make a tent.

Camberwell beauty showing yellow-bordered wings

Fur-like scales on inner surface of wings

Camouflaged underside to hindwings

ABOVE *The small tortoiseshell hibernates as an adult. It often shelters in buildings, where the central heating may well wake it up before spring arrives.*

RIGHT *Peacock butterflies have large eye-spots on their wings. If a bird attacks a peacock butterfly, it tends to peck at the eye-spots rather than the insect's body, giving it a chance to make an escape.*

CAMBERWELL BEAUTY

This large, brownish-black butterfly is known in America as the mourning cloak. Its wings have pale yellow borders that make it easy to identify in flight.
The Camberwell beauty lays its eggs on willows, poplars and other trees. Its spiny caterpillars live and feed in large groups. They react to danger by jerking their bodies in a threatening-looking way. Where there are lots of these caterpillars, they can strip young trees of their leaves.

SCIENTIFIC NAME *Nymphalis antiopa*
DISTRIBUTION Europe, Asia, North America, South America
SIZE Wingspan up to 8.5cm

SMALL TORTOISESHELL

This orange and red butterfly is one of the most common species in Europe. It can be seen almost anywhere, from city gardens to seaside cliffs. It lays its eggs on nettles, and once the eggs have hatched, the caterpillars work together to make large silk nests. As the caterpillars grow, they often eat all the leaves around the nest. If their food supplies start to run out, they move to new plants before pupating and becoming adults.

SCIENTIFIC NAME *Aglais urticae*
DISTRIBUTION Europe
SIZE Wingspan up to 5.5cm

PEACOCK

Adult butterflies often die before the winter begins, but the peacock hibernates. In the autumn, they take shelter in dry places, camouflaged by their mottled hindwings. They wake in the spring. Adult peacocks feed at many kinds of flowers and lay their eggs on nettles.

SCIENTIFIC NAME *Inachis io*
DISTRIBUTION Europe, Asia
SIZE Wingspan up to 6cm

QUEEN CRACKER BUTTERFLY

Male cracker butterflies have an unusual way of signalling to attract females – they make a loud clicking sound as they fly about. The noise is produced by their forewings, which have a hard ridge that clicks when the wings beat. Cracker butterflies are found only in the American tropics, where there are many different species. The queen cracker, with its brilliant blue and white colouring, is one of the largest examples.

SCIENTIFIC NAME *Hamadryas arethusa*
DISTRIBUTION Central America, South America
SIZE Wingspan up to 7cm

EIGHTY-EIGHT BUTTERFLY

This small tropical butterfly gets its name from the markings on the underside of its hindwings, which look like the number 88. The upperside of its wings are a plain brown colour. There are nearly 40 species of butterfly related to the eighty-eight, living mostly in the tropical forests of South America.

SCIENTIFIC NAME *Diaethria clymena*
DISTRIBUTION South America
SIZE Wingspan up to 4.5cm

Thistle flower

Fully extended wings, showing the black tips

The underside of the painted lady's wings are as colourful as the upperside

Eye-spots confuse or deter predators

tongue to reach nectar deep inside flowers. Towards the end of the summer, the young butterflies head south to escape the winter cold. Many do not survive the journey because they are killed by early frosts.

SCIENTIFIC NAME	*Cynthia cardui*
DISTRIBUTION	Worldwide, except Australia and New Zealand
SIZE	Wingspan up to 6cm

COMMON SNOUT BUTTERFLY

Snout butterflies are easy to recognize because they have a pair of unusually long mouthparts that look like a slender snout. They use these mouthparts, called palps, to find suitable foodplants for their eggs. There are about ten species of these butterflies worldwide. They include the common snout from North America, the nettle-tree butterfly from Europe *(Libythea celtis)* and the beak butterfly from Southeast Asia and Australia *(Libythea geoffroyi)*.

SCIENTIFIC NAME	*Libytheana bachmanii*
DISTRIBUTION	North America
SIZE	Wingspan up to 5cm

INDIAN LEAF BUTTERFLY

This Asian insect is one of the best examples of camouflage in the butterfly world. When it is resting on a twig, it looks exactly like a dry, brown leaf. Its forewings have a sharp point like the tip of a leaf, and its hindwings end in a long tail like a leaf's stalk. The disguise works only when the butterfly has its wings closed. As soon as it opens them to fly, it reveals the bright orange and purple colours on the upper surface of its wings. Leaf butterflies live in tropical forests, and their caterpillars are protected by spines and hairs.

SCIENTIFIC NAME	*Kallima inachus*
DISTRIBUTION	Southern Asia, Far East
SIZE	Wingspan up to 12cm

PAINTED LADY

The painted lady is one of the world's most widespread butterflies. It is also one of the greatest insect travellers. Every summer, billions of these fast-flying insects head northwards across America and Europe in search of foodplants for their young. They travel through mountain passes and across open water, often reaching areas north of the Arctic Circle. Painted ladies lay their eggs on thistles, nettles and hollyhocks. Their black and yellow spiny caterpillars feed on vegetation inside tents made from folded leaves. The adults have an extra-long

MONARCH

This large black and orange insect is a renowned traveller and one of the best-known butterflies in the world. In North America, it travels more than 3,200km between its winter quarters in Mexico and its breeding-grounds further north.

In late summer, monarchs return south to escape the worst of the winter cold. They spend the winter clustered on trees, jostling for space and a chance to bask in the sun. Monarchs absorb poisons from their diet of milkweeds. The poison is stored in their bodies, making them a dangerous meal for birds that are not put off by their bright warning colours.

Monarch with open wings

SCIENTIFIC NAME	*Danaus plexippus*
DISTRIBUTION	Originally from the Americas; now also found in parts of Europe, Southeast Asia, Australia
SIZE	Wingspan up to 10cm

TOP *Male monarchs have scent pockets on their hindwings and tufts of scented hairs on the tip of their abdomen. These release a perfume that attracts female monarchs during courtship.*
ABOVE *Morphos skim through forests, flapping their giant wings much more slowly than most other butterflies.*

BLUE MORPHO

Male morphos have beautiful blue wings that flash in the sunshine as they fly through the rainforests where they live. There are more than 50 species of morpho and they all come from the American tropics. They were once caught in huge numbers so that their wings could be used to make jewellery, but today many species are protected. The male's brilliant colour is produced by microscopic ridges on the surface of its scales. These reflect the light in a certain way, making the wings glisten with a metallic blue sheen. Female morphos usually have less blue on their wings, although in some species they are orange or brown.

SCIENTIFIC NAME	*Morpho* species
DISTRIBUTION	South America
SIZE	Wingspan up to 14cm

VICEROY

It is not easy to tell this butterfly from the monarch, because the two species are almost identical in shape and colour. The similarity is not accidental. Viceroys have come to resemble monarchs because it helps to protect them from predators. Viceroys are not poisonous but, because they look like monarchs, birds and other animals avoid them. This kind of defence, called mimicry, is common in the insect world.

SCIENTIFIC NAME	*Limenitis archippus*
DISTRIBUTION	North America, Central America
SIZE	Wingspan up to 7.5cm

GLASSWING BUTTERFLY

Glasswings have transparent wings. In some species, the wings are covered in see-through scales, but in others the scales fall off soon after the butterfly emerges from its chrysalis. Glasswings are found in tropical climates. Most of them live close to the ground in forests, where their clear wings make them difficult to spot.

SCIENTIFIC NAME	*Acraea* and other genera
DISTRIBUTION	Worldwide
SIZE	Typical wingspan 6cm

OWL BUTTERFLY

This giant butterfly has brown and grey wings and two large eye-spots that show when its wings are closed. These look like an owl's eyes and may help to scare off birds searching for insects to eat. Owl butterflies feed mainly on rotting fruit. They lay their eggs on banana plants and flowers called lobster claws. The caterpillars may grow up to 11cm long. They have large appetites, and can cause major problems in banana plantations.

SCIENTIFIC NAME	*Caligo idomeneus*
DISTRIBUTION	South America
SIZE	Wingspan up to 15cm

EVENING BROWN

This tropical butterfly feeds at dusk and hides among fallen leaves during the day. In some parts of the world, evening browns look the same all year round but, in places that have wet and dry seasons, butterflies that emerge at different times have different patterns. In western Africa, the wet-season browns have several eye-spots, but the dry-season butterflies have none.

SCIENTIFIC NAME	*Melanitis leda*
DISTRIBUTION	Africa, southern Asia, Australia
SIZE	Wingspan up to 8cm

MEADOW BROWN

This large, plain butterfly is a relative of the evening brown. It lays its eggs on grasses, sometimes dropping them as it flutters overhead. Its caterpillars are bright green – a colour that camouflages them as they feed. Meadow browns have eye-spots on their forewings, but they are too small to scare off most predators. Instead, they probably work as decoys. Birds peck at the spots instead of the butterfly's body, giving it a better chance of surviving to fly away.

SCIENTIFIC NAME	*Maniola jurtina*
DISTRIBUTION	Europe, North Africa, Middle East
SIZE	Wingspan up to 5.5cm

POSTMAN BUTTERFLY

The postman belongs to a group of butterflies called the heliconians, which are found only in warm parts of the Americas. Heliconians have long, narrow wings and their colours – red or yellow stripes on a black background – warn birds that they taste unpleasant and are not worth attacking. Like all heliconians, the postman lays its eggs on climbing plants called passionflowers. Heliconians usually ignore plants that already have eggs on them and some passionflowers grow special 'decoy eggs' to stop these butterflies from laying eggs on their leaves.

SCIENTIFIC NAME	*Heliconius melpomene*
DISTRIBUTION	Central America, tropical South America
SIZE	Wingspan up to 9cm

Meadow brown with open wings

Meadow brown caterpillar

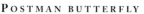

Long antennae help to detect foodplants

Hindwings are much shorter than forewings

Bright colours warn predators that the butterfly tastes unpleasant

Three pairs of slender legs

Coiled tongue

ABOVE *The meadow brown is one of the most common butterflies in Europe. Its caterpillars feed at night to avoid being seen and eaten, and the adult butterfly keeps close to the ground, relying on its eye-spots for protection.*

LEFT *The postman butterfly lives in hot, damp forests. It flies close to the ground on its elegant, rounded wings.*

MOTHS

Butterflies and moths are so closely related that it is sometimes difficult to tell them apart. Moths have a similar coiled 'tongue' to butterflies, and are covered by scales, but their antennae are often feathery, instead of club-shaped, and they fly mostly by night. Moths usually rest with their wings opened flat, whereas butterflies rest with their wings folded up. Most moths are dull in colour, but day-flying species can be as colourful as butterflies. There are more species of moth than of butterfly and they are more varied.

ABOVE *The peppered moth's speckled wings provide camouflage against tree-trunks. This moth rests with its wings partly spread.*

BELOW *The atlas moth's body is dwarfed by its four gigantic wings. This moth spends the first part of its life as a bright green caterpillar covered with long spines.*

PEPPERED MOTH

This insect is a member of a huge family of moths called the geometrids, which includes more than 15,000 species. Like other geometrids, its caterpillars move by forming their bodies into a loop, instead of by walking with their legs. The peppered moth demonstrates evolution in action. It is normally speckled black and white but, during the 19th century, a black form evolved near British cities where tree-trunks were covered in soot. This new-look moth was better camouflaged, so it became more widespread.

SCIENTIFIC NAME	*Biston betularia*
DISTRIBUTION	Europe, Asia
SIZE	Wingspan up to 6cm

WINTER MOTH

Unlike most moths, this species is active throughout the winter months. The males have rounded, greyish-brown wings, and they often flutter around lighted windows, particularly on mild, damp nights. The females have tiny wings, and cannot fly. Winter moth caterpillars feed on trees of all kinds, and they can be a serious pest where apples are grown.

SCIENTIFIC NAME	*Operophtera brumata*
DISTRIBUTION	Europe, northern Asia, Canada
SIZE	Wingspan up to 3cm

MADAGASCAN SUNSET MOTH

This day-flying moth is so colourful that it is easily mistaken for a butterfly. It has brilliant metallic markings – just like a spectacular sunset – and the long 'tails' on its hindwings make it look like a swallowtail butterfly (page 72). Sunset moths eat poisonous plants and they are brightly coloured to warn birds that they are inedible. The Madagascan sunset moth is a favourite with collectors and is now raised in captivity to protect the species in the wild.

SCIENTIFIC NAME	*Chrysiridia riphearia*
DISTRIBUTION	Madagascar
SIZE	Wingspan up to 10cm

ATLAS MOTH

With wings wide enough to cover a dinner plate, this is one of the largest moths in the world. Its wings are coloured with many shades of brown, and they have triangular 'windows' that are almost transparent. Atlas moths live in tropical forests and lay their eggs on a variety of trees.

SCIENTIFIC NAME	*Attacus atlas*
DISTRIBUTION	India, Southeast Asia, Far East
SIZE	Wingspan up to 30cm

There are no scales on the see-through 'windows'

Triangular hindwings have rounded tips

Forewings have a streamlined, swept-back tip

LEFT *The American moon moth often rests hanging from twigs and plant stems in woodland areas. It was once widespread in North America but has been endangered by pesticide use and collectors.*

Forewings have a reddish-purple band along the front edge

Each hindwing has a long twisted tail

ABOVE *Hummingbird hawkmoths have a short, stubby body and a fan-shaped tail. They spend all day on the move – just like real hummingbirds.*

ABOVE *These silkmoths have just emerged from their cocoons. Two of them are already mating. After this, the female will lay her eggs.*

DEATH'S-HEAD HAWKMOTH

Compared to other moths, hawkmoths are fast and powerful, with heavy bodies and streamlined wings. There are about 1,000 species worldwide and the death's-head is one of the fastest. It can cruise at about 40km/h, and fly even faster in short bursts. It lays its eggs on potatoes and related plants, and often migrates long distances to breed. The death's-head gets its name from markings on its back which resemble a skull. If the adult moth is picked up, it can make a loud squeaking sound. Some people believe that it is bad luck if a death's-head hawkmoth enters their house.

SCIENTIFIC NAME	*Acherontia atropos*
DISTRIBUTION	Northern Africa, Europe
SIZE	Wingspan up to 14cm

AMERICAN MOON MOTH

Moon moths have a plump, furry body and pale wings with long curling 'tails'. The American moon moth is a ghostly green colour and it has four bright eyespots – one on each wing. Like many moths, the males have large, feathery antennae. They use these to detect the scent of females, sometimes over distances of more than 3km. This moth lays its eggs on a variety of trees, including hickories and walnuts, and usually produces two generations a year. However, in Canada, where summers are short, moon moths breed just once between May and July. In Mexico, where it is warmer, they may fit up to three generations in a single year.

SCIENTIFIC NAME	*Actias luna*
DISTRIBUTION	Southern Canada, USA, Mexico
SIZE	Wingspan up to 11cm

HUMMINGBIRD HAWKMOTH

When it is feeding, this day-flying hawkmoth flutters its wings so fast that they are little more than a blur. Like its namesake the hummingbird (page 205), it hovers in front of flowers, takes a quick drink of nectar with its long tongue, and then dashes off to find its next meal. Despite its small size, the hummingbird hawkmoth is an adventurous traveller. It migrates north through Europe in early summer to breed. It sometimes crosses the sea to reach the British Isles, and ventures as far north as the Arctic Circle.

SCIENTIFIC NAME	*Macroglossum stellatarum*
DISTRIBUTION	Europe, Asia
SIZE	Wingspan up to 5cm

MULBERRY SILKMOTH

This brown or white flightless moth has been farmed as a source of silk for more than 4,000 years. Its caterpillars spin a strand of silk up to 1.5km long when making their cocoons. People harvest the silk by floating the cocoons on water and winding the strands on reels. Silkworms eat the leaves of mulberry trees in silk-producing countries such as China. There are no longer any in the wild – only captive silkmoths survive.

SCIENTIFIC NAME	*Bombyx mori*
DISTRIBUTION	Worldwide
SIZE	Wingspan up to 6cm

ABOVE AND RIGHT *The brightly coloured six-spot burnet moth is easily confused with a butterfly. After climbing out of its cocoon, it rests before taking off.*

Two pairs of slender wings

The burnet moth's antennae have thickened tips

Contrasting colours on the wings warn birds that this moth would make an unpleasant meal

PINE PROCESSIONARY MOTH

This moth lays its eggs on pine trees, and its caterpillars are serious pests. During the daytime, the caterpillars crowd together inside ball-shaped tents made of tough silk and, as night falls, they set off to feed. The caterpillars move in single file, as many as 200 travelling head-to-tail. After splitting up to feed on pine needles, the procession reforms and the caterpillars return to their silky tents. Processionary moth caterpillars follow each other by instinct – if a few are put on the rim of a cup, they crawl around in circles.

SCIENTIFIC NAME *Thaumetopia pityocampa*

DISTRIBUTION Southern Europe, northern Africa

SIZE Wingspan up to 5cm

GYPSY MOTH

The gypsy moth looks harmless enough, but its caterpillars cause tremendous damage in North American forests. They feed on leaves, and strip them so quickly that affected trees can die. Unlike most moths and butterflies, the gypsy moth is not fussy about where it lays its eggs. Its caterpillars thrive on a wide range of broadleaved and evergreen trees. Gypsy moths originally came from Europe. They were introduced into North America in 1869 as a source of silk, but the project failed and the moths escaped into the wild, where they are now common.

SCIENTIFIC NAME *Lymantria dispar*

DISTRIBUTION Europe, Asia, North America

SIZE Wingspan up to 6cm

HORNET MOTH

With its transparent wings and brown and yellow body, this harmless moth looks exactly like a stinging hornet (page 88). To make the disguise even more convincing, it also moves in a hornet-like way. A closer look shows that it has a much smaller head than a hornet and, more importantly, it does not have a sting. Hornet moths lay their eggs on poplar and willow trees and the adults feed at flowers. They belong to a family of moths called clearwings, all of which protect themselves by mimicking stinging insects.

SCIENTIFIC NAME *Sesia apiformis*

DISTRIBUTION Europe, Asia, North America

SIZE Wingspan up to 4.5cm

SIX-SPOT BURNET MOTH

Burnet moths fly by day, and have red and black markings to warn predators that they are poisonous. Like most of their relatives, they fly quite slowly and never get far above the ground. Burnets lay their eggs in grassy places and their caterpillars eat meadow plants. The caterpillars become adult moths inside papery cocoons, and often find a partner waiting to mate as soon as they emerge.

SCIENTIFIC NAME *Zygaena filipendulae*

DISTRIBUTION Europe

SIZE Wingspan up to 4cm

CLOTHES MOTH

This small, dusty-gold moth spends its whole life indoors. It can fly, but it normally prefers to scuttle away if it is disturbed. Clothes moths lay their eggs on anything containing wool or fur, including carpets, blankets and clothes. Their caterpillars live inside tents made of silk, making holes as they feed. If they are shaken out, they trek across floors or even up windows to find something else to eat. The adult moths live for two or three weeks – long enough for them to find a mate and lay the next generation of eggs.

SCIENTIFIC NAME *Tineola bisselliella*

DISTRIBUTION Worldwide

SIZE Wingspan up to 1.5cm

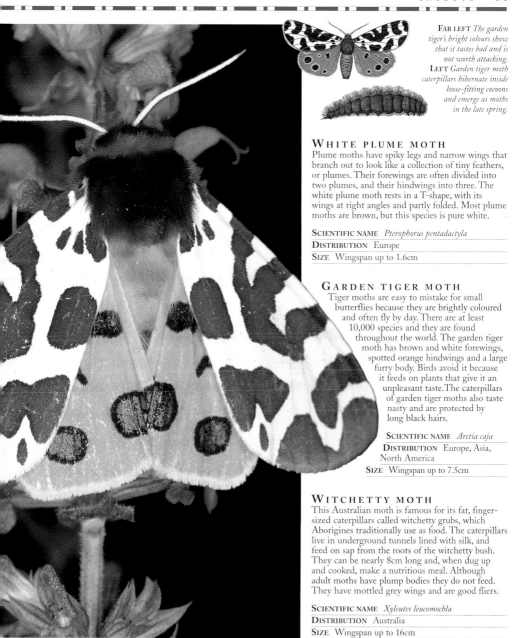

WHITE PLUME MOTH

Plume moths have spiky legs and narrow wings that branch out to look like a collection of tiny feathers, or plumes. Their forewings are often divided into two plumes, and their hindwings into three. The white plume moth rests in a T-shape, with its wings at right angles and partly folded. Most plume moths are brown, but this species is pure white.

SCIENTIFIC NAME	*Pterophorus pentadactyla*
DISTRIBUTION	Europe
SIZE	Wingspan up to 1.6cm

GARDEN TIGER MOTH

Tiger moths are easy to mistake for small butterflies because they are brightly coloured and often fly by day. There are at least 10,000 species and they are found throughout the world. The garden tiger moth has brown and white forewings, spotted orange hindwings and a large furry body. Birds avoid it because it feeds on plants that give it an unpleasant taste. The caterpillars of garden tiger moths also taste nasty and are protected by long black hairs.

SCIENTIFIC NAME	*Arctia caja*
DISTRIBUTION	Europe, Asia, North America
SIZE	Wingspan up to 7.5cm

WITCHETTY MOTH

This Australian moth is famous for its fat, finger-sized caterpillars called witchetty grubs, which Aborigines traditionally use as food. The caterpillars live in underground tunnels lined with silk, and feed on sap from the roots of the witchetty bush. They can be nearly 8cm long and, when dug up and cooked, make a nutritious meal. Although adult moths have plump bodies they do not feed. They have mottled grey wings and are good fliers.

SCIENTIFIC NAME	*Xyleutes leucomochla*
DISTRIBUTION	Australia
SIZE	Wingspan up to 16cm

ANTS, BEES AND WASPS

These three types of insect belong to the same group of animals. They have a slender 'waist' between the thorax and the abdomen and often have a sting. Bees and wasps have four narrow, transparent wings. Ants are usually wingless, but many develop winged forms when they reproduce. Most bees get their food from flowers, using their long tongues to suck up nectar. Adult wasps eat similar food, but they feed their young on insects. Ants have the most varied diet. Some are hunters, others are vegetarians, but many are scavengers – collecting whatever food they can find. Most of these insects are social species, living in colonies or family groups. A female – the queen – lays all the colony's eggs and the other members have different roles. There are more than 100,000 species of ant, bee and wasp, and they live all over the world.

BULLDOG ANT

These ants are large and fierce, with big jaws and powerful stings. If they are threatened, they sprint towards their enemy, sometimes leaping 30cm off the ground. Bulldog ants live in small colonies, usually of less than 1,000 insects. As with most ants, the colonies consist of worker ants, which collect food and build, and soldier ants, which defend the nest. Bulldog ants eat nectar and other insects.

SCIENTIFIC NAME	*Myrmecia* species
DISTRIBUTION	Australia
SIZE	Up to 3.5cm long

WOOD ANT

In the evergreen forests of Europe, large mounds of twigs and pine-needles show where wood ants have set up home. Their nests can be 1.5m high and they often house several queens. Wood ants feed mainly on small insects. They do not have a sting, but they have a powerful bite and can squirt formic acid at attackers.

SCIENTIFIC NAME	*Formica rufa*
DISTRIBUTION	Europe
SIZE	About 1cm long

HONEY ANT

Insects that live in dry places have to find ways to survive periods of drought. Honey ants get around this problem by using specialized workers to store water and food. These workers, called repletes, live underground permanently, hanging upside down. In the wet season, they are fed with nectar and honeydew – a sugary liquid produced by sap-sucking insects. The repletes store this mixture, swelling up like miniature balloons. During droughts, they release the food to keep their nest-mates alive. Native Americans once used these ants as food.

SCIENTIFIC NAME	*Myrmecocystus melliger*
DISTRIBUTION	North America, Central America
SIZE	Workers about 1cm long

RIGHT *These wood ants are tending a group of aphids high up in a tree. The ants guard the aphids and collect drops of honeydew that the aphids produce as they feed.*

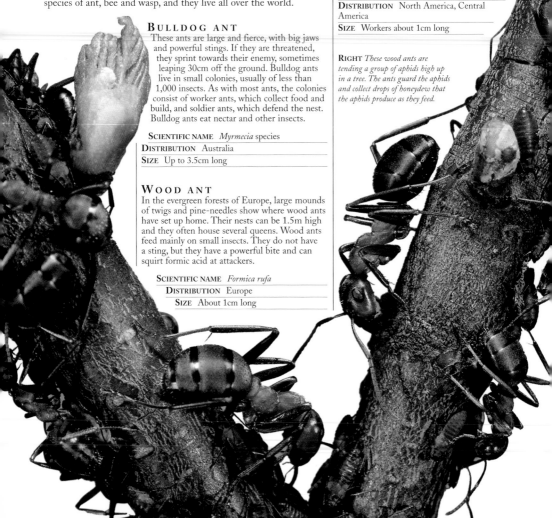

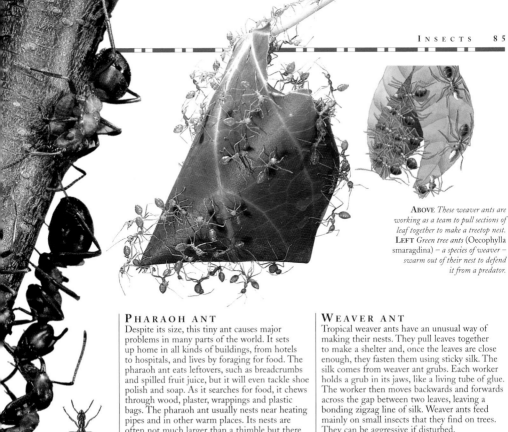

ABOVE *Ants, such as
this wood ant, use their
antennae to taste food
and to communicate. The
antennae have 'elbows'
where they bend.*
BELOW *Army ants have
tiny eyes, and find their
prey by touch. Each army
of ants can contain more
than 500,000 insects.*

PHARAOH ANT

Despite its size, this tiny ant causes major
problems in many parts of the world. It sets
up home in all kinds of buildings, from hotels
to hospitals, and lives by foraging for food. The
pharaoh ant eats leftovers, such as breadcrumbs
and spilled fruit juice, but it will even tackle shoe
polish and soap. As it searches for food, it chews
through wood, plaster, wrappings and plastic
bags. The pharaoh ant usually nests near heating
pipes and in other warm places. Its nests are
often not much larger than a thimble but there
may be several hundred in a single building,
which makes them difficult to control.

SCIENTIFIC NAME	*Monomorium pharaonis*
DISTRIBUTION	Worldwide
SIZE	Workers about 2mm long

ARMY ANT

Instead of making a permanent nest, army ants
are often on the move. They pour across the
forest floor at the run, using their formidable
jaws to overpower animals many times larger
than themselves. Army ants spend their nights
in temporary camps called bivouacs, which often
hang from fallen logs. The ants themselves form
the walls of the bivouacs by clinging to each
other with their feet. Driver ants, which are
found in Africa, live in a similar way.

SCIENTIFIC NAME	*Eciton* species
DISTRIBUTION	Central America, South America
SIZE	Up to 1.5cm long

WEAVER ANT

Tropical weaver ants have an unusual way of
making their nests. They pull leaves together
to make a shelter and, once the leaves are close
enough, they fasten them using sticky silk. The
silk comes from weaver ant grubs. Each worker
holds a grub in its jaws, like a living tube of glue.
The worker then moves backwards and forwards
across the gap between two leaves, leaving a
bonding zigzag line of silk. Weaver ants feed
mainly on small insects that they find on trees.
They can be aggressive if disturbed.

SCIENTIFIC NAME	*Oecophylla* species
DISTRIBUTION	Tropical Africa, southern Asia, Australia
SIZE	About 1cm long

LEAFCUTTER ANT

There are several species of leafcutter ant, but
they are found only in the Americas. Leafcutter
ants live in rainforests, where they excavate large
underground nests. They spend the night in their
nests but, at dawn, the workers pour out and
climb to the tree tops, where they cut out pieces
of leaves. They carry these leaf-pieces back to
their nests, following well-worn trails over the
forest floor. Instead of eating the leaf-pieces,
leafcutters use them to build spongy 'compost
heaps' underground. A fungus grows on the
heaps and the ants harvest it as food.

SCIENTIFIC NAME	*Atta* species
DISTRIBUTION	Central America, South America
SIZE	Largest workers about 1.2cm long

HONEY BEE

Originally from southern Asia, this useful insect has been spread around the world by people, partly because it makes honey and partly because it pollinates flowers, helping to produce fruits and seeds. Worker honey bees have a compact body and strong wings. Their back legs each have a hair-lined basket that they use for collecting pollen. The queen bee is slightly larger and spends all the time in the nest, laying several hundred eggs a day. In the wild, honey bees nest in hollow trees, and they raise their young in hanging sheets of wax made up of six-sided cells. Some of the cells contain eggs or larvae but others store honey, which the bees use as a winter food. Beekeepers design beehives to be like a tree hollow, but with a wooden frame so that they can take the honey out to eat.

SCIENTIFIC NAME	*Apis mellifera*
DISTRIBUTION	Worldwide
SIZE	Workers up to 1.5cm long

BUMBLEBEE

Throughout much of the northern hemisphere, the year's first bumblebees are a sure sign that spring has arrived. These bees have a large, hairy body, and they can fly when many other insects are still grounded by the cold. Many bumblebees build small nests underground, often in holes made by mice. When the eggs hatch, they produce workers that collect food and look after the developing young. Unlike honey bees, bumblebees do not store up food for the winter. The queens mate and then hibernate but, when the weather turns cold, the worker bees die.

SCIENTIFIC NAME	*Bombus* and other genera
DISTRIBUTION	Mainly northern hemisphere
SIZE	Up to 4cm long

LEFT *A garden bumblebee* (Bombus hortorum) *uses its long tongue to get nectar from a teasel flower.*

Six-sided cells make the honeycomb light, but strong

RIGHT *A worker honey bee (in the centre of the picture) does a special dance to tell the other workers where there is food. The dance shows in which direction the food is and how far away.*

MINING BEE

Unlike honey bees and bumblebees, mining bees are solitary species, not social ones. This means that the adult bees go their separate ways when they grow up. During spring, the female mining bee digs a small tunnel in loose ground. After laying her eggs and stocking the tunnel with food, she closes it up and flies away. The larvae develop on their own, and eventually emerge from the tunnel as adults. There are hundreds of species of mining bee. They nest in dry ground, and also in lawns.

SCIENTIFIC NAME	*Andrena* species
DISTRIBUTION	Worldwide
SIZE	Up to 2.5cm long

ABOVE *Mining bees like this tawny mining bee* (Andrena fulva) *look similar to honey bees, but they are usually more hairy and do not have pollen-collecting baskets.*

CARPENTER BEE

Carpenter bees are large insects with a dark, shiny body, hairy legs and tinted wings. These solitary bees build nest burrows in old timber and dead trees, chewing their way into the wood with their powerful jaws. A typical carpenter tunnels up to 30cm deep and lays its eggs at intervals along its burrow. It gives each egg a stock of pollen and then separates it from the next egg with a partition made of chewed wood. The young bees emerge in sequence, with the ones furthest in leaving last.

SCIENTIFIC NAME	*Xylocopa* species
DISTRIBUTION	Worldwide
SIZE	Typical length 2.5cm

LEAFCUTTER BEE

This bee looks like a honey bee but its abdomen is fringed with golden hairs. It gets its name from the way it slices semicircular pieces out of leaves, which it then takes away to its nest. The nest is usually in a hollow stem, although leafcutters also nest in crevices and even upturned flowerpots. In the nest, the bee rolls up each piece of leaf to make a parcel, then stocks it with pollen and one egg. Gardeners are not fond of leafcutter bees because they attack roses and other plants.

SCIENTIFIC NAME	*Megachile centuncularis*
DISTRIBUTION	Europe
SIZE	Up to 2cm long

Leafcutter bee in flight

ABOVE *A female leafcutter bee cuts out a piece of leaf using its sharp jaws like a pair of scissors.*

CUCKOO BEE

Cuckoo bees look like bumblebees, but they raise their eggs in a very different way. Instead of making their own nests, they search out the nests of bumblebees, and force their way inside. Once a cuckoo bee has entered a nest, it starts to lay its eggs. The workers look after the cuckoo bee's eggs, while the intruder often attacks and kills the queen bumblebee. Cuckoo bees often resemble their hosts very closely, but unlike bumblebees, they do not have pollen baskets on their legs, because they do not collect food.

SCIENTIFIC NAME	*Psithyrus* and other genera
DISTRIBUTION	Mainly northern hemisphere
SIZE	Typical length 2cm

STINGS

Animals use stings to defend themselves and also to attack their prey. A sting works by injecting poison into another animal's body and its effects range from mild pain and discomfort that soon wears off, to severe injury or death.

A scorpion's sting is easy to see because it is in the open on the end of its tail. The stings of ants, bees and wasps are also at the end of their bodies but they are normally hidden away by folding scales. If the insect decides to attack, the scales open up and the sting slides out. The sting has two barbed spikes that slide against each other along a central shaft. As the insect pushes the sting into its victim, the spikes move up and down to work the sting into its body. Poison flows along a hollow in the centre of the sting and into the animal.

What happens next depends on the type of stinging insect. Ants and wasps can pull their stings out quite easily because the barbs on them are small. Bumblebees take a little longer and honey bees often cannot pull their stings out at all, because their stings have large barbs that stick tight in skin. When a honey bee tries to fly away, the sting gets torn from its body and the bee eventually dies.

Poison sac

Sting

A wasp's sting

LEFT *Potter wasps, like other solitary wasps, feed alone instead of living in family groups or colonies. Their eggs are laid separately, so their young are solitary from the moment they hatch.*

POTTER WASP

Unlike common wasps, potter wasps are solitary insects. They raise their young in nests made of clay. The nests are about the size of a blueberry and they look like tiny vases stuck to the branches of shrubs. When the female wasp has made a nest, she lays a single egg inside. She then fills the nest with living caterpillars that she has paralysed with her sting. She seals up the pot and moves on to make another. When the potter wasp larvae hatch, they eat the living food.

SCIENTIFIC NAME	*Eumenes* species
DISTRIBUTION	Worldwide
SIZE	Typical length 1.3cm

TARANTULA HAWK WASP

These solitary wasps hunt large spiders, which they use as living food for their young. They rush over the ground looking for their prey, and use their long legs to overtake spiders and pin them down. Once a tarantula hawk wasp has trapped a spider, it paralyses it with its sting and then buries it in sandy ground, laying a single egg on its body. When the wasp grub hatches, it feeds on the buried spider. Other spider-hunting wasps are found all over the world, but most live in the tropics.

SCIENTIFIC NAME	*Hemipepsis ustulata*
DISTRIBUTION	North America
SIZE	Up to 2cm long

TOP *A common wasp feeds on a drop of sugary apple juice.*
ABOVE *Bold yellow and black colours warn that wasps have a sting.*

COMMON WASP

These black and yellow wasps build ball-shaped paper nests in attics or underground. They are quick to use their stings, often causing people to panic when they appear in search of sugary food. Common wasps make the paper for their nests by chewing fibres of dead wood to form a paste. A single queen starts the nest but she soon hands over to a growing band of workers. Common wasp nests can house more than 5,000 workers and can be more than 50cm across. The workers die in winter, but new queens survive to nest the following spring. Yellow jackets, American relatives of this wasp, live in a similar way.

SCIENTIFIC NAME	*Vespula vulgaris*
DISTRIBUTION	Europe, Asia
SIZE	Workers up to 1.5cm

Adult oak apple wasp

HORNET

These woodland insects nest in hollow trees. They are larger than common wasps, with yellow and brown markings and smoky wings. The adults eat nectar but they also hunt insects for themselves and for their young. Hornets cut off the head and legs of their prey before taking the remains to their nest. They have dangerous stings, but they usually avoid people.

SCIENTIFIC NAME	*Vespa crabro*
DISTRIBUTION	Europe, Asia, North America
SIZE	Up to 3cm long

Worker hornet showing brown and yellow markings

OAK APPLE WASP

Instead of making nests, oak apple wasps lay their eggs on oak twigs. When the eggs hatch, they cause the tree to form small growths called galls. The oak apple wasp larvae live inside the galls and feed on plant juices contained in them. Hundreds of types of small wasp live in this way on a wide variety of plants. Gall wasps have complicated life-cycles, often involving several generations a year. Some gall wasps make two different types of gall, one in the spring and the other in the summer. The shape of the gall depends on the species of wasp that lays the egg.

SCIENTIFIC NAME	*Biorrhiza pallida*
DISTRIBUTION	Europe
SIZE	About 3mm long

BELOW *The ruby-tailed wasp is a parasite. It lives off other wasps and bees, laying eggs in their nests so that its grubs can feed on the nest-owner's grubs.*

Reinforced body-shell is resistant to stings from other wasps and bees

Giant ichneumon wasp with its long ovipositor

GIANT ICHNEUMON WASP

Ichneumons lay their eggs inside caterpillars and other insect grubs. Once the eggs have hatched, the ichneumon larvae eat their host alive, leaving behind the empty corpse when they become adult. Gruesome though this sounds, ichneumons are useful in controlling a wide variety of insect pests. There are more than 10,000 species of ichneumon. Giant ichneumon wasps are impressive insects. The females have long ovipositors that they use to drill through wood to lay their eggs on grubs inside trees.

SCIENTIFIC NAME	*Rhyssa persuasoria*
DISTRIBUTION	Europe, Asia
SIZE	Up to 8cm long, including ovipositor

RUBY-TAILED WASP

With its brilliant green body and shiny red abdomen, this small but colourful wasp scuttles around busily in bright sunshine, tapping the surface underfoot with its antennae. Like cuckoo bees (page 87), it uses the nests of other bees and wasps as foster homes for its young. The ruby-tailed wasp has an armoured body to protect it when it breaks into a nest.

SCIENTIFIC NAME	*Chrysis ignita*
DISTRIBUTION	Europe, Asia
SIZE	About 1cm long

HORNTAIL

Also known as wood wasps, horntails belong to a group of insects called sawflies, which are common in woodland areas. Sawflies are named after the saw-like teeth on their ovipositors that allow them to bore through wood or tough plants to deposit their eggs. Sawflies differ from true wasps in two important ways: they do not have a sting or a narrow 'waist'. Horntail larvae feed on plant matter, spending their early life tunnelling through trees and other plants. They are often attacked by ichneumon wasps.

SCIENTIFIC NAME	*Urocerus* and other genera
DISTRIBUTION	Worldwide
SIZE	Typical length 4cm

Ovipositor drills deep into wood

LEFT *This female horntail is about to use her ovipositor to lay an egg inside a fallen branch.*

ECHINODERMS

STARFISH, SEA ANEMONES AND SEA CUCUMBERS ARE TYPES
OF ECHINODERM. THEY ARE THE ONLY ANIMALS BUILT ON A
FIVE-PART PLAN. MANY HAVE FIVE ARMS, FIVE SETS OF
MOUTHPARTS AND FIVE SETS OF TUBE-SHAPED FEET.

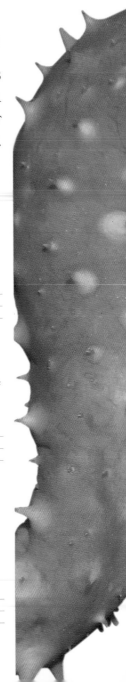

As well as a unique shape, echinoderms also have unique skeletons of chalky plates, covered by a thin layer of skin. In some species, the plates are joined to long spines – echinoderm means 'spiny skin'. Echinoderms live in the sea, ranging from shallow water to the greatest depths. They feed on plants, small animals such as bivalves, and dead remains. About 6,500 species have been identified.

EDIBLE SEA URCHIN

Sea urchins have round, spine-covered bodies. When they die and their spines fall off, they leave empty skeletons called tests. Their mouths, on their undersides, have five pointed teeth that the urchins use to scrape algae from rocks. Sea urchins' spines provide protection against predators. Edible sea urchins have sharp spines that snap off and stick in skin. Other urchins have blunt spines that they use to jam themselves safely into rocky crevices.

SCIENTIFIC NAME	*Echinus esculentus*
DISTRIBUTION	Eastern North Atlantic Ocean
SIZE	Skeleton up to 17cm wide

RIGHT *The violet heart urchin (Spatangus purpureus) has short, fur-like spines.*

ABOVE *The edible sea urchin has dense pink, red or purple spines. It gets its name from its edible eggs, or roes.*

HEART URCHIN OR SEA POTATO

Instead of creeping over rocks, heart urchins burrow into seabed sand. They plough along slowly beneath the surface, pointed end first, using their tube-feet to collect particles of food. On their upper sides, heart urchins have long tube-feet that they use to dig tunnels up to the surface of the sand. They use the tunnels as water vents and these enable them to breathe.

SCIENTIFIC NAME	*Spatangus* and other genera
DISTRIBUTION	Worldwide
SIZE	Typical length 10cm

SAND DOLLAR

These sea urchins have a flat, biscuit-shaped body and short spines. Their skeletons have a flower-like pattern of tiny holes, which connect to five rows of tube-feet. Sand dollars live on the seabed, where they crowd together close to the shore. They produce sticky mucus, which traps particles of food floating in the water.

SCIENTIFIC NAME	*Dendraster* and other genera
DISTRIBUTION	Worldwide
SIZE	Typical width 8cm

SEA CUCUMBER

These sausage-shaped animals creep across the seabed, using a set of frilly tentacles to collect food. Unlike other echinoderms, their mouths are at one end of their bodies. Sea cucumbers are protected by tough skin and a skeleton of chalky spikes. If an enemy comes too close, a threatened sea cucumber has another defence – it turns its anus towards its attacker and ejects a tangle of sticky threads.

SCIENTIFIC NAME	*Stichopus* and other genera
DISTRIBUTION	Worldwide
SIZE	Typical length 40cm

Upper surface is studded with thorn-shaped swellings

LEFT *The common starfish can be pale yellow through red to violet in colour. It has five long arms.*

COMMON STARFISH

There are about 1,500 species of starfish living in oceans all over the world. Most of them have five arms, but some have as many as 50. Some starfish have such short arms that they look like five-sided cushions, and most can replace their arms if any are broken or bitten off. The common starfish lives in shallow water and eats mussels and other bivalve molluscs. It creeps over its victims and prises open their shells with its tube-feet. Once a small gap has opened up, the starfish slips its stomach inside its prey and digests the soft body.

SCIENTIFIC NAME	*Asterias rubens*
DISTRIBUTION	Atlantic Ocean, Mediterranean Sea
SIZE	Up to 20cm across

LEFT
The Californian sea cucumber (Stichopus californicus) *lives in water up to 100m deep.*

Common brittlestar

CROWN-OF-THORNS STARFISH

This tropical starfish has up to 23 arms covered with poisonous spines. It feeds on reef-building corals, eating their soft bodies and leaving the skeletons behind. In recent decades, plagues of these starfish have attacked the Great Barrier Reef off the northeastern coast of Australia, raising fears about whether the reef would survive. Biologists now think that these plagues are natural events that have occurred many times before. After each onslaught, the starfish die off and the reefs slowly recover.

SCIENTIFIC NAME	*Acanthaster planci*
DISTRIBUTION	Indian Ocean, Pacific Ocean
SIZE	Up to 40cm across

COMMON BRITTLESTAR

Brittlestars look like starfish but they are much more slender and faster on the move. Their arms are joined to a disc-shaped body. The arms are flexible but break off easily if touched – which is how brittlestars got their name. The common brittlestar lives close to the shore, but many spend their lives in deep water. They eat dead remains or small particles of food that drift down from the water above.

SCIENTIFIC NAME	*Ophiothrix fragilis*
DISTRIBUTION	Atlantic Ocean
SIZE	Up to 20cm across

RIGHT
The common brittlestar's five arms are flanked by rows of small spines. The spines help the brittlestar to collect food and fend off other animals.

CHORDATES

ALL CHORDATES SHARE ONE KEY FEATURE – A
STRENGTHENING ROD, OR NOTOCHORD, THAT RUNS THE
LENGTH OF THEIR BODIES. THIS GROUP OF ANIMALS INCLUDES
SIMPLE CREATURES THAT BARELY MOVE, AS WELL AS THE
LARGEST, FASTEST, MOST INTELLIGENT ANIMALS ON EARTH.

*Leathery trunk is
sensitive to touch*

I n simple chordates, such as lancelets and sea squirts, the notochord is the
only hard part of the body. But in advanced chordates, such as fish, birds
and mammals, it is surrounded by a column of interlocking bones. These
bones are called vertebrae, and they form part of a complete internal skeleton.
After millions of years of evolution, animals with vertebrae now outnumber
simple chordates many times over, and they dominate life on our planet.

SIMPLE CHORDATES

There are about 1,300 species of simple
chordate found in oceans worldwide. They
are all quite small, and easy to overlook.
Some of them burrow through sand, but
others spend their lives fastened to rocks,
or drifting in open water. Because simple
chordates do not have backbones, they are
classified as invertebrates. However, they are
invertebrates with a difference, because they
have a notochord for all or part of their
lives. This feature means that they are
related to vertebrates, including ourselves.

LANCELET

A lancelet looks like a small transparent fish,
with an extremely narrow body. It lurks on the
seabed, half-buried in sand, and uses tentacles
to pump water into its mouth. Once the water
is inside, sieve-like slits filter out small particles
of food, and the waste water is pumped away.
Lancelets do not have eyes or jaws, and they
have only the beginnings of a brain. However,
many of the features that they do have, such
as muscles arranged in blocks, also appear in
fish and other vertebrates.

SCIENTIFIC NAME *Branchiostoma* species

DISTRIBUTION Warm seas worldwide

SIZE About 5cm long

SEA SQUIRT

Adult sea squirts live fastened to solid objects,
and feed by pumping water through their bag-
like body. When they are young, they look
completely different. They have a tadpole-shaped
body, reinforced by a notochord, and swim in
open water. Young sea squirts settle on rocks to
turn into adults, and their notochord disappears.

SCIENTIFIC NAME *Ciona* and other genera

DISTRIBUTION Worldwide

SIZE Typical height 15cm

*Sea squirts often
live in colonies of
many individuals*

VERTEBRATES

Vertebrates are animals that have backbones,
and a complete internal skeleton. Unlike a shell
or exoskeleton, this kind of skeleton can grow
to a large size without becoming
too heavy or too clumsy to move.
Compared to other animals,
vertebrates have large brains
and elaborate nervous systems, and
they often behave in complex ways.
There are seven groups or classes of
vertebrates – three groups of fish,
amphibians, reptiles, birds and
mammals. Fish are divided
into three classes because they
are built in three different ways.

ABOVE *The pike* (Esox
lucius) *is a bony fish.*

LEFT *Like most
amphibians, the painted
frog* (Discoglossus
pictus) *must keep
moist to survive.*

LEFT *The
common wall
lizard* (Podarcis
muralis) *basks in the sun
to raise its body temperature.*

LEFT *The common sea squirt* (Ciona intestinalis) *lives on rocks in shallow water. If touched, it contracts instantly.*

Small opening expels water

Large opening sucks in water

JAWLESS FISH

Fish without jaws were the first vertebrates to exist on Earth. They lived on the seabed, and sucked up their food. Most jawless fish died out more than 300 million years ago but a few species, called lampreys and hagfish, still exist. They have snake-like bodies, round mouths and tiny eyes. Their gill openings are shaped like port-holes and they have scaleless and often slimy skin.

ATLANTIC HAGFISH

These slimy deep-sea scavengers feed on dead or dying fish. They find food by using their keen sense of smell, and often slither right inside dead remains. A hagfish does not have jaws, but has small teeth that it uses to fasten its mouth on to prey. It then forms a knot at the end of its tail, and slides the knot towards its head, pushing hard until a mouthful of food is sucked away. Hagfish lay elongated eggs, and their young look like small adults when they hatch.

SCIENTIFIC NAME	*Myxine glutinosa*
DISTRIBUTION	Atlantic Ocean
SIZE	Up to 70cm long

SEA LAMPREY

Adult sea lampreys are parasites that feed on the blood of other fish. They have sharp teeth that they use to clamp on to their prey. Lampreys can cling on for weeks, taking so much blood that the victim often dies. Like all lampreys, the sea lamprey breeds in fresh water. Its young – called ammocoete larvae – are blind and toothless. They spend up to six years filtering food from the water before they develop into adults and travel downriver to the sea.

SCIENTIFIC NAME	*Petromyzon marinus*
DISTRIBUTION	North Atlantic Ocean, Mediterranean Sea; adjoining rivers and lakes
SIZE	Up to 90cm long

RIGHT *A young brook lamprey slithers over the bed of a stream.*

ABOVE *The jay* (Garrulus glandarius) *is a typical bird.*

ABOVE *The rabbit* (Oryctolagus cuniculus) *is a typical mammal, with dense fur.*

ABOVE *Sea lampreys have seven round gill openings, and small fins near the ends of their bodies.*

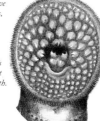

RIGHT *The sea lamprey's mouth has no jaws, but it is studded with small teeth.*

BROOK LAMPREY

Unlike sea lampreys, brook lampreys spend all their lives in fresh water. They are not a threat to other fish because the adults do not feed. The female lays her eggs in gravel or sand. These eggs produce filter-feeding larvae that take about five years to grow, before finally turning into adults. After spawning, the adults die.

SCIENTIFIC NAME	*Lampetra planeri*
DISTRIBUTION	Europe
SIZE	Up to 25cm long

CARTILAGINOUS FISH

SHARKS, SKATES AND RAYS ARE KNOWN AS
CARTILAGINOUS FISH BECAUSE THEIR
SKELETONS ARE MADE OF CARTILAGE. THIS IS
THE SAME RUBBERY SUBSTANCE THAT LINES
OUR JOINTS AND GIVES OUR EARS AND NOSES
THEIR SHAPE. CARTILAGE IS WEAKER THAN
BONE, BUT IT IS STRONG ENOUGH TO SUPPORT
SOME OF THE LARGEST ANIMALS IN THE SEAS.

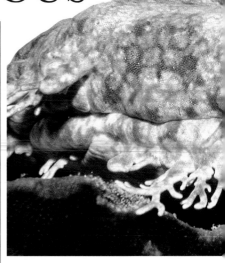

Cartilaginous fish have streamlined bodies covered with rough skin like sandpaper, and stiff fins that cannot be folded away. Their jaws are powerful, and armed with an endless supply of biting or crushing teeth. Most of these fish are predators, but the largest species feed on planktonic animals, scooping up huge quantities in their gaping mouths as they swim along. There are about 600 species of cartilaginous fish and they live mainly in the sea, with only a few venturing into fresh water. Some lay eggs, but many species give birth to live young.

SHARKS

Sharks are the best-known cartilaginous fish and the most feared. There are more than 340 species and, although only about 20 of them are known to attack humans, they kill several hundred people every year. Most sharks are shaped for non-stop swimming. They have large, oily livers that work like on-board floats, and a keen sense of smell that alerts them to food far away. Most sharks are open-water animals, but some are bottom dwellers with effective camouflage colours that protect them from predators.

MONKFISH

This bottom-dwelling shark lives in water as deep as 100m. It has a flat body and broad pectoral fins, which make it look quite like a ray (page 100). Monkfish eat small seabed fish. Like other sharks, they can sense the faint electrical field that surrounds a fish's body, so they can find prey buried in the sand. Monkfish eggs hatch inside the mother's body, producing live young.

SCIENTIFIC NAME	*Squatina squatina*
DISTRIBUTION	Eastern Atlantic Ocean, Mediterranean Sea
SIZE	Up to 1.8m long

ABOVE *A monkfish, or angel shark, lies on the seabed. Monkfish have breathing-holes on the tops of their heads so they can lie flat on the sand and still be able to breathe.*

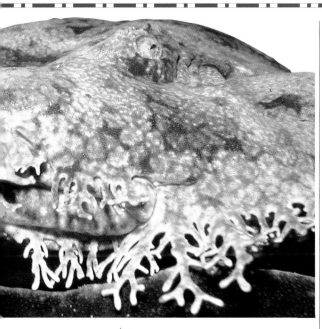

ABOVE *The extraordinary tassels around this spotted wobbegong's body help it to hide as it lies on the seabed. From above, its camouflage makes it almost invisible.*

BELOW *The dwarf shark was first discovered in the sea off Japan. It lives in deep water and rises to the surface at night to feed.*

COOKIECUTTER SHARK
Instead of killing and swallowing its prey, the cookiecutter bites off small chunks of flesh. It attacks animals much larger than itself, including dolphins and whales, and it has even been known to bite off the rubber fittings of submarines. Cookiecutters live mainly in deep water, travelling up towards the surface after dark to feed on other fish.

SCIENTIFIC NAME	*Isistius brasiliensis*
DISTRIBUTION	Indian Ocean, Pacific Ocean, South Atlantic Ocean
SIZE	Up to 50cm long

PORT JACKSON SHARK
With its blunt head, spiny fins and downward-pointing mouth, this fish looks quite different from most other sharks. It feeds after dark on molluscs and crabs, crushing them with its flattened back teeth. Port Jackson sharks breed in shallow water and lay large eggs with tough, spiral-shaped cases. The females sometimes push their eggs into crevices, where they have the best chance of surviving until they hatch.

SCIENTIFIC NAME	*Heterodontus portusjacksoni*
DISTRIBUTION	Southern Pacific Ocean
SIZE	Up to 1.5m long

Hard spine on dorsal fin

Port Jackson shark

SPOTTED WOBBEGONG
Wobbegongs do not actively search for their prey. Instead, they lie in wait, camouflaged on the seabed. Their shape is broken up by a pattern of light brown markings and by fleshy tassels along the edge of their jaws. Wobbegongs can lie still for hours but, if anything edible comes within range, they strike instantly. Wobbegongs do not normally attack humans, but they can be very dangerous if they are stepped on accidentally.

SCIENTIFIC NAME	*Orectolobus maculatus*
DISTRIBUTION	Western Pacific Ocean
SIZE	Up to 3m long

DWARF SHARK
This is probably the world's smallest shark, with a body that is often shorter than a human hand. Dwarf sharks rise up to shallow water at night and have a luminous underside that they can 'switch on' when they feed near the surface of the water. The pale light may help to disguise their silhouette from below, making it hard for predators to spot them.

SCIENTIFIC NAME	*Squaliolus laticaudus*
DISTRIBUTION	Worldwide
SIZE	Up to 25cm long

GREENLAND SHARK
This large cold-water shark feeds on fish, seals and waste thrown overboard from fishing-boats. It is a sluggish animal that spends much of its time near the seabed. Its flesh is poisonous to humans, but the sharks sometimes eat each other. Adult Greenland sharks usually have finger-sized parasitic crustaceans attached to their eyes. Scientists think that the crustaceans may help to lure prey towards the sharks.

SCIENTIFIC NAME	*Somniosus microcephalus*
DISTRIBUTION	North Atlantic Ocean, Arctic Ocean
SIZE	Up to 6.5m long

RIGHT AND BELOW
*The whale shark has
the huge mouth and tiny
eyes typical of a harmless
plankton-eater.*

WHALE SHARK

The largest fish in the world, this immense shark can weigh more than 20 tonnes. Its tail can be more than 2.5m from tip to tip, and its mouth is wide enough to swallow a human swimmer sideways-on. Fortunately, this giant animal is not interested in people because it feeds entirely on plankton and tiny fish. As it cruises close to the surface, it takes large gulps of water and then sieves out food through its gills. Whale sharks sometimes collide with ships, but are otherwise rarely seen. They lay the world's largest eggs, measuring up to 30cm in length. Little is known about how they grow because sightings of young whale sharks are extremely rare.

SCIENTIFIC NAME *Rhincodon typus*

DISTRIBUTION Tropical seas worldwide

SIZE Maximum length unknown but possibly about 18m

BASKING SHARK

This is the second largest species of shark, weighing up to four tonnes. It is a filter-feeder, though its shape is more typical of a hunting shark, with a streamlined body and pointed snout. When the basking shark feeds, it opens its mouth until it is almost circular, and strains large amounts of water through its huge gills. It swims slowly as if it is basking in the sunshine, which is how it gets its name. Basking sharks give birth to live young after a gestation period of more than a year.

SCIENTIFIC NAME *Cetorhinus maximus*

DISTRIBUTION Cool seas worldwide

SIZE Up to 10m long

NURSE SHARK

Nurse sharks spend most of their time on the seabed and are found as far north as New York, USA. They have much smaller mouths than most sharks of their size, and feed with a vacuum-cleaner action, sucking up molluscs and crustaceans. Nurse sharks look dangerous, but they are generally harmless to people. If they are provoked, however, they can attack. Once a nurse shark has bitten, its jaws often lock shut and have to be forced apart. Nurse sharks give birth to live young.

SCIENTIFIC NAME *Ginglymostoma cirratum*

DISTRIBUTION Eastern Pacific Ocean, Atlantic Ocean

SIZE Up to 4m long

MEGAMOUTH SHARK

The megamouth shark was discovered in 1976, when the first known specimen was brought ashore in Hawaii. Like the whale shark and basking shark, it is a filter-feeder, but it lives in deep water instead of near the surface. It has a blackish-brown tapering body and, true to its name, a huge mouth. Its teeth are tiny, but it has luminous organs inside its mouth that probably help it to attract its food. The megamouth is seldom seen, and so little is known about its breeding habits or numbers.

SCIENTIFIC NAME *Megachasma pelagicus*

DISTRIBUTION Unknown

SIZE About 4m long

THRESHER SHARK

A thresher shark's tail is almost as long as the rest of its body. The lower tail lobe is small, but the upper one is large and arched, ending in a pointed tip. Threshers feed alone or in groups on shoals of fish. They thrash their tails from side to side to round up or wound their prey. When they are near the surface, they can even use their tails to knock low-flying seabirds out of the air. Threshers give birth to up to four live young at a time. They produce more, but some of the young eat the others while they are inside their mother's body.

Thresher shark showing its long arched tail

SCIENTIFIC NAME *Alopias vulpinus*

DISTRIBUTION Worldwide

SIZE Up to 6m long

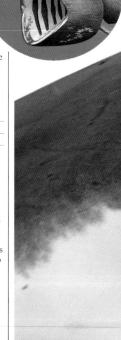

BELOW The basking shark's mouth swells up like a balloon as it filters plankton from the sea.

GREAT WHITE SHARK

The great white is the world's largest and most dangerous predatory shark. It attacks seals, dolphins and other fish, and eats all kinds of leftovers and remains, including dead whales and rubbish thrown overboard. It has a reputation as a man-eater, and has been known to attack small boats, biting or punching them with its snout until they sink. The great white's reputation means that it is highly prized by sea anglers and by souvenir hunters who collect shark teeth and jaws. As a result, fully grown great white sharks are far less common than they once were.

SCIENTIFIC NAME	*Carcharodon carcharias*
DISTRIBUTION	Warm waters worldwide
SIZE	Up to 8m long

MAKO

With a top speed of nearly 90km/h, the mako is the fastest-swimming shark. It needs this speed because it feeds on tuna and mackerel – fish that are also among the swiftest in the seas. Makos have been known to attack people, and they are sought after by sea anglers because they fight back ferociously if hooked. Female makos keep their eggs inside their bodies until they have hatched, and then give birth to live young.

SCIENTIFIC NAME	*Isurus oxyrhynchus*
DISTRIBUTION	Worldwide, mainly in warm waters
SIZE	Up to 4m long

Large dorsal fin

ABOVE *The mako shark uses its large tail to produce spectacular bursts of speed when swimming.*

BELOW *The great white shark's teeth can be more than 6cm long. They are constantly replaced throughout the shark's life.*

PORBEAGLE

A close relative of the mako (page 97), the porbeagle is also a swift surface-dwelling hunter. It feeds on mackerel and herring and also chases squid. Although sharks are normally cold-blooded, porbeagles and makos can keep their body temperature slightly higher than the water around them. This enables their muscles to contract more quickly, so they can produce a burst of speed. Porbeagles give birth to live young. They feed on their mother's unfertilized eggs before they are born.

SCIENTIFIC NAME *Lamna nasus*

DISTRIBUTION Worldwide, particularly common in cold water

SIZE Up to 3m long

LESSER SPOTTED DOGFISH

This slender-bodied fish is Europe's most common shark. Its upper surface is sandy brown with dark spots, and its upright dorsal fin is far down its body, nearer to its tail than to its head. Dogfish hunt on the seabed in shallow water, and feed on molluscs, crustaceans and slow-moving fish. Like other bottom-dwelling sharks, they have a well-developed electrical sense. This allows them to find their prey, even when it is

Sleek shape enables swift movement

completely buried. Dogfish lay flat, square eggs with spiral tendrils at the corners. These tendrils wind around seaweed, anchoring the eggs until they hatch. The empty cases, called mermaids' purses, are often washed up on the shore.

SCIENTIFIC NAME *Scyliorhinus canicula*

DISTRIBUTION Eastern Atlantic Ocean, Mediterranean Sea

SIZE Up to 1m long

LEOPARD SHARK

Leopard sharks get their name from their dark brown spots, which look like the pattern on a leopard's fur. They have large pectoral fins and a series of hard ridges that run the length of their bodies. These common and harmless sharks swim on the seabed, where they feed on clams and other burrowing molluscs. They thrive in captivity, and are often kept in marine aquariums.

SCIENTIFIC NAME *Triakis semifasciata*

DISTRIBUTION Pacific coast of North America

SIZE Up to 1.8m long

BULL SHARK

This is one of the few sharks that swims up estuaries into fresh water. It can be seen far inland, in the River Amazon in South America, the River Zambezi in Africa and the River Ganges in India. Bull sharks feed on animals of all kinds, including other sharks. They can be dangerous because they hunt where people swim.

SCIENTIFIC NAME *Carcharhinus leucas*

DISTRIBUTION Tropical rivers and coasts

SIZE Up to 3.4m long

BLACKTIP SHARK

Many sharks get excited when they sense food, but blacktips get more frantic than most. During 'feeding frenzies', they swirl around in chaotic packs, competing for food. They swim near land, but rarely attack people.

SCIENTIFIC NAME *Carcharhinus limbatus*

DISTRIBUTION Tropical coasts and seas

SIZE Up to 2.2m long

BELOW *The blue shark is a slender and graceful fish, with long pectoral fins. It feeds near the surface, and is more tolerant of cold than most sharks. It often ventures into regions where the water temperature is lower than 10°C.*

BELOW *A tiger shark bursts through the water's surface. Compared to other open-water sharks, the tiger shark has an unusually short snout.*

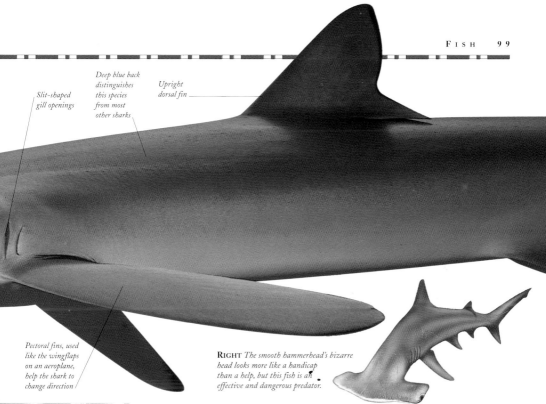

Slit-shaped
gill openings

Deep blue back
distinguishes
this species
from most
other sharks

Upright
dorsal fin

Pectoral fins, used
like the wingflaps
on an aeroplane,
help the shark to
change direction

RIGHT *The smooth hammerhead's bizarre
head looks more like a handicap
than a help, but this fish is an
effective and dangerous predator.*

BLUE SHARK

This steel-blue streamlined fish is one of the
most widespread sharks in the world. It has
long, curved pectoral fins that it uses to twist
and turn through the water after prey. Blue
sharks have a reputation as man-eaters, and
they also cause problems for fishermen by
raiding nets to feed on trapped fish. They
feed inshore and also in the open ocean, often
hunting in packs. They attack and overpower
whales and other animals larger than themselves.

SCIENTIFIC NAME	*Prionace glauca*
DISTRIBUTION	Tropical and temperate waters worldwide
SIZE	Up to 3.8m long

TIGER SHARK

Some shark specialists believe that this fish
is responsible for more attacks on humans than
any other species – including the infamous great
white (page 97). A huge and formidable hunter,
the tiger shark attacks and eats almost anything,
from turtles and other sharks to lobster pots and
old oil drums. In 1935, one specimen caught off
Australia regurgitated a human arm – it was
identified by a tattoo, but the rest of the body
was never found. Tiger sharks have a stripy
pattern when they are young, but this fades
as they grow. They live both inshore and in
the open sea, and give birth to live young.

SCIENTIFIC NAME	*Galeocerdo cuvieri*
DISTRIBUTION	Warm seas worldwide
SIZE	Up to 7m long

SMOOTH HAMMERHEAD

The ten species of hammerhead are the world's
most strangely shaped sharks. They have a
typical shark shape, except for their heads,
which have long flaps that stick out on either
side. Scientists do not know for certain what
these flaps are for. One possibility is that they
help the hammerhead to pinpoint its prey;
another is that they provide lift as the shark
swims along. Smooth hammerheads have
been known occasionally to attack people.
They often swim close to the surface, and can
be found near to the shore as well as out at sea.

SCIENTIFIC NAME	*Sphyrna zygaena*
DISTRIBUTION	Warm waters worldwide
SIZE	Up to 4m long

SKATES, RAYS AND RABBITFISH

Skates and rays are cartilaginous fish with flattened bodies and wing-like fins. Many live on the seabed, where they are often superbly camouflaged, but a few spend most of their lives near the surface, flapping through the sea like underwater birds. Unlike sharks, these fish crush their food up with blunt teeth. Their mouths and gill openings are on the undersides of their bodies and they have breathing-holes on their upper surfaces, just behind their eyes. There are more than 300 species of both skate and ray and most of them live in the sea. Rabbitfish belong to a different group of cartilaginous fish. There are about 25 species and all are marine.

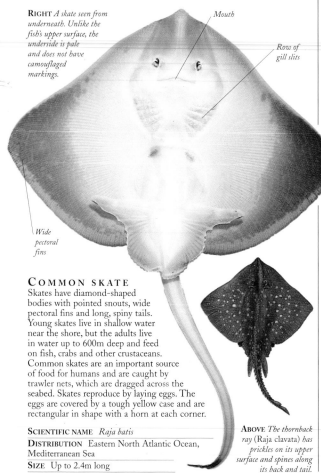

RIGHT *A skate seen from underneath. Unlike the fish's upper surface, the underside is pale and does not have camouflaged markings.*

Mouth

Row of gill slits

Wide pectoral fins

COMMON SKATE

Skates have diamond-shaped bodies with pointed snouts, wide pectoral fins and long, spiny tails. Young skates live in shallow water near the shore, but the adults live in water up to 600m deep and feed on fish, crabs and other crustaceans. Common skates are an important source of food for humans and are caught by trawler nets, which are dragged across the seabed. Skates reproduce by laying eggs. The eggs are covered by a tough yellow case and are rectangular in shape with a horn at each corner.

SCIENTIFIC NAME   *Raja batis*

DISTRIBUTION   Eastern North Atlantic Ocean, Mediterranean Sea

SIZE   Up to 2.4m long

ABOVE *The thornback ray (Raja clavata) has prickles on its upper surface and spines along its back and tail.*

MANTA RAY

With a 'wingspan' of nearly 7m, this is the largest ray in the world. Like many of the largest sea animals, it feeds on plankton, which it scoops up as it swims along. It has two fleshy paddles on either side of its head that help to funnel food into its mouth. In the past, manta rays inspired many legends about sea monsters but, as far as humans are concerned, these enormous fish are totally harmless.

SCIENTIFIC NAME   *Manta birostris*

DISTRIBUTION   Warm seas worldwide

SIZE   Up to 5m long

STINGRAY

These fish are closely related to skates, but they have a blunter snout. They have one or two spines near the base of their tail that can inject a strong poison if they are attacked. Stingray wounds are rarely deadly to humans but they can be painful, sometimes paralysing part of the body until the poison has worn off. Stingrays eat molluscs and crustaceans and produce live young.

SCIENTIFIC NAME *Dasyatis* and other genera

DISTRIBUTION   Worldwide

SIZE   Typical length 1.5m

EAGLE RAY

These active swimmers feed on the seabed but often come to the surface, sometimes jumping clear of the water. They have poisonous spines in their tail, which they use for self-defence. Eagle rays eat small seabed animals, flapping their fins to expose them in the sand or mud.

SCIENTIFIC NAME   *Myliobatis* and other genera

DISTRIBUTION   Worldwide

SIZE   Typical length 1.5m

Atlantic torpedo ray attacking and engulfing a fish

RIGHT *A manta ray glides through the sea, funnelling plankton into its mouth. This one is giving a lift to some remoras (page 125).*

LEFT
The Atlantic torpedo ray's pectoral fins give it an almost perfectly circular outline. This electric ray can deliver a severe shock, but it rarely harms people.

Rounded pectoral fins

ATLANTIC TORPEDO RAY

The Atlantic torpedo is the largest electric ray, weighing as much as 90kg. Species of electric ray are found in seas all over the world. They trap prey in their fins and give it a powerful electric shock. They have two sets of muscles just behind the head that can generate a brief jolt of up to 220 volts, which is enough to stun or kill a medium-sized fish.

SCIENTIFIC NAME	*Torpedo nobiliana*
DISTRIBUTION	Atlantic Ocean, Mediterranean Sea
SIZE	Up to 1.8m long

Sawfish using its long snout to scatter a shoal of fish

SAWFISH

The sawfish looks like a cross between a shark and a skate, but its most conspicuous feature is its remarkable saw-like snout. Shaped like a flattened blade, it can be more than 1m long and is edged with more than 50 sharp teeth. The sawfish uses this implement to rake over the seabed in search of buried animals, and to attack fish. Female sawfish produce live young that have soft saws when they are born. Large adults can weigh more than two tonnes. Although sawfish look highly dangerous, there are no reliable records of them ever attacking people.

SCIENTIFIC NAME	*Pristis* species
DISTRIBUTION	Worldwide
SIZE	Up to 7m long

RABBITFISH OR RATFISH

Roughly translated, this strange looking fish's scientific name means 'multi-animal monster'. It is easy to understand why, because the rabbitfish has a large bulbous head, a rabbit-like mouth and a long rat-like tail. Rabbitfish are bottom-feeders, and they eat molluscs and other seabed animals. Unlike sharks, skates and rays, the rabbitfish's gills are hidden by a flap of skin – a feature that is more often found in bony fish (page 102). Rabbitfish reproduce by laying eggs. Each egg is enclosed in a long, slender case.

SCIENTIFIC NAME	*Chimaera monstrosa*
DISTRIBUTION	Eastern North Atlantic Ocean, Mediterranean Sea
SIZE	Up to 1.5m long

BONY FISH

MORE THAN 24,000 SPECIES OF BONY FISH
ARE KNOWN TO SCIENCE. SOME WEIGH MORE
THAN TWO TONNES WHILE OTHERS WEIGH A
FRACTION OF A GRAM. BONY FISH LIVE IN
EVERY IMAGINABLE WATERY HABITAT, FROM
SUNLIT OCEAN SURFACES TO THE PERPETUAL
DARKNESS OF UNDERGROUND LAKES.

RIGHT *The common sturgeon,
like all sturgeons, has a skeleton
made of cartilage as well as bone.
Sturgeons are primitive bony fish.*

T hese fish have bony skeletons and, in most species,
their bodies are covered with scales. Their gills
are concealed by a moveable flap, and they have
an internal 'float', or swimbladder, which gives them
buoyancy. Their shapes depend on how they live. Most
are streamlined while others are flat, but some have such
strange shapes that it is hard to tell they are fish. Bony
fish usually lay eggs that are fertilized in the water and
they typically leave their young to fend for themselves.

LUNGFISH, BICHIRS AND BONYTONGUES

This diverse collection of bony fish includes some species that have
hardly changed for millions of years, such as coelacanths – the only
fish with fleshy fins. Bichirs and their relatives have features in
common with sharks. Bonytongues are typical bony fish, although
they have some primitive features. There are about 230 species
of these fish, living in either fresh water or the sea.

BICHIR

Bichirs live in large rivers in Africa. They have
long bodies, stubby fins and a row of finlets
along their backs that they can raise or lower
like little sails. They breathe by gulping air and
can also crawl along the riverbed, using their
front fins to haul themselves along. Bichirs feed
on fish and other small water animals, creeping
up on their prey using this crawling motion.

SCIENTIFIC NAME	*Polypterus* species
DISTRIBUTION	Tropical Africa
SIZE	Up to 1m long

COELACANTH

Until 1938, scientists thought that this fleshy-
finned fish had died out 65 million years ago.
Then a museum curator spotted one that had
been caught by fishermen off the coast of South
Africa, and had it identified by an expert fish
biologist. The discovery caused great excitement
because coelacanths are the closest living relatives
of vertebrates that have legs instead of fins.
Coelacanths live close to the coast in water
up to 750m deep. They feed on fish, and the
females are thought to give birth to live young.

SCIENTIFIC NAME	*Latimeria chalmunae*
DISTRIBUTION	Indian Ocean; off the Comoros islands and Madagascar
SIZE	Up to 2m long

ABOVE RIGHT CENTRE
*The elephant-trunk fish's
'trunk' looks like a nose, but
it is a long lower jaw with
a flexible chin. This fish has
an unusually large brain
and will play with toys
when in an aquarium.*
ABOVE RIGHT BOTTOM
*Like all ten species of bichir,
this species (Polypterus
ornatus) has an eel-like
body and widely separated
pectoral and pelvic fins.*

SOUTH AMERICAN LUNGFISH
This fish lives in places where there is a long
dry season each year. As the water dries up, each
lungfish digs a burrow in the mud and breathes
air until the wet weather returns. The fish then
breaks out of its burrow and takes up normal life
again. There are six species of lungfish. South
American and African lungfish have two pairs
of lungs, but the Australian lungfish has just
one and does not make burrows.

SCIENTIFIC NAME	*Lepidosiren paradoxa*
DISTRIBUTION	Tropical South America
SIZE	Up to 1.2m long

COMMON STURGEON

Sturgeon are among the largest and most endangered river fish. The common sturgeon can weigh up to 275kg, while the heaviest sturgeon on record – a Russian sturgeon, or beluga – weighed nearly one and a half tonnes. Sturgeon have shark-like bodies with long, flat snouts and five rows of large, bony plates instead of scales. They feed on the bottom of the sea and in rivers, and they have fleshy barbels, or whiskers, beneath their mouths that help them search for food. Female sturgeon lay millions of sticky black eggs. People collect these eggs and sell them as caviar – one of the world's most expensive foods.

SCIENTIFIC NAME	*Acipenser sturio*
DISTRIBUTION	European coasts and rivers
SIZE	Up to 3m long

ELEPHANT-TRUNK FISH

This nocturnal freshwater fish has a long lower jaw that looks like an elephant's trunk. It uses this to stir up sand and mud to find small animals buried beneath the surface. Elephant-trunk fish often live in murky water, and they find their way by creating a weak electrical field around themselves. Underwater objects distort the field, and the fish sense this and steer away.

SCIENTIFIC NAME	*Gnathonemus petersi*
DISTRIBUTION	Tropical Africa
SIZE	Up to 23cm long

PIRARUCU OR ARAPAIMA

The pirarucu looks like a gigantic pike (page 107) and is one of the largest fish to spend all of its life in fresh water. It is a member of the bonytongue group of fish, and lives in South American rivers and swamps. Pirarucus feed mainly on smaller fish, but they also eat snakes, turtles, frogs and insects. In the tropics, slow-flowing water can get very warm and it often contains only a little oxygen. Pirarucus survive in these conditions by gulping air. The air enters the swimbladder, which works like a lung.

SCIENTIFIC NAME	*Arapaima gigas*
DISTRIBUTION	South America
SIZE	Up to 2.5m long

RIGHT *The ornate bichir is a primitive fish. It has diamond-shaped scales and a swimbladder that is connected to the stomach.*

HERRING AND THEIR RELATIVES

This group of fish contains nearly 400 species, including many that are important as food for humans and wild animals. They live mainly in the sea, and often form large shoals. Shoaling protects them from other fish by making it harder for predators to single them out, but it also means that they are easy to catch in nets. Most of these fish have streamlined silvery bodies and scales that rub off easily. They feed on planktonic animals, which they filter from the water with their gills. Marine species live near the shore and in shallow seas, and are most varied where the water is warm.

HERRING

Adult herring live in the open sea, where they rise up to the surface at night to feed on swarms of plankton. They have tiny teeth, but their gills work like sieves, trapping tiny animals that they swallow as they swim. Female herring produce up to 40,000 eggs each year, scattering them into the water. The eggs sink to the seabed, and many are eaten by haddock and other predators before they have a chance to hatch. Those that do survive produce tiny young fish that swim upwards towards the surface, attracted by the light. In Europe, people have fished for herring since prehistoric times but, in recent years, so many have been caught that their numbers have dwindled.

SCIENTIFIC NAME	*Clupea harengus*
DISTRIBUTION	North Atlantic Ocean
SIZE	Up to 40cm long

SPRAT

This small fish looks like a miniature version of the herring because it has the same torpedo-shaped silvery body. It is one of the smallest members of the herring family, but is still an important food fish for many marine animals. Sprats spawn close to the shore in late winter and spring. Their eggs float on the water.

SCIENTIFIC NAME	*Clupea sprattus*
DISTRIBUTION	Atlantic coast of Europe, Mediterranean Sea
SIZE	Up to 15cm long

NORTHERN ANCHOVY

There are more than 100 species of anchovy and, although all of them are small and slender, they play an important part in ocean life. These silvery fish live in large shoals and they are eaten by all kinds of animals, from seabirds to seals. Anchovies themselves eat tiny planktonic animals, but instead of snapping them up one by one, they swim with their mouths open and scoop them up as they move along. Northern anchovies live in the Pacific Ocean and a similar species lives near the coasts of Europe.

SCIENTIFIC NAME	*Engraulis mordax*
DISTRIBUTION	Pacific coast of North America
SIZE	Up to 23cm long

SARDINE OR PILCHARD

Sardines live close to the shore in spring and summer, but move into deeper water during the rest of the year. When they are inshore, they are often attacked by seabirds. They are also caught by people to be processed and canned. Sardines are attracted to light at night and, in southern Europe, they are lured by fleets of small boats fitted with lamps. When the sardines are close enough to a boat, a net is tightened around them and the fish are hauled aboard. Sardines and pilchards belong to the same species – sardines are young fish, and pilchards are those that are fully grown.

SCIENTIFIC NAME	*Sardina pilchardus*
DISTRIBUTION	European coasts
SIZE	Up to 25cm long

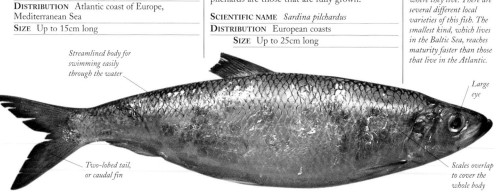

BELOW *Herring can live to be 20 years old, although their life-span depends on where they live. There are several different local varieties of this fish. The smallest kind, which lives in the Baltic Sea, reaches maturity faster than those that live in the Atlantic.*

Streamlined body for swimming easily through the water

Large eye

Two-lobed tail, or caudal fin

Scales overlap to cover the whole body

European anchovy
(Engraulis encrasicolus)

TOP *A shoal of northern anchovies off the coast of California, USA. A single shoal can contain over one hundred thousand fish, swimming in a tightly packed group. For seabirds, these shoals make easy targets.*

ALEWIFE

This North American fish lives along coasts and also in lakes, but it always lays its eggs in fresh water. Like all its close relatives, it has a silvery body with a row of sharply pointed scales along its underside. Many alewives travel back into the sea after they spawn, but those that live in landlocked lakes, or in rivers with dams, spend their whole lives inland. Freshwater alewives are not as large as their sea-going relatives, and their numbers vary considerably from year to year.

SCIENTIFIC NAME *Alosa pseudoharengus*

DISTRIBUTION Atlantic coast and Great Lakes of North America

SIZE Marine fish up to 38cm long; freshwater fish up to 25cm long

ALLIS SHAD

Like the alewife, the shad has sharp scales along its underside, forming a ridge like a small-toothed saw. It spends most of its life in deep water offshore but, in the spring, it swims up rivers to breed. The adults return to the sea after they have spawned, but the young fish spend up to two years in rivers before venturing out to sea.

SCIENTIFIC NAME *Alosa alosa*

DISTRIBUTION European coasts, including Mediterranean Sea

SIZE Up to 60cm long

ATLANTIC MENHADEN

Like herring, Atlantic menhadens live in large shoals. They are always on the move, looking for plankton-rich waters in which to feed. They have stocky silvery bodies, with distinctive black spots on their sides. They lay their eggs in the sea and their young hatch near the surface. Menhadens are an important food for many other fish, for seabirds and also for humpback whales.

SCIENTIFIC NAME *Brevoorta tyrannus*

DISTRIBUTION Atlantic coast of North America

SIZE Up to 50cm long

SALMON AND THEIR RELATIVES

There are more than 300 species in this group, which includes some of the world's best-known migratory fish. Most of them are predators, and they either chase their prey through the water or lurk among water weeds for fish and other animals to come close by. Salmon and their relatives reproduce by laying eggs. In some species, the males change colour and shape just before the breeding season begins. This group of fish includes species that are found in both fresh water and the sea. They are most common in the northern hemisphere.

ABOVE *Two Atlantic salmon leap a waterfall on their way to their spawning grounds. During their journey upstream, the adult salmon do not feed, although they will often snap at flies and fishing lures. They use so much energy that they can lose more than half their bodyweight during the journey.*

ATLANTIC SALMON

This large and powerful fish starts life in rivers, where it eats insect larvae and worms. When it has grown to about 15cm long, it swims downriver to begin life in the sea. Adult salmon roam far out into the Atlantic but, after two to four years, they head back towards fresh water to breed. Using its sense of smell, each fish navigates its way to the river where it developed, fighting its way up stream against the current. Female salmon lay their eggs in riverbed gravel. Once breeding is over, the thin and exhausted adults set off back to the sea, leaving their young to mature on their own. Atlantic salmon are valuable food fish for humans. Some are caught in nets, but many are bred and raised in fish farms close to the shore.

SCIENTIFIC NAME	*Salmo salar*
DISTRIBUTION	North Atlantic Ocean, Arctic Ocean; adjoining lakes and rivers
SIZE	Up to 1.5m long

SOCKEYE SALMON

Like the Atlantic salmon, this fish spends most of its adult life at sea, returning to rivers to breed. At sea, the males are sleek and silvery, but during the breeding season they turn bright red and develop a humped back and hooked jaws. Sockeye salmon can travel 2,000km up rivers, leaping waterfalls and dodging predators. After they have laid their eggs, the adults die.

SCIENTIFIC NAME	*Oncorhynchus nerka*
DISTRIBUTION	Northern Pacific Ocean
SIZE	Up to 85cm long

EUROPEAN SMELT

Smelts are slender-bodied fish with large mouths and long teeth. Like many of their relatives, such as the pike, they have teeth in the roofs of their mouths as well as in their jaws, which makes it difficult for their prey to escape. Smelts feed on fish and crustaceans, and they swim up rivers to lay their eggs. The eggs are sticky and attach to stones and underwater plants.

SCIENTIFIC NAME *Osmerus eperlanus*

DISTRIBUTION Coasts and rivers of northern Europe

SIZE Up to 30cm long

RAINBOW TROUT

Originally from North America, this fast-swimming fish is a favourite with anglers, and has been introduced into lakes and rivers in many parts of the world. Wild rainbow trout lay their eggs in gravelly streams and feed on insects and other small animals, sometimes leaping right out of the water to catch those fluttering above. The adults usually return to the sea after they have spawned, but fish that live in large lakes often spend their whole lives in fresh water.

SCIENTIFIC NAME *Salmo gairdneri*

DISTRIBUTION Originally from northeastern Pacific Ocean, North America; introduced worldwide

SIZE Migratory fish up to 1m long; non-migratory fish usually less than 60cm long

NORTHERN PIKE

Pike are fierce freshwater predators that live in quiet lakes and rivers. They hunt by lying in wait for their victims – mainly fish – which they grab with a sudden burst of speed. Their beak-like jaws are strong enough to deal with animals as large as a third of the pike's own size. In the spring, a pike's diet may also include ducklings and young coots, which it ambushes from below. Pike have cylindrical-shaped bodies and large fins that are positioned close to their tail.

SCIENTIFIC NAME *Esox lucius*

DISTRIBUTION Northern hemisphere

SIZE Up to 1.3m long

GRAYLING

The grayling is easy to recognize because it has an unusually large fin in the middle of its back. During the breeding season the male's fin turns red and he arches it over the female as she lays her eggs. Graylings live in rivers and lakes, and lay their eggs on gravel. They feed on insect larvae, other small animals and on other fish's eggs. A similar species, called the Arctic grayling, is found as far north as Canada and Alaska.

SCIENTIFIC NAME *Thymallus thymallus*

DISTRIBUTION Northern Europe, northern Asia

SIZE Up to 46cm long

ARCTIC CHAR

This member of the salmon family is one of the world's most northerly freshwater fish. It lives in rivers and lakes inland, as well as in the Arctic Ocean, and survives in places where the water's surface is iced up for many months of the year. Arctic chars look similar to trout, but their colour varies, depending on where they live. Males usually develop orange-red undersides during the breeding season, but in some lakes they keep this colour all year round.

SCIENTIFIC NAME *Salvelinus alpinus*

DISTRIBUTION Seas, lakes and rivers throughout the far north

SIZE Up to 96cm long

Arctic char with reddish underside

TOP *Rainbow trout come from North America, but they have been introduced into other parts of the world that have cool, fast-flowing rivers and streams.* **ABOVE** *The brown trout* (Salmo trutta) *is a European fish. Like the rainbow trout, it can either spend its whole life in fresh water or migrate between fresh water and the sea.*

ABOVE *Although it is young, this northern pike is already a fierce predator. Its large eyes are good for spotting movement.* **LEFT** *The grayling is very sensitive to pollution. Graylings quickly disappear from rivers contaminated with fertilizers washed off fields.*

BRISTLEMOUTHS AND HATCHETFISH

This group of about 250 species includes some of the world's most common saltwater fish. Most of them live in the oceans' depths and are rarely seen. They are very varied in size and shape, but all of them have hinged teeth and rows of light-producing organs on their bodies. Bristlemouths and hatchetfish feed on other fish, or on small animals that drift in plankton. They live in oceans worldwide.

BIOLUMINESCENCE

Sunlight is absorbed by sea water, so the deeper you dive the darker it gets. Below depths of 1,000m, the water is inky black. In these conditions, many fish make their own light. They use it to keep in touch or to lure prey within striking distance of their mouths.

Fish are not the only animals that can light up. Other light-producing animals include jellyfish, sea gooseberries, molluscs and insects. Light production by living things is called bioluminescence. Some animals glow all over, but most have light-producing organs that they can flash. The light is usually produced by a protein called luciferin that glows when oxygen is used to break it down. The flashlight fish from the Indian Ocean uses bacteria to make light. The bacteria are kept in a pouch with a shutter that can cover the pouch to hide the light.

Flashlight fish (Photoblepharon palpebratus)

VIPERFISH

The viperfish gets its name from the long fangs that stick out from its jaws, even when its mouth is closed. It has a slender, jet-black body, and one of its fins has a long spine with a luminous tip. The fish probably uses this to lure other animals towards its mouth. Like many deep-sea hunters, the viperfish can swallow animals that are almost its own size. Its stomach has an extra-dark lining that works like a curtain, stopping light from its swallowed prey being spotted by other hunters.

SCIENTIFIC NAME	*Chauliodus sloani*
DISTRIBUTION	Worldwide
SIZE	Up to 30cm long

Overlapping teeth

DEEP-SEA HATCHETFISH

When sound waves were first used to survey the seabed, about 50 years ago, scientists were puzzled by echoes that seemed to move up during the night and sink down during the day. These 'deep scattering layers' turned out to be shoals of deep-sea hatchetfish feeding by night on planktonic animals. Hatchetfish have very narrow silvery bodies, and their undersides have a sharp edge, just like the blade of an axe. The fish keep in touch with each other by using rows of lights, which give off a yellowish glow when seen from below. In turn, hatchetfish have tubular eyes that point upwards so they can see others swimming above them.

SCIENTIFIC NAME	*Argyropelecus aculeatus*
DISTRIBUTION	Warm seas worldwide
SIZE	Up to 7.5cm long

DEEP-SEA BRISTLEMOUTH

Although little is known about them, deep-sea bristlemouths are thought to be the most abundant saltwater fish on Earth. They feed on small planktonic animals and have bristle-lined jaws that help them to scoop up their prey. They have light-producing organs on their undersides, visible from below.

SCIENTIFIC NAME	*Cyclothone* species
DISTRIBUTION	Worldwide
SIZE	About 6cm long

ABOVE *The viperfish is covered with a layer of slimy jelly, which is thought to make it harder for other fish to catch.*

EELS

With their long, snake-like bodies, eels look very different from most other fish. Most eels do not have scales, but many do have a ribbon-shaped fin that runs along their backs, around their tails and underneath their bodies. True eels live in fresh water and the sea, but they all start life as transparent leaf-shaped larvae that drift in the surface waters of the oceans. Some species migrate back to rivers to breed, an epic journey that can take several years. There are 700 species of eel and they are found all over the world.

ABOVE *The gulper eel has an enormous mouth. Scientists do not know if the eel actively hunts or lies in wait for fish.*

EUROPEAN EEL

These eels spend most of their adult life in fresh water, where they feed on small animals after dark. For many years, their life-cycle was a mystery, but in 1920, a research expedition showed that the adults travel across the Atlantic Ocean to lay their eggs in the Sargasso Sea. The adults then die, leaving the tiny larvae to make their way back to Europe – a journey that takes three years. A similar eel lives in North America. Its journey from the Sargasso Sea takes only one year.

RIGHT *During its lifetime, the European eel travels nearly 10,000km.*

BELOW *The conger's snake-like shape allows it to slide through rocky crevices in search of its prey.*

SCIENTIFIC NAME
Anguilla anguilla

DISTRIBUTION Europe, North Atlantic Ocean

SIZE Up to 1m long

CONGER EEL

This eel's grey body is thicker than a man's arm. It lives in shallow water close to the shore, but during the day, it hides in rocky crevices and old wrecked ships, with only its head exposed. At night, it swims out of its lair to feed on fish, crabs, octopuses and sometimes lobsters caught in fishermen's lobster pots. In summer, fully mature congers migrate to the open sea to breed.

SCIENTIFIC NAME *Conger conger*

DISTRIBUTION North Atlantic Ocean

SIZE Up to 2.7m long

Lower jaw much shorter than the upper jaw

MORAY EEL

Brightly coloured and highly aggressive, moray eels spend most of their adult lives half-hidden in rocky lairs. They feed by grabbing fish that come within reach, using a swift, snake-like action, and sometimes bite divers' hands and feet. Moray bites can be dangerous because they easily become infected. There are more than 200 species of these eels and they are most common in the tropics, particularly on coral reefs.

SCIENTIFIC NAME *Muraena* and other genera

DISTRIBUTION Worldwide

SIZE Up to 3m long

GULPER EEL

The gulper eel has a slender body and a huge mouth – fully open, it could swallow a football. Gulper eels live in the deep sea and it is not known how they feed. They either trap fish by swimming with their mouths open, or use light to lure them into their jaws.

SCIENTIFIC NAME *Eurypharynx pelecanoides*

DISTRIBUTION Warm seas worldwide

SIZE Up to 60cm long

Small pectoral fin

SPINY EEL

Unlike true eels, spiny eels have scales and underslung mouths. They also have a row of spines along their backs, which is how they get their name. These fish live on seabed mud in deep water and feed on slow-moving animals.

SCIENTIFIC NAME *Macroganthus* and other genera

DISTRIBUTION Worldwide

SIZE Typical length 1m

ABOVE
Spiny eels are found in tropical and temperate waters. They live on soft seabed sediment, often at great depths.

CARP AND THEIR RELATIVES

Carp and their relatives are among the world's most numerous freshwater fish. They are found all over the world except in South America, Australia and New Zealand, and range in size from minnows and other 'tiddlers' to fish more than 2m long. Carp eat a wide variety of food, including other fish, water snails and water plants. They do not have any teeth in their jaws, but they do have them at the back of their mouths. These teeth push against a hard pad, grinding up any food that they swallow. There are about 2,000 species of these fish and they all reproduce by laying eggs.

COMMON CARP

This deep-bodied fish lives in lakes and slow-flowing rivers, where it feeds by sucking up animals and small plants from the mud. It has four fleshy feelers, or barbels, at the corners of its mouth that help it to find food in murky water. Carp have been bred by people for food since ancient times and, over the centuries, several different varieties have evolved. One type, the mirror carp, has lines of extra-large scales along its back and sides, while another, the golden carp, is orange. Carp can live for up to 40 years – a long time for a freshwater fish.

SCIENTIFIC NAME *Cyprinus carpio*

DISTRIBUTION Originally from central Asia; introduced into many parts of the world

SIZE Up to 1m long

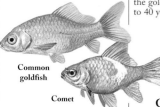

Common goldfish

Comet

ABOVE *Goldfish have been specially bred in captivity for longer than any other kind of fish.*

GRASS CARP

In the Far East, the slender, silvery grass carp is one of the most important 'farmed' freshwater fish. It is easy to raise because it feeds on water plants and can survive in small village ponds. Grass carp have large appetites and, in the wild, they help to stop rivers and lakes becoming clogged up with vegetation. Because of this useful habit they have been introduced into Europe and North America.

SCIENTIFIC NAME *Ctenopharyngodon idella*

DISTRIBUTION Originally from China; introduced into other parts of Asia, Europe, North America

SIZE Up to 1.25m

BELOW *The rudd usually feeds near the surface because its sloping mouth prevents it from picking up food from the bottom.*

RUDD

With its bright red fins and olive-yellow body, this common freshwater fish looks as though it should be easy to spot. But it is actually well camouflaged in murky water. Rudd live in lakes and slow-flowing rivers and eat plants and small animals, such as worms and insect larvae. In late spring, the females lay as many as 200,000 eggs. The eggs stick to underwater plants, and the young fish hatch about a week later.

SCIENTIFIC NAME *Scardinius erythrophthalmus*

DISTRIBUTION Originally from Europe, parts of Asia; introduced into North America

SIZE Up to 30cm long

GOLDFISH

Goldfish are the world's most popular ornamental fish. Over the past thousand years, hundreds of varieties have been bred. Some have bright colours and patterns, whilst others have bulging eyes and misshapen bodies and fins. Wild goldfish live in pools and lakes. They are grey when young, but turn orange as they grow.

SCIENTIFIC NAME *Carassius auratus*

DISTRIBUTION Originally from Europe, Asia; now kept in ornamental ponds worldwide

SIZE Up to 30cm long

FAR LEFT *Golden carp are often kept in lakes and ornamental ponds. They are descended from the common carp and are specially bred for their colour.*
LEFT *The finger-sized European minnow is common in clean rivers and streams. It is caught by kingfishers, which dive into the water to catch fish near the surface.*

EUROPEAN MINNOW

This small, dark-coloured fish lives in cool, fast-flowing streams, where it feeds on water plants, insect larvae and shrimps. Because it lives in clear water, it relies on speed to keep out of trouble, darting away at the first sign of danger. European minnows gather in shoals to spawn, and they lay their eggs among gravel and stones.

SCIENTIFIC NAME *Phoxinus phoxinus*
DISTRIBUTION Europe, northern Asia
SIZE Up to 10cm long

BITTERLING

Bitterlings are small, silvery fish that have a remarkable way of reproducing. Instead of laying eggs in open water, the female uses a long egg-tube, or ovipositor, to lay them inside the shell of a live freshwater mussel. The male then sheds his sperm into the mussel and guards the mussel while the eggs develop inside. When the eggs hatch, the young leave their nursery and swim away. Bitterlings lay far fewer eggs than other fish in the carp family, but their unusual behaviour gives their eggs a much better chance of survival.

SCIENTIFIC NAME *Rhodeus sericeus*
DISTRIBUTION Originally from Europe, northeastern Asia; introduced into North America
SIZE Up to 9cm long

COMMON SHINER

This is a widespread river fish of eastern North America. It is covered with silvery scales and has an olive-coloured back, although the male turns pink just before the breeding season begins. There are more than 100 species of shiner in North America and it can be difficult to tell them apart. To make matters more complicated, several species, including the common shiner, interbreed with other species.

SCIENTIFIC NAME *Luxilus cornutus*
DISTRIBUTION North America
SIZE Up to 18cm long

TOP *A female bitterling lays her eggs inside a freshwater mussel while a male waits nearby.*
ABOVE *The common shiner lives in rocky pools in rivers, and sometimes in lakes.*

LEFT *Female danios are plumper than males. The upper fish of this pair of zebra danios is the female.*
BELOW *Tench feed on insect larvae in summer but, in winter, they hardly feed at all.*

ZEBRA DANIO

Danios are tiny, highly active freshwater fish that live in streams and lakes in India and other warm parts of Asia. They have slender bodies, often with a silvery sheen. This particular species gets its name from the horizontal stripes that run from its head to the tip of its tail and across its fins. It is a popular aquarium fish and several ornamental varieties have been bred.

SCIENTIFIC NAME	*Brachydanio rerio*
DISTRIBUTION	India
SIZE	Up to 5cm long

TENCH

This greenish-brown, heavy-bodied fish feeds on the bottom of slow-moving lakes or rivers, where it finds its prey by touch and smell. The tench has leathery skin covered with a layer of slippery mucus. Female tench can lay nearly a million eggs a year, but many get eaten and only a tiny fraction survive to become adult fish.

SCIENTIFIC NAME	*Tinca tinca*
DISTRIBUTION	Originally from Europe, parts of northern Asia; widely introduced elsewhere
SIZE	Up to 70cm long

COLORADO SQUAWFISH

Squawfish are the largest fish in the carp family in North America. They have streamlined bodies, long heads and large mouths, and they feed mainly on other fish. The Colorado squawfish is the largest of all, weighing more than 35kg. The building of dams has caused the population to dwindle and it is now an endangered species.

SCIENTIFIC NAME	*Ptychocheilus lucius*
DISTRIBUTION	Southwestern USA
SIZE	Up to 1.8m long

BARBEL

This slender freshwater fish has a round body with a flat underside to suit its bottom-dwelling lifestyle. It is named after the four fleshy feelers, or barbels, that hang from its jaws. The feelers have taste-sensitive tips, and are used to probe riverbeds for insect larvae and other small animals. Barbels lay their eggs in gravel or on stones.

SCIENTIFIC NAME	*Barbus barbus*
DISTRIBUTION	Europe
SIZE	Up to 90cm long

ABOVE *The barbel is a typical bottom-feeder, with a downward-facing mouth.*
BELOW *The red-tailed black shark will often fight if it is kept with others in an aquarium.*

RED-TAILED BLACK SHARK

Despite its name, this small freshwater fish is not a shark, but it does have an aggressive streak. It lives in streams and feeds on algae, which it rasps off plants and stones. The most striking thing about this fish is its colour. Its body is jet-black, its tail is bright red and its fins are sometimes orange. The red-tailed black shark has many close relatives living in rivers in Africa and Asia.

SCIENTIFIC NAME	*Labeo bicolor*
DISTRIBUTION	Southeast Asia
SIZE	Up to 15cm long

LONGNOSE SUCKER

Suckers are freshwater fish with a downward-pointing mouth and large sucker-like lips. They live on the bottom of rivers and lakes, sucking up their prey like vacuum cleaners. There are about 100 species of sucker and almost all of them live in North America. The longnose sucker is one of the few that is also found in Asia. It lives in rivers in the far north and survives in waters right up to the edge of the Arctic Ocean.

SCIENTIFIC NAME *Catastomus catastomus*

DISTRIBUTION North America, northern Asia

SIZE Up to 60cm long

JAPANESE WEATHERFISH

Although they live in water, fish are sometimes affected by conditions outside. The Japanese weatherfish is one of these species. It is most active when the atmospheric pressure is low and when the weather is changing. In the past, it was sometimes kept as a living weather forecaster because it warned of approaching rain – the atmospheric pressure often drops before it begins to rain and the weatherfish signals the change ahead. Weatherfish live in mud on the bottom of lakes and streams, where they sometimes burrow beneath the surface.

SCIENTIFIC NAME *Misgurnus anguillicaudatus*

DISTRIBUTION Originally from Far East; introduced into North America

SIZE Up to 10cm long

CLOWN LOACH

Loaches are bottom-dwelling fish that live in streams. Some have a snake-like shape but the clown loach is thickset with clear orange and black markings. There are about 200 species of loach worldwide and some of them, including the clown loach, are popular aquarium fish. Because loaches feed on the bottom, they keep out of the way of other fish and help to keep the aquarium gravel clean.

SCIENTIFIC NAME *Botia macracantha*

DISTRIBUTION Indonesia, Papua New Guinea

SIZE Up to 30cm long

BELOW *Clown loaches normally feed at night. Like many other loaches, they defend themselves with two spines – one underneath each eye.*

Dark vertical bands of colour

Small scales give the skin a smooth texture

Defensive spine is usually folded flat but flips up if the fish is threatened

Downward-facing mouth

CHARACINS AND THEIR RELATIVES

Characins are freshwater fish that live in warm parts of the Americas and in tropical Africa. Some are small and highly active with jewel-like colours, but this group also includes fish that are large, slow-moving and well camouflaged. Characins often have sharp teeth, and they eat a wide range of different foods. Many are vegetarians, but predatory characins include highly aggressive piranhas, which hunt in packs and can strip large fish and other animals down to their bones. Characins usually scatter their eggs among water plants, and they leave their young to develop on their own. There are about 1,400 species of characin, mostly in South America.

RED PIRANHA

There are more than 50 species of piranha, all of them living in the rivers of South America. Many are fruit-eaters, but the red piranha is a highly efficient predator. It has a blunt face with an underslung lower jaw – an ideal shape for biting pieces of flesh out of animals much larger than itself. Red piranhas hunt in large shoals, normally feeding on fish. However, if a large land animal becomes stranded in the water, a piranha shoal will attack in a deadly feeding frenzy. Although piranhas usually ignore humans, their unpredictable nature makes them dangerous. In the early 1980s, more than 300 people died when a shoal of piranhas attacked after a boat overturned in a river in Brazil.

SCIENTIFIC NAME	*Serrasalmus nattereri*
DISTRIBUTION	South America
SIZE	Up to 30cm long

RIGHT *A red piranha peers out from some waterside vegetation. Its upper and lower teeth fit together exactly when it closes its jaws, so it can chop out pieces of flesh.*

STRIPED HEADSTANDER

Headstanders are small South American fish that spend most of their lives head-down on riverbeds. This position is convenient for getting at riverbed plants, but headstanders often stay like this even when they are resting. The striped headstander has dark bands that run the length of its body, and a narrow mouth that is good for probing into riverbed mud for food.

SCIENTIFIC NAME	Anostomus anostomus
DISTRIBUTION	South America
SIZE	Up to 18cm long

GIANT TIGERFISH

This African fish is one of the largest characins, often weighing more than 30kg. It is built for speed, with a streamlined body and a deeply forked tail. The giant tigerfish lives in slow-flowing rivers and lakes, where it feeds on other fish. Tigerfish are naturally aggressive and put up a furious fight if they are hooked by an angler.

SCIENTIFIC NAME	Hydrocynus goliath
DISTRIBUTION	Central Africa
SIZE	Up to 1.8m long

MARBLED HATCHETFISH

Not to be confused with the deep-sea hatchetfish (page 108), this small, deep-bodied characin is one of the few fish in the world that is capable of powered flight. If it is chased by a predator, it leaps clear of the water and beats its pectoral fins to skim just above the surface. Marbled hatchetfish cannot fly far, but their brief journey through the air is often enough to help them escape being eaten by larger fish.

SCIENTIFIC NAME	Carnegiella strigata
DISTRIBUTION	Tropical South America
SIZE	Up to 5cm long

NEON TETRA

With its electric-blue sides and bright red tail, the tiny neon tetra is easily recognized. In the wild, neon tetras live in the upper reaches of the Amazon in Brazil. They feed in shoals and, like other characins, they scatter their eggs among plants. Their placid nature means that they are easy to keep in aquariums.

SCIENTIFIC NAME	Pracheirodon innesi
DISTRIBUTION	Tropical South America
SIZE	Up to 4cm long

X-RAY FISH

Instead of being brightly coloured, the x-ray fish is almost transparent. It has see-through muscles and skin, and its backbone is clearly visible, just like an x-ray picture. Its other organs are surrounded by a silvery covering that glints as it catches the light. X-ray fish live in rivers, and feed on plants and water animals.

SCIENTIFIC NAME	Pristella maxillaris
DISTRIBUTION	South America
SIZE	Up to 2.5cm long

BLIND CAVE CHARACIN

The blind cave characin lives in water underground. It has a pale pink body with colourless fins, but its most remarkable feature is that it has no eyes. It finds its food by smell and navigates using its lateral line – a row of sensors down each side of its body that warn it of anything nearby. Most fish have a lateral line but, in the cave characin, it is highly developed.

SCIENTIFIC NAME	Astyanax fasciatus
DISTRIBUTION	Mexico
SIZE	Up to 9cm long

TOP *The neon tetra needs to live in warm water.*
ABOVE *The x-ray fish gets its name because it has a see-through body.*

ABOVE *As blind cave characins swim along, they sense faint waves of pressure that bounce back from nearby objects.*

Deep body stabilizes fish during take-off

Deeply forked tail

Metallic scales

LEFT
The marbled hatchetfish has a low-slung body and two pectoral fins high up near its back. It uses these fins as wings to flutter over the surface of the water.

CATFISH AND ELECTRIC EELS

Catfish spend their lives on the bottom of rivers and lakes. Most of these fish are nocturnal, and they probe for food with the thread-like barbels that hang from their lips and jaws like whiskers. Catfish do not have scales, but their pectoral fins are armed with sharp spines that make it uncomfortable for other animals to swallow them. In some species, these spines are poisonous, giving the catfish extra protection. There are at least 2,500 species of catfish and they are found in most parts of the world, except where it is extremely cold. Electric eels do not look much like catfish, but they are related to them and not to other eels.

RIGHT *The glass catfish is active during the day. Being transparent helps it to avoid being spotted by predators, such as herons and other fishing birds.*

BELOW *The upside-down catfish, seen here the right way up, has three pairs of long barbels that it uses to find its food.*

GLASS CATFISH

Many fish have a see-through body, but the glass catfish is remarkable for being almost transparent. Its muscles contain oil that makes them nearly as clear as glass, so it is easy to see its bones, intestines, reproductive organs and eyes. The glass catfish lives in streams and rivers, where it feeds on small animals such as water fleas, and plants. It usually lives in shoals.

SCIENTIFIC NAME	*Kryptopterus bicirrhis*
DISTRIBUTION	Southeast Asia
SIZE	Up to 10cm long

UPSIDE-DOWN CATFISH

Instead of getting its food from riverbed mud, like most catfish, this African species often feeds at the surface of the water. It swims upside down, which makes it easier for it to eat flies and other insects that have landed on the water. It even rests like this under water plants and overhanging branches. This catfish has a mottled pattern that helps to camouflage it from predators as it feeds.

SCIENTIFIC NAME	*Synodontis multipunctatus*
DISTRIBUTION	Lake Tanganyika (Tropical Africa)
SIZE	Up to 10cm long

Long barbels attached to upper lip

Short central barbels attached to lower lip

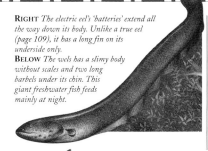

RIGHT *The electric eel's 'batteries' extend all the way down its body. Unlike a true eel (page 109), it has a long fin on its underside only.*
BELOW *The wels has a slimy body without scales and two long barbels under its chin. This giant freshwater fish feeds mainly at night.*

WELS

The wels is one of the largest freshwater fish in the world. The heaviest one ever caught – in Russia in the 19th century – weighed over 330kg, although it is unlikely that such examples still exist today. Wels live in large, slow-flowing rivers and feed entirely on animals. Fish are the most important items on their menu, but they also eat crayfish and ducks, and have been reputed to tackle dogs. They breed in mid-summer, when the male excavates a 'nest' in the mud. The female can lay more than 100,000 eggs and the male guards them until they hatch.

SCIENTIFIC NAME	*Silurus glanis*
DISTRIBUTION	Europe, parts of central Asia
SIZE	Up to 5m long

ELECTRIC EEL

This South American river fish can produce strong electric currents. When it is hunting, it can stun other fish with a shock of up to 550 volts. Once the fish has been stunned, the eel switches off the current and swallows its prey. Like the elephant-trunk fish (pages 102–103), the electric eel uses special muscles as batteries. Large eels have the largest batteries – a shock from one can knock a person off their feet.

SCIENTIFIC NAME	*Electrophorus electricus*
DISTRIBUTION	South America
SIZE	Up to 2.4m long

Long barbels have sensitive tips for finding food

TOADFISH AND ANGLERFISH

These two groups of fish contain some of the strangest-looking animals in the seas. Most of them hunt on the seabed or in open water, and use a combination of stealth and camouflage to catch unwary prey. Some look like pieces of living seaweed, while others resemble stones or sediment, but all of them have large mouths that can open in a split-second to suck in their victims. There are about 70 species of toadfish, mostly living in shallow water near the coast. Anglerfish are more varied, with at least 300 species. They live in a range of habitats from shallow water to the deep ocean floor.

ATLANTIC MIDSHIPMAN

A member of the toadfish family, the Atlantic midshipman lurks on the bottom in shallow water and feeds on crustaceans and other fish. Unusually for an inshore fish, it produces light to lure its victims. Like many toadfish, it can make grunting and squeaking sounds with its swimbladder, and it is particularly noisy when it breeds. The females fasten their eggs to rocks and the males guard them until they hatch.

SCIENTIFIC NAME	*Porichthys porosissimus*
DISTRIBUTION	Western Atlantic Ocean
SIZE	Up to 23cm long

EUROPEAN ANGLERFISH

With its huge, flat head and stumpy tail, this grotesque fish looks as if it has been squashed by a car. Its body is superbly camouflaged, and it has a row of leafy flaps around the edge, helping it to blend in with the seabed. When the anglerfish hunts, the only part of its body that moves is a special spine on its head. The fleshy tip of the spine jiggles and entices fish. The anglerfish's mouth opens and shuts so quickly that its victims appear to vanish into thin air.

SCIENTIFIC NAME	*Lophius piscatorius*
DISTRIBUTION	Eastern North Atlantic Ocean
SIZE	Up to 2m long

SARGASSUM FISH

The Sargassum fish is an anglerfish that lives close to the surface of the sea. It hides among rafts of floating weed, and is camouflaged so well that it is seldom spotted. Its body is the same colour and pattern as seaweed and, for extra effect, it is covered with leafy flaps. Like other anglerfish, the Sargassum fish catches its prey with the help of a lure on its head.

SCIENTIFIC NAME	*Histrio histrio*
DISTRIBUTION	Warm seas worldwide
SIZE	Up to 20cm long

ABOVE *The European anglerfish lurks on the seabed, often in shallow water. Many smaller anglerfish hunt in the dark depths of the open sea, attracting prey with luminous lures.*

CODFISH AND THEIR RELATIVES

There are about 500 species of codfish. They are found mainly in the cool seas of the northern hemisphere, mostly near the seabed or in open water, although a few live in lakes and rivers inland. These fish are all carnivorous and they eat a wide range of water animals. Codfish have small scales, but their eyes are often large – an essential feature for animals that hunt partly by sight. Compared to other fish, codfish lay vast numbers of eggs, but they abandon them once they have been laid. The young fish usually drift in the plankton and only a tiny fraction survive. As adults, they face another threat – many of them are caught to feed people.

ATLANTIC COD

This thick-bodied creature is one of the world's most important commercial fish, and nearly two million tonnes are caught each year. In some places, so many fish have been caught that stocks have been badly damaged and may take many years to recover. The cod often feeds near the seabed, in water up to 600m deep. During the breeding season, large shoals gather in shallow waters and the females lay as many as nine million eggs each. The eggs float upwards and the young start life feeding close to the surface. The largest cod on record weighed more than 90kg, but today's fish are much smaller.

SCIENTIFIC NAME	*Gadus morhua*
DISTRIBUTION	North Atlantic Ocean
SIZE	Up to 1.2m long

WHITING

Unlike many of its relatives, the whiting usually stays close to the shore. This sleek, silvery-sided fish eats other fish and shrimps, catching its food both in open water and on the seabed. It is often caught by anglers and by fishing-boats out at sea. Newly hatched whiting feed on plankton. When they are big and strong enough to swim against the current, they often live among the tentacles of jellyfish. As they are immune to jellyfish stings, this protects them from predators.

SCIENTIFIC NAME	*Merlangius merlangus*
DISTRIBUTION	European coasts
SIZE	Up to 60cm long

HADDOCK

Haddock live near the seabed in water up to 300m deep. They feed on worms, molluscs and other small animals. They have a dark patch on each side of their bodies and pointed dorsal fins. Haddock eggs float on the water for about two weeks until they hatch. Adult haddock are often caught in trawler nets towed across the seabed.

SCIENTIFIC NAME	*Melanogrammus aeglefinus*
DISTRIBUTION	North Atlantic Ocean
SIZE	Up to 75cm long

RIGHT
*The whiting is one
of the most common sea fish
in the eastern North Atlantic.*

HAKE

Unlike some of their relatives, which have three fins on their backs, hake have only two, but their rear fins reach as far as their tails. They have sharp teeth and a black lining on the inside of their mouths. Hake are fierce predators, preying on smaller fish, including their own young. They usually live in deep water, but come close to the shore to spawn.

SCIENTIFIC NAME
Merluccius merluccius

DISTRIBUTION European coasts

SIZE Up to 75cm long

ABOVE
A common ling looks
out from a rock crevice.

COMMON LING

The ling has a totally different shape to its relative the cod. It is slender and eel-like, with two extra-long fins along the top and underside of its body. Adult ling live in water up to 400m deep. They hide among rocks and sunken ships, where they attack fish and other animals. They spawn in deep water but their eggs drift to the surface.

Single barbel under the chin

SCIENTIFIC NAME *Molva molva*

DISTRIBUTION North Atlantic Ocean

SIZE Up to 2m long

Large gill covers

Burbot showing its long dorsal fin

BURBOT

This long-bodied fish is one of the few codfish relatives that live in fresh water. A bottom-dweller, it is found in rivers and lakes, as well as in salty water near the sea. Burbots feed on other fish, attacking after dark. They do most of their feeding in winter months, and spend the summer resting in deep pools. Female burbots can lay as many as five million eggs. Their eggs would float if they were laid in the sea but, in fresh water, they sink to the bottom.

ABOVE
The Atlantic cod eats worms, crustaceans and also other fish.

SCIENTIFIC NAME *Lota lota*

DISTRIBUTION North America, Europe, northern Asia

SIZE Up to 1m long

ROUGH-HEADED GRENADIER

The grenadier belongs to a group of fish called rat-tails, which live in water up to 6,000m deep. They all have large heads with large eyes and downward-pointing mouths. They get their name because their bodies quickly taper away to thin and spindly tails. Rat-tails are just as common as many of their edible relatives but, because they are harder to catch, less is known about how they live. The rough-headed grenadier feeds on the seabed. It has powerful jaws, which it uses to crunch up molluscs and deep-water starfish. Like other species of rat-tail, it can use its swimbladder to make noises.

SCIENTIFIC NAME *Macrourus berglax*

DISTRIBUTION North Atlantic Ocean

SIZE Up to 1m long

LIONFISH, DORIES AND OARFISH

These three groups of fish are only distantly related and very different in size. There are more than 1,200 species of lionfish and their relatives, about 40 kinds of dory and only about 20 species of oarfish. Lionfish and their relatives live in both fresh water and the sea, and are particularly common in coral reefs. Some of these reef species are brilliantly coloured and many have highly poisonous spines. Dories live in shallow water close to coasts, while oarfish and their relatives usually live out in the open ocean. As well as having a very narrow body, oarfish are immensely long and brightly coloured, making them some of the world's most spectacular fish.

LIONFISH

Lionfish have fan-shaped fins and eye-catching brown, red and white vertical stripes. They live on coral reefs, eating small fish and shrimps. If they are threatened, lionfish stay in the open with their fins spread out wide. Their fins are tipped with sharp spines that can inject poison into an attacker's skin. By facing up to an enemy, they show that they will fight back if attacked.

SCIENTIFIC NAME	*Pterois* species
DISTRIBUTION	Indian Ocean, Pacific Ocean
SIZE	Typical length 30cm

STONEFISH

This is one of the deadliest animals in the sea. Unlike its relative the lionfish, it is well camouflaged among coral and rocks. The fins on its back have sharp spines, and if the stonefish is accidentally stepped on, these can inject a fast-acting poison that is strong enough to kill. The stonefish feeds on fish that come within reach of its large, upturned mouth.

Stonefish hidden on a coral reef

SCIENTIFIC NAME	*Synanceia verrucosa*
DISTRIBUTION	Indian Ocean, Pacific Ocean
SIZE	Up to 30cm long

RED GURNARD

Gurnards are bottom-dwelling members of the lionfish group. They are usually red or grey, and have a large, bony head, a slender body and spiky fins. They have three rays on their pectoral fins that can move like fingers, and they use these to 'walk' on the seabed, feeling for food. Red gurnards make a grunting sound, which probably helps them to keep in touch with each other.

SCIENTIFIC NAME	*Trigla lucerna*
DISTRIBUTION	European coasts
SIZE	Up to 75cm long

LUMPSUCKER OR LUMPFISH

The lumpsucker lives in shallow water close to the coast, where it feeds on worms and other small animals. It has a plump body, a small mouth and is covered with knobbly lumps. Its most interesting feature is its pelvic fins. These are underneath the deepest part of its body, and form a powerful sucker that it uses to fasten itself to rocks. In spring, female lumpsuckers lay about 200,000 eggs among rocks near the shore. The male guards the eggs with great devotion and fans water over them until they hatch.

SCIENTIFIC NAME	*Cyclopterus lumpus*
DISTRIBUTION	North Atlantic Ocean
SIZE	Up to 60cm long

JOHN DORY

The John Dory is shaped like a plate standing on its edge. Its body is deep but extremely narrow with a central black spot, and is edged at the top and bottom by large, spiny fins. Its face is flat and bony with a large drooping mouth. John Dories eat other fish but they are not built for speed. Instead, they hunt by stealth, shooting out their mouths and swallowing their food in a fraction of a second. Despite their unappetising appearance, John Dories are highly valued as food.

SCIENTIFIC NAME	*Zeus faber*
DISTRIBUTION	Eastern North Atlantic Ocean
SIZE	Up to 65cm long

ABOVE *The red gurnard is one of the few fish that uses its fins to feel for food.*
LEFT *John Dories are solitary hunters, feeding in water up to 200m deep. When they are young, they often lurk in seaweed.*

ABOVE *This picture shows two species of lionfish – the common lionfish* (Pterois volitans) *on the left and the clearfin lionfish* (Pterois radiata) *on the right.*

OARFISH

The oarfish looks like a gigantic silvery ribbon edged with a single, brilliant red fin. This ocean-going fish is rarely seen, but it grows to such an immense size that it is easily mistaken for a sea monster rising from the depths. Despite its great length, it is harmless to people – it has no teeth and feeds on small crustaceans and fish, which it catches in its funnel-like mouth. Oarfish swim by rippling their body, and they normally stay out of sight, well beneath the surface.

SCIENTIFIC NAME	*Regalecus glesne*
DISTRIBUTION	Worldwide
SIZE	Up to 17m long

OPAH

Like oarfish, the opah spends most of its time in the middle depths of the ocean and is hardly ever seen near the surface. It has a bright blue body with bright red fins, lips and eyes. Although it looks narrow when seen head-on, it is a heavy fish with a deep body. Large examples can weigh as much as 70kg. Opahs are fast-moving creatures and they chase squid and other fish, catching them with their beak-like mouths.

SCIENTIFIC NAME	*Lampris guttatus*
DISTRIBUTION	Warm waters worldwide
SIZE	Up to 1.25m long

FLYINGFISH, GRUNIONS AND SEAHORSES

These three groups contain some freshwater fish, but most of the species live in the sea. Flyingfish are famous for gliding over the water on outstretched fins, while grunions wriggle on to sandy beaches to lay their eggs. Seahorses never leave the water, but they are poor swimmers and live mainly among water weeds. Altogether, these fish total about 900 species and they are most common in warm parts of the world.

ABOVE *An Atlantic flyingfish bursts into the air. This fish can 'fly' at a height of more than 5m – high enough to land accidentally on small boats.*

BELOW *The leafy seadragon lives in seaweed off the coast of Australia. It has tiny fins and is an extremely slow swimmer.*

ATLANTIC FLYINGFISH

Many fish jump out of the water to escape danger, but flyingfish go one better – they skim through the air on their outstretched fins for up to 200m. After take-off, flyingfish often trail the bottom lobe of their tails in the water. This works like a ship's propeller, pushing them along. Flyingfish all have large pectoral, or 'shoulder', fins and many species fly on these alone. The Atlantic flyingfish also has large pelvic fins to give it extra lift as it soars along.

SCIENTIFIC NAME	*Cypselurus melanurus*
DISTRIBUTION	Warm seas worldwide
SIZE	Up to 40cm long

HOUNDFISH

The houndfish is a relative of flyingfish, but its shape could hardly be more different. It has a slender, spear-like body with small fins and a needle-sharp, tooth-filled 'beak'. Houndfish are predators and they use their long jaws to grab other fish sideways-on. They have a habit of leaping at bright lights after dark and have been known to impale people aboard boats, occasionally even killing them.

SCIENTIFIC NAME	*Tylosurus crocodilus*
DISTRIBUTION	Warm seas worldwide
SIZE	Up to 1.5m long

SEAHORSE

Seahorses are like no other fish. They are covered in bony armour and they swim upright, pushed along by tiny fins. They have angular horse-like heads at right angles to their bodies and grasping, or prehensile, tails that can wrap around rocks and weeds. Seahorses feed on minute animals that they suck up through their tiny mouths. When they breed, the males and females pair up during a long and complicated courtship dance. The female then passes her eggs to the male, who incubates them in a special pouch on his front. After hatching, the young swim out through a hole at the top of the pouch.

SCIENTIFIC NAME	*Hippocampus* and other genera
DISTRIBUTION	Worldwide, except in cold regions
SIZE	Typical length 15cm

LEAFY SEADRAGON

Seadragons are closely related to seahorses. They have the same overall shape as seahorses, but they are disguised by some of the most elaborate camouflage in the animal world. They live in beds of underwater weeds, and their bodies have a collection of leafy flaps that make them almost impossible to see.

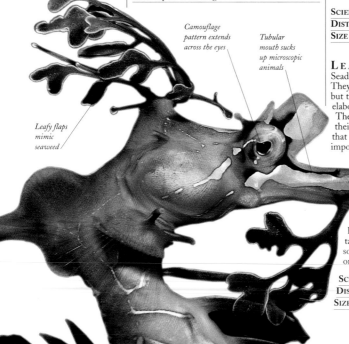

Camouflage pattern extends across the eyes

Tubular mouth sucks up microscopic animals

Leafy flaps mimic seaweed

Seadragons do not have prehensile tails. They are sometimes washed on to shores in storms.

SCIENTIFIC NAME	*Phycodurus eques*
DISTRIBUTION	Australia
SIZE	Up to 30cm long

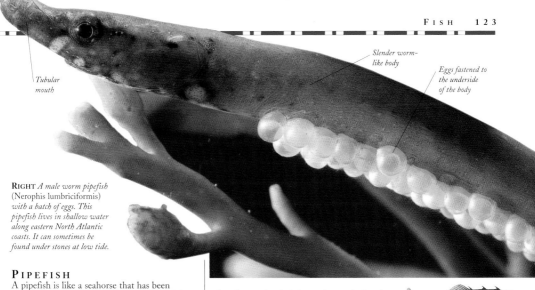

Slender worm-like body

Eggs fastened to the underside of the body

Tubular mouth

RIGHT *A male worm pipefish* (Nerophis lumbriciformis) *with a batch of eggs. This pipefish lives in shallow water along eastern North Atlantic coasts. It can sometimes be found under stones at low tide.*

PIPEFISH

A pipefish is like a seahorse that has been stretched out until its body is perfectly straight. It has the same kind of bony armour, and a tubular mouth and tiny fins. Some pipefish swim vertically, but most swim horizontally, gliding slowly through eelgrass and other underwater plants. Pipefish share another feature with seahorses – when they breed, the male carries the eggs until they hatch. Pipefish live close to the shore, and rely mainly on their camouflage to avoid being attacked.

SCIENTIFIC NAME	*Nerophis* and other genera
DISTRIBUTION	Worldwide
SIZE	Typical length 25cm

THREE-SPINED STICKLEBACK

This freshwater fish gets its name from the three spines on its back. During the breeding season, the greenish-brown males develop bright red undersides. Each male builds a nest from underwater plants. He lures females into the nest to lay their eggs and then guards the young fish. Despite their small size, male sticklebacks are pugnacious fish, and fights often break out between rivals.

SCIENTIFIC NAME	*Gasterosteus aculeatus*
DISTRIBUTION	Europe
SIZE	Up to 8cm long

CALIFORNIA GRUNION

This small, silvery fish lives in shoals and is famous for the unusual way in which it breeds. On spring and summer nights, during extra-high tides, thousands of adult grunions wriggle ashore on sandy beaches. The females lay eggs in the wet sand. After 15 days, the next series of high tides wets the eggs and they hatch. The young grunions then make their way out to sea.

SCIENTIFIC NAME	*Leuresthes tenuis*
DISTRIBUTION	Pacific coast of southern California and Mexico
SIZE	Up to 19cm long

ABOVE
Male three-spined sticklebacks develop bright colours in the spring.

PARENTAL CARE

Seahorses, pipefish and sticklebacks take care of their eggs, and sometimes of their young when they hatch. Although they lay only a few eggs each time they breed, careful parenting gives each one a good chance of survival. The jewel cichlid (page 126) is also a good parent, but most other fish are not. Fish usually lay thousands, or even millions, of eggs but, because they leave them to develop on their own, only a small percentage of their young survive.

Parental care varies throughout the animal world. Most invertebrates have little to do with their eggs or young, but there are exceptions, such as scorpions, spiders and some insects. Amphibians and reptiles often abandon their eggs once they have been laid, but some of these animals stand guard over them until they hatch, and a few even carry their young to the water. With birds and mammals, parental care is an important part of life. Compared to other animals, birds and mammals have small families, but they put a lot more effort into helping their young to survive.

Male common seahorse 'giving birth' to young

PERCH AND THEIR RELATIVES

There are about 9,500 species of these fish – more than a third of the world's total – making them the largest single group of bony fish. They live in a huge range of habitats, from mountain streams to the open sea. The largest species can grow to more than 4.5m long, while the smallest species, measuring just 1cm long, is the shortest animal with a backbone. Perch and their relatives have a bewildering variety of shapes but they all have a spiny dorsal fin – the front, and sometimes only, fin on their backs. They reproduce by laying eggs. Some species scatter their eggs in the water, so most do not survive, but other species are much more careful parents, looking after their young both before and after they hatch.

NILE PERCH

The Nile perch is the largest freshwater fish in Africa, and can weigh as much as 130kg. It lives in rivers and lakes and is often caught for food. Nile perch have olive-grey bodies, large mouths and spiny front dorsal fins. They feed mainly on other fish and have decimated species where they have been introduced.

SCIENTIFIC NAME   *Lates niloticus*

DISTRIBUTION   Originally found in River Nile; widely introduced into other parts of Africa

SIZE   Up to 2m long

ABOVE The European perch lives in lowland rivers, lakes and ponds, usually in small shoals close to tree roots or weed beds.

EUROPEAN PERCH

Compared to some of its exotic relatives, the European perch is an inconspicuous fish. It has a deep body, and its colour camouflages it well among water plants. It has two fins on its back. The rear one is soft but the front one has strong spines. Perch hunt other fish by lurking among underwater plants. Their usual technique is to rush out from cover to grab a passing fish by the tail. Once the fish has been disabled, the perch turns it around so that it can swallow it headfirst. Perch lay thousands of eggs in long strings, wrapping them around plants and stones.

SCIENTIFIC NAME   *Perca fluviatilis*

DISTRIBUTION   Originally from Europe, northern Asia; introduced into other parts of the world

SIZE   Up to 50cm long

GIANT GROUPER

Groupers are warm-water fish that often live on coral reefs. Heavy and slow-moving, they have stocky bodies and wide, fleshy mouths with lots of teeth. Many of them are striped or spotted and their markings often change as they grow. There are more than 400 species of these impressive carnivorous fish and the giant grouper is the largest, weighing up to 300kg. It feeds on lobsters and fish, including small sharks. Groupers have been reported to attack divers,

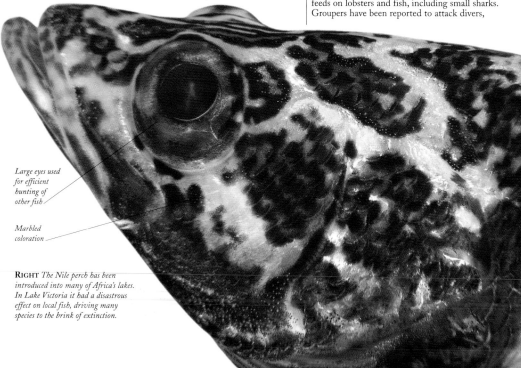

Large eyes used for efficient hunting of other fish

Marbled coloration

RIGHT *The Nile perch has been introduced into many of Africa's lakes. In Lake Victoria it had a disastrous effect on local fish, driving many species to the brink of extinction.*

but they are probably not as dangerous as they look. Because they move slowly, they are easy targets for spear-fishers, and many species are now endangered.

SCIENTIFIC NAME
Epinephalus lanceolatus

DISTRIBUTION   Red Sea, Indian Ocean, Pacific Ocean

SIZE   Up to 2.7m long

Sucker seen from above

Spotted pattern

ABOVE *The giant grouper is the largest bony fish that lives in coral reefs. It often lurks in caves and wrecks.*

ABOVE
The remora's sucker has two rows of ridges. When the remora presses the sucker against another fish, the ridges flatten and the sucker sticks tight.

Ridges are flattened because the sucker is fastened to a tank

PILOTFISH
Pilotfish spend their adult lives swimming close to large sea animals, such as sharks, rays, turtles and whales. Their hosts seem to ignore them completely, although they are brightly striped and often swim right in front of their mouths. At one time, people thought that pilotfish acted as guides to lost animals. A more likely explanation is that pilotfish gain protection from the larger animals. They do not share their host's food, but they do dart after any small fish that swim off as a host animal approaches.

SCIENTIFIC NAME   *Naucrates ductor*

DISTRIBUTION   Warm seas worldwide

SIZE   Up to 70cm long

DOLPHIN-FISH
This relative of the remora has a confusing name. It is not a true dolphin but probably got this name because it feeds on flyingfish, often bursting out of the water like a dolphin as it chases its prey. Dolphin-fish have very narrow bodies that are brilliant yellowish-green, with a metallic sheen. They have large pointed tails that give them an impressive swimming speed of up to 64km/h.

SCIENTIFIC NAME   *Coryphaena hippurus*

DISTRIBUTION   Warm seas worldwide

SIZE   Up to 2m long

REMORA OR SHARKSUCKER
The remora gets a free ride through the seas by fastening itself with an oval sucker to animals such as sharks, whales and porpoises. The sucker is a specially modified fin just behind the top of its head. It locks tight when the remora presses against its host, but it loosens if the remora swims ahead to feed. The sucker is amazingly strong – if a remora is put in a bucket of water, the whole bucket can be lifted up by holding on to the remora's tail.

SCIENTIFIC NAME   *Echeneis naucrates*

DISTRIBUTION   Warm seas worldwide

SIZE   Up to 1.1m long

SPANGLED EMPEROR
Emperors are coastal fish with long, sloping foreheads and large staring eyes. They feed mostly at night, catching other fish or crunching up crabs and molluscs with their powerful jaws. There are about 40 species of emperor fish, but they can be difficult to identify because they are able to change colour extremely quickly. The spangled emperor is one of the largest species. It lives on coral reefs and among beds of seagrass, and often feeds in shoals.

SCIENTIFIC NAME   *Lethrinus nebulosus*

DISTRIBUTION   Indian Ocean, Pacific Ocean

SIZE   Up to 85cm long

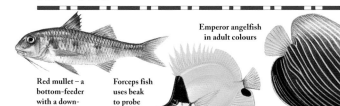

Red mullet – a bottom-feeder with a down-turned mouth

Forceps fish uses beak to probe into crannies

Emperor angelfish in adult colours

Jewel cichlid showing speckled coloration

RED MULLET

Mullet – also known as goatfish – are mainly tropical fish that live on the seabed in shallow water. They have two long feelers, or barbels, and they use these to stir up the sand. They eat worms and other bottom-dwelling creatures, and once they have finished feeding, they fold away their barbels into grooves underneath their jaws. The red mullet is one of the few species found along the shores of Europe.

SCIENTIFIC NAME *Mullus surmuletus*

DISTRIBUTION Eastern North Atlantic Ocean, Mediterranean Sea

SIZE Up to 40cm long

COMMON ARCHERFISH

The archerfish is one of the most unusual hunters in the animal world. It lives along muddy coasts, estuaries and in mangrove swamps, and feeds on insects and other small animals. It sometimes jumps out of the water to catch its prey, but it can also knock insects off overhanging branches by spitting at them. The archerfish does this by closing its gill covers suddenly. This forces a mouthful of water past its tongue and jaws, and out in a well-aimed jet. The fish can hit animals 1m above the surface.

SCIENTIFIC NAME *Toxotes chatareus*

DISTRIBUTION Indian Ocean

SIZE Up to 40cm long

EMPEROR ANGELFISH

Angelfish live in coral reefs and are famous for their striking patterns and colours. Young emperor angelfish are dark blue with white rings, but the adults are yellow with pale blue stripes – so different that they look like a separate species. Like all angelfish, they feed on coral and sponges. They have small beak-like mouths and narrow bodies, which helps them to squeeze between coral branches.

SCIENTIFIC NAME *Pomacanthus imperator*

DISTRIBUTION Indian Ocean, Pacific Ocean

SIZE Up to 30cm long

FORCEPS FISH

The forceps fish lives on the seaward edge of coral reefs, where breakers roll in from the open ocean. Its mouth looks like a pair of forceps or tweezers. With this precision instrument, the forceps fish can pick up small animals from inaccessible places, such as among sea urchin spines. Like its relatives, this fish has a dark spot near its tail. This looks like an eye and probably helps to divert predators away from its head.

SCIENTIFIC NAME *Forcipiger longirostris*

DISTRIBUTION Indian Ocean, Pacific Ocean

SIZE Up to 18cm long

CLOWN ANEMONE FISH

A brilliant orange body marked with three broad white bands gives this small fish one of the brightest colour schemes in the seas. It shelters and feeds among the stinging tentacles of large sea anemones. Here it is safe from most of its enemies, because its skin produces chemicals that stop the anemones from attacking it. While the fish clearly benefits from the partnership, it is not known if anemones get anything in return.

SCIENTIFIC NAME *Amphiprion percula*

DISTRIBUTION Great Barrier Reef, coasts of New Guinea

SIZE Up to 11cm long

JEWEL CICHLID

Cichlids are freshwater fish of tropical Africa, India, and Central and South America. The jewel cichlid lives in streams, and eats a variety of food including plants and small animals, such as water fleas. As with all cichlids, it is a careful parent. Once the young have hatched, both adults protect them by sheltering them in their mouths. There may be more than 2,000 species of cichlid, but counting them is difficult because many are found in only one river or lake.

SCIENTIFIC NAME *Hemichromis bimaculatus*

DISTRIBUTION Western Africa

SIZE Up to 10cm long

Clown anemone fish among the stinging tentacles of an anemone

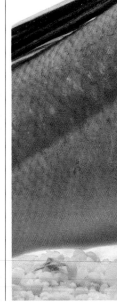

MUDSKIPPER

These small fish live in mangrove swamps and on muddy coasts. When the tide rises, they hide in burrows but, at low tide, they skip across the mud on their fins and even climb up tree roots. They survive out of water because they breathe partly through their gills and partly through their skin. Their eyes are on top of their heads, helping them to spot food and watch for danger.

SCIENTIFIC NAME
Periophthalmus and other genera

DISTRIBUTION Warm coasts worldwide

SIZE Typical length 15cm

Protruding eyes give all-round vision, and the mudskipper keeps them moist by rolling them back into the sockets

BELOW *A mudskipper peers out of the water. This fish can stay out of the water for hours at a time, as long as it keeps its skin moist. Mudskippers carry water in their gill chambers, which enables them to live in air.*

Skin absorbs oxygen from the air

Pectoral fins act like legs

PARROTFISH

Parrotfish get their name from their teeth, which are joined together to form a shape like a parrot's beak. They live in coral reefs and use their teeth to bite off plants and pieces of the reef itself. They have a second set of teeth inside their throat, which they use to grind up their food. Their loud crunching sounds can be heard several metres away. Parrotfish are often beautifully coloured, and they come out to feed during the day. At night, they wrap themselves up in a 'sleeping bag' of mucus, which helps to keep their enemies at bay.

SCIENTIFIC NAME	*Scarus* and other genera
DISTRIBUTION	Tropical seas worldwide
SIZE	Typical length 30cm

animals to swim nearby. Stargazers can produce mild electric shocks using 'batteries' behind their eyes. They probably use the electric shocks to help them to catch their prey.

SCIENTIFIC NAME	*Astroscopus guttatus*
DISTRIBUTION	Atlantic Ocean
SIZE	Up to 56cm long

LEFT *The powder-blue surgeonfish* (Acanthurus leucosternon) *has blades that can cut through skin.*

POWDER-BLUE SURGEONFISH

Surgeonfish look quite harmless as they feed among coral reefs. But if anything threatens one, it can fight back with hidden weapons – two foldaway blades at the base of its tail. The surgeonfish slashes its blades from side to side and can inflict a painful wound. Surgeonfish have deep, narrow bodies, and are often beautifully coloured. They eat plants, and usually feed in small shoals. Like many coral reef fish, they scatter their eggs in the water, leaving their young to develop on their own.

SCIENTIFIC NAME	*Acanthurus* and other genera
DISTRIBUTION	Tropical seas worldwide
SIZE	Typical length 25cm

ABOVE *Spectacled parrotfish* (Scarus perspicillatus) *live around the Hawaiian Islands.* **LEFT** *A juvenile twin-spot wrasse is brightly coloured.*

TWIN-SPOT WRASSE

Wrasse are slender fish with several strange features. They often change colour as they grow and, like parrotfish, they sometimes change sex as well. The twin-spot wrasse starts life with a pale yellow body with black and red spots on its back. Adult females are also yellow, although they do not have spots, but adult males are greenish-black. Twin-spot wrasse live in coral reefs and feed on molluscs, crabs and sea urchins. At night, they hide away in sand.

SCIENTIFIC NAME	*Coris aygula*
DISTRIBUTION	Indian Ocean, Pacific Ocean
SIZE	Up to 1.2m long

NORTHERN STARGAZER

The stargazer has an almost vertical mouth, and eyes on the top of its head. It keeps its thick body partly buried in sand and lies in wait for

SIAMESE FIGHTING FISH

This small freshwater fish is famous for its territorial behaviour. The females are inconspicuous and placid, but the males are brightly coloured with large fins. They are also much more aggressive than the females. If one male swims into another's territory, a fight almost always breaks out. The territory's resident holds out his fins like fans and, if the intruder does not give way, he launches an attack. Males on home ground usually win. Fighting fish are often kept in aquariums. Many breeds have been developed and, in some, the males' fins are much longer than their body.

SCIENTIFIC NAME	*Betta splendens*
DISTRIBUTION	Southeast Asia
SIZE	Up to 6cm long

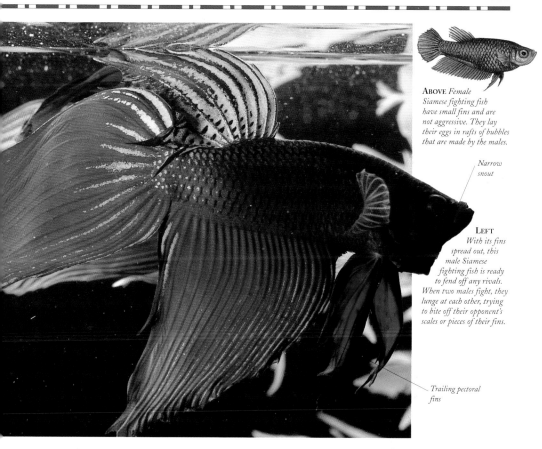

ABOVE *Female Siamese fighting fish have small fins and are not aggressive. They lay their eggs in rafts of bubbles that are made by the males.*

Narrow snout

LEFT
With its fins spread out, this male Siamese fighting fish is ready to fend off any rivals. When two males fight, they lunge at each other, trying to bite off their opponent's scales or pieces of their fins.

Trailing pectoral fins

SYMBIOSIS

In coral reefs, many fish improve their chances of survival by forming partnerships with other animals. For example, clown anemone fish (page 126) shelter in the tentacles of sea anemones, while small fish called cleaner wrasse remove parasites and damaged scales from larger fish. This kind of teaming-up is known as symbiosis. In some symbiotic partnerships, only one partner benefits but, in most partnerships, both of the partners gain. This is the situation with cleaner wrasse – the cleaner benefits by getting a meal and, in return, it helps its 'clients' to stay healthy. Symbiotic partnerships occur not just with fish, but throughout the living world. Many animals use symbiotic microbes to help them digest food, and many plants use animals to spread their pollen. In some partnerships, the partners can live without each other if they have to, but other partners depend on each other for survival.

Cleaner wrasse (Labroides species) with a grouper fish

CLIMBING PERCH
Climbing perch are close relatives of Siamese fighting fish and, like them, they live in slow-flowing rivers and coastal lagoons. The water in these habitats often contains little oxygen, and both types of fish survive by breathing air as well as using their gills. Climbing perch are particularly good at this, and can survive out of the water for long periods provided they stay wet. Like some catfish (page 116), climbing perch can crawl overland using their front fins like legs. They tend to come out on land when it is raining, but will crawl over land to move home if their surroundings start to dry up.

SCIENTIFIC NAME *Anabas testudineus*

DISTRIBUTION Southeast Asia

SIZE Up to 25cm long

RIGHT *Travelling in tight formation, a school of great barracuda search for prey. Barracuda are inquisitive fish and they often circle divers and boats.*

GREAT BARRACUDA

With its lean, torpedo-shaped body, jutting lower jaw and sharp, dagger-like teeth, the great barracuda is a highly dangerous predator. Although stories about these fish are often exaggerated, they are known to attack divers and swimmers, particularly if they are carrying shiny objects that look like fish. Barracuda hunt in packs, and they live in a wide range of habitats, from inshore water to the open sea. They are sometimes caught and eaten, but this is dangerous because their flesh can be poisonous.

SCIENTIFIC NAME	*Sphyraena barracuda*
DISTRIBUTION	Warm seas worldwide
SIZE	Up to 2m long

ATLANTIC MACKEREL

Mackerel look like small-scale versions of the barracuda, with the same sleek and slender shape. They are camouflaged by iridescent blue and green stripes, and their fins can be flattened against their body – an adaptation that helps them swim at speed. Atlantic mackerel live in large shoals that migrate into shallow water to breed. They are famous for snapping at almost anything that moves, from fish to pieces of brightly coloured plastic.

SCIENTIFIC NAME	*Scomber scombrus*
DISTRIBUTION	Atlantic Ocean
SIZE	Up to 60cm long

ABOVE *The Atlantic mackerel begins life in mid-water, where it feeds on tiny animals in the plankton. Females lay up to half a million eggs each time they spawn.*

RIGHT AND BELOW *Three of the fastest fish in the world are the sailfish, the blue marlin and the swordfish. All these fish have two different types of muscle. One type is used for steady cruising, and the other for bursts of speed. Like tuna, these fish can keep their bodies warmer than the water around them.*

Swordfish

Blue marlin

Sailfish

SAILFISH

Over short distances, the metallic-blue sailfish is probably the fastest fish in the sea. It can reach an amazing 109km/h. A sailfish can manage these bursts of speed because its body is superbly streamlined and packed with muscle. Its stiff, crescent-shaped tail is ideal for hitting high speeds, and its high dorsal fin, or 'sail', slices through the water like a knife. A sailfish's snout tapers to a sharp spear-like point. It eats fish and squid, and scatters its eggs in the open sea.

SCIENTIFIC NAME *Istiophorus platypterus*

DISTRIBUTION Warm seas worldwide

SIZE Up to 3.6m long

BLUE MARLIN

A close relative of the sailfish, the blue marlin is one of the largest predatory fish in the world. Using its sharply pointed snout, it slashes its way through shoals of smaller fish, swallowing them once they are stunned. Blue marlins are not as fast as sailfish – the top speed on record is 80km/h – but they can beat most other fish for speed in open water.

SCIENTIFIC NAME *Makaira nigricans*

DISTRIBUTION Warm seas worldwide

SIZE Up to 4.5m long

SWORDFISH

From a distance, the swordfish looks like a blue marlin because of its purple-blue colour and streamlined shape, but its snout is flattened like a sword and up to 1.4m long. The swordfish probably uses its snout to kill or stun its prey. It has a reputation for being dangerous, which may come from accidental collisions with old sailing ships. In the early 1800s, one swordfish stabbed through a ship's hull, penetrating a layer of copper plating and 30cm of solid oak.

SCIENTIFIC NAME *Xiphias gladius*

DISTRIBUTION Warm seas worldwide

SIZE Up to 4.9m long

SKIPJACK TUNA

Tuna live in shoals, and are famous for their speed and for their long migrations through the seas. In the 1950s, a tagged tuna was caught after swimming from Mexico to Japan, a distance of at least 9,000km. Tuna can manage feats like this because they keep their bodies warmer than the water around them. The warmth makes their muscles work more effectively, but they have to keep on the move to get the oxygen that their muscles need. There are more than six species of these fish. Some of them are becoming rare because they are heavily fished for food.

SCIENTIFIC NAME *Euthynnus pelamis*

DISTRIBUTION Warm seas worldwide

SIZE Up to 1m long

ANTARCTIC COD

This fish is one of only about 120 species that manage to survive in the icy waters close to Antarctica. It lives on the seabed, where it feeds on molluscs and crustaceans that thrive in a cold but clean environment. Around Antarctica, the temperature on the seabed is often slightly below freezing point, and the sea would freeze solid if it did not contain dissolved salt. The Antarctic cod copes with these conditions by having a natural antifreeze in its blood.

SCIENTIFIC NAME *Notothenia coriiceps*

DISTRIBUTION Southern Ocean

SIZE Up to 60cm long

ICE FISH

Antarctica's ice fish are the only vertebrates that do not have haemoglobin – the red pigment that normally carries oxygen in blood. Their blood is almost colourless, and it collects oxygen in the same way that water does – by simply dissolving it. Ice fish have to survive with about a tenth as much oxygen as normal fish, and they do this by swimming slowly, and by spending long periods without moving. They live on the seabed, feeding on small animals such as crustaceans.

SCIENTIFIC NAME *Chaenocephalus aceratus*

DISTRIBUTION Southern Ocean

SIZE Up to 60cm long

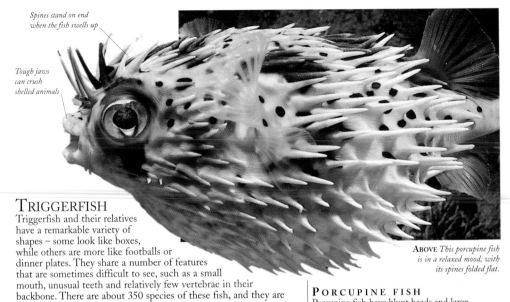

Spines stand on end when the fish swells up

Tough jaws can crush shelled animals

ABOVE *This porcupine fish is in a relaxed mood, with its spines folded flat.*

TRIGGERFISH

Triggerfish and their relatives have a remarkable variety of shapes – some look like boxes, while others are more like footballs or dinner plates. They share a number of features that are sometimes difficult to see, such as a small mouth, unusual teeth and relatively few vertebrae in their backbone. There are about 350 species of these fish, and they are found worldwide. Most of them live in shallow water near coasts, but the ocean sunfish, which is the largest, roams far out to sea.

PICASSO TRIGGERFISH

Triggerfish get their name from two spines on their back. One spine can hinge upright, and the other works like a trigger, locking the first one in place. Many of these fish have extraordinary colours and markings, as if they had been painted by an artist. The Picasso triggerfish lives on coral reefs and sandy seabeds. It feeds on sea urchins, which it turns upside down by blowing water at them. It can then reach the spineless undersides.

TOP *The Picasso triggerfish has a large head with a tiny mouth.*
ABOVE *Like all its relatives, the blue boxfish (Ostracion lentiginosum) is a slow swimmer. It has few enemies because of its effective 'armour'.*

SCIENTIFIC NAME	*Rhinecanthus aculeatus*
DISTRIBUTION	Indian Ocean, Pacific Ocean
SIZE	Up to 30cm long

BOXFISH

Also known as trunkfish, these fish are covered with hard bony plates that protect them from attack. This is not their only form of defence. A powerful poison oozes over the surface of their skin. There are many species of boxfish and almost all of them live on coral reefs.

SCIENTIFIC NAME	*Ostracion* and other genera
DISTRIBUTION	Warm seas worldwide
SIZE	Typical length 20cm

PORCUPINE FISH

Porcupine fish have blunt heads and large eyes, and a remarkable way of fending off their enemies. If one of these fish is threatened, it swallows a large amount of water, and swells up like a balloon. The fish's skin is covered with large spines, and these stand on end, making it almost impossible for predators to eat it. The only disadvantage of this survival technique is that the puffed-up fish is far too cumbersome to swim. Porcupine fish live among rocks and seaweed close to the shore.

SCIENTIFIC NAME	*Diodon hystrix*
DISTRIBUTION	Warm seas worldwide
SIZE	Up to 90cm long, often much smaller

OCEAN SUNFISH

The sunfish is one of the world's largest and most strangely shaped fish. Its body is round and flat, like an immense saucer. It has a long pointed fin above and underneath, but its tail is almost non-existent, making the fish look as if it has been cut off at the back. The ocean sunfish feeds mainly on jellyfish, which it scoops up with its tiny mouth. It often basks on the surface of the water and, despite its clumsy shape, sometimes jumps right out of the water.

SCIENTIFIC NAME	*Mola mola*
DISTRIBUTION	Warm seas worldwide
SIZE	Up to 4m long

FLATFISH

Flatfish start life in the open sea, but most of them spend their adult life on the seabed, lying on one side. As a flatfish grows, its body changes. It starts to lean over and its downward-pointing eye moves around its head until it is next to the eye that points upwards. The side that will be on top develops camouflaged colours, while the other side turns pale. There are about 500 species of flatfish. Most live in shallow sea water, from the tropics to much colder regions in the far north and south.

PLAICE

An adult plaice lies on its left-hand side, which means that both of its eyes are on its right. It swims in characteristic flatfish fashion, by rippling along close to the seabed. The plaice has smooth scales and distinctive bright orange spots on its upper side. It feeds on bottom-dwelling invertebrates, and finds food mainly by touch, using the sensitive skin on the left-hand side of its head.

SCIENTIFIC NAME	*Pleuronectes platessa*
DISTRIBUTION	Eastern Atlantic Ocean
SIZE	Up to 90cm long

DAB

Like the plaice, this small fish feeds in shallow water, and ranges northwards beyond the Arctic Circle. Its breeding technique is typical of flatfish as a whole. It releases its eggs into the water, and they float up to the surface. The young fish drift among the plankton, and are already lopsided by the time they are 2cm long. Once they have changed shape, they leave the surface and lie on the seabed.

SCIENTIFIC NAME	*Limanda limanda*
DISTRIBUTION	Eastern Atlantic Ocean
SIZE	Up to 40cm long

PEACOCK FLOUNDER

This colourful flatfish belongs to a family called the left-eye flounders, which have their eyes on their left-hand sides. This side of their bodies has a pattern of bright blue rings, which stretch from the mouth to the tail. Peacock flounders live along shallow coasts and on coral reefs.

SCIENTIFIC NAME	*Bothus lunatus*
DISTRIBUTION	Western Atlantic Ocean, Caribbean Sea
SIZE	Up to 45cm long

Dab

Plaice

ATLANTIC HALIBUT

This is the world's largest flatfish, weighing up to 300kg. Unlike most other flatfish, it is an active predator that feeds in open water, instead of living on the seabed. It has a large mouth with sharp teeth and, for a flatfish, its eyesight is unusually good. Atlantic halibut have been fished for centuries, partly because they grow so big. Today, specimens of more than 175kg are rare, and the species is endangered because of overfishing.

SCIENTIFIC NAME	*Hippoglossus hippoglossus*
DISTRIBUTION	North Atlantic Ocean
SIZE	Up to 2.4m long

Mouth twisted round to one side

Left eye moved round to be on the right side, now the upper side, of the fish

BELOW *The plaice lives on sand and gravel on the seabed, up to 200m deep.*

ABOVE
The peacock flounder is difficult to see when it lies on the seabed.

AMPHIBIANS

AMPHIBIANS INCLUDE FROGS, TOADS, NEWTS AND SALAMANDERS, AS WELL AS SOME LESSER-KNOWN ANIMALS CALLED CAECILIANS. MOST OF THEM START LIFE AS LEGLESS TADPOLES THAT LIVE IN WATER AND BREATHE THROUGH GILLS.

COMMON FROG

This greenish-brown frog spends almost all of its adult life on land but, in early spring, the males and females return to ponds and ditches to breed. Each female lays up to 4,000 jelly-coated eggs, which float in masses called frogspawn. When the tadpoles hatch, they fasten themselves to underwater plants. Like other amphibians, the common frog's development depends partly on the water temperature. If it is warm, the tadpoles can turn into froglets within six weeks, but in cold weather this process takes much longer.

SCIENTIFIC NAME	*Rana temporaria*
DISTRIBUTION	Europe, parts of Asia
	SIZE Up to 10cm long, excluding legs

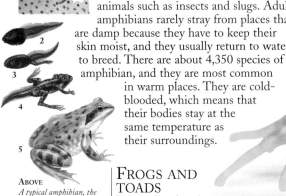

Large, circular eardrum just behind the eye

D uring their early lives, amphibians slowly change shape, so that they can live on land. Tadpoles often eat tiny water plants, but the adults gulp down small animals such as insects and slugs. Adult amphibians rarely stray from places that are damp because they have to keep their skin moist, and they usually return to water to breed. There are about 4,350 species of amphibian, and they are most common in warm places. They are cold-blooded, which means that their bodies stay at the same temperature as their surroundings.

ABOVE
A typical amphibian, the common frog changes shape completely as it develops from tadpole to adult.
1 *The female lays eggs in early spring.* **2** *The eggs hatch into legless tadpoles with tails.* **3** *A few weeks later, the tadpoles develop hind legs.* **4** *The tadpoles develop front legs.* **5** *The tail and gills are absorbed and the tadpoles become small adults with lungs, ready for life on land.*

FROGS AND TOADS

Frogs and toads make up about nine-tenths of all the world's amphibians. They are easy to recognize, because they have short bodies, powerful back legs and no tail. Their back feet have webs between the toes, which they use for swimming as well as jumping. Frogs usually move by hopping, and live either on the ground or in trees. Toads normally move by crawling, and nearly always live on the ground. Many of these animals have loud calls, which they use during the breeding season to attract a mate.

Front feet have four toes

ABOVE *Like many amphibians, the common frog breathes partly through its lungs and partly through its skin. It cannot suck air into its lungs – instead, it takes it in by gulping with its mouth. Common frogs hunt mainly by sight, lunging at any small animals that move, including insects and spiders.*

RIGHT *The whistling frog is so small that it could fit inside a matchbox. The male has a whistle-like courtship call.*

BELOW *A horned frog lies in wait for its prey. This predator is large enough to swallow small mammals.*

range of habitats, from mountain meadows to coastal swamps, and feeds on insects and other small animals. Leopard frogs have green skin, but they get their name from the black spots that are scattered over their legs and backs.

SCIENTIFIC NAME *Rana pipiens*

DISTRIBUTION North America

SIZE Up to 9cm long, excluding legs

GOLIATH FROG

This is the world's largest frog, with a body almost the size of a dinner plate. The heaviest one ever found weighed more than 3.5kg and had a legspan of 87cm. Goliath frogs live in the rivers of tropical western Africa and were once quite common. Today, they are threatened with extinction, due to the building of dams and also because they are hunted and sold as unusual pets.

SCIENTIFIC NAME *Conraua goliath*

DISTRIBUTION Cameroon and neighbouring countries

SIZE Up to 30cm long, excluding legs

WHISTLING FROG

This tiny frog is unusual because it lays its eggs on land and its young hatch out as miniature adults, but with tiny tails. The female lays about 25 eggs at a time, usually among damp, fallen leaves. This way of reproducing allows it to live in forests and other habitats where standing water is hard to find. The whistling frog has about 400 relatives that also breed on land. All these frogs come either from Central or South America, or from islands in the Caribbean.

SCIENTIFIC NAME *Eleutherodactylus johnstonei*

DISTRIBUTION Caribbean islands, northern South America

SIZE Up to 4cm long, excluding legs

AMERICAN BULLFROG

Adult bullfrogs lurk in the weed-choked shallows of lakes and streams, where they eat anything they can swallow. They are the largest frogs in North America and their diet includes fish, turtles, rats, and even bats and young waterbirds. Bullfrogs hunt mainly by night. This is also when they call. The males have a pouch, or vocal sac, under their chin that blows up like a balloon to amplify the sound. Bullfrogs take between two and five years to develop into adults.

SCIENTIFIC NAME *Rana catesbiana*

DISTRIBUTION Originally from eastern and central North America; introduced into parts of Europe

SIZE Up to 20cm long, excluding legs

Webbed back feet

NORTHERN LEOPARD FROG

Unlike the bullfrog, this streamlined North American frog often wanders away from water, although it goes back to breed. It lives in a wide

HORNED FROG

This large, fat-bodied frog has a huge mouth and two protruding eyes topped by stubby 'horns'. It has electric blue and brilliant green markings, though these are usually hidden because the frog buries itself in mud, with only its eyes visible. It stays completely still and lies in wait for an insect or other animal to wander within range. It then bursts out of the mud and swallows its victim. Unlike most frogs, the tadpoles of the horned frog are also predatory.

SCIENTIFIC NAME *Ceratophrys cornuta*

DISTRIBUTION South America

SIZE Up to 20cm long, excluding legs

ABOVE *A red-eyed treefrog clings to a twig high up in the canopy of a Central American rainforest.*

RED-EYED TREEFROG

Treefrogs spend most of their lives high above the ground in trees. They have long, spindly legs and their fingers and toes end in flat pads that work like suckers. A treefrog can stick to a vertical leaf and can even climb up a pane of glass. The red-eyed treefrog lives in rainforests and the females lay their eggs on large leaves overhanging pools. The tadpoles drop into the water when they hatch, and climb up into the trees as froglets.

SCIENTIFIC NAME	*Agalychnis callidryas*
DISTRIBUTION	Central America
SIZE	Up to 7cm long, excluding legs

EURASIAN GREEN TREEFROG

Most treefrogs live in the tropics, where there are insects to eat all year round. This species lives as far north as Holland and Denmark and hibernates for several months each year. Green treefrogs are mainly nocturnal. During the spring, the females lay eggs in ponds and water-tanks. The males attract them to good laying sites at night by making a loud, duck-like quacking noise.

SCIENTIFIC NAME	*Hyla arborea*
DISTRIBUTION	Central and southern Europe, Asia
SIZE	Up to 5cm long, excluding legs

SPRING PEEPER

The high-pitched call of this North American treefrog signals that spring is on the way. Spring peepers live among plants close to water but, unlike most treefrogs, they rarely climb far from the ground. They set up a loud chorus when it rains, but because they are small and brown in colour, they are very difficult to find. Female peepers lay their eggs one by one on water plants. After the tadpoles hatch, they take about three months to turn into froglets and move onto land.

SCIENTIFIC NAME	*Pseudacris crucifer*
DISTRIBUTION	Eastern North America
SIZE	Up to 3cm long, excluding legs

ABOVE *Using an inflatable sac under its throat, a grey treefrog* (Hyla versicolor) *calls to attract a mate.*
BELOW *The Eurasian green treefrog often climbs up rushes and reeds. This one is getting ready to jump from its perch.*

Smooth skin

The treefrog's toe-pads give it a firm grip on a slippery sheet of glass

Slender toes with pads at tips

Moist skin sticks to smooth surfaces

ROCKET FROG

This small Australian frog belongs to the treefrog family, but it spends much of its life on the ground. It has a sharply pointed nose, well-developed back legs and dark stripes running down its body. The rocket frog is exceptionally agile – it jumps for cover at the first sign of trouble, disappearing into the undergrowth or into water. Rocket frogs breed in streams, or in grassland flooded by storms in the wet season.

SCIENTIFIC NAME	*Litoria nasuta*
DISTRIBUTION	Northern and eastern Australia
SIZE	Up to 5cm long, excluding legs

WHITE'S TREEFROG

Also known as the green treefrog, this amphibian is a relative of the rocket frog, but it is not so streamlined. It is one of Australia's most widespread frogs and is often seen in gardens. Compared to most other treefrogs, it survives well in dry conditions, thanks to its thick skin.

SCIENTIFIC NAME	*Litoria caerulea*
DISTRIBUTION	Australia
SIZE	Up to 10cm long

BELOW White's treefrog is well camouflaged among leaves. Its slender legs and toes allow it to move agilely through the trees.

WATER-HOLDING FROG

The water-holding frog lives in deserts – a remarkable habitat for any amphibian. It spends most of its life underground, coming to the surface only after heavy rain. Like many desert species it breeds in temporary pools created after rare storms. Between the storms, the frog digs into the ground, burying itself up to a metre deep. It has a water supply in its bladder and seals itself inside a watertight cocoon.

SCIENTIFIC NAME	*Cyclorana platycephalus*
DISTRIBUTION	Australia
SIZE	Up to 7cm long, excluding legs

MARSUPIAL FROG

This plump South American treefrog raises its young in an unusual way. The male helps the female to gather her eggs into a pouch on her back, which is covered by a flap of skin. The female frog carries the eggs for three or four months. When the tadpoles are ready to live on their own, the female reverses into a pool and uses her back feet to push them into the water.

SCIENTIFIC NAME	*Gastrotheca marsupiata*
DISTRIBUTION	South America
SIZE	Up to 4cm long, excluding legs

Male peacock *(Pavo cristatus)* displaying its tail feathers to attract females

COMMUNICATION

Most animals have to communicate with their own kind. Often the message is a simple one. It may show that an animal is ready to breed, or is about to launch an attack. But whatever the message, it is vital that it gets across.

Animals communicate in many different ways. Visual signals are very common, particularly with animals that have good eyesight. Many animals also signal by scent – this has the added advantage that it can work at close quarters or at a distance, and the message remains when the animal that left it has moved on. Sound is a good way of sending signals, particularly in dense areas such as forests, where trees get in the way. Frogs and toads are experts at communicating by sound. They amplify their calls by inflating throat pouches or vocal sacs, which swell up like miniature balloons. Although their calls can sound alike to us, each species has its own 'song' – a set of signals understood only by others of the same species.

Black ants *(Lasius niger)* communicating by touching antennae

Edible frog *(Rana esculenta)* calling with inflatable air sacs

FLYING FROG

Flying frogs cannot really fly, but they are experts at gliding from tree to tree in their rainforest home. They manage this remarkable trick by using their hands and feet as parachutes. For their size, flying frogs have huge fingers and toes, linked together by webs of skin. They also have flaps of skin that stick out from their legs. Together, these webs and flaps slow their fall, enabling them to glide through the air. Flying frogs lay their eggs high above the ground in nests of foam, which they whip up by mixing mucus with rainwater.

SCIENTIFIC NAME *Rhacophorus nigripalmatus*

DISTRIBUTION Southeast Asia

SIZE Up to 4cm long, excluding legs

GLASS FROG

There are about 60 species of glass frog and they live along rainforest streams, often in cloud-draped mountains. Most have semi-transparent skin and, as a result, some of their internal organs can be clearly seen. Like many rainforest frogs, they lay their eggs on leaves overhanging shallow pools, and their tadpoles drop into the water when they hatch. *Centrolenella fleischmanni* has bright red tadpoles that bury themselves in submerged mud and decaying leaves.

SCIENTIFIC NAME *Centrolenella* species

DISTRIBUTION Central America, South America

SIZE Typical length 5cm, excluding legs

POISON-ARROW FROG

Poison-arrow frogs live on the rainforest floor, where predators are all around. But these tiny frogs do not hide – instead they feed in broad daylight, showing off their brilliant colours. The reason for this boldness is that their skin contains poisons so deadly that they are used by forest people to poison the tips of arrows for hunting. The bright colours of the frogs warn predators to keep away. There are more than 100 species of these frogs – the most dangerous one, *Phyllobates terribilis*, was discovered in Colombia in 1973. Poison-arrow frogs have an unusual life-cycle. The female lays her eggs on damp ground. When the tadpoles hatch, the male carries them around on his back. Once they are large enough to fend for themselves, the male carefully releases them into water.

SCIENTIFIC NAME *Dendrobates* and other genera

DISTRIBUTION Central America, South America

SIZE Up to 4cm long, excluding legs

ABOVE *With its feet spread out, a flying frog glides through the air far above the forest floor.*

RIGHT *These two Surinam toads are preparing to mate. Once the female has laid her eggs, the male will press them into the soft skin on her back.*

BELOW *Poison-arrow frogs have a variety of showy colour schemes. Males use their colours to defend their territories as well as to warn predators that they are poisonous.*

Mottled skin provides camouflage in muddy streams

MOUTH-BROODING FROG OR DARWIN'S FROG

For all amphibians, the early part of life is the most dangerous. The male mouth-brooding frog helps its tadpoles to survive by swallowing them as they start to hatch. The tadpoles shelter in the frog's vocal sac, and feed on the yolk from their eggs. Three weeks later, when the tadpoles have become small adults, the male spits them out into water. This frog lives in streams in the forests of the southern Andes Mountains. It is small and well camouflaged, but its sharply pointed nose makes it easy to identify.

ABOVE *A male mouth-brooding frog sits with a froglet that has just emerged from its vocal sac.*

SCIENTIFIC NAME *Rhinoderma darwinii*

DISTRIBUTION Chile, Argentina

SIZE Up to 3cm long, excluding legs

Star-shaped fingertips help the toad to find food

RIGHT *A young Surinam toad emerges from a pouch on its mother's back. It is far smaller than its mother, but otherwise looks like an adult.*

slender fingers. This toad has a remarkable life-cycle – the female acts as a living nursery for her eggs. When the female lays her eggs, the male uses his body to press them into the spongy skin on her back. The skin then grows over the eggs, protecting them from hungry predators. Three or four months later, the eggs hatch, producing up to one hundred tiny, but fully formed, toads.

SCIENTIFIC NAME	*Pipa pipa*
DISTRIBUTION	Northern South America
SIZE	Up to 20cm long, excluding legs

AFRICAN CLAWED TOAD
This flat-bodied toad lives in ponds and lakes in southern Africa. Like its close relative the Surinam toad, it spends its entire life in water. Its eyes and nostrils face upwards above the surface, which allows it to see and breathe. Females lay their eggs one by one on water plants or pieces of wood, and their tadpoles feed on microscopic plants, insect larvae and other small animals.

SCIENTIFIC NAME	*Xenopus laevis*
DISTRIBUTION	Southern Africa
SIZE	Up to 13cm long, excluding legs

PARADOXICAL FROG
A paradox is something that seems absurd but is true. With this frog, the paradox is that the tadpoles are three times as long as their parents. Adult paradoxical frogs are small enough to sit in a coffee cup, but the largest tadpole on record was 25cm long. Adult paradoxical frogs spend most of their lives in water. No one knows why they have such gigantic young.

SCIENTIFIC NAME	*Pseudis paradoxus*
DISTRIBUTION	South America
SIZE	Adult up to 6cm long, excluding legs

SURINAM TOAD
With its flattened body, triangular head and warty skin, the Surinam toad is one of South America's most unusual amphibians. It lives in rivers and streams, and finds food partly by touch, using its

BELOW *The African clawed toad has a wedge-shaped body with a narrow head and large back legs. Like the Surinam toad, it does not have a tongue.*

Front legs feel for food

Egg-laying and
fertilization
happen when the
toads are in water

Female's body
is swollen
with eggs

LEFT *Gripping his
partner with his front
legs, a male common toad
stays with his mate until
she has laid her eggs. The
male will fertilize the eggs
as they are laid so that
they can start to develop.*

COMMON TOAD

Unlike frogs, most toads have
warty skin and short back
legs, and spend most of
their adult lives on
land. They usually
hide away during
the day and feed
at night, when
the air is damp. The common toad is one of
the largest toads in Europe. It has a dark brown
body and golden eyes. In cold places, these toads
hibernate during the winter. The adults gather at
ponds to breed in the early spring. Each female
lays a double string of up to 4,000 eggs, which
she wraps around underwater plants.

*Male grasps the female
under her front legs –
rough pads help him
to maintain his grip*

BELOW *As in
most toads, the
giant toad
has poison-
producing
parotid glands
behind each eye.
Large giant
toads can squirt
poison at an
attacker.*

SCIENTIFIC NAME	*Bufo bufo*
DISTRIBUTION	Europe, northern Asia
SIZE	Up to 15cm long, excluding legs

AMERICAN TOAD

The American toad lives in a wide variety of
habitats, and is a frequent visitor to gardens and
backyards. It is a useful guest because, during its
nocturnal wanderings, it eats many small garden
pests, such as insects and slugs. The females
produce up to 8,000 eggs in early spring, and
they lay them in all kinds of places, from swamps
to temporary pools. Many toads have croaky
voices, but this species is much more musical –
in spring, it makes a long trilling sound.

SCIENTIFIC NAME	*Bufo americanus*
DISTRIBUTION	Eastern North America
SIZE	Up to 10cm long, excluding legs

GIANT TOAD OR CANE TOAD

This is the world's largest toad.
In the wild, females often weigh more
than 1kg, and in captivity they can grow
to more than twice this weight. They
feed at dusk and have little fear of
predators because their skin contains
glands that produce a powerful
poison. Giant toads originally
lived only in the American tropics
but they eat so many insects that
they have been introduced into
other parts of the world – often
with disastrous results. They
were released in Australia in
1935 to control beetles that were
destroying sugar cane crops, but
they ate lizards, frogs and small
rodents as well. Because they had
no natural predators, they multiplied
rapidly and have seriously harmed
many native Australian animals.

SCIENTIFIC NAME	*Bufo marinus*
DISTRIBUTION	Originally from Central America, South America; introduced into West Indies, Hawaii, Philippines, Australia
SIZE	Up to 25cm long, excluding legs

**American toad
with red parotid glands**

The green toad is well camouflaged

The natterjack toad is brown, grey or greenish in colour

BELOW AND BOTTOM
Male midwife toads carry their partner's eggs. Midwife toads have good eyesight, and emerge only after dark.

GREEN TOAD

This toad has patches of bright green colour on a pale brown background, making it look as if it were wearing military camouflage. In warm places, it often lives near houses, and adults sometimes gather around streetlights to feed on insects that have fallen to the ground. Green toads sound like crickets when they call. They lay their eggs in ponds and shallow lakes.

SCIENTIFIC NAME	*Bufo viridis*
DISTRIBUTION	Eastern and southern Europe, northern Africa, parts of Asia
SIZE	Up to 10cm long, excluding legs

NATTERJACK TOAD

The European natterjack is easy to recognize because it has a bright yellow stripe running down its back. It has an exceptionally loud call that sounds like a piece of machinery. Each burst of sound lasts for only a few seconds but, on still evenings, it can be heard up to 2km away. This toad often lives in sandy places close to the sea.

SCIENTIFIC NAME	*Bufo calamita*
DISTRIBUTION	Europe
SIZE	Up to 10cm long, excluding legs

Male carries up to 60 eggs wrapped around his back legs

FIRE-BELLIED TOAD

From above, this small toad is an unremarkable grey-green colour, but underneath it has a startling scarlet and black pattern. If it is threatened by a predator, it arches its head and raises its legs, showing these bright markings, which warn that it is poisonous and dangerous to attack. Fire-bellied toads live in ditches and ponds, and often float on the water.

SCIENTIFIC NAME	*Bombina bombina*
DISTRIBUTION	Eastern Europe, parts of Asia
SIZE	Up to 5cm long, excluding legs

MIDWIFE TOAD

Midwife toads mate and lay their eggs on land. The female produces a string of eggs and, after they have been fertilized, the male wraps them around his back legs. For a month or more he carries the eggs, helping to protect them from predators, and dipping them in water to keep them wet. Just before they are ready to hatch, he lowers them into shallow water. Midwife toads live in woodlands and rocky places, and spend the day hiding in holes and crevices.

SCIENTIFIC NAME	*Alytes obstetricans*
DISTRIBUTION	Western Europe
SIZE	Up to 5cm long, excluding legs

SPADEFOOT TOAD

Spadefoot toads are expert burrowers. They have a ridge of hard skin on each back foot, which they use like spades to dig into loose, sandy ground. Spadefoot toads live in dry places, and they often spend months hidden away underground. If it rains, they scramble to the surface, where they mate and lay their eggs. Spadefoot tadpoles can turn into toadlets in just two weeks – helping them to survive in places where water soon dries out. There are ten species of spadefoot toad.

SCIENTIFIC NAME	*Scaphiophus* and *Pelobates* species

DISTRIBUTION	North America, Europe, northern Africa, Middle East
SIZE	Typical length 6cm, excluding legs

LEFT *Couch's spadefoot toads* (Scaphiophus couchii) *can spend up to nine months underground.*

SALAMANDERS AND CAECILIANS

Unlike frogs and toads, salamanders and caecilians keep their tails when they are adults. Apart from this, these two groups of animals look quite different and behave in different ways. Salamanders have long bodies and four, or occasionally two, legs. As adults, some live in damp woods, but many spend their lives in ponds and streams. There are nearly 400 species of salamander, and they are found all over the world. Caecilians are rarer, with about 150 species. They look like giant earthworms because they do not have legs and their bodies are divided up into rings. Caecilians live mainly in the tropics. Some live in water, but most of them burrow through soil.

CHINESE GIANT SALAMANDER

This is the largest amphibian in the world. It has a large, broad head, small eyes and dark, wrinkly skin. It lives in cool mountain streams, where it eats insects, frogs and fish. Chinese giant salamanders are very rare. They are threatened by pollution, and they are also collected for food and for use in traditional medicine.

SCIENTIFIC NAME *Andrias davidianus*

DISTRIBUTION China

SIZE Up to 1.8m long, including tail

AXOLOTL

This pale pink salamander has a remarkable life-cycle – it can breed without fully growing up. Instead of losing its gills and developing into an adult shape, it often stays as a giant four-legged tadpole for the whole of its life, although some axolotls do change shape and take up life on land. Axolotls are sometimes kept in aquariums. Their only natural habitat is in lakes near Mexico City, where they are now quite rare.

SCIENTIFIC NAME *Ambystoma mexicanum*

DISTRIBUTION Mexico

SIZE Up to 30cm long, including tail

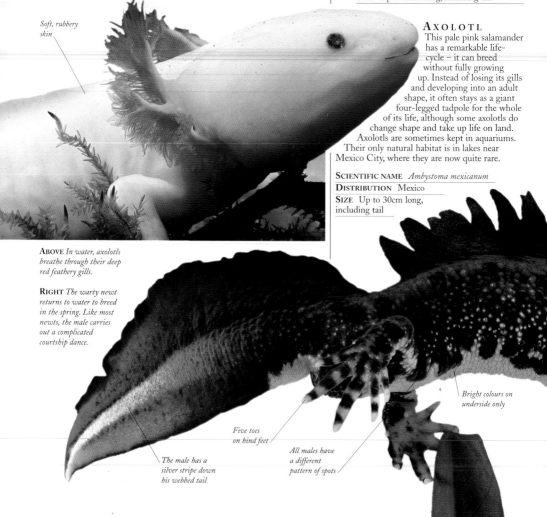

Soft, rubbery skin

ABOVE *In water, axolotls breathe through their deep red feathery gills.*

RIGHT *The warty newt returns to water to breed in the spring. Like most newts, the male carries out a complicated courtship dance.*

The male has a silver stripe down his webbed tail

Five toes on hind feet

All males have a different pattern of spots

Bright colours on underside only

HELLBENDER

North America is home to a large proportion of the world's salamanders, and the hellbender is the largest and possibly the ugliest of them all. It is a close relative of the Chinese giant salamander, and has a similar shape with short legs, an outsize head and wrinkly, slimy skin. Hellbenders live in fast-flowing rivers and streams, and spend the day hiding under rocks. In summer, female hellbenders lay strings of eggs on the riverbed, and the male guards them until they hatch.

SCIENTIFIC NAME	*Cryptobranchus alleganiensis*
DISTRIBUTION	Eastern North America
SIZE	Up to 70cm long, including tail

WARTY NEWT OR GREAT CRESTED NEWT

Newts are small or medium-sized salamanders that often have webbed tails as adults. During the breeding season, the male warty newt also develops a jagged crest that runs all the way down his back. His underside is orange or yellow, with contrasting black spots. Warty newts carry out their courtship underwater, and the female lays about 300 eggs. She fastens them individually to the leaves of water plants, using a sticky fluid to fold the leaf around the egg.

SCIENTIFIC NAME	*Triturus cristatus*
DISTRIBUTION	Europe
SIZE	Up to 16cm long, including tail

Only the male has a crest

Four toes on front feet

FIRE SALAMANDER

The brilliantly coloured fire salamander spends its adult life on land. Its yellow and black markings warn that its skin is poisonous, which keeps enemies at bay as it searches for food. Fire salamanders live in forests and other damp habitats. They emerge at night, often after rain, to hunt prey such as earthworms. They mate on land, but female fire salamanders give birth to live young in pools and streams.

SCIENTIFIC NAME	
Salamandra salamandra	
DISTRIBUTION	Europe, except British Isles and Scandinavia
SIZE	Up to 28cm long, including tail

RED SALAMANDER

The red salamander is equally at home in and out of water, and is found in springs, woodlands and wet meadows. When it has reached maturity it is brilliant red, though its colour fades as it grows older. The red salamander is one of about 200 species that do not have lungs when they grow up. Lungless salamanders breathe through their skin, or through the lining of their mouths. Almost all of the world's lungless salamanders live in the Americas.

SCIENTIFIC NAME	*Pseudotriton ruber*
DISTRIBUTION	Eastern North America
SIZE	Up to 18cm long, including tail

CAECILIAN

Compared to other amphibians, little is known about caecilians because their burrowing behaviour keeps them out of sight. Most live in the leaf litter and soft soil on the floor of tropical rainforests. They have blunt heads and small eyes, and push headfirst through the soil, finding their food mainly by touch. Like all amphibians, adult caecilians are carnivorous, but their prey depends on their size. The smallest ones eat insects, centipedes and worms, but the largest species can tackle frogs and snakes. Some caecilians give birth to live young, but most species have swimming tadpoles – a feature that demonstrates their links with salamanders, frogs and toads.

SCIENTIFIC NAME	*Siphonops*
and other genera	
DISTRIBUTION	Central America, South America, tropical Africa, India, Southeast Asia
SIZE	Up to 1.5m long

TOP AND ABOVE *Fire salamanders are marked with yellow lines or spots. The poison in their skin burns the mouth and eyes of any animal that tries to eat them.*

LEFT *A female South American caecilian (Siphonops annulatus) curls around her newly laid clutch of eggs.*

REPTILES

REPTILES WERE THE FIRST ANIMALS WITH BACKBONES TO BECOME FULLY EQUIPPED FOR LIFE ON DRY LAND. DURING THE AGE OF THE DINOSAURS, REPTILES RULED THE EARTH, AND INCLUDED THE LARGEST ANIMALS THE WORLD HAS EVER SEEN.

U nlike amphibians, reptiles have a tough skin covered by scales, and their eggs have waterproof shells. These two features allow them to live away from water in some of the driest habitats on Earth. Although reptiles are cold-blooded, they often warm themselves up by basking in sunshine – once they are warm they can move about at speed. Altogether, there are nearly 6,000 species of reptile. They are found in most parts of the world, except places where it gets very cold.

CROCODILES AND ALLIGATORS

This group of about 23 species includes the largest reptiles alive today. Crocodiles and alligators live in or near water, and they have armoured scales and long jaws with sharp teeth. When they swim, they are almost invisible because only their eyes and nostrils break the surface – an adaptation that helps them ambush animals coming down to drink. Crocodiles and alligators lay leathery-shelled eggs, and they often carry their young to water when they have hatched. These animals are hunted for their skins, and many are endangered.

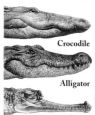

Crocodile

Alligator

Gavial

ABOVE *Crocodiles and alligators have broad snouts, but the gavial's snout is very narrow for catching fish.*

ESTUARINE CROCODILE

Known in Australia as the 'saltie', this is the world's largest and most dangerous crocodile. Unlike other crocodiles, it lives in sea water as well as lakes and rivers. Fully grown estuarine crocodiles can kill animals as large as water buffaloes, and may be responsible for 1,000 human deaths each year. The female lays up to 90 eggs in a mound of sand and leaves. She guards the nest fiercely, but when her young hatch, she gently carries them to water.

SCIENTIFIC NAME	*Crocodylus porosus*
DISTRIBUTION	Bay of Bengal (Indian Ocean), Southeast Asia, northern Australia
SIZE	Up to 6m long

ABOVE *The estuarine crocodile is famous for its aggressive nature.*

NILE CROCODILE

This freshwater crocodile lives in lakes and rivers. It preys on animals coming to drink, dragging them underwater and drowning them. The crocodile twists around in the water to rip its food apart. It has a spectacular courtship display. The male defends a stretch of bank, roaring at any intruders. When a female is attracted by the noise, the male thrashes his body and shoots water into the air from his nostrils.

SCIENTIFIC NAME	*Crocodylus niloticus*
DISTRIBUTION	Africa, Madagascar
SIZE	Up to 5m long

DWARF CROCODILE

This is the smallest and least-known of the world's crocodiles. It lives in rainforest rivers and swamps, and climbs up tree-trunks to bask in the sun. The female lays up to 17 eggs and guards them for three months. Unusually, it has armoured scales on its underside as well as its back.

SCIENTIFIC NAME	*Osteolaemus tetraspis*
DISTRIBUTION	Western and central Africa
SIZE	Up to 2m long

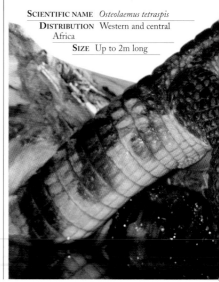

ABOVE *Like most of their relatives, Nile crocodiles spend many hours each day basking in the sunshine.*

BELOW *American alligators hunt when the temperature is above about 20°C. When it is colder, they become sluggish.*

GAVIAL

This large freshwater crocodile has an extremely slender snout equipped with masses of small but needle-sharp teeth. Although its snout looks fragile, it is ideal for catching fish – the gavial's main food. Once it has made a catch, the gavial lifts its snout into the air, and then flicks the fish around so it can swallow it headfirst. Compared to other crocodiles, gavials spend a lot of time in the water, and their back feet are fully webbed.

SCIENTIFIC NAME	*Gavialis gangeticus*
DISTRIBUTION	Pakistan, India, Bangladesh, Nepal
SIZE	Up to 7m long

AMERICAN ALLIGATOR

The American alligator is the largest reptile in the western hemisphere. In the 1960s, after decades of being hunted, it was declared an endangered species and, since then, it has made a spectacular recovery. Alligators live in rivers and swamps, and feed on anything they can overpower, from turtles to birds. During the summer, they often wallow in water-filled hollows called 'gator holes' but, in winter, they hibernate in shallow dens, where the temperature sometimes hovers just above freezing. Alligators are very similar to crocodiles – the easiest way to tell them apart is that a crocodile's lower front teeth protrude when its mouth is closed, while an alligator's fit into sockets in its upper jaw.

SCIENTIFIC NAME	*Alligator mississippiensis*
DISTRIBUTION	Southeastern USA
SIZE	Up to 5.5m long

SPECTACLED CAIMAN

A caiman is a small crocodile from Central and South America. There are five different species, and the spectacled caiman is the most common. It lives in rivers, lakes and swamps, and it can survive droughts by burrowing into the mud. The spectacled caiman gets its name from ridges around its eyes, which look like a pair of glasses.

SCIENTIFIC NAME	*Caiman crocodilus*
DISTRIBUTION	Central America, South America
SIZE	Up to 2m long

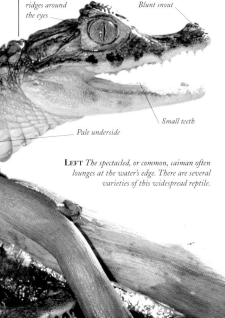

Spectacle-shaped ridges around the eyes

Blunt snout

Small teeth

Pale underside

LEFT *The spectacled, or common, caiman often lounges at the water's edge. There are several varieties of this widespread reptile.*

LIZARDS AND TUATARAS

Lizards make up just over half the world's reptiles. There are about 3,500 species, and most of them live in places with warm climates. Lizards usually have long legs and tails. In emergencies, many can escape attack by shedding their tail – later, they grow a new one in its place. Most lizards live on the ground and feed on insects, although these reptiles also include many nimble climbers, such as geckoes and chameleons. Lizards normally reproduce by laying small, leathery-shelled eggs, but some species give birth to live young. Tuataras look like lizards, but they belong to a completely different group of reptiles that first appeared more than 200 million years ago. There are only two species, and both live in New Zealand.

fixed to their jaws, instead of being set in sockets. Tuataras are nocturnal. They hide away in burrows during the day, emerging at night to eat birds' eggs and small animals such as insects. Compared to lizards, they are long-lived, and cope well with the cold. Tuataras were once common in New Zealand, but are now among the rarest animals in the world. They live only on a few islands, where they are carefully protected against rats and other introduced mammals.

SCIENTIFIC NAME *Sphenodon punctatus* and *Sphenodon guntheri*

DISTRIBUTION New Zealand

SIZE Up to 65cm long

BELOW *Tuataras grow slowly and take about 20 years to reach breeding age – a record for any reptile. It is thought that they can live for as long as 100 years.*

TUATARA

These powerfully built animals have large heads, stocky feet and a spiky crest running down their backs. They resemble lizards on the outside, but they have unusually shaped skulls and backbones, and their teeth are permanently

Iguanas have good eyesight

Ear opening behind eye

COMMON IGUANA

This impressive animal is one of the world's largest plant-eating lizards. It spends most of its time basking high up in waterside trees. It has powerful feet with sharp claws, and a long, muscular tail. Despite its size, it can be difficult to see, because its green colour keeps it well camouflaged. Adult iguanas are large enough to defend themselves against most attackers, but if they are taken by surprise, they have an unusual way of escaping – they leap out of the trees and crash into the water, before quickly swimming away.

RIGHT AND ABOVE
Although it has a fearsome appearance, the common iguana is a harmless vegetarian.

SCIENTIFIC NAME *Iguana iguana*

DISTRIBUTION Central America, South America

SIZE Up to 2m long

CHUCKWALLA

Chuckwallas are plant-eating lizards that live in deserts and rocky places. They have broad, red and grey bodies with fat tails, and loose skin covered with rough, sandpapery scales. Chuckwallas feed during the day. If they are threatened, they often run into rocky crevices and then gulp air – this makes them swell up, wedging them in place. Female chuckwallas lay clutches of about ten eggs and, like most lizards, they leave their young to fend for themselves.

SCIENTIFIC NAME	*Sauromalus obesus*
DISTRIBUTION	Southern USA, Mexico
SIZE	Up to 40cm long

MARINE IGUANA

This remarkable reptile is the world's only sea-going lizard. It feeds on seaweed growing around the rocky shores of the Galapagos Islands, and can stay underwater for up to 20 minutes. The water around the Galapagos is cold, and the iguana survives the low temperatures by slowing its heart-rate when it dives, so that its blood does not lose too much heat through its skin. Marine iguanas are shaped for their unusual way of life – they have blunt heads, wide jaws and a flattened tail that works like a cross between a propeller and a rudder.

SCIENTIFIC NAME	*Amblyrhynchus cristatus*
DISTRIBUTION	Galapagos Islands
SIZE	Up to 1.5m long

HORNED LIZARD

Most lizards run away if threatened, but horned lizards stand their ground. Their squat bodies are protected by an array of horns and spines, and they can squirt blood from their eyes at an attacker. Also known as horned toads, horned lizards live in deserts in North America. There are 14 species, and most of them feed on ants.

SCIENTIFIC NAME	*Phrynosoma* species
DISTRIBUTION	North America; from southern Canada to Mexico
SIZE	Up to 18cm long

BASILISK OR CRESTED WATER DRAGON

The bright green basilisk has an eyecatching bony flap on its head, as well as a crest on its back and tail. But the most unusual thing about it is that it can run on its two back legs. It only does this in emergencies, but it can splash its way across several metres of water, as well as run on dry land. Basilisks are able to do this because they have large back feet with a fringe of scales

on each of their toes. These lizards live in forests, and they find their food on the ground as well as in trees.

SCIENTIFIC NAME	*Basilicus plumifrons*
DISTRIBUTION	South America
SIZE	Up to 80cm long

ANOLE

Anoles are small, bright green lizards with slender bodies and long tails. They feed on insects in trees. They can race along branches with amazing speed because their fingers and toes have rounded pads and sharp claws, giving them a good grip. Most male anoles have a brightly coloured flap that can fold down underneath their chin, and they use this to attract females during the breeding season. There are more than 250 species of anole, and they are found only in the Americas.

SCIENTIFIC NAME	*Anolis* species
DISTRIBUTION	Southeastern USA, Central America, South America
SIZE	Up to 20cm long

LEFT *Chuckwallas jam themselves tightly into crevices to stop predators removing them.*
BELOW *With its tail up and its throat-flap extended, a male anole tries to attract a mate.*

ABOVE *Marine iguanas bask on the shores of the Galapagos Islands.*

BELOW *The Texas horned lizard (Phrynosoma cornutum) usually stays out in the open, but it can bury itself in loose soil.*

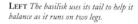

LEFT *The basilisk uses its tail to help it balance as it runs on two legs.*

GALAPAGOS LAND IGUANA
Unlike the marine iguana (page 147), this large lizard stays on dry land. It feeds almost entirely on the leaves and fruit of prickly pear cacti, breaking off the cacti's spines with its jaws before swallowing the rest. Female land iguanas bury their eggs in the ground. They leave the dry lowlands and trek up mountains to find moist ground that is suitable for laying.

SCIENTIFIC NAME	*Conolophus subcristatus*
DISTRIBUTION	Galapagos Islands
SIZE	Up to 1.2m long

FRILLED LIZARD
This is one of Australia's most spectacular lizards. Its colour varies from dull red to brown but, if the lizard is cornered, it responds with a striking threat display. It opens up a brilliant red and yellow frill around its neck, and bares its bright red mouth. At the same time, it sways and hisses, so that it looks as if it is about to attack. This is often enough to make the lizard's enemies back away but, if not, it folds up its frill and runs up the nearest tree.

SCIENTIFIC NAME	*Chlamydosaurus kingii*
DISTRIBUTION	Australia
SIZE	Up to 50cm long

FLYING DRAGON
This lizard lives in forests, and glides from tree to tree. Its 'wings' are specially enlarged ribs that open out like the struts of a fan, stretching a flap of loose skin. Once the lizard has completed a flight, the ribs hinge back along its body, folding the wings away. Flying dragons feed on small insects, and lay their eggs on the ground.

SCIENTIFIC NAME	*Draco volans*
DISTRIBUTION	Southeast Asia
SIZE	Up to 22cm long

THORNY DEVIL
The thorny devil lives in the deserts of western Australia, where it feeds mainly on ants. Its body is covered with prickles and spines that extend from its head to its tail, and along its legs. It needs these because ants take time to eat, and while it is feeding it is vulnerable to attack.

SCIENTIFIC NAME	*Moloch horridus*
DISTRIBUTION	Australia
SIZE	Up to 15cm long

BELOW *With its frill opened out like an umbrella, a frilled lizard tries to bluff its way out of trouble with a spectacular defensive display.*

RIGHT *Jackson's chameleon* (Chamaeleon jacksoni) *catches a moth. It is fast and accurate in the use of its long, sticky tongue.*

Turret-shaped swivelling eyes

ABOVE *The spikes on a thorny devil serve another purpose besides defence. In the desert, dew condenses on them and the water drips into the lizard's mouth.*

FLAP-NECKED CHAMELEON
This African lizard is one of about 90 species of chameleon, all adapted for life in trees. Like other chameleons, its body is humped and narrow, and its eyes can swivel independently. It can also change colour – either to match its background, or to show its mood. If it spots an insect, it shoots out its sticky-tipped tongue, which is as long as the rest of its body. Some chameleons give birth to live young, but this particular species lays eggs.

SCIENTIFIC NAME	
	Chamaeleon dilepis
DISTRIBUTION	
	Southern Africa
SIZE	Up to
	35cm long

Long tongue retracts into the chameleon's throat when not in use

Colour changes as a pigment moves in or out of the outer layers of skin

Fingers and toes are especially designed for grasping twigs and branches

SIX-LINED RACERUNNER

Racerunners are among the world's fastest lizards. Over short distances, they can reach speeds of 30km/h – almost as fast as the world's best human sprinters. They have slender bodies with very long tails, and they live in grassland, sand dunes and other open places, relying on speed to keep out of trouble. Racerunners belong to a family of lizards called whiptails, which total more than 200 species, and are found only in the Americas. Some are of particular interest to scientists because they are all female, and can breed without having to mate.

SCIENTIFIC NAME *Cnemidophorus sexlineatus*

DISTRIBUTION Central and eastern USA

SIZE Up to 20cm long

Large eyes for seeing prey in the dark

Toes have sharp claws and narrow pads

LEFT *The flap-necked chameleon uses stealth to catch food. Perfectly camouflaged on a branch, it waits patiently for food to come within reach of its long tongue.*

TOKAY GECKO

Across much of Southeast Asia, the tokay gecko is a common visitor to houses. It scuttles up walls in search of insects and other lizards, and can even run across ceilings upside down. It can grip so well because it has flattened toe-pads covered with up to a million microscopic clinging hairs. It feeds at night, and gets its name from the loud call that the males make to attract mates. This acrobatic animal is one of more than 800 species in the gecko family. Geckoes are most common in the tropics, and they often gather around lights after dark to catch their prey. Most lay two eggs at a time. These are soft and sticky at first, but soon harden.

SCIENTIFIC NAME *Gekko gekko*

DISTRIBUTION Southern and Southeast Asia

SIZE Up to 28cm long

LEAF-TAILED GECKO

When it is pressed flat against a tree, the leaf-tailed gecko is almost impossible to see because of its superb camouflage. Its body has a mottled pattern that looks just like patches of lichen growing on bark. It also has a leaf-shaped tail that helps to break up its outline. Like most geckoes, this forest lizard cannot blink – instead, it uses its tongue to clean its eyes.

SCIENTIFIC NAME *Phyllurus cornutus*

DISTRIBUTION Australia

SIZE Up to 18cm long

Prehensile tail can wrap around branches for extra grip

TOP *This tokay gecko is in a defensive posture.*
ABOVE *A leaf-tailed gecko uses its long tongue to clean its eyes. Geckoes have larger eyes than most lizards, which helps them to spot their prey after dark.*

Long snake-like body

ABOVE *The sand skink, like its relatives, has smooth, flat scales that allow it to burrow without getting dirty.*

BELOW AND BOTTOM *The green lizard is one of the largest in Europe. It can shed its tail and grow a new one if it is attacked. The close-up shows how the green lizard's scales vary in size across its body.*

Tail breaks off at this point

COMMON BLUE-TONGUED SKINK

Skinks make up one of the largest families of lizards, with at least 1,000 species. Most of them have smooth, shiny scales and small legs, and almost all of them live on the ground. The common blue-tongued skink is a large species from eastern Australia that often comes into gardens. It has a large head and short tail, but its most conspicuous feature is its blue tongue. If it is threatened, it sticks this out and makes a hissing noise. This performance frightens off many predators – and some humans as well. There are several kinds of blue-tongued skink, and they all give birth to live young.

SCIENTIFIC NAME *Tiliqua scincoides*

DISTRIBUTION Eastern Australia

SIZE Up to 50cm long

SAND SKINK

The sand skink is one of North America's strangest lizards. It has a long, streamlined body and a sharply pointed nose, but its legs are so small that they are often difficult to see. Its back feet each have two toes, but its front feet have just one. Sand skinks spend much of their lives underground. Instead of digging with their legs, they wriggle their bodies and 'swim' through the sand. They are very sensitive to movement, which helps them to find termites and insect grubs to eat.

SCIENTIFIC NAME *Neoseps reynoldsi*

DISTRIBUTION Florida (USA)

SIZE Up to 13cm long

GREEN LIZARD

This handsome bright green lizard has a tail that is almost twice as long as its body. It lives on the ground and in trees, and feeds on insects, spiders and occasionally young birds. Green lizards breed by laying eggs, and during the winter months they hibernate in tree hollows and rocky crevices. The viviparous lizard *(Lacerta vivipara)*, a small brown relative of this species, is the only lizard that breeds north of the Arctic Circle. Unlike the green lizard, it gives birth to live young, which is what viviparous means.

SCIENTIFIC NAME *Lacerta viridis*

DISTRIBUTION Central and southern Europe

SIZE Up to 45cm long

Ear opening

Large scales cover the head

SLOW WORM

The slow worm looks like a small snake, but it is actually a lizard with no legs. Slow worms are different from snakes in many ways. They can close their eyes, and they can shed their tails if they are attacked. They also have bony plates beneath their scales, which make their bodies hard and stiff. Slow worms come out at dawn and dusk, often after rain. They feed on insects, spiders and slugs. Females produce up to 12 eggs that hatch as they are being laid.

Slow worm curled like a snake

SCIENTIFIC NAME	*Anguis fragilis*
DISTRIBUTION	Europe, Asia, northern Africa
SIZE	Up to 50cm long

GILA MONSTER

The fat and lumbering Gila monster is one of only two poisonous lizards in the world – the other is the Mexican beaded lizard *(Heloderma horridum)*. The Gila monster has bright orange and black colours that warn other animals to leave it alone. Gila monsters live in deserts and other dry places, and usually hunt after dark. They eat small mammals and other lizards, gripping them in their jaws and injecting venom as they chew. Although their bite is extremely painful, it is rarely fatal to humans. A Gila monster's tail works like a camel's hump, storing fat for times when food is scarce.

SCIENTIFIC NAME	*Heloderma suspectum*
DISTRIBUTION	Southwestern USA, northern Mexico
SIZE	Up to 60cm long

KOMODO DRAGON

The Komodo dragon is the world's largest lizard. It is a meat-eater, and feeds by hunting and scavenging. It is strong enough to bring down a horse. Komodo dragons belong to a group of giant lizards called monitors, which have powerful legs and long, forked tongues. They use their tongues to taste the air for living prey or dead remains. Komodo dragons once roamed over a large part of Indonesia, but they now live on only a handful of islands. There are about 5,000 left, and they are protected by law.

SCIENTIFIC NAME	*Varanus komodoensis*
DISTRIBUTION	Komodo and neighbouring islands (Indonesia)
SIZE	Up to 3m long

Tongue is deeply forked

Loose skin stretches as prey is swallowed

GOULD'S MONITOR OR GOULD'S GOANNA

Australia has more monitor lizards, or goannas, than anywhere else in the world, and Gould's monitor is the most widespread species. It is brown or golden in colour, with a small head, but has large, powerful feet and claws that it uses for ripping apart its prey. Its tail is long and thick, and acts as a prop when the lizard stands on its back legs to look for food. Gould's monitor eats mammals, snakes and other lizards, and was once an important source of food for Australian Aborigines.

SCIENTIFIC NAME	*Varanus gouldii*
DISTRIBUTION	Australia
SIZE	Up to 1.5m long

WORM LIZARD OR AMPHISBAENIAN

Worm lizards are burrowing reptiles with blunt heads, tiny eyes and scales arranged in rings. Most of them have no legs, but three species – all from Mexico – have small front legs with five strong toes. These bizarre animals are not true lizards, and they live very differently from them. They build a system of underground tunnels by using their heads to bulldoze through the soil, and they feed on insects and worms. There are about 130 species of these reptiles. Some lay eggs, but others give birth to live young.

SCIENTIFIC NAME	*Amphisbaena* and other genera
DISTRIBUTION	Worldwide, mainly in warm regions
SIZE	Typical species about 30cm long

ABOVE *Gould's monitor can detect dead animals more than 1km away by tasting the air with its forked tongue.*

BELOW *The Gila monster has a slow, lumbering walk, but it can suddenly lunge forwards to inflict a poisonous bite.*

ABOVE *The Komodo dragon is bulkier than other monitors, and also more dangerous. It can weigh more than 100kg, and its tail takes up about half its length.*

SNAKES

Snakes are legless reptiles that hunt other animals and swallow their prey whole. They can eat animals wider than themselves because they have flexible jaws that inch their way forwards around the victim's body. Unlike lizards, snakes cannot move their eyelids, their ears are not visible and their vision is poor. They have an excellent sense of smell, flicking out their forked tongues to pick up scents in the air. Some snakes kill their prey by squeezing them to death, or constriction, but most use their teeth. Some inject poison, or venom, through special teeth called fangs to stun or kill their victims. Most snakes lay eggs, which often hatch as soon as they are laid. There are about 2,300 species of snake, and they are most common in warm climates.

Emerald tree boa coiled on a branch

Body curled around a branch for support

TOP *This emerald tree boa has almost finished swallowing a rat whole. While it is swallowing, its windpipe is pushed out of the way. If this did not happen, the snake would not be able to breathe.*
ABOVE *A boa constrictor swallows its prey. Although snakes cannot chew their food, they can digest almost everything they eat, except fur, feathers and claws.*

BOA CONSTRICTOR

Like all the snakes on these two pages, the boa is non-venomous. It kills by constriction, tightening its coils around its victims until they cannot breathe. Contrary to what people often imagine, boas do not crush their prey and few bones are broken. Boas are among the top six largest snakes in the world. They live in a variety of habitats from deserts to dense forests. Their markings vary, but they are always well camouflaged. Boas prey mainly on birds and mammals, and sometimes farm livestock. They produce up to 50 eggs a year, which hatch as they are laid.

SCIENTIFIC NAME	*Boa boa*
DISTRIBUTION	Central America, South America
SIZE	Up to 5.5m long

EMERALD TREE BOA

This beautifully coloured rainforest snake spends most of its life in trees. With its bright green body clamped around a branch, it waits for birds and other animals to come within range. Once it has made an attack, the boa has to deal with its prey. It hangs in the air while clinging on with its tail. After it has constricted and swallowed its prey, it pulls itself back up. The green tree python *(Chondropython viridis)* from Australia is also bright green and hunts in a similar way.

SCIENTIFIC NAME	*Corallus caninus*
DISTRIBUTION	South America
SIZE	Up to 1.2m long

ANACONDA OR WATER BOA

The olive-green anaconda is one of the world's longest and heaviest snakes. One captive anaconda measured more than 8.6m from head to tail, but it is not known what size this snake can reach in the wild. The anaconda is a good climber, but it spends much of its time in or near water, catching animals coming down to drink. Capybaras (page 257)

BELOW *A fully grown anaconda can weigh more than 200kg. Its dark colours camouflage it well on the ground and in water.*

are among its favourite prey, but it also eats turtles and caimans. When young anacondas are born, they can be 1m long.

SCIENTIFIC NAME	*Eunectes murinus*
DISTRIBUTION	Tropical South America
SIZE	Up to 9m long, possibly more

BURMESE PYTHON

This is one of the most common pythons in Southeast Asia. The true Burmese python is dark in colour, but a sub-species called the Indian python is paler and also smaller. Burmese pythons hunt by both day and night for rodents, young deer and other animals. They have been known to bite humans, but like other pythons they are not venomous.

SCIENTIFIC NAME	*Python molurus*
DISTRIBUTION	Southeast Asia
SIZE	Up to 6.5m long

RETICULATED PYTHON

This is the longest snake in the world, and it is the only snake that is known to have reached a length of 10m. Reticulated pythons live in tropical forests, where they prey on birds and small mammals. Like other pythons, they have a pair of heat-sensitive pits on their snouts to help them track down their prey. They lay up to 100 eggs, which the female guards until they hatch.

SCIENTIFIC NAME	*Python reticulatus*
DISTRIBUTION	Southeast Asia
SIZE	Up to 10m long

ANIMAL EGGS

Most of the world's animals reproduce by laying eggs. Water animals usually lay jelly-like eggs. On land, eggs like these would dry out, so most land animals lay eggs with waterproof shells. The smallest shelled eggs, laid by insects, can be seen only with a microscope, but the largest, laid by ostriches, can be 20cm long, with shells as thick as a plate. Once an egg has been laid, the animal inside has to develop. To do this, it often needs warmth. Birds incubate or sit on their eggs, but because reptiles are cold-blooded they rely on warmth from their surroundings. In cold places, snakes seek out 'hot spots' such as compost heaps, and lay their eggs inside. Pythons are the only snakes that are known to incubate their eggs. They wrap their bodies around them, and twitch their muscles to produce heat.

A common king snake
(*Lampropeltis getulus*)
hatching from its egg

WART SNAKE

There are three species of wart snake, found from India to northern Australia. Wart snakes are thick and heavily built, and they have baggy skin that looks as if it is several sizes too large. They spend their lives in shallow water in rivers and estuaries or the sea, and have great difficulty moving about on land. They feed on fish, killing them with a powerful bite. *Acrochordus javanicus*, sometimes known as the Javan wart snake, is the largest species. It gives birth to live young.

SCIENTIFIC NAME	*Acrochordus* species
DISTRIBUTION	Southeast Asia, northern Australia
SIZE	Up to 2.5m long

BELOW The Burmese python's coloration camouflages it well in the dappled light on the forest floor.
BOTTOM Like other large snakes, the reticulated python can go for months between meals. Because it is cold-blooded, it uses up relatively little energy for its size.

Interlocking scales produce a smooth surface

Heat sensitive pit

COMMON KING SNAKE

This widespread snake is one of the most varied in North America. In California, it is often black or brown with white bands, but further south it is much paler. King snakes kill their prey by constriction. Like all the snakes on these two pages, they belong to a family called the colubrids, which includes more than three-quarters of the world's snake species. Colubrids have solid teeth rather than true fangs, and most of them are harmless.

ABOVE *The common king snake's head is barely wider than the rest of its body – a common feature of the colubrid family of snakes.*
BELOW *This rat snake is swallowing a vole. It has to stretch its jaws slowly around its prey.*

SCIENTIFIC NAME	*Lampropeltis getulus*
DISTRIBUTION	North America, Central America
SIZE	Up to 2m long

ABOVE *With its mouth gaping open, this grass snake is trying to avoid attack by looking as if it is dead. Grass snakes also have another defence – they can expel a fluid that has a very unpleasant smell.*

GRASS SNAKE

The grass snake is a daytime hunter that spends much of its time near water. It is a good swimmer, and feeds mainly on frogs and toads, although it also eats small mammals and young birds. Its olive-green body is well camouflaged, and its slender shape is ideal for slipping through waterside vegetation. If a grass snake is threatened out in the open, it defends itself in an unusual way – it stays completely still and pretends to be dead. Many predators avoid dead animals, so this ruse sometimes saves the snake's life. Grass snakes reproduce by laying clutches of up to 40 eggs, which can take two months to hatch.

SCIENTIFIC NAME	*Natrix natrix*
DISTRIBUTION	Europe, northern Africa, northern Asia
SIZE	Up to 2m long

RAT SNAKE

The rat snake can be plain or striped, and black, yellow, grey or brown, but it has one characteristic feature – its underside is completely flat, and turns up at sharp corners along its flanks. Rat snakes climb well, and eat mice and rats, which makes them useful visitors on farms. Rat snakes kill their prey by constriction. If a rat snake is in danger, it rears up, hissing.

SCIENTIFIC NAME	*Elaphe obsoleta*
DISTRIBUTION	North America
SIZE	Up to 2.5m long

COMMON GARTER SNAKE

This North American snake gets it name from its stripes, which look like the patterns on old-fashioned garters. It is very widespread, and is found further north than any other North American reptile, within a few hundred kilometres of the Arctic Circle. There, large numbers of snakes gather in writhing heaps during the mating season in autumn. After mating, they hibernate together, which helps them to survive in places with freezing winters. Garter snakes give birth to live young.

SCIENTIFIC NAME	*Thamnopsis sirtalis*
DISTRIBUTION	North America
SIZE	Up to 1.3m long

Unusually small teeth

LEFT *This egg-eating snake has found and is swallowing an egg. At this stage, the egg is still intact, but the shell will be broken as it travels down the snake's throat.*

Spines inside the throat break the egg's shell

Jaws dislocate when the egg is swallowed

Skin between the scales stretches so that the mouth can expand

The tongue can sense other animals nearby

WESTERN WHIP SNAKE

This snake is a greenish-yellow daytime hunter with well-developed eyes. It lives on rocky hillsides and in scrub, and specializes in catching lizards. Compared to many snakes, it is fast and agile – characteristics needed for hunting fast-moving prey. Whip snakes lay about 12 eggs each time they breed, and hide them in crevices among the rocks.

Snakes constantly flick their tongues in and out to taste the air

SCIENTIFIC NAME	*Coluber viridiflavus*
DISTRIBUTION	Southern and western Europe
SIZE	Up to 1.5m long

ABOVE *Snakes use their tongues to smell. They collect a tiny amount of scent with their tongues and carry it to a sensitive pit in the roof of their mouths. Here, a common garter snake (above centre) and a western whip snake (above) sample the air.*

BROWN VINE SNAKE

Vine snakes live in trees and mainly eat lizards. They are long, but very slender. They have pointed snouts, and their shape allows them to creep up on their prey. Vine snakes inject venom through grooved teeth at the back of their jaws. 'Back-fanged' snakes are rarely dangerous to humans, as most of them can bite only small animals.

SCIENTIFIC NAME	*Oxybelis aeneus*
DISTRIBUTION	Southern Arizona (USA), Central America, South America
SIZE	Up to 2m long

EGG-EATING SNAKE

This snake is a rare exception to the rule that snakes hunt things that move. It feeds on birds' eggs, and it has become so well adapted for this unusual diet that it rarely eats anything else. Like other snakes, it cannot chew, and swallows the eggs whole. As an egg moves down its neck, the snake arches its body, and downward-pointing spines on its backbone break open the shell. The contents of the egg travel onwards into the snake's stomach, but the snake regurgitates the pieces of broken shell. There are six species of egg-eating snake, and all of them live in Africa.

SCIENTIFIC NAME	*Dasypeltis scaber*
DISTRIBUTION	Africa
SIZE	Up to 75cm long

BOOMSLANG

The African boomslang is one of the few members of the colubrid family that has a bite poisonous enough to kill people. Like the vine snake, it also lives in trees, but its venom is far stronger. Unusually for a colubrid, it has three pairs of fangs instead of two. and they are set further forwards, making it easier for it to strike and bite. Boomslangs are camouflaged brown or green, and they lie in wait in trees for their prey, often with the front of their bodies sticking out in the air. Birds sometimes mistake them for branches and land on them, only to become an easy meal for the snake.

SCIENTIFIC NAME	*Dispholidus typhus*
DISTRIBUTION	Central and southern Africa
SIZE	Up to 2m long

KING COBRA OR HAMADRYAD

This giant cobra is the largest venomous snake in the world. The largest on record, which was kept at London Zoo in England, reached a length of 5.7m. King cobras produce large quantities of highly toxic venom, and prey entirely on other snakes. They are generally secretive, but can be aggressive, hunting by day, and sometimes attacking people without any provocation. King cobras are unusual in the snake world because they make nests out of sticks and leaves. The female lays up to 40 eggs, and remains on top of the nest until her young slither out.

SCIENTIFIC NAME *Ophiophagus hannah*

DISTRIBUTION India, Southeast Asia

SIZE Up to 5.5m long

RINGHALS OR SPITTING COBRA

The ringhals is one of three types of cobra that defend themselves by spitting venom. The ringhals' fangs have venom ducts that open forwards, so the venom squirts out of its open mouth. It can spray its venom up to a distance of 2.5m, and it leans its head backwards to target the venom on its enemy's eyes. The effect is extremely painful, and can sometimes cause permanent blindness. This snake eats rodents and frogs, and it is one of the few members of the cobra family that gives birth to live young.

SCIENTIFIC NAME
Haemachatus haemachatus

DISTRIBUTION
Southern Africa

SIZE Up to 1m long

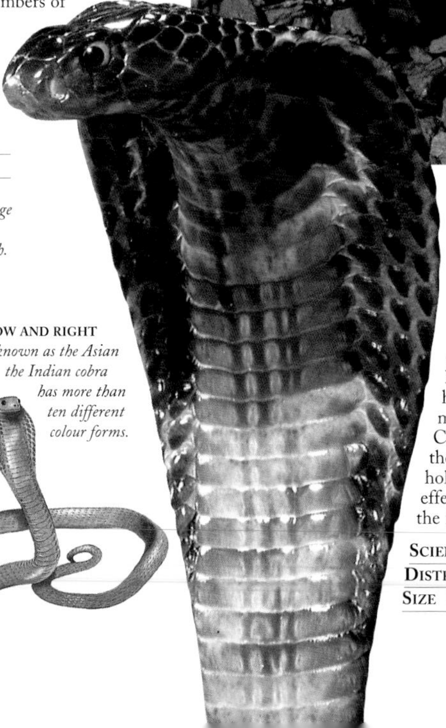

BELOW *The king cobra can lunge more than 2m when it strikes, making it dangerous to approach. Its spread hood warns that it is preparing to attack.*

BELOW AND RIGHT
Also known as the Asian cobra, the Indian cobra has more than ten different colour forms.

ABOVE *A death adder bites a lizard. Before antidotes became available, people often died after being bitten by this snake.*

INDIAN COBRA

For centuries, this poisonous snake has been popular with Indian snake charmers. When disturbed, it rears up and spreads out its ribs to form a hood as it gets ready to strike. It cannot hear, so it responds to snake charmers' movements rather than their music. Cobras have hollow fangs at the front of their mouths. They make a quick stab and hold their prey until the poison has taken effect. Indian cobras lay 20 or 30 eggs, and the female guards them until they hatch.

SCIENTIFIC NAME *Naja naja*

DISTRIBUTION India, Southeast Asia

SIZE Up to 2.2m long

dangerous of all. It is the world's third largest venomous snake, and is unpredictable when threatened. The taipan lives in the sparsely populated north of Australia, and although it sometimes hunts in sugar cane fields, it rarely attacks people. It has a dark brown body and a slim, creamy-coloured head.

SCIENTIFIC NAME *Oxyuranus scutellatus*
DISTRIBUTION Australia
SIZE Up to 3m long

ABOVE
The eastern coral snake has powerful venom, but its mouth and teeth are small, making it difficult for it to bite people.

EASTERN CORAL SNAKE
Coral snakes are nocturnal and they spend much of their time under leaves or logs. They have cylindrical bodies and small heads, and their colouring of black, yellow, red or white hoops is often so bright that they look freshly painted. No one knows why burrowing nocturnal snakes should be so vividly coloured – it is most likely that the colours warn potential predators that the snakes are dangerous. There are about 40 species of true coral snake, all from warm parts of the Americas.

SCIENTIFIC NAME *Micrurus fulvius*
DISTRIBUTION Southeastern USA, Mexico
SIZE Up to 1.2m long

BLACK MAMBA
The black mamba is the largest poisonous snake in Africa. It is actually grey rather than black, and it hunts in trees and bushes as well as on open ground. Black mambas are probably the fastest-moving land animals without legs. In short bursts, they can move at up to 20km/h – fast enough to overtake someone running away.

SCIENTIFIC NAME *Dendroaspis polylepis*
DISTRIBUTION Africa south of the Sahara Desert
SIZE Up to 4.3m long

YELLOW-BELLIED SEA SNAKE
About 40 species in the cobra family live in the sea. These snakes have flat tails that work like paddles, nostrils that shut when they dive, and highly toxic venom. The yellow-bellied sea snake is often found hundreds of kilometres out to sea. Huge shoals of them are sometimes seen from ships, but it is not known why so many gather together. Some sea snakes lay their eggs on land, but the yellow-bellied sea snake gives birth to live young, and never comes ashore.

SCIENTIFIC NAME *Pelamis platurus*
DISTRIBUTION Tropical seas worldwide
SIZE Up to 1m long

ABOVE *Raising its head above the grass, a black mamba investigates its surroundings. Black mambas are extremely venomous – fortunately, they live in places that are thinly populated.*

DEATH ADDER
This highly venomous snake is not a true adder, but an unusually short and fat member of the cobra family. It feeds on rodents, lizards and birds, and spends the day coiled up beneath leaves or in loose soil. Like a real adder, it often lies in wait for prey instead of searching it out. Its body tapers very sharply into a narrow tail, and it waves this to attract animals within range. Death adders are dangerous because they strike instantly if they are disturbed.

SCIENTIFIC NAME *Acanthopis antarcticus*
DISTRIBUTION Australia
SIZE Up to 50cm long

TAIPAN
Nine-tenths of Australia's snakes belong to the cobra family, which explains why most of them are poisonous. The taipan is probably the most

COMMON VIPER

Vipers do not pursue their prey, but wait for food to come their way, then strike with deadly efficiency. The common viper is a typical member of this small group of poisonous snakes. It has a large head, narrow neck and thick body with a zigzag pattern for camouflage. Its fangs are normally folded away, but they swing forwards as the snake attacks. Once a viper has struck, it waits for its venom to work – only feeding when its prey is dead. The common viper eats lizards, frogs and small mammals. The female produces to up to 20 young in late summer.

SCIENTIFIC NAME *Vipera berus*

DISTRIBUTION Europe, northern Asia

SIZE Up to 50cm long

ABOVE *The body of a fully grown puff adder is thicker than a man's arm.*
RIGHT *Compared to its larger relatives, the common viper is rarely a threat to humans, but it attacks small animals with deadly efficiency.*

ABOVE *A Gaboon viper waits for passing animals to come within reach of its giant fangs.*

GABOON VIPER

This rainforest snake is one of the fattest vipers, and also one of the best camouflaged. Its back is covered with intricate brown and black wedge-shaped markings, making it very difficult to spot among fallen leaves. Its eyes face upwards – an adaptation that helps it to spot other animals as it lies on the forest floor. The Gaboon viper's fangs can be up to 5cm long, and they are sharp enough to stab through clothes and shoes. Like the common viper, it produces eggs that hatch as, or just after, they are laid.

SCIENTIFIC NAME *Bitis gabonica*

DISTRIBUTION Western, central and southern Africa

SIZE Up to 2m long

PUFF ADDER

The puff adder is one of Africa's most dangerous snakes, because it often lies in wait on roads and tracks after dark, staying still but fully alert. It is then all too easy to tread on it. It lives in a wide range of habitats, from woodlands to semi-desert, and feeds on ground-living animals, such as reptiles and rodents. This snake gets its name from its habit of puffing itself up if it is threatened.

SCIENTIFIC NAME *Bitis arietans*

DISTRIBUTION Africa, Middle East

SIZE Up to 2m long

FER-DE-LANCE

This large, dangerous snake belongs to a family of reptiles called the pit vipers. Pit vipers track down warm-blooded animals by using heat-sensitive pits between their eyes and nostrils. This works so well that many of them can strike accurately in total darkness. The fer-de-lance is one of the largest pit vipers, and is responsible for more human deaths than any other snake in the American tropics. It lives in low-lying areas, and often hunts in fields and sugar plantations.

SCIENTIFIC NAME *Bothrops atrox*

DISTRIBUTION Central America, South America

SIZE Up to 2.5m long

EYELASH VIPER

This small pit viper is one of a handful of species that live and feed in trees. Many eyelash vipers are green or brown, but some are golden with speckles of red. Eyelash vipers eat lizards and frogs, but they also lurk near flowers to catch hummingbirds as they hover and feed.

SCIENTIFIC NAME *Bothrops schlegelii*

DISTRIBUTION Central America, northern South America

SIZE Up to 1m long

Zigzag pattern along back

*Rival males
wrestle, but do
not bite each other*

*Rattle
gets longer
each year*

*Wide scales on
the underside
for gripping
the ground*

WESTERN DIAMONDBACK

The western diamondback is one of the
largest and most dangerous of the 35 species
of rattlesnake. These snakes are pit vipers with
a special feature – a built-in rattle at the tips of
their tails. The rattle consists of up to 12 loose,
bony rings, which make a buzzing or rattling
sound when the tail vibrates. Rattlesnakes use
their rattles to warn their enemies to keep away,
but they may also help to distract small animals
while the snake gets ready to strike. The western
diamondback lives in dry places and woodlands,
and eats mammals, birds and lizards. Like all
rattlesnakes, it gives birth to live young.

SCIENTIFIC NAME	*Crotalus atrox*
DISTRIBUTION	Southern USA, Mexico
SIZE	Up to 2m long

SIDEWINDER

This desert rattlesnake lives in sandy
places, where the loose surface makes it
difficult to move about. Instead of creeping,
it throws its body sideways across the sand,
leaving a series of parallel J-shaped tracks.
Called sidewinding, this way of moving uses
less energy than creeping, and it also helps the
snake to keep cool. Sidewinders have another
adaptation to desert life – a pair of horns over
their eyes that work like sunshades.

SCIENTIFIC NAME	*Crotalus cerastes*
DISTRIBUTION	Southwestern USA, northwestern Mexico
SIZE	Up to 80cm long

FANGS AND VENOM

Vipers and pit vipers have fangs that fold
away when not in use. Most of these snakes
can eat small animals without using their
fangs, but they bring them into action to deal
with larger prey. Unlike other snakes, their
fangs are at the front of their mouths – ideal
for making a quick, deadly stab. Snake venom
contains many substances, and the way it
works varies from one group of snakes to
another. Viper venom breaks down the prey's
blood cells, but cobra venom acts on the
victim's nervous system. The Gaboon
viper produces
more venom
than any other
snake – about
0.5g each
time it bites
and enough to
kill ten people.

*Hole
in tip
of fang*

Venom sac

TURTLES AND TORTOISES

Turtles and tortoises are the only living reptiles with hard shells. Their shells wrap around the whole of the body apart from the head, legs and tail, and are made of solid bone covered by large, thin scales. Most turtles and tortoises can pull their heads inside their shells if they are threatened, and many can also pull in their legs and tails. Land-dwelling tortoises have stubby legs with blunt claws, while sea-going turtles have flat legs that work like flippers. Freshwater and coastal species have legs that can be used for swimming, walking and sometimes climbing as well. There are about 230 species of turtle and tortoise, and they all reproduce by laying eggs. Many species have become endangered in recent years.

1 2

3 4

LEFT *Although they live in the sea, green turtles lay their eggs on land.* **1** *The female uses her front flippers to haul herself up a sandy beach.* **2** *After excavating a nest, she lays a clutch of soft-shelled eggs.* **3** *The young turtles usually hatch beneath the sand, tearing open their eggs with their snouts.* **4** *Once they have reached the surface of the sand, they instinctively head towards the sea.*

BELOW *Leatherbacks feed on jellyfish and can dive more than 1,500m to catch their food.*

GREEN TURTLE

This turtle is one of seven species that spend almost all of their lives at sea. Like other marine turtles, its shell is smooth and streamlined, and its front legs beat like wings, pulling it through the water. It feeds on seagrass and seaweed, nipping off mouthfuls with its sharp-edged jaws. It can hold its breath underwater for more than half an hour. Green turtles lay their eggs on sandy beaches, hauling themselves ashore under the cover of darkness. Each female lays about one hundred eggs, and three months later, the baby turtles dig their way to the surface and scuttle towards the waves. This is the most dangerous moment of a turtle's life, because seabirds often attack young turtles before they can swim away. Green turtle nesting-sites are often in remote places, and the adult turtles may travel more than 1,600km to breed. Scientists think that they navigate in the same way as fish, by recognizing the taste of the water where they hatched.

SCIENTIFIC NAME *Chelonia mydas*

DISTRIBUTION Warm seas worldwide

SIZE Up to 1.2m long

LEATHERBACK TURTLE

The leatherback is the world's largest turtle, sometimes weighing more than half a tonne. Its enormous front flippers look like wings, and can measure 2.5m from tip to tip. Unlike other marine turtles, its shell does not have scales, and it has a rubbery feel, with deep grooves running from front to back. They are also great travellers, and may wander far out into the oceans. One leatherback tagged off South America turned up on the opposite side of the Atlantic Ocean – nearly 7,000km away. The leatherback is now critically endangered because it has been hunted so heavily by people.

SCIENTIFIC NAME *Dermochelys coriacea*

DISTRIBUTION Worldwide, in temperate or warm water

SIZE Up to 1.8m long

WOOD TURTLE

This North American turtle is equally at home on land and in water. It hibernates in ponds and lakes, but in summer it often wanders across farms and through woods, looking for fruit and animals such as insects and worms. It is a good swimmer, but also climbs well and sometimes clambers up tree-trunks. Wood turtles have rough shells, and their scales look as if they have been cut into steps. The skin on their neck and forelegs is often orange.

SCIENTIFIC NAME *Clemmys insculpta*

DISTRIBUTION Northeastern USA; adjoining areas of Canada

SIZE Up to 23cm long

DIAMONDBACK TERRAPIN

Terrapins are small turtles that live in or near water. Most of them are freshwater animals, but the diamondback lives in estuaries and saltmarshes, where it feeds mainly on worms and snails. Its colours can vary greatly but, like most terrapins, its underside is usually much more eyecatching than the top of its shell, often with orange or yellow streaks and patches of black. Diamondback terrapins nest above the high tide mark. The females dig several holes, and lay up to 12 eggs in each one. The young terrapins are only about 2.5cm long when they hatch, and they grow up slowly. They often do not breed until they are ten years old.

SCIENTIFIC NAME *Malaclemys terrapin*
DISTRIBUTION Atlantic and Gulf coasts of USA
SIZE Up to 23cm long

ALLIGATOR SNAPPING TURTLE

This giant turtle is the largest species that lives in fresh water, and also the most dangerous. It has a knobbly shell, a spiky neck and a long tail. Instead of moving about to find food, this turtle lurks on the bottom of rivers and lakes with its mouth wide open, wiggling a pink, worm-like thread of skin on the end of its tongue. If a fish approaches to investigate, the turtle's massive jaws snap shut. Because the turtle stays still, it uses up very little oxygen, and it can stay underwater for hours without surfacing to breathe. No one knows exactly how large these turtles can grow. One example, seen in 1948, probably weighed more than 225kg, and was said to be as large as a kitchen table.

SCIENTIFIC NAME *Macrochelys temmincki*
DISTRIBUTION Mississippi Basin (Southern USA)
SIZE Up to 1.2m, including tail

SPUR-THIGHED TORTOISE

There are about 40 kinds of land tortoise – this medium-sized species is one of the few that lives in Europe. It gets its name from the small spur on each of its front legs. Spur-thighed tortoises are vegetarians, and they live in scrub and rocky places. They feed during the morning and evening, resting during the hottest part of the day. The females lay two or three eggs each year, which take about three months to hatch. In the past, large numbers of these tortoises were collected and sold as pets, but they are now protected by law.

SCIENTIFIC NAME *Testudo graeca*
DISTRIBUTION Southern Europe
SIZE Up to 30cm long

GALAPAGOS GIANT TORTOISE

Weighing up to 350kg, the Galapagos giant tortoise looks almost too heavy to move. It is one of only two species of giant tortoise in the world – the other one lives on the remote Aldabra islands, north of Madagascar. Galapagos giant tortoises feed on cacti and other plants. The tortoises vary from one island to another, and some have extra-long necks that help them to reach their food. These huge animals can live for more than one hundred years, but they face an increasing struggle to survive. In the past, they were often used as food by sailors, and now only a few thousand are left.

SCIENTIFIC NAME *Geochelone elephantopus*
DISTRIBUTION Galapagos Islands
SIZE Up to 1.2m long

Alligator snapping turtles' jaws have razor-sharp edges for slicing prey

ABOVE *Wiggling its tongue, an alligator snapping turtle lures a fish into its mouth. It swallows small fish whole – larger ones will often be cut in two.*

BELOW *Tearing open their eggs, two baby spur-thighed tortoises begin life in the outside world. Like other tortoises and turtles, they look like miniature versions of their parents when they hatch, complete with tiny shells.*

Tortoise's shell hardens soon after hatching

BIRDS

APART FROM BATS, BIRDS ARE THE ONLY
ANIMALS WITH BACKBONES THAT CAN FLY.
THEY ARE THE UNRIVALLED EXPERTS AT
FLIGHT, TRAVELLING FURTHER AND FASTER
THAN ANY OTHER LIVING CREATURES.

Birds have several features that help them to save
weight and get off the ground. These include
hollow bones, slender legs and a beak instead of
heavy jaws and teeth. But their most important features
are feathers and wings. Feathers are useful in a number
of ways. They provide lift and make the birds' bodies
streamlined so they can slip easily through the air.
Feathers also help to keep in body heat. There are about
9,000 species of bird. They all reproduce by laying hard-
shelled eggs and most of them look after their young.

FLIGHTLESS BIRDS
Over millions of years, some birds have
gradually lost the ability to fly. Today,
flightless birds include giant species,
such as the ostrich and emu, as well
as kiwis and penguins. On land,
flightless birds move about by
walking or running on their
powerful legs. Penguins have
short legs so they cannot run
fast, but they use their wings
like flippers to
speed through
sea water.

LEFT *Male
ostriches have
black and white
plumage, but the females
are brownish-grey.*

OSTRICH
The ostrich is the world's largest
bird, and the only one with two-
toed feet. It lives on open plains,
where its height gives it a good view
of approaching predators. Ostriches
can run at up to 70 km/h but, if they
are cornered, they kick out with their
feet, using their claws as weapons.
They nest on the ground, and their
eggs are the largest of any bird,

measuring as much as 20cm long. Each female
lays up to 12 eggs, and several females often
lay in the same nest. When the eggs hatch, the
male takes charge of the young, and may gather
several families of young together. Ostriches are
easy to tame, and are often kept in captivity. In
the wild, they feed mainly on seeds and fruit,
but captive birds will swallow almost anything.

SCIENTIFIC NAME	*Struthio camelus*
DISTRIBUTION	Africa
SIZE	Up to 2.75m high

GREATER RHEA
Rheas are like small versions of ostriches, and
they live in the open plains of South America.
There are two species – the greater and the
lesser rhea *(Pterocnemia pennata)*. They both
have brown plumage and live in flocks. Like
ostriches, rheas use shared nests, with up to six
females laying their eggs in the same hollow in
the ground. Unlike most birds, the females take
no part in incubating the eggs or looking after
the young. Instead, the males do it all.

SCIENTIFIC NAME	*Rhea americana*
DISTRIBUTION	Southern South America
SIZE	Up to 1.5m high

EMU
The emu is Australia's tallest bird. It has
brownish-grey plumage, with a distinctive pale
blue throat. Emus feed on seeds and insects, and
can be serious pests on farmland. In the 1930s,
a team of army machine-gunners tried to keep
emu flocks out of the wheat-growing region of
western Australia but, despite this, emus still
managed to thrive. Emus lay dark green eggs.
The male incubates them on his own, and the
stripy chicks hatch after about eight weeks.

SCIENTIFIC NAME	*Dromaius novaehollandiae*
DISTRIBUTION	Australia
SIZE	Up to 2m high

COMMON CASSOWARY
Cassowaries are solitary birds that
live in rainforests. They have black
plumage, blue and red necks and a
large bony shield – called a casque –
on the top of their heads. Compared
to other flightless birds, cassowaries are
unpredictable and dangerous. Instead
of running away from people, they may

LEFT *The cassowary's casque and coarse plumage
protect it as it runs through dense undergrowth.*

attack with their claws, sometimes with fatal results. Cassowaries lay their eggs on a bed of leaves on the forest floor. The male takes care of incubation, but both parents look after the chicks.

SCIENTIFIC NAME
Casuarius casuarius

DISTRIBUTION
New Guinea, northern Australia

SIZE Up to 2m high

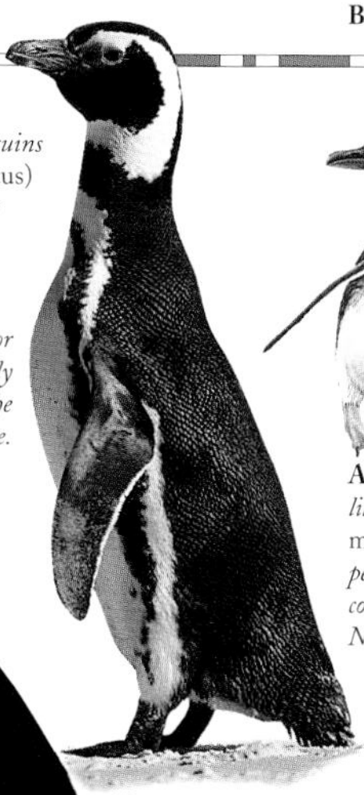

RIGHT *Magellanic penguins (Spheniscus magellanicus) lay their eggs in burrows and sleep underground.*

BELOW *The chicks of emperor penguins grow extremely quickly to enable them to survive in the Antarctic climate.*

ABOVE *At 30cm high, the little penguin* (Eudyptula minor) *is the smallest penguin. It breeds on the coasts of Australia and New Zealand.*

BROWN KIWI

Kiwis live in New Zealand's forests, and they come out to feed after dark. They eat earthworms and other small animals and, unusually for birds, they sniff out their food using nostrils at the end of their beaks. Their wings are tiny, but their hair-like plumage provides protection from the rain. Female kiwis often lay just one egg, but this can be a quarter of their total weight.

A kiwi finds food mainly by smell

SCIENTIFIC NAME *Apteryx australis*

DISTRIBUTION New Zealand

SIZE Up to 50cm long

EMPEROR PENGUIN

This is the world's largest penguin, and is one of the few that breeds on Antarctic ice. The female lays one egg in late autumn, and then swims out to sea. The male protects his partner's egg through the dark winter, keeping it warm under a flap of skin on his feet. When the female returns in early spring, the chick has hatched, and the male urgently needs food. Emperor penguins can dive to a depth of 250m to find their food of fish and krill.

SCIENTIFIC NAME
Aptenodytes forsteri

DISTRIBUTION Antarctica, Southern Ocean

SIZE Up to 1.2m high

DIVERS, GREBES AND PETRELS

These birds spend most of their lives on or over water. Divers and grebes live mainly on lakes and rivers, where they catch fish beneath the surface. Their legs are set far back along their bodies, and their webbed feet work like propellers, helping them to dive and swim. Petrels and their relatives live at sea. They also have webbed feet, but they snatch up food as they flutter or glide over the waves. Some of these birds stay close to shore. Others, such as albatrosses, wander across the oceans, coming back to land only to breed. There are four species of diver and about 20 species of grebe. Petrels and their relatives make up a larger group of birds, containing more than 100 species.

RIGHT *The great northern diver's calls sound like ghostly howling or eerie laughter.*
BELOW *Like its relatives, the southern giant petrel has tubular nostrils and a well-developed sense of smell.*

Nostrils open near the end of the beak

GREAT NORTHERN DIVER

The loud cry of this bird is one of the most haunting sounds in the lonely northern lakes where it feeds and breeds. It has a long, sharp beak, and handsome black and white breeding plumage. Divers are expert swimmers and fast fliers, but their legs are set so far back that they have difficulty moving about on land. They spend the spring and summer on rivers and lakes but, after raising a pair of chicks, they usually head for the coast for the winter months.

SCIENTIFIC NAME	*Gavia immer*
DISTRIBUTION	Northern North America, Iceland, northwestern Europe
SIZE	Up to 90cm long

GREAT CRESTED GREBE

During the breeding season, this grebe's feathery crest makes it one of the most elegant birds on the water. It shows off the crest during its courtship displays, and moults it once the breeding season is over. Grebes are not deep divers, but they are very agile. Their toes have individual webbing and, if danger threatens, they can sink like submarines, until only the tops of their heads are visible above the water. Great crested grebes usually raise three or four chicks a year. The chicks often ride on their parents' backs, held underneath their wings, and they stay on board even during a dive.

SCIENTIFIC NAME	*Podiceps cristatus*
DISTRIBUTION	Europe, Asia, Africa, Australia, New Zealand
SIZE	Up to 48cm long

PIED-BILLED GREBE

This small, pale brown grebe gets its name from the black ring around its beak, which appears just before the breeding season. Compared to the great crested grebe, it has a stocky body and a short neck, and it feeds on freshwater insects and snails as well as fish. It builds its nest in typical grebe fashion, heaping water plants into a soggy, floating pile.

SCIENTIFIC NAME	*Podylimbus podiceps*
DISTRIBUTION	North America, Central America, South America; from Canada to Argentina
SIZE	Up to 35cm long

SOUTHERN GIANT PETREL

The southern giant petrel is a scavenger, feeding on the shore as well as out at sea. It looks like a heavyweight brown seagull, and has a powerful, hooked beak, which it uses to tear open dead animals and to carry off seabird chicks. Its nostrils form two tubes along the top of its beak – a feature that petrels and their relatives all share. Giant petrels nest on the ground. If anything comes too close, they can defend themselves by spitting a foul-smelling oil.

SCIENTIFIC NAME *Macronectes giganteus*

DISTRIBUTION Southern oceans and coasts, as far south as Antarctica

SIZE Up to 1m long

Northern fulmar in flight

NORTHERN FULMAR

Holding out its wings stiffly from its sides, the fulmar rides the wind over rocks and waves, soaring and swooping with amazing agility. This grey and white bird nests on cliffs, where it lays its eggs on rocky ledges. The adults feed their chicks on regurgitated, half-digested food. They often follow fishing-boats to eat waste thrown overboard, and the species has become common because modern boats produce a lot of waste.

SCIENTIFIC NAME *Fulmarus glacialis*

DISTRIBUTION Northern Pacific Ocean, North Atlantic Ocean

SIZE Up to 48cm long

SHORT-TAILED SHEARWATER

Shearwaters roam the open oceans, skimming over the waves as they search for food. They are common all over the world, but they often go unnoticed – partly because they come ashore only at night. They nest in burrows on rocky islands, laying just one egg each time they breed. Shearwaters are great travellers, and the short-tailed shearwater flies further than any other bird on its annual migration. It breeds on islands near Tasmania, and each year the adults fly a figure-of-eight loop around the whole Pacific Ocean – a distance of about 32,000km.

SCIENTIFIC NAME *Puffinus tenuirostris*

DISTRIBUTION Pacific Ocean

SIZE Up to 43cm long

WANDERING ALBATROSS

This giant seabird has the largest wingspan of any flying animal – up to 3.6m. Its wings are long and narrow, and it uses them to glide on storm-force winds in the Southern Ocean, snatching jellyfish and other animals from the waves. Its flight is so efficient that it hardly ever has to beat its wings. Wandering albatrosses nest on remote islands, and they lay a single egg each time they breed. Their eggs are the largest of any

seabird, and take more than 80 days to hatch. This is the longest incubation period of any bird. Wandering albatrosses take a long time to mature, and are almost a year old before they are ready to fly.

SCIENTIFIC NAME *Diomedea exulans*

DISTRIBUTION Southern Ocean

SIZE Up to 1.35m long

ABOVE *The northern fulmar is often mistaken for a seagull, but its tubular nostrils show that it is one of the petrel family.*
BELOW *The wandering albatross glides on air that rises from the waves.*

COURTSHIP

Before animals mate, they have to make sure they have found the right partner. Many birds do this by carrying out courtship displays, which are like dances with precise movements. The great crested grebe's displays are among the most complicated in the whole bird world. During one of the dances, the two partners paddle towards each other until they are almost touching, and then shake their heads from side to side. In another dance, the weed ceremony, they suddenly dive down to the lakebed, and surface with weed in their beaks. Paddling furiously, they tread water, with their bodies and necks bolt upright. Displays like these enable both partners to show that they are healthy, and that they belong to the same species. They also help them to get used to each other – an important step if they are to raise a family together.

ABOVE *These great crested grebes are in the middle of a courtship dance, while a rival male looks on from the right.*

PELICANS AND THEIR RELATIVES

Pelicans are famous for their enormous beaks, but they also have another unusual feature – unlike most waterbirds, they have webs of skin connecting all four of their toes. This is also true of cormorants, gannets and frigatebirds, which are among the pelican's closest relatives. These birds all feed on fish, and most of them live at sea. They are all strong fliers, but many find it difficult to move about on land. There are about 60 species in this group of birds; some are found all over the world, but tropicbirds and frigatebirds are found only where it is warm.

RIGHT *Northern gannets are friendly with their mates, but aggressive towards their neighbours.*

Pouch for carrying fish hangs beneath huge beak

LEFT *While one white pelican feeds, the other rests with its closed beak propped on its chest.*

ABOVE *Brown pelicans always fish close to the coast. They often follow fishing-boats into port in the hope of catching scraps.*

GREAT WHITE PELICAN

This pelican has a wingspan of up to 3m, making it one of the world's largest freshwater birds. It is a powerful and skilful flier, but it is even more impressive when it sets about catching a meal. Great white pelicans live and feed in flocks. They form circles around shoals of fish, driving them together to make them easier to catch. Each pelican lunges after its food, filling its pouch with as much as 14 litres of water. Once the water has drained from its beak, the pelican swallows its prey.

SCIENTIFIC NAME *Pelecanus onocrotalus*

DISTRIBUTION Southern Europe, Africa, Asia

SIZE Up to 1.75m long

BROWN PELICAN

Instead of scooping the water for food, brown pelicans are more like low-level dive-bombers. They cruise along in long lines close to the shore, watching for fish below. If they spot a shoal, the lead bird swoops upwards and then dives, and all the others follow suit. Within seconds, the pelicans are bobbing back up to the surface, usually with fish in their pouches. Brown pelicans nest on rocky ground or in low trees, and they lay two or three eggs at a time.

SCIENTIFIC NAME *Pelecanus occidentalis*

DISTRIBUTION Pacific and Atlantic coasts of North, Central and South America

SIZE Up to 1.3m long

ABOVE *A blue-footed booby guards its clutch of eggs. These birds lay their eggs on bare rock, and keep them warm with their feet.*

NORTHERN GANNET

Gannets and boobies are the bird world's record high-divers. They dive at fish from a height of 30m or more, folding back their narrow wings just before they slice through the surface of the sea. A superbly streamlined shape – together with a strong skull and air pockets under the skin – means that they can hit the water at great speed without risk of injury. Northern gannets nest on rocky islands in the North Atlantic. At first, the young birds are speckled brown, but after four or five years they develop their adult plumage, with white bodies and black wingtips.

SCIENTIFIC NAME *Sula bassana*

DISTRIBUTION North Atlantic Ocean

SIZE Up to 90cm long

BLUE-FOOTED BOOBY

This close relative of the northern gannet has a grey beak, brown wings and bright blue webbed feet. Like the gannet, it catches fish by plunge-diving, and it also has close-set eyes that enable it to look directly ahead as it drops towards the water. Boobies often dive at a more gentle angle than gannets, and they are experts at catching flyingfish (page 122) disturbed by boats.

SCIENTIFIC NAME *Sula nebouxii*

DISTRIBUTION Pacific coast of Central and South America, Galapagos Islands

SIZE Up to 84cm long

RED-BILLED TROPICBIRD

Tropicbirds often wander far out to sea, soaring and flapping their way across hundreds of kilometres of open water. They feed on fish and squid, and usually hover for a few seconds before diving into the water. There are three species of these birds, and all of them are mainly white, with two long tail feathers that look like streamers. The red-billed tropicbird is the largest of the three. It nests on rocky coasts and remote islands, and raises a single chick each year.

SCIENTIFIC NAME *Phaeton aethereus*
DISTRIBUTION Tropical eastern Pacific and Atlantic Oceans, Arabian Sea, Persian Gulf
SIZE Up to 1.05m long, including tail-streamers

AMERICAN DARTER, ANHINGA OR SNAKE-BIRD
Darters are sleek relatives of cormorants that live in lakes and swamps. They often swim with most of their body submerged, leaving just their head and neck above the surface. A darter's beak is straight and sharp – unlike a cormorant's, which is hooked – and it is used to impale fish underwater. Once a darter has made a catch, it surfaces, flicks its prey into the air and swallows it headfirst. Darters nest in trees near the water's edge, and their young can swim before they can fly.

SCIENTIFIC NAME *Anhinga anhinga*
DISTRIBUTION Southeastern USA, Central America, tropical South America
SIZE Up to 90cm long

GREAT CORMORANT
Cormorants are fish-eating birds that chase their prey underwater. They propel themselves mainly with their feet, and can dive for more than a minute, reaching a depth of about 10m. Unlike most waterbirds, cormorants' feathers are not completely waterproof, and they hold their wings out to dry when they return to land. There are about 30 species of cormorant, and the great cormorant is by far the most widespread. It lives in lakes and estuaries as well as on coasts, and builds its nest on cliffs or in trees. Apart from its white throat, it is almost entirely black.

SCIENTIFIC NAME *Phalacrocorax carbo*
DISTRIBUTION Fresh water and coasts worldwide, except South America
SIZE Up to 90cm long

RIGHT *The great cormorant spends much of its time perched at the water's edge.*

MAGNIFICENT FRIGATEBIRD
Frigatebirds often have a wingspan of more than 1.8m, but their skeletons can weigh as little as 114g – less than the weight of their feathers. This amazing combination of size and lightness enables them to soar effortlessly over the sea, where they keep a watchful eye on other birds. If a frigatebird sees another bird catching a fish, it immediately sets off in pursuit. It snaps at the bird until it drops its catch, and deftly catches the food before it hits the water. Frigatebirds nest in trees and shrubs, and the males attract females by inflating throat pouches that look like red balloons. They hardly ever land on water.

SCIENTIFIC NAME *Fregata magnificens*
DISTRIBUTION Tropical eastern Pacific and Atlantic Oceans
SIZE Up to 1.14m long

BELOW *Perched in a bush, a male magnificent frigatebird inflates his throat to attract a mate. Frigatebirds nest in groups, and use twigs to make platform-shaped nests.*

Great cormorant holding out its wings to dry

HERONS AND THEIR RELATIVES

These birds all share two eye-catching features – long legs and equally long necks. Most of them feed by wading into shallow water, where they either watch for fish, or use their beaks to feel for small animals, such as molluscs and crabs. Flamingoes strain their food from the water, using bent beaks that work like sieves. Storks look as if they should wade as well, but they rarely feed in water. Instead, most of them stride across open ground, catching small animals, including insects and frogs. There are about 120 species of heron and their relatives, and they are found all over the world. Where wetlands have been drained, many of these birds have become rare.

GREY HERON

This is the largest heron in Europe, with a wingspan of up to 1.7m. It catches fish by stealth, wading into the shallows and then waiting for its prey to swim within reach. When a fish comes near, the heron suddenly flicks out its neck, stabbing the fish on the end of its long, pointed beak. Like other herons, this bird folds its neck into an S-shape when it is flying or resting. It nests in groups, usually high in trees, and the males and females greet each other by making loud clattering sounds with their bills.

SCIENTIFIC NAME *Ardea cinerea*

DISTRIBUTION Europe, Africa, Asia

SIZE Up to 1.25m long

BLACK-CROWNED NIGHT HERON

When most birds are settling down for the night, this small heron comes out to feed. Compared to some of its relatives, it looks short and squat, but it is just as effective at finding food. Night herons have good eyesight, and they patrol the water's edge, watching for fish and other small animals. They nest in trees and bushes, making flimsy platforms out of sticks.

SCIENTIFIC NAME *Nycticorax nycticorax*

DISTRIBUTION Worldwide, except cool regions of northern hemisphere and Australia

SIZE Up to 64cm long

EURASIAN BITTERN

Bitterns live in reedbeds, where their camouflage makes them hard to spot. Their plumage blends in against dead reed stalks. When threatened, they stretch out their necks and sway like reeds blowing in the wind. In the breeding season, male Eurasian bitterns make booming calls that sound like someone blowing across an empty bottle. This can be heard up to 5km away.

SCIENTIFIC NAME *Botaurus stellaris*

DISTRIBUTION Europe, parts of central Asia, parts of Africa

SIZE Up to 80cm long

RIGHT The great blue heron (Ardea herodias) is one of the tallest birds in North America.

BELOW AND RIGHT
The Eurasian bittern is a secretive bird that feeds mainly on frogs and fish. Although it flies well, it spends most of its time creeping through its marshy reedbed home. During the last 100 years, many reedbeds have been drained and turned into farmland, so this bird is less common than it once was.

S-shaped curve of neck

ABOVE
Balancing on one leg, a grey heron stretches its wings.
RIGHT *The black-crowned night heron has strong toes and is a good climber. It often perches on overhanging branches to watch for fish or frogs.*

Grey wings with black flight feathers

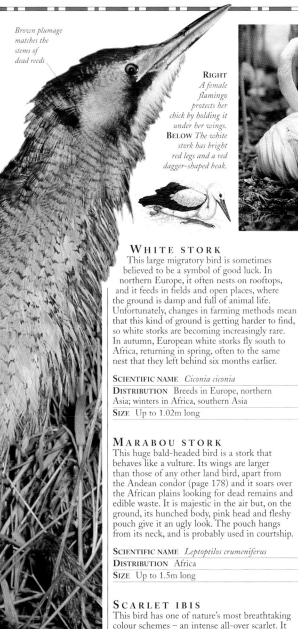

Brown plumage matches the stems of dead reeds

RIGHT *A female flamingo protects her chick by holding it under her wings.* **BELOW** *The white stork has bright red legs and a red dagger-shaped beak.*

ABOVE *Young scarlet ibises are grey with white undersides. Their scarlet plumage develops when they are old enough to breed.*

WHITE STORK

This large migratory bird is sometimes believed to be a symbol of good luck. In northern Europe, it often nests on rooftops, and it feeds in fields and open places, where the ground is damp and full of animal life. Unfortunately, changes in farming methods mean that this kind of ground is getting harder to find, so white storks are becoming increasingly rare. In autumn, European white storks fly south to Africa, returning in spring, often to the same nest that they left behind six months earlier.

SCIENTIFIC NAME *Ciconia ciconia*

DISTRIBUTION Breeds in Europe, northern Asia; winters in Africa, southern Asia

SIZE Up to 1.02m long

MARABOU STORK

This huge bald-headed bird is a stork that behaves like a vulture. Its wings are larger than those of any other land bird, apart from the Andean condor (page 178) and it soars over the African plains looking for dead remains and edible waste. It is majestic in the air but, on the ground, its hunched body, pink head and fleshy pouch give it an ugly look. The pouch hangs from its neck, and is probably used in courtship.

SCIENTIFIC NAME *Leptoptilos crumeniferus*

DISTRIBUTION Africa

SIZE Up to 1.5m long

SCARLET IBIS

This bird has one of nature's most breathtaking colour schemes – an intense all-over scarlet. It lives along muddy coasts and in mangrove swamps, and feeds and nests in groups. Scarlet ibises eat small molluscs and crustaceans, feeling for them in the mud with their curved beaks.

SCIENTIFIC NAME *Eudocimus ruber*

DISTRIBUTION Northeastern coast of South America

SIZE Up to 61cm long

WHITE SPOONBILL

It is easy to see how this bird gets its name. Its beak has a rounded tip, making it look like a spoon. As it wades through lakes or lagoons, the spoonbill dips its beak beneath the surface of the water, and sweeps its head from side to side. Its sensitive beak snaps shut instantly if it touches anything that might be food.

SCIENTIFIC NAME *Platalea leucorodia*

DISTRIBUTION Southern Europe, Asia, northern and western Africa

SIZE Up to 90cm long

GREATER FLAMINGO

Flamingoes are the only birds that filter-feed – a method of eating also used by many whales (page 26). Flamingoes dip their beaks in the water and collect tiny plants and animals by pumping water through slits on their beak and tongue. There are five species of flamingo, and this is the most common. It feeds in shallow lakes, sometimes in flocks of more than one million birds.

SCIENTIFIC NAME *Phoenicopterus ruber*

DISTRIBUTION Southern Europe, Africa, southern Asia, Central America, Caribbean islands

SIZE Up to 1.45m long

SWANS, GEESE AND DUCKS

Swans, geese and ducks are also known as waterfowl because they spend their lives on or near water. They have flat, shovel-shaped beaks, and most of them get their food either from the water itself, or from underwater mud. Geese are exceptions to this rule – they feed on land, pulling up grass and other plants with their beaks. Waterfowl have webbed feet and waterproof feathers, and most nest on the ground. Their chicks can swim only a few hours after hatching. There are more than 150 species of these birds. Ducks are found all over the world, but most geese live in the northern hemisphere and breed in the Arctic.

Red beak with pale tip

Long muscular neck

BLACK SWAN

This Australian bird is the world's only all-black swan, although it does have white wingtips. It lives on large, shallow lakes and mudflats, and is highly sociable, often gathering in flocks thousands strong. Black swans nest near the water's edge or on small islands, and the parent birds are careful to nest just beyond pecking distance of their neighbours. Black swans were introduced into New Zealand in the 1860s, and are now widespread throughout the country.

SCIENTIFIC NAME *Cygnus atratus*

DISTRIBUTION Originally from Australia; introduced into New Zealand

SIZE Up to 1.4m long

Flight feathers have curled edges

White wingtips

MUTE SWAN

This elegant all-white bird originally comes from the lakes of central Asia, but it is now common on parkland lakes all over the world. It uses its long neck to reach water plants, molluscs and other bottom-dwelling animals, often tipping up on end as it feeds. Its young – called cygnets – are grey-brown when they hatch, and it takes them nearly a year to turn white. Mute swans fly well, but they need a long run-up to take off. They usually come in to land on water, using their large black feet as brakes.

SCIENTIFIC NAME *Cygnus olor*

DISTRIBUTION Originally from Europe, central Asia; semi-tame birds also in North America, Australia, New Zealand

SIZE Up to 1.55m long

SNOW GOOSE

These geese breed in the Arctic tundra of North America. They fly up from the south each spring, and their young hatch when the days are getting longer and the food supply is at its best. Even in late spring, the tundra can be very cold, and the geese line their nests with feathers to keep their eggs warm. Snow geese have two quite different colour forms; many are white all over, apart from their black wingtips, but some are blue-grey.

SCIENTIFIC NAME *Anser caerulescens*

DISTRIBUTION Breeds in North American Arctic; winters in southern USA, northern Mexico

SIZE Up to 84cm long

FAR LEFT *Black swans are nomadic birds. They are constantly on the move, searching for good places to feed.*
LEFT *Mute swans are often seen in pairs, but will gather in flocks in the winter.*
BELOW LEFT *Snow geese may fly 5,000km to breed.*
BELOW RIGHT *In parts of Europe, Canada geese are common parkland birds.*

CANADA GOOSE

This handsome goose has a brown and white body and a black head, with a white 'chinstrap' on its throat. It breeds near lakes and in wetlands throughout Canada and northern USA, and its size varies according to where it lives. The largest geese, from the American Great Plains, can be seven times heavier than those from Alaska – a record difference for the same species of bird. In the early evening, Canada geese usually return to water to roost, and they make a loud honking sound as they fly.

SCIENTIFIC NAME	*Branta canadensis*
DISTRIBUTION	Originally from North America; introduced into northern Europe, New Zealand
SIZE	Up to 1.1m long

GREYLAG GOOSE

Greylags breed near water and they often feed in pasture and grassland close to the water's edge. They have grey-brown bodies with pink legs and feet, and heavy beaks that are good for pulling up grass and water weeds. They are the ancestors of most farmyard geese, and make useful security guards because they honk loudly at strangers.

SCIENTIFIC NAME	*Anser anser*
DISTRIBUTION	Breeds from Iceland eastwards to China; winters in the British Isles, southern Europe, southern Asia
SIZE	Up to 90cm long

MIGRATION

Every year, millions of geese travel northwards to the Arctic to breed. They fly in a V-formation, and they make their long journey for one reason – food. In warm parts of the world, the days are more or less the same length all year round, and the food supply depends mainly on how much rain there is. Further north and south, the days are much longer in the summer than they are in the winter. In winter it is dark and cold, but in summer long days mean that plants can grow rapidly, producing lots of food for animals to eat. For geese and many other birds, this huge but short-lived surge of food makes it worth travelling a long way. Animal travellers are called migrants. Migratory species include whales, antelope, turtles, butterflies and fish, but birds migrate furthest – up to 32,000km a year.

ABOVE When they migrate, greylags and other geese often fly in a V-shaped formation. This saves energy because each bird is helped along by air currents produced by the one in front. The geese take turns to lead.

Horny crest helps males to attract females

LEFT The magpie goose is one of the world's strangest looking waterbirds. It is easy to tell the males from the females because they have a high, bony crown on the top of their heads.

MAGPIE GOOSE OR PIED GOOSE

The black and white magpie goose is unusual in several ways. It has much longer legs than most geese and its feet are only slightly webbed. It is also the only waterfowl species that feeds its young – all the others simply lead their chicks to food. Magpie geese live in large flocks close to rivers, and in swamps and grassland. They feed on land and in water and, although they live in open places, they are good at perching in trees.

SCIENTIFIC NAME	*Anseranas semipalmata*
DISTRIBUTION	Australia, New Guinea
SIZE	Up to 85cm long

Soft down feathers are hidden beneath outer plumage

Feathers are kept waterproof by a special oil

Male mallard in breeding plumage

ABOVE AND RIGHT *Like all ducks, mallards spend a lot of time making sure that their feathers are clean and waterproof.*

Female mallard with wings spread

MALLARD

The mallard is one of the world's most widespread ducks. It lives on almost any patch of fresh water, from the fringes of the Arctic to suburban lakes and ponds. To feed, it either 'dabbles' at the surface, or tips up on end to reach food on the bottom. Like most ducks, the males and females look quite different. During the breeding season, the males have bright green heads and curly tails. Females are brown all year round, which camouflages them when they nest.

SCIENTIFIC NAME *Anas platyrhynchos*
DISTRIBUTION Originally found throughout northern hemisphere; introduced into Australia, New Zealand
SIZE Up to 65cm long

MANDARIN

During the breeding season, the male mandarin has a bright red beak, orange 'whiskers' and two orange wing feathers that stick up like a pair of sails. Mandarins live in forested rivers and lakes in the Far East, and they nest in holes in trees. Within a day of hatching, the ducklings have to leave the nest to follow their mother to water. They cannot fly, but they are light and covered with soft down, so the jump is not as dangerous as it sounds.

SCIENTIFIC NAME *Aix galericulata*
DISTRIBUTION Originally from eastern Russia, China, Japan; introduced into the British Isles
SIZE Up to 49cm long

Female

Male

Male

Female

Male

Female

ABOVE TOP *Northern shovelers often swim in circles to stir up food.*
ABOVE CENTRE *In the winter, pintails will feed in fields of harvested corn.*
ABOVE *Tufted ducks have a distinctive backswept crest on their heads.*

NORTHERN SHOVELER

Shovelers are easy to recognize from their huge, shiny black beaks. They use them to sieve tiny plants and animals from the surface of lakes and ponds. Unlike other freshwater ducks, they rarely tip up on end. There are four other species of shoveler – one in South America, one in South Africa and another in Australia. The northern shoveler is much more widespread than the other three, and migrates as far as 6,000km in order to breed.

SCIENTIFIC NAME *Anas clypeata*
DISTRIBUTION Breeds in northern North America, Europe, Asia; winters on Atlantic and Pacific coasts of USA, in Central America, southern Europe, Africa, southern Asia, Japan
SIZE Up to 51cm long

NORTHERN PINTAIL

In its breeding plumage, the male pintail is one of the most elegant freshwater ducks, with a chocolate-brown head, grey and white body and long, pointed tail. Pintails are sociable birds. They breed near rivers and on marshy ground, and they feed by dabbling on the water's surface, and by up-ending. Most ducks are good at flying, and the pintail is no exception. It can take off almost vertically when alarmed, and speeds through the air on its powerful, fast-beating wings.

SCIENTIFIC NAME *Anas acuta*
DISTRIBUTION Breeds in northern North America, Europe, Asia; winters in southern USA, Central America, southern Europe, Africa, southern Asia, Japan
SIZE Up to 58cm long

TUFTED DUCK

This black and white duck lives on lakes but, instead of feeding from the surface of the water, it dives for food. It disappears with a splash, and then bobs back to the surface with water plants and small animals, such as molluscs and insects, from the lakebed. Adult tufted ducks usually feed in water up to 2m deep, and the ducklings can dive for food within a few hours of leaving the nest. At night, tufted ducks often doze in groups, bobbing on the surface of the water.

SCIENTIFIC NAME *Aythya fuligula*
DISTRIBUTION Breeds in northern Europe, northern Asia; winters in southern and western Europe, Africa, southern Asia
SIZE Up to 47cm long

RED-BREASTED MERGANSER

Mergansers are saw-billed ducks – so-called because their beaks have serrated edges for gripping slippery fish. They live on fresh water and on the coast, and they dive after their prey, bringing it to the surface to eat. Compared to other ducks, they have long, slender bodies, and also untidy, backswept crests. Red-breasted mergansers lay up to 12 eggs in a nest hidden among plants. The female covers her eggs with feathers when she leaves the nest to feed.

SCIENTIFIC NAME *Mergus serrator*

DISTRIBUTION Breeds in northern North America, Europe, Asia; winters on coasts in North America, southern Europe, Far East

SIZE Up to 58 cm long

COMMON EIDER

Eiders live on rocky coasts, where they feed on crabs and other small animals. They have stocky bodies, powerful sloping beaks and some of the warmest plumage in the world. Eiders need good insulation because they breed further north than any other birds. They nest on the ground, and keep their eggs warm by lining their nests with down.

Before synthetic fibres were invented, eider down was harvested and used as stuffing for pillows and bedding. Small amounts are still collected today.

SCIENTIFIC NAME *Somateria mollissima*

DISTRIBUTION Breeds on northern coasts, including edges of Arctic Sea; winters on coasts of North America, Iceland, northern Europe

SIZE Up to 71cm long

FALKLAND ISLANDS STEAMER DUCK

There are four species of steamer duck and they all live on the cold coasts around the tip of South America. Like most steamer ducks, the Falkland Islands steamer duck has difficulty getting into the air. Instead of flying, it usually escapes danger by paddling and splashing its way to safety, which is how it gets its name. This duck dives in beds of seaweed to find its food of small animals, such as molluscs, and water plants.

SCIENTIFIC NAME *Tachyeres brachypterus*

DISTRIBUTION Falkland Islands

SIZE Up to 74cm long

Female

Male

Female

Male

TOP *Red-breasted mergansers are very good at catching fish, which makes them unpopular with anglers.*

ABOVE *The common eider duck has a distinctive profile, with a flat forehead that merges with its beak.*

BELOW *The Falkland Islands steamer duck nests in tussock grass on coasts and lagoons close to the shore. It is very territorial and chases away any other ducks that come too close.*

Close-fitting feathers are fully waterproof

Wings are small compared to body

BIRDS OF PREY

Birds of prey hunt other animals, particularly those that it takes speed and strength to overpower. They catch their prey with their feet, which are armed with needle-sharp claws called talons. Once they have made a kill, they use their hooked beaks to tear their food into pieces small enough to swallow. Unlike owls (page 200), which hunt after dark, birds of prey are active during the day. Most swoop down to snatch their victims on the ground, although some can catch animals in mid-air. There are about 280 species of birds of prey and they are found worldwide. They include eagles, hawks, kites and falcons, and also vultures – birds that feed on dead remains.

Powerful neck muscles aid in tearing up prey

Sharp talons for gripping and piercing

Good forward vision helps with judging distances

Sharply hooked beak tip

ABOVE AND RIGHT
Like all birds of prey, the golden eagle has superb eyesight. Its hooked beak looks dangerous, but comes into play only once it has made a kill. Its real weapons are its talons.

GOLDEN EAGLE

An inhabitant of wild mountainous country, the golden eagle preys on rabbits, marmots and other mammals, as well as on other birds. It often makes a fast low-level attack, catching its prey from behind. Golden eagles nest on crags or in trees, making a large platform, or eyrie, out of sticks. They lay two eggs a year, and often use the nest for many years in succession, adding further nesting material each time they breed. People have always admired the golden eagle's power, but its reputation for attacking lambs and game birds has meant that it has been persecuted. As a result, and because its eggs are sometimes stolen from nests by collectors, this magnificent bird of prey is now quite rare.

SCIENTIFIC NAME	*Aquila chrysaetos*
DISTRIBUTION	Europe, northern Asia, Middle East, North America
SIZE	Up to 1m long

Head feathers are golden in colour and body plumage is brown

MARTIAL EAGLE

This powerful bird is Africa's largest eagle. It attacks a wide range of animals, including hyraxes (page 283) and snakes, usually by diving on them from high in the air. Like many birds of prey, male and female martial eagles are different in size, the females being larger than their mates. Martial eagles nest high up in trees, and often use the same nest for many years.

SCIENTIFIC NAME	*Polemaetus bellicosus*
DISTRIBUTION	Africa south of the Sahara Desert
SIZE	Up to 97cm long

WEDGE-TAILED EAGLE

The wedge-tailed eagle lives in a wide range of habitats, from open plains to dense forest. With a wingspan of more than 2.5m, it can catch animals as large as young kangaroos, and it launches its attack either from the air or from a perch high up in a tree. In Australia, before rabbits were introduced, wedge-tailed eagles ate mostly marsupials, though they now eat rabbits as well. They also gather around dead sheep and other animal remains.

SCIENTIFIC NAME	*Aquila audax*
DISTRIBUTION	Australia, Tasmania, New Guinea
SIZE	Up to 1.04m long

AMERICAN HARPY EAGLE

Harpy eagles live in tropical forests. They have short, broad wings, which make them slow but highly manoeuverable. Harpy eagles fly over the forest canopy, snatching prey in the treetops. They eat monkeys and lizards, but specialize in attacking sloths. Female harpy eagles, which are larger than the males, can lift animals weighing 5.5kg – roughly equal to their own body weight. Deforestation has had a severe effect on these birds and, particularly in Central America, they are now extremely rare.

SCIENTIFIC NAME	*Harpia harpyja*
DISTRIBUTION	Central America, tropical South America
SIZE	Up to 1.10m long

PHILIPPINE EAGLE OR MONKEY-EATING EAGLE

The Philippine eagle is one of the world's most endangered birds of prey, with perhaps as few as 150 birds left in the wild. Like the American harpy eagle, it lives in dense forest, and has been

RIGHT *Like other large birds of prey, the Philippine eagle needs access to large areas of undisturbed forest to survive. If deforestation continues, the bird's future looks bleak.*

Strong beak can tear large animals apart

BELOW *With its talons at the ready, an American harpy eagle swoops through the trees to catch a monkey. Harpy eagles build their nests at the top of rainforest trees, so their chicks start life up to 70m above the ground.*

brought to the edge of extinction by the rapid clearance of its forest home. As well as monkeys, the Philippine eagle attacks squirrels, pigs and flying lemurs, or colugos. It searches for food either by flying above the trees, or by perching beneath the treetops, where it silently watches, waiting for any animals to come within reach.

SCIENTIFIC NAME	*Pithecophaga jefferyi*
DISTRIBUTION	Philippines
SIZE	Up to 1.02m long

BALD EAGLE

The bald eagle is the national bird of the USA, and one of the world's largest birds of prey. It lives near rivers, lakes and coasts, and feeds mainly on fish, though it also eats other birds. There were once about 50,000 bald eagles in North America but, by the 1970s, the numbers had dropped to 2,000 due to poisoning from the pesticide DDT. This has now been banned and the population is making a gradual recovery.

SCIENTIFIC NAME	*Haliaeetus leucocephalus*
DISTRIBUTION	North America
SIZE	Up to 1.10m long

ABOVE *The bald eagle takes five years to develop its black and white adult plumage. It does not always hunt live prey – dead or dying animals, especially salmon, make up a large part of its diet.*

AFRICAN FISH EAGLE

With its white head and chest, and loud yelping call, this eagle is a distinctive bird of prey. It perches on waterside trees, watching the water for signs of food. If it sees a fish, it glides down from its vantage-point, and snatches the prey up with one foot before returning to its perch to eat.

SCIENTIFIC NAME	*Haliaeetus vocifer*
DISTRIBUTION	Africa south of the Sahara Desert
SIZE	Up to 75cm long

Flight feathers splay out like fingers

Powerful feathered legs

ABOVE *With its wings spread wide, this black kite shows the long, outer flight feathers that help it to soar.*

BELOW *The red-tailed hawk is closely related to the Eurasian buzzard, and has the same powerful build.*

Streamlined head helps the hawk to glide smoothly

Only the male has grey wing feathers

ABOVE *Northern harriers have slender bodies and legs. Unlike most birds of prey, harriers glide with their wings held up in a V-shape.*

BLACK KITE

An efficient hunter and scavenger, the black kite is one of the world's most widespread birds of prey. It is also the one that is least scared of people. In Asia, it often lives in towns and cities, where it swoops down to snatch up scraps of food, even where there is busy traffic. The black kite also follows bush fires, looking for animals flushed out by the smoke and flames. Like other kites, it has a forked tail, which it uses like a rudder to help it dodge any obstacles in its path.

SCIENTIFIC NAME *Milvus migrans*

DISTRIBUTION Central and southern Europe, Africa, Asia, Australia

SIZE Up to 60cm long

RED-TAILED HAWK

This heavily-built bird of prey is the most common hawk in North America. It is also one of the most variable, with more than 12 local varieties, each one different in size and colour. Red-tailed hawks live in woods, open plains and deserts, and they feed mainly on rodents. In Canada, red-tailed hawks are only summer visitors, but in most of the USA they stay all year round.

SCIENTIFIC NAME *Buteo jamaicensis*

DISTRIBUTION North America, Central America, Caribbean islands

SIZE Up to 63cm long

EURASIAN BUZZARD

Over large parts of Europe and Asia, the buzzard can often be seen soaring high in the air. Even when it is far away, its high-pitched mewing cry is easy to hear. It feeds on a wide range of live animals, from rabbits to earthworms, and will also eat dead remains. At the start of the breeding season, in early spring, buzzards perform spectacular courtship displays. The male and female pass sticks to each other in mid-air, and sometimes lock their feet together and tumble towards the ground. In North America, the turkey vulture (page 178) is sometimes known as a buzzard, but it is not a close relative of the Eurasian buzzard.

SCIENTIFIC NAME *Buteo buteo*

DISTRIBUTION Europe, Asia, parts of Africa

SIZE Up to 54cm long

SNAIL KITE OR EVERGLADES KITE

This remarkable bird feeds almost exclusively on a single kind of freshwater snail. It has an unusually long and slender beak, which is ideal for prising the snails from their shells. It finds its food by flapping along at a low level over marshes and reedbeds. When it locates a snail, it picks it up with one foot, and carries it to a perch to feed.

SCIENTIFIC NAME *Rostrhamnus sociabilis*

DISTRIBUTION Florida (USA), Caribbean islands, Central America, tropical South America

SIZE Up to 43cm long

HEN HARRIER OR NORTHERN HARRIER

Harriers hunt by flying low over the ground, flapping and gliding backwards and forwards across the same stretch of country. If they spot food – for example, a mouse or a young bird – they drop down to the ground and snatch it up with their feet. Unusually for most birds of prey, harriers nest on the ground, and both parents are involved in feeding the nestlings until they are old enough to fly. Female hen harriers are brown, but the slightly smaller males are light grey with black wingtips.

SCIENTIFIC NAME *Circus cyaneus*

DISTRIBUTION North America, South America, Europe, northern Asia; migratory in north of range

SIZE Up to 58cm long

A peregrine falcon dives with its wings folded by its sides

Small beak with narrow hook

Prey is held fast in strong talons

Narrow wingtips

PEREGRINE FALCON

The peregrine is the world's fastest bird. It attacks other birds by diving on them in mid-air, and can reach speeds of more than 160km/h as it plummets towards its prey. It can knock a pigeon from the air with a single slash of its talons, following its victim to the ground. Like other falcons, the peregrine has a slender body, a long narrow tail and pointed wings. It usually breeds on mountains or cliffs, but some live in cities, nesting on window ledges.

SCIENTIFIC NAME *Falco peregrinus*

DISTRIBUTION Worldwide, except Greenland, Central America, South America

SIZE Up to 48cm long

GYRFALCON

There are about 50 species of falcon, and this Arctic species is the largest of them all. Females can weigh more than 2kg – twice as much as many of the males. Gyrfalcons live in and near the Arctic, where they feed on ptarmigans, ducks and other birds. They also prey on hares and rodents, speeding close to the ground to make a kill. Some gyrfalcons have grey plumage, but others are largely white – a useful feature in a snow-covered landscape.

SCIENTIFIC NAME *Falco rusticolus*

DISTRIBUTION Breeds north of the Arctic Circle; winters further south

SIZE Up to 64cm long

COMMON KESTREL

Kestrels are small falcons that eat rodents and insects. They have superb eyesight, and hover over open ground watching for food, with their tails splayed out and their wings beating rapidly. Kestrels are the largest birds that can hover for long periods. Unlike hummingbirds (pages 204-205), they need a gentle headwind to keep them in the air. Common kestrels may take over other birds' nests. They lay up to five eggs a year in one clutch and the nestlings can fly a month after hatching.

SCIENTIFIC NAME *Falco tinnunculus*

DISTRIBUTION Europe, Asia, Africa; migratory in north of range

SIZE Up to 35cm long

ABOVE *In the evening, turkey vultures gather together to roost in trees and on cliff ledges. This protects them from surprise attacks and also gives them a head start in the morning, when they take off to search for food.*

TURKEY VULTURE

Vultures are birds of prey that feed on dead remains instead of catching live animals. They have extremely good eyesight, and they watch for food from the air, soaring high in the sky. The turkey vulture, often mistakenly called a buzzard, is the most widespread vulture in the Americas. It lives in a variety of habitats, and can often be seen over roads, where it watches for animals that have been hit by cars. Like other vultures, it has a bald head – an adaptation that helps it to stay clean when it feeds. Adult turkey vultures have bright red heads, which contrast with their dark brown plumage.

SCIENTIFIC NAME *Cathartes aura*

DISTRIBUTION North America, Central America, South America; from Canada to Tierra del Fuego

SIZE Up to 80cm long

Bald head avoids feathers becoming matted with blood

CENTRE *Andean condors are graceful in the air, but clumsy on land. The males have a fleshy ridge on their foreheads – this probably helps to attract females.*
ABOVE *Adult California condors are black with orange-red head feathers.*

ANDEAN CONDOR

The Andean condor is the largest vulture in the world. Its wings can measure up to 3.2m from tip to tip, a size equalled by only one other land bird, the marabou stork (page 169). Its head and neck are bald, but it has a white feathery 'collar', and black and white wings. Condors soar over high mountains, and nest and roost on inaccessible ledges. They lay between one and three eggs a year, and their young take up to six months to leave the nest.

SCIENTIFIC NAME *Vultur gryphus*

DISTRIBUTION South America

SIZE Up to 1.32m long

CALIFORNIA CONDOR

Andean condors are still quite common, but their largest living relative, the California condor, is in danger of extinction. This giant vulture was once found throughout the mountains of central and southern California, but today only about 150 birds are left, and most of them are in captivity. A programme is underway to breed captive condors and release their young into the wild.

SCIENTIFIC NAME *Gymnogyps californianus*

DISTRIBUTION California (USA)

SIZE Up to 1.2m long

RÜPPELL'S GRIFFON

This vulture is one of more than six species that soars over the African plains. It takes off shortly after sunrise, when the air has started to warm up, and finds its food partly by watching the ground below, and partly by watching other vultures. If one vulture spots a carcase and drops down to feed, others quickly arrive from many kilometres around. Rüppell's griffons are stronger than most other African vultures, and they push aside the smaller species to feed.

SCIENTIFIC NAME *Gyps ruepellii*

DISTRIBUTION Tropical Africa

SIZE Up to 94cm long

LAMMERGEIER

The lammergeier is unlike other vultures in looks and in the way it feeds. It has a feathered head and neck, and a 'moustache' of bristles around its beak. It specializes in eating the tough parts of carcases, such as the skin and bone. Lammergeiers live in mountains, and drop bones from high up in the air. The bones smash when they

Lammergeier perched on a rock land, allowing the birds to feed on the marrow inside.

SCIENTIFIC NAME *Gypaetus barbatus*

DISTRIBUTION Southern Europe, Africa, central Asia

SIZE Up to 1.15m long

EGYPTIAN VULTURE

This small, off-white vulture is one of the few animals that uses tools to get at its food. It normally eats insects and dead remains but, if it finds an ostrich egg, it picks up a stone and throws it at the egg until it breaks. Egyptian vultures often gather on rubbish tips near towns.

SCIENTIFIC NAME *Neophron percnopterus*

DISTRIBUTION Southern Europe, Africa, Middle East, southern Asia

SIZE Up to 70cm long

RIGHT *A crested caracara guards its nest. Caracaras build their nests in trees or on rocky ledges, and they lay either two or three eggs at a time. They often feed alongside vultures, harassing them and forcing them to give up their food.*

CRESTED CARACARA

Caracaras feed mainly on dead animals, but they are not true vultures. Their closest relatives are the falcons (page 177). Like falcons, they usually fly by flapping their wings instead of by soaring, but their long legs make them good at walking on the ground. The crested caracara lives on the edge of forests and in open country, and it often feeds on animals that have been killed on roads.

SCIENTIFIC NAME *Polyborus plancus*

DISTRIBUTION North America, Central America, South America; from southern USA to Tierra del Fuego

SIZE Up to 53cm long

Relatively short hook at tip of beak

SECRETARY BIRD

The secretary bird is a bird of prey, but it is so unusual that biologists classify it in a family all of its own. It has a hooked beak, a red face and a feathery crest, but its most distinguishing features are its two extremely long legs that end in relatively small feet. The secretary bird lives on the ground, and often stamps its prey to death. It eats frogs, lizards and small rodents, but snakes are its favourite food. When it attacks a snake, it uses its wings as shields, making it difficult for the snake to strike. Secretary birds fly well and nest in the tops of trees.

SCIENTIFIC NAME *Sagittarius serpentarius*

DISTRIBUTION Africa south of the Sahara Desert

SIZE Up to 1.5m long

Crest of feathers is raised when the bird is excited or trying to attract a mate

ABOVE AND RIGHT *The secretary bird gets its name from the long feathers on its head. These look like the old-fashioned quill pens that secretaries used to tuck behind their ears. Unlike other birds of prey, the secretary bird can run fast, but its feet are too small for picking up prey.*

GAMEBIRDS

Gamebirds got their name because many of them were hunted for food. Some are still hunted today, but several species are raised on farms. Gamebirds have plump bodies and short legs. Most of them feed on the ground. They eat seeds, insects and grubs, often using their feet to scratch for food. They can fly short distances, but many run if they are threatened. Most gamebirds are ground-nesters and lay large numbers of eggs. There are more than 230 species, found in various inland habitats from tropical forests to Arctic tundra.

Many gamebirds have bright coloured flesh on their heads, which is used in courtship displays

BELOW *The mallee fowl's shape is typical of most gamebirds. Its plump body is supported by sturdy legs.*

Long fleshy wattles hang down over the beak

Fleshy neck wattles

MALLEE FOWL

This Australian gamebird and its relatives do not incubate their eggs. Instead of sitting on them to keep them warm, they bury them in gigantic nest-mounds made of sand and fallen leaves. As the leaves begin to rot, the mounds start to warm up, allowing the eggs to develop. Every day, the male checks his mound's temperature by testing it with his beak. By opening the mound or building it up, he keeps the eggs at a steady 33°C. Mallee fowl chicks take about seven weeks to hatch. The young chicks dig their way to the surface of the mound, and are left to fend for themselves.

SCIENTIFIC NAME	*Leipoa ocellata*
DISTRIBUTION	Southern and western Australia
SIZE	Up to 61cm long

GREAT CURRASOW

Unlike other gamebirds, currasows nest in trees, and also fly up into the branches if they are disturbed. They lay fewer eggs than most gamebirds – usually between two and four – but their young develop quickly, and can fly within a few days of hatching. The great currasow is one of the most spectacular species, with long legs and a feathery crest. The males are black, and the females are rusty red with black and white heads.

SCIENTIFIC NAME	*Crax rubra*
DISTRIBUTION	Central America, South America; from Mexico to Colombia
SIZE	Up to 1m long

WILD TURKEY

Wild turkeys are woodland birds that feed on acorns, other seeds and insects. Both the males and females have bare heads and copper-coloured plumage, but the males also have fleshy

LEFT AND CENTRE *Male wild turkeys display to females by fluffing out their feathers and fanning their wings and tails. Their calls can be heard nearly 2km away.*

flaps called wattles hanging from their heads and necks, and a tuft of feathers dangling from their chests. Wild turkeys were first domesticated in Mexico more than 1,000 years ago but, by the early 1900s, they had disappeared from large parts of the USA. In recent years, turkeys have been reintroduced into places where they once lived, and they have managed to stage a successful comeback.

SCIENTIFIC NAME	*Meleagris gallopavo*
DISTRIBUTION	USA, Mexico
SIZE	Up to 1.17m long

GREATER PRAIRIE CHICKEN

Many gamebirds carry out impressive courtship displays, but the display of the prairie chicken is one of the most remarkable of all. The males have an inflatable yellow sac on either side of their necks, and they pump these full of air to attract potential mates. At the same time, they make a loud booming sound as they dance up and down. These displays take place at courtship grounds called leks, which are often used for many years. Unfortunately for prairie chickens, much of their habitat has been turned into farmland, and they are becoming increasingly rare.

SCIENTIFIC NAME	*Tympanuchus cupido*
DISTRIBUTION	Central USA
SIZE	Up to 43cm long

GREY PARTRIDGE

Partridges are small gamebirds that often feed in fields. They usually live in flocks, scuttling away at the first sign of danger, or speeding low over the ground on whirring wings. The grey partridge is one of the most widespread European species. Its body is actually brown, but it gets its name from its grey legs. Grey partridges can lay more than 20 eggs each time they breed, making them among the most prolific egg-laying birds in the world. However, many of their chicks are eaten by predators.

SCIENTIFIC NAME	*Perdix perdix*
DISTRIBUTION	Western and central Europe
SIZE	Up to 30cm long

HIMALAYAN SNOWCOCK

The snowcock looks rather like a giant partridge, and it is one of the partridge's closest relatives. It can weigh as much as 3kg, but its white and grey plumage helps to hide it against snow and rocks. Snowcocks live in flocks of up to 20 birds. In their bleak mountain habitat, where food is

ABOVE AND LEFT *Like all gamebirds, grey partridges feed on the ground. They keep a constant lookout for predators.*

Female   Male

Male   Female

ABOVE *The top pair of willow grouse are in their summer plumage. The other birds are in their winter whites. The red grouse – a British form – stays brown all year round.*

always scarce, Himalayan snowcocks are always on the move, searching for food. They nest on the ground under overhangs and in caves.

SCIENTIFIC NAME	*Tetraogallus himalayensis*
DISTRIBUTION	Himalayan Mountains (southern Asia)
SIZE	Up to 56cm long

WILLOW GROUSE OR RED GROUSE

Willow grouse are among the world's hardiest birds. They live in the Arctic tundra, where they eat leaves, twigs and seeds. In winter, they dig into snow-banks to keep out of the freezing wind. To help them to survive, their feet are covered with warm feathers, and the birds change colour to stay camouflaged all year. In the summer, they are mottled brown, but their winter plumage is white, except for a black-tipped tail.

SCIENTIFIC NAME	*Lagopus lagopus*
DISTRIBUTION	Throughout the far north, except Greenland
SIZE	Up to 38cm long

BELOW *The California quail spends the day on the ground, but it roosts in trees and shrubs. Many gamebirds behave in this way as a protection against predators hunting after dark. The bird below is a male; the female does not have a black throat and her crest is smaller.*

CALIFORNIA QUAIL

With its dainty forward-pointing crest, the California quail is one of the most elegant small gamebirds in North America. Its plumage is neat and tidy, with speckles and stripes on its face, neck and underside. The California quail lives mainly on open ground and in woodlands, but it sometimes ventures into the edges of towns. It feeds in small groups during the breeding season but, in the winter, birds gather together, forming flocks of up to 300 strong. These winter flocks have a better chance of avoiding attack than lone birds because, while some birds are feeding, others are always on the lookout for danger.

SCIENTIFIC NAME	*Callipepla californica*
DISTRIBUTION	Western North America; from British Columbia to Baja California
SIZE	Up to 25cm long

COMMON QUAIL

The tiny, stubby-tailed common quail is one of the few gamebirds that migrates to breed. It spends the winter as far south as central Africa, but breeds thousands of kilometres away in Europe and parts of western Asia. Common quails feed in grassy places and cornfields. They are so small that they are difficult to spot, but their soft, three-note calls sometimes give them away. Despite being such experienced travellers, common quails usually run from danger instead of flying away. They nest in hollows in the ground, and lay up to 12 camouflaged eggs.

SCIENTIFIC NAME	*Coturnix coturnix*
DISTRIBUTION	Europe, Africa, Middle East, central Asia, India
SIZE	Up to 18cm long

Main plumage colour can vary from grey to brown

Teardrop-shaped crest

Male

Female

A pair of common quails, camouflaged in dead grass

One leg tucked up under plumage

Female

Male

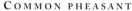

LEFT *The male common pheasant has a more colourful head and a much longer tail than the female.*

COMMON PHEASANT

Pheasants are gamebirds with long trailing tails. Female common pheasants are brown all over, but males have coppery bodies, an iridescent greenish-purple neck and a patch of bright red skin around their eyes. Common pheasants originally lived in Asia, but they have been introduced into many other parts of the world for sport and for food. In their natural home, they live in forests and open grasslands, but they adapt well to life in wooded farmland and fields.

SCIENTIFIC NAME	*Phasianus colchicus*
DISTRIBUTION	Originally from central and Southeast Asia; introduced into North America, Europe, Australia, New Zealand
SIZE	Up to 83cm long

Peacock

Peahen

bird, called a peahen, is mainly brown and white with a short tail. The male bird, called a peacock, has a brilliant blue body, and his tail has up to 150 extra-long feathers, each tipped with an iridescent 'eye'. When a peacock courts a peahen, he opens these feathers to make a fan, and shakes them so that they rustle. The male also has a distinctive piercing call. Peacocks are kept in parks and gardens worldwide.

SCIENTIFIC NAME *Pavo cristatus*

DISTRIBUTION Originally from India, Sri Lanka; semi-captive birds introduced into many parts of the world

SIZE Up to 2.15m long

RED JUNGLEFOWL

The red junglefowl is the ancestor of domestic fowl, or cockerels and chickens, which are raised all over the world. It lives on the edges of forests, and finds seeds and insects by scratching up the ground with its feet. Male junglefowl look similar to farmyard cockerels, and they make the same noisy crowing sound. The hens are slimmer than domesticated chickens, and they are always brown. Domesticated junglefowl now outnumber wild ones many times over.

SCIENTIFIC NAME *Gallus gallus*

DISTRIBUTION Northern India, Southeast Asia

SIZE Up to 55cm long

HELMETED GUINEAFOWL

Guineafowl live in plains and forests, where they eat seeds, edible roots and insects. They have dark blue bodies with light blue spots, short tails and powerful legs. All species of guineafowl have bare, blue heads, and the helmeted guineafowl also has a hard shield, or casque, on the top of its head. Originally from Africa, the helmeted guineafowl is bred for food all over the world. Even in captivity, it reacts to danger with a piercing alarm call that sounds like the screeching of broken machinery.

SCIENTIFIC NAME *Numidia meleagris*

DISTRIBUTION Tropical Africa

SIZE Up to 58cm long

GREAT ARGUS PHEASANT

This rainforest pheasant is one of the most spectacular gamebirds in Southeast Asia. The male and female both have blue heads and grey-brown bodies, but the male also has giant flight feathers along the rear edges of his wings. These are decorated with eye-spots, and the male opens them out during his courtship display to form a gigantic fan. As with many other spectacular birds, the male puts all his efforts into attracting females, though he plays no part in building a nest or raising young.

SCIENTIFIC NAME *Argusianus argus*

DISTRIBUTION Thailand, Malaysia, Indonesia

SIZE Up to 1.85m long

PEAFOWL OR PEACOCK

Male gamebirds are usually more impressive than their mates but, with the peafowl, these differences reach amazing extremes. The female

ABOVE *A peacock fans out his tail feathers in a spectacular display.*

Female Lady Amherst's pheasant

Male Lady Amherst's pheasant

Female golden pheasant

Male golden pheasant

ABOVE *Lady Amherst's pheasants* (Chrysolophus amherstiae) *come from Southeast Asia. Golden pheasants* (Chrysolophus pictus) *live in China.*

CRANES AND THEIR RELATIVES

Cranes and their relatives include some birds that stand as high as an adult human, as well as others that could easily nestle in the palm of a hand. Despite their outward differences, they have similar internal features, such as the shape of their skeletons, that show that they are closely related. Many of these birds live near water or on marshy ground, and most of them have long necks and legs. When they fly, they hold their necks out straight, and their legs usually trail behind them. Most of these birds nest on the ground. There are about 200 species, and they include some of the most endangered birds in the world.

COMMON CRANE

Cranes are birds of open places. They stride across the ground on their long legs, snapping up seeds and insects with their sharply pointed beaks. They live in flocks, and many of them, including the common crane, migrate long distances to breed. Like other cranes, the common crane pairs up for life, and has a spectacular courtship display. The males and females strut about and bow, and leap high into the air. Cranes have a very long windpipe, or trachea, and they make loud trumpeting sounds that can be heard 2km away. Common cranes were once widespread, but their numbers have declined because they need to live in an undisturbed habitat to survive.

SCIENTIFIC NAME *Grus grus*
DISTRIBUTION Breeds in Europe, Asia; winters in southern Europe, Asia, northern Africa
SIZE Up to 1.12m long

Common crane standing on one leg

WHOOPING CRANE

This stately white bird is the rarest crane in North America, and also the largest, with a wingspan of about 2.1m. At one time it lived in marshes across the western side of the continent, but today only about 200 birds are left. Most of them breed in the Wood Buffalo National Park in Canada, though they spend the winter more than 4,000km away, on the coast of the Gulf of Mexico. The whooping crane gets its name from its loud call, which sounds like a high-pitched trumpeting.

SCIENTIFIC NAME
Grus americana
DISTRIBUTION
Canada, USA
SIZE Up to 1.32m long

RIGHT *The whooping crane will sometimes wade into water, but it finds most of its food on land.*

GREAT BUSTARD

Bustards are long-legged, ground-dwelling birds that live in open, grassy places. Most of them are found in Africa, but the great bustard comes from the plains of Europe and Asia. It weighs up to 18kg, making it one of the heaviest flying birds in the world. Male and female great bustards look similar, with grey heads and brown and white bodies, and the males put on a spectacular display during the breeding season, puffing out their chests and turning their tails over their backs. Great bustards have been hunted for centuries, and are now much rarer than they once were.

SCIENTIFIC NAME *Otis tarda*
DISTRIBUTION Spain, central Europe, central and eastern Asia
SIZE Up to 1m long

COMMON COOT

Coots are small, solidly built freshwater birds with short beaks and jet-black plumage. They spend most of their time on the water, picking food from the surface or diving to the bottom. Although their feet are not webbed, their toes are edged with flexible flaps that push against the water when they swim. Although small, these birds are noisy and aggressive. They often chase each other across the water during the breeding season, and sometimes eat the young of other waterbirds. Coots build their nests close to the water's edge, laying up to ten camouflaged eggs at a time. A very similar species lives in North America.

Flexible flaps along sides of toes

SCIENTIFIC NAME *Fulica atra*
DISTRIBUTION Originally from Europe, Asia, Australia; introduced into New Zealand
SIZE Up to 43cm long

TOP *If it is in danger, a moorhen can sink like a submarine, until only its beak is above the surface.*
ABOVE *The water rail 'freezes' to avoid being seen if it is caught out in the open.*
LEFT *Moorhen chicks leave the nest when they are just two or three days old. At this age they are already good swimmers.*

Speckled pattern camouflages eggs

Greyish-black plumage

ABOVE *Unlike ducks, male and female coots look exactly the same. The females usually raise one family a year, but they often lay eggs in their neighbours' nests as well as in their own.*

COMMON MOORHEN

The moorhen looks similar to the coot, but it is a smaller, more timid bird, and is also more secretive. It swims well, but it finds a lot of its food on land, in damp mud and grassy fields. At the first sign of danger, it runs for cover, hiding away among waterside plants. During the breeding season, moorhens and coots are easy to tell apart, because moorhens have red beaks.

SCIENTIFIC NAME *Gallinula chloropus*
DISTRIBUTION Worldwide, except Australia, New Zealand, the far north
SIZE Up to 33cm long

TAKAHE

The takahe is a large flightless relative of the moorhen. It has a dark blue body, red legs and a powerful, bright red beak. It uses its beak to eat tussock grass, holding the stems down with one foot while it feeds. Takahes are found only in New Zealand. At one time, they were thought to have been driven into extinction by introduced

mammals such as cats, but in 1948, a small group was discovered in the Murchison Mountains of South Island. These birds are now protected, and the species looks likely to survive.

SCIENTIFIC NAME *Porpyrio mantelli*
DISTRIBUTION South Island of New Zealand
SIZE Up to 63cm long

WATER RAIL

Rails are narrow-bodied birds that live among waterside plants. Their shape is ideal for slipping through dense vegetation, but they are cautious about coming into the open. Although they are usually hidden away, they reveal themselves with their loud and unearthly calls. The water rail's call sounds like a squealing and grunting pig – an amazingly loud sound for a small bird.

SCIENTIFIC NAME *Rallus aquaticus*
DISTRIBUTION Europe, central Asia, Far East, northern Africa
SIZE Up to 28cm long

SHOREBIRDS

Shorebirds, also known as waders, live on coasts, lakes, marshes and meadows all over the world. Most of them are small or medium-sized birds with slender legs and long, sensitive beaks. They often probe wet

sand, mud or grass, finding worms, molluscs and other small animals to eat mainly by touch. Shorebirds lay their eggs on the ground and are careful parents, sometimes dive-bombing animals that come too close. There are more than 200 species of these birds worldwide. Many breed in the far north, migrating in flocks tens of thousands strong.

ABOVE *Jacanas often make their nests on floating water plants. The male looks after the nest and the young.*

Winter

Summer

CENTRE *Even when they are resting, oystercatchers are always on the lookout for danger.*
ABOVE *In summer, the male black-winged stilt has a black head.*

COMB-CRESTED JACANA

Jacanas live on plant-covered lakes and ponds. Although they can swim if they have to, they usually trot and flutter across the surface, using lilypads and leaves as floating stepping-stones. Jacanas can do this because they have immensely long toes that help to spread out their weight. The comb-crested jacana has a brown and white body and a fleshy crest on its head. Like other jacanas, it has a sharp spur on the front edge of each wing, and it uses these when it fights.

SCIENTIFIC NAME *Irediparra gallinacea*

DISTRIBUTION Philippines, Indonesia, New Guinea, Australia

SIZE Up to 26cm long

EURASIAN OYSTERCATCHER

Oystercatchers are large, noisy birds that live on rocky coasts and beaches, or sometimes near water inland. There are 11 species, and most of them are either black, or brown and white, with long orange or red beaks. Eurasian oystercatchers make use of their their beaks in two ways. Some birds use them to hammer open the tough shells of mussels and cockles, but others operate them like pincers to pull up worms out of the sand. Oystercatchers nest on shingle beaches, and lay up to four camouflaged eggs each year.

SCIENTIFIC NAME *Haematopus ostralegus*

DISTRIBUTION Breeds in Europe, central Asia, Far East; winters in western and southern Europe, parts of Africa, Middle East, India

SIZE Up to 43cm long

BLACK-WINGED STILT

Compared with the rest of its body, the black-winged stilt has the longest legs of any bird. They are bright pink, and they trail far beyond its tail when it takes to the air. Stilts live on insect larvae and other small animals, and they use their long legs to wade out into lakes and lagoons, where they feed on the surface of the water. They build their nests on open mud, and when they sit down to incubate their eggs, their legs stick out behind them like a pair of back-to-front knees.

SCIENTIFIC NAME *Himantopus himantopus*

DISTRIBUTION Breeds in North America, Europe, central Asia; winters throughout most of the southern hemisphere

SIZE Up to 38cm long

PIED AVOCET

Avocets are the only shorebirds with sharply upturned beaks. Instead of probing for their food, they stride through shallow water, sweeping the tips of their beaks from side to side just beneath the surface. If an avocet touches anything it can eat, it grabs it using its beak like a pair of tweezers, and the animal is quickly swallowed. Avocets live on lagoons and brackish lakes, and they nest on muddy islands. There are four different kinds of avocet and the pied avocet is the most widespread species. During the northern winter, tens of thousands gather on some lakes in East Africa.

SCIENTIFIC NAME *Recurvirostra avosetta*

DISTRIBUTION Breeds in Europe, central Asia, parts of Africa; winters mainly in Africa, Persian Gulf

SIZE Up to 45cm long

LEFT *Like many other shorebirds, the pied avocet can find food simply by feeling with its beak. This highly developed sense of touch allows it to feed in muddy water.*

Beak has
thickened
tip

Double band
around breast

RIGHT *A kildeer stands over
its nest. If a predator comes
too close, the parent bird will
lure it away by pretending
to have a broken wing.
This trick is used by
many shorebirds.*
BELOW *Northern lapwings
are not as common as they
once were because their
habitat is often drained
and ploughed up.*

KILLDEER
This brightly marked shorebird gets its name
from its piercing call, which sounds like 'kill-dee,
kill-dee'. It has a slender body and conspicuous
stripes on its breast, and lives in a wide variety of
habitats, including fields, riverbanks and shores.
Killdeers nest on shingle and gravel, and they
sometimes lay their eggs on flat roofs.

SCIENTIFIC NAME *Charadrius vociferus*

DISTRIBUTION Breeds throughout North America,
except the Arctic; winters in southern North
America, Central America, parts of South America

SIZE Up to 25cm long

NORTHERN LAPWING
Unlike most shorebirds, lapwings usually
live inland. Damp, grassy fields are one of the
northern lapwing's favourite habitats, although
other species of lapwing prefer to live closer
to water. The northern lapwing has an elegant
crest, a greenish-black back and a short, sharply
pointed beak. During the breeding season,
the males perform spectacular aerial displays,
tumbling down from the sky towards the
ground. Because lapwings build their nests
on the ground, they always have to be on the
lookout for predators. If a crow or fox appears

near the nest, the parent birds immediately go
on the attack to try to drive it away.

SCIENTIFIC NAME *Vanellus vanellus*

DISTRIBUTION Breeds in northern Europe, central
Asia; winters in western and southern Europe,
northern Africa, Middle East, southern Asia

SIZE Up to 30cm long

LESSER GOLDEN PLOVER
Every year, this small shorebird carries out one
of the longest migrations of any land-living bird.
It spends the winter in central South America,
then flies north to the high Arctic to breed. This
northward journey is mostly over land but, on
the return trip, the adult birds follow a shorter,
more hazardous route. They head out into the
Atlantic Ocean from eastern Canada and fly due
south until they hit land in Brazil. This shortcut
saves energy, but it means flying nearly 4,000km
non-stop. These plovers are a golden colour
during the breeding season, but grey during
the rest of the year.

SCIENTIFIC NAME *Pluvialis dominica*

DISTRIBUTION Breeds in Alaska, northern
Canada; winters in central South America

SIZE Up to 27cm long

ABOVE *American lesser
golden plovers prepare
themselves for their
southward migration
by fattening up on berries
along the Canadian coast.
They cannot fly back along
the same route because
spring comes very late in
this part of the world. The
ground is frozen, making
food very difficult to find.*

RUDDY TURNSTONE

This small, solidly built shorebird lives on rocky coasts, and feeds in an unusual way. Using its short beak, it flicks stones and seaweed aside to reveal animals hidden underneath. There are two species of turnstone; the black turnstone *(Arenaria melanocephala)* lives on the Pacific coast of North America, but the ruddy turnstone can be seen almost anywhere from Alaska to Australia.

SCIENTIFIC NAME *Arenaria interpres*

DISTRIBUTION Breeds throughout the Arctic; winters in western Europe, southern North America, Australia, New Zealand, throughout the tropics

SIZE Up to 23cm long

BELOW The ruddy turnstone has quick reactions. When it flicks away a stone or pebble, it can peck up insects and sandhoppers before they escape.

GREENSHANK

Every spring, large flocks of greenshanks fly north to the Siberian tundra to breed. These birds have grey wings and white undersides, but they get their name from their legs, which are coloured olive-green. Greenshanks nest in boggy ground or forest clearings and, as with all shorebirds, they have fast-developing young. Their chicks can feed themselves soon after they hatch, and they instinctively crouch down if any predators fly overhead.

SCIENTIFIC NAME *Tringa nebularia*

DISTRIBUTION Breeds in northern Europe, Siberia; winters mainly in Africa, southern Asia, Australia

SIZE Up to 34cm long

EURASIAN CURLEW

Curlews are among the largest shorebirds, and have speckled brown or grey plumage and long downcurved beaks. They live on coasts and in damp places inland, and are experts at finding worms and other animals hidden in wet sand and mud. When a curlew is searching for food, it probes the ground with its beak closed. If it feels

food, it can open just the tip of its beak, to grip the animal and pull it to the surface of the mud. Eurasian curlews nest in damp grassland and other boggy places, and are famous for their beautiful bubbling call.

SCIENTIFIC NAME *Numenius arquata*

DISTRIBUTION Breeds in northern Europe, northern Asia; winters in western and southern Europe, Africa, southern Asia

SIZE Up to 60cm long

WRYBILL

The wrybill is the only bird in the world to have a beak with a sideways bend. It lives in New Zealand, spending the summer months on stony riverbanks in South Island, and the winter on the North Island coast. The wrybill's beak turns to the right, and is an ideal tool for getting at insect larvae and other animals hidden beneath stones. The bird sweeps its beak in a clockwise direction, flipping over stones and quickly snapping up its meal. Wrybills nest on bare river gravel and lay just two eggs a year.

SCIENTIFIC NAME *Anarhychus frontalis*

DISTRIBUTION New Zealand

SIZE Up to 21cm long

RED-NECKED PHALAROPE

In most birds, the male is more brightly coloured than the female, and the female does most of the work of raising the young. With the red-necked phalarope, things are the other way around. During the breeding season, the female has a bright red neck, and she uses her colourful plumage to attract a mate. Once the eggs have been laid, the male takes sole charge of the incubation of the clutch, and of the care of the young. Phalaropes are also unusual because they are good swimmers, and pick food from the water's surface. Most other waders feed by walking.

SCIENTIFIC NAME *Phalaropus lobatus*

DISTRIBUTION Breeds in northern regions, the Arctic; winters at sea in the tropics

SIZE Up to 18cm long

RIGHT In the winter, both male and female red-necked phalaropes have pale plumage. In the summer, the female is brighter then her mate.

Winter

Male (summer)

Female (summer)

TOP With a beak up to 19cm long, the Eurasian curlew can reach worms buried deep in wet mud.
ABOVE When a wrybill hatches, its beak is short and straight. It develops a bend to the right as the bird matures.

RUFF

During the winter, ruffs look much like other shorebirds, but in spring the males develop extraordinary feathery 'ruffs' around their necks, with extra tufts over their heads. These ruffs have many different colours, and the males show them off at their traditional display grounds, or leks, where they attract females and compete for the chance to mate. Once a female has mated, she leaves the display ground and raises her young alone. Ruffs live in marshland and grassy places, and they feed mainly on insects.

SCIENTIFIC NAME *Philomachus pugnax*

DISTRIBUTION Breeds in northern Europe, Siberia; winters mainly in Africa

SIZE Up to 29cm long

Male ruff in winter

Female ruff

BELOW *A female common snipe carefully settles down on her clutch of eggs.*

ABOVE *In their summer breeding plumage, male ruffs are unmistakable.*

PURPLE SANDPIPER

The purple sandpiper feeds on rocky shores, where it dodges the surf to pick up molluscs exposed by the tide. This small, dumpy bird nests on some of the most northerly land on Earth – within 1,000km of the North Pole. Unlike other Arctic shorebirds, the purple sandpiper does not migrate very far south. Some individuals stay close to the Arctic Circle right through the winter, when there are only a few hours of daylight each day.

SCIENTIFIC NAME *Calidris maritima*

DISTRIBUTION Breeds in high Arctic; winters in northeastern North America, Iceland, northwestern Europe

SIZE Up to 22cm long

COMMON SNIPE

The common snipe is a small, secretive bird with brown plumage and a long, straight beak. It lives in woodlands and other damp places, and leaves trails of small holes in damp mud where it has been feeding. Snipe are well camouflaged, but if they are caught unawares, they burst into the air with a sudden screech, disappearing in a zigzag flight. During the breeding season, male snipe make a remarkable humming sound as they plunge through the air. This sound is made by their two outermost tail feathers, which vibrate as the air rushes past them.

SCIENTIFIC NAME *Gallinago gallinago*

DISTRIBUTION Breeds in North America, northern Europe, northern Asia; winters in North America, Central America, western and southern Europe, Africa, southern Asia

SIZE Up to 27cm long

SKUAS, GULLS AND TERNS

There are seven species of skua, and about 85 species
of gull and tern. Skuas breed mainly in cold places,
but gulls and terns are found worldwide on or near coasts,
and sometimes far inland. They all have webbed feet and
waterproof feathers and are skilful fliers. Terns live by fishing, but
most gulls scavenge on the shore, or in waste thrown from boats.
Gulls and terns can be bold, but skuas are even
more aggressive. They eat eggs and chicks,
often stealing food from other seabirds.

ABOVE *The great skua
often steals food from birds
that are larger than itself.*

ARCTIC SKUA

The Arctic skua is a skilful airborne pirate.
It will hunt rodents or steal eggs, but it gets
most of its food by making other seabirds
drop any fish that they have caught. The skua
grabs the falling fish in mid-air. Arctic skuas
breed in groups in treeless tundra or open
ground near the sea. They spend the winter
flying over the ocean and often follow fishing-
boats hundreds of kilometres out from land.

ABOVE *Arctic skuas vary
in colour. Some are dark
brown all over, but others
have brown backs and
pale undersides.*
BELOW *Herring gulls
crack open mollusc shells by
dropping them from the air.*

SCIENTIFIC NAME *Stercorarius parasiticus*

DISTRIBUTION Breeds
in the far north;
winters as far
south as the
Southern
Ocean

SIZE Up
to 46cm
long

GREAT SKUA

This powerfully built, dark brown seabird
makes its living largely at the expense of other
birds. It eats young seabirds and eggs, and chases
adult birds to make them regurgitate their catch.
It also eats dead animals, ripping open their
remains with its hooked beak. Great skuas nest
on the ground, and usually produce two eggs
each time they breed. The great skua is closely
related to the Antarctic skua, which lives in the
Southern Ocean, and often attacks penguin
chicks. These two kinds of skua are so similar
that they were once thought to be the same.

SCIENTIFIC NAME *Catharacta skua*

DISTRIBUTION North Atlantic Ocean

SIZE Up to 66cm long

HERRING GULL

This noisy and quarrelsome bird
is one of the most widespread
and adaptable gulls in the
northern hemisphere. It
feeds on fields and around
rubbish dumps as well as along the shore, and
often follows fishing-boats and ferries, waiting
for any scraps that are thrown overboard.
Herring gulls breed in groups, and make their
nests out of seaweed and other plants. They
usually nest on the ground, but in some coastal
towns they set up home on rooftops. If anything
comes too close to their eggs or chicks, the
parent gulls circle overhead, producing a
deafening chorus of loud, yelping cries.

Powerful beak

SCIENTIFIC NAME *Larus argentatus*

DISTRIBUTION Coasts and inland areas
throughout the northern hemisphere

SIZE Up to 60cm long

GREAT BLACK-
BACKED GULL

This is one of the world's largest
gulls, with a wingspan of up to
1.7m. It has a powerful yellow
beak, a white body and head,
and a black back and wings.
Black-backed gulls scavenge
for dead remains, but they
are also highly effective

**Great black-
backed gull on
the ground**

predators. They can kill animals as large as rabbits, and gobble up seabird chicks and ducklings, swallowing them whole. Unlike the herring gull, this bird often hunts on its own or in pairs. It nests on rocky coasts, and lays three eggs each time it breeds.

SCIENTIFIC NAME	*Larus marinus*
DISTRIBUTION	North Atlantic Ocean
SIZE	Up to 79cm long

COMMON BLACK-HEADED GULL

In the winter, this small gull is almost totally grey and white, but when it is wearing its breeding plumage, it looks as though its head has been dipped in dark brown ink. Black-headed gulls sometimes feed on the coast, but they are just as much at home inland. They often follow ploughs to pick up earthworms and other small animals. They roost on lakes and reservoirs, and nest on marshy ground.

SCIENTIFIC NAME	*Larus ridibundus*
DISTRIBUTION	Breeds in Europe, northern Asia; winters throughout Europe, northern Africa, Asia, Atlantic coast of North America
SIZE	Up to 36cm long

Juvenile

Breeding adult

Winter adult

LEFT *Great black-headed gulls* (Larus ichthyaetus) *breed around the inland seas of central Asia. Like most of their relatives, their heads turn grey in the winter.*
BELOW *These common black-headed gulls are scavenging for food around European bison. They catch insects and other small animals that are disturbed by the bison.*

KITTIWAKE

Kittiwakes get their name from their call – a shrill 'kitti-week, kitti-week'. They are smaller and daintier than many gulls, and get almost all of their food from the sea. Kittiwakes breed in noisy groups on steep cliff ledges. Unlike most of their relatives, they build elaborate cup-shaped nests, using mud to cement them to the rock. After they have raised their chicks, parent kittiwakes go their separate ways, but they return to the same breeding site the following year, and pair up again to raise their next family.

SCIENTIFIC NAME	*Rissa tridactyla*
DISTRIBUTION	North Atlantic Ocean, northern Pacific Ocean
SIZE	Up to 41cm long

SILVER GULL OR RED-BILLED GULL

This seabird is the most common gull in Australia. It has a rounded white body with a silvery-grey back and wings, and a bright red beak and legs. Silver gulls are versatile creatures, and they are quite at home in towns and on inland lakes, as well as far out at sea. They often gather in fields and around rubbish dumps to feed, particularly in stormy weather. Silver gulls nest on the ground, and lay one to three eggs each year.

SCIENTIFIC NAME	*Larus novaehollandiae*
DISTRIBUTION	Australia, New Zealand
SIZE	Up to 43cm long

ABOVE *Kittiwakes have sharp claws, which help them to cling to rocky ledges when they nest.*
BELOW *Measuring just 25cm long, the little gull* (Larus minutus) *is the world's smallest gull.*

ARCTIC TERN

Terns are more graceful than gulls, and have pointed beaks, narrow wings and forked tails. Instead of scavenging for food along the shore, they flutter over the water, diving down to catch small fish. These lightly built birds are tireless fliers, and the Arctic tern is one of greatest travellers of them all. Arctic terns breed in cool parts of the northern hemisphere, laying their camouflaged eggs in hollows scraped in shingle. Once they have finished breeding, they fly all the way to the Southern Ocean, feeding as they go. During the northern spring, they fly back north again, completing a return journey that can be more than 35,000km long.

SCIENTIFIC NAME *Sterna paradisea*

DISTRIBUTION Breeds in northern Europe, northern North America, along shores of the Arctic Sea; winters mainly in Southern Ocean

SIZE Up to 35cm long

INCA TERN

Many terns have white and grey plumage, but the Inca tern has a completely different colour scheme. Its beak and feet are bright red and its body is dark grey, but it has white plumes that sprout from the base of its beak like a pair of long, curling whiskers. Inca terns feed in large flocks, and they often catch fish trying to escape from cormorants and sealions.

SCIENTIFIC NAME *Larosterna inca*

DISTRIBUTION Pacific coast of South America

SIZE Up to 42cm long

WHITE TERN

This all-white tern flutters across the vastness of the open ocean. It is unusually tame, and often circles boats before continuing on its way. White terns breed on remote islands, and lay a single egg each year. Instead of laying on the ground like most terns do, they lay their eggs on the bare branches of low trees. The parent holds the egg in position with its body, and the chick jumps to the ground a few days after hatching.

SCIENTIFIC NAME *Gygis alba*

DISTRIBUTION Tropical oceans worldwide, except eastern Pacific

SIZE Up to 33cm long

BLACK SKIMMER

Skimmers are the only birds with a lower beak that is much longer than the part on top. They skim the surface of lakes and lagoons with their beaks open and, if the beak touches a fish or other small animal, the top part snaps shut and the bird swallows its catch. There are three species of these birds. The black skimmer is the largest, and is the only one that sometimes flies out over the sea.

SCIENTIFIC NAME
Rhyncops niger

DISTRIBUTION North, Central and South America

SIZE Up to 50cm long

ABOVE *Arctic terns share the work of feeding their chicks. Here, one parent returns with a fish while the other keeps the chick warm.*
BELOW *This Atlantic puffin has a beak full of sand-eels for its chick. Puffins abandon their young when they are about six weeks old, leaving them to flutter down to the sea.*

Narrow wings for fast, agile flight

FAR LEFT *White terns lay just one egg each time they breed, and the parents share the task of incubation. They have to swap places with care to stop the egg from falling from the precarious nest site.*
LEFT *An Inca tern spreads its wings and calls. Inca terns breed on desert coasts, and lay their eggs in rocky crevices or burrows made by other birds.*

AUKS

There are no penguins in the northern hemisphere, but auks look like them and feed in a similar way. Like penguins, they have dumpy bodies, and they speed through the water by beating their wings. There are about 22 species in the auk family, and most of these birds nest on rocky ledges or in burrows, although a few nest in trees. Unlike real penguins, auks can fly, and they soar over the water on whirring wings.

The largest auk ever known, called the great auk, was completely flightless. It became extinct in 1844.

Beak is at its brightest during the breeding season

Fish arranged head to tail

Little auks (left) and razorbills (right) in summer and whiter winter plumage

Summer

Winter

Common guillemots in summer and winter plumage

ATLANTIC PUFFIN

With their bright red feet and multi-coloured beaks, puffins are comical-looking seabirds. They nest in burrows on rocky coasts, and eat sand-eels and other small fish. During the breeding season, puffins speed back to their burrows with deliveries of fish for their chicks. They catch up to 12 fish on each trip to the sea, holding them in their beaks. Remarkably, a puffin can add to its catch without dropping any of the fish it has already caught.

SCIENTIFIC NAME	*Fratercula arctica*
DISTRIBUTION	North Atlantic Ocean
SIZE	Up to 32cm long

LITTLE AUK

The tiny black and white little auk is one of the most common seabirds on the edges of the Arctic. It has a short beak, and a plump body with legs set far back. Little auks feed on planktonic animals, and they sometimes bob up and down on the water in large flocks. They nest in rocky crevices or burrows and, like most other auks, lay just one egg a year.

SCIENTIFIC NAME	*Alle alle*
DISTRIBUTION	North Atlantic Ocean, Arctic Ocean
SIZE	Up to 21cm long

RAZORBILL

These large auks have flat, hooked beaks. They nest on ledges and in crevices on rocky coasts, laying single eggs. Razorbill chicks leave their nesting ledges when they are about two weeks old, still with plenty of growing to do. Once they are safely at sea, one of their parents feeds them until they are able to feed themselves.

SCIENTIFIC NAME	*Alca torda*
DISTRIBUTION	North Atlantic Ocean
SIZE	Up to 41cm long

COMMON GUILLEMOT

Guillemots are the largest auks, with streamlined bodies and long, pointed beaks. They breed on inaccessible rocky ledges, crowding together just a few metres above the waves. Guillemots lay their single egg directly on the rock, and the parents take turns to incubate it. Guillemot eggs are sharply pointed, so they roll in circles instead of rolling off the edge into the sea.

SCIENTIFIC NAME	*Uria aalge*
DISTRIBUTION	North Atlantic Ocean, northern Pacific Ocean
SIZE	Up to 45cm long

PIGEONS
AND DOVES

Pigeons and doves are
plump-bodied birds,
with small heads that flick
backwards and forwards when
they walk. They have short beaks
and most of them are vegetarians,
feeding on seeds, fruit or leaves. Apart from the
largest species, all of them are strong fliers, exploding
into the air at the first sign of danger, and speeding
away on fast-flapping wings. They nest in trees,
on ledges or sometimes on the ground, and
make flimsy nests out of sticks and twigs.
One of their most unusual features is that
they feed their young on a milky fluid made
in their throats. Flamingoes (page 169) are
the only other birds known to behave in this
way. Pigeons and doves are unique in that they
can suck up water
when they drink – all other birds
have to take a mouthful and then
tip back their heads. There are about
300 species in the pigeon and dove
family, and the greatest variety is
found in Southeast Asia and Australia.

ABOVE LEFT *The wood
pigeon (Columba
palumbus) is a farmland
pest in parts of Europe.*
ABOVE RIGHT *Stock doves
(Columba oenas) are
smaller than wood pigeons,
with shorter tails.*

ROCK DOVE

The slate-grey rock dove is the original
ancestor of all the world's street pigeons.
Centuries ago, rock doves were kept for food,
and over the years many of them escaped.
The escaped birds learned how to find food in
built-up areas, and they have been increasingly
successful ever since. Wild rock doves nest on
cliff ledges, often near the sea. Street pigeons
have inherited this head for heights. They treat
buildings like cliffs, nesting on high window
ledges or under bridges. In the wild, rock doves

lay two eggs at a time, often raising two or three
families each year. In towns and cities, where
food is easy to find, street pigeons may breed
all through the year.

SCIENTIFIC NAME *Columba livia*

DISTRIBUTION Rock dove: southern Europe,
northern Africa, southern Asia
Street pigeon: worldwide

SIZE Up to 33cm long

MOURNING DOVE

The mourning dove is well known for its call.
It makes a soft, mournful cooing sound, which
is how it gets its name. Mourning doves nearly
always feed in pairs or small flocks, and they are
common in many different habitats, including
fields, farmyards and gardens. They have brown
wings, pinkish-brown bodies and long, sharply

pointed tails. During the breeding season, male mourning doves perform special display flights, climbing high on noisily clapping wings, and then gliding down to the ground.

SCIENTIFIC NAME	*Zenaida macroura*
DISTRIBUTION	North America, Central America, Caribbean islands
SIZE	Up to 32cm long

TURTLE DOVE

Like the mourning dove, this dove is famous for its call – a purring sound that can be heard wherever it nests. As with most pigeons and doves, the males and females look very similar, with pinkish-grey bodies and brown and black wings. Turtle doves spend the winter in Africa, but they fly northwards to Europe and central Asia to breed.

SCIENTIFIC NAME	*Streptopelia turtur*
DISTRIBUTION	Breeds mainly in Europe, Middle East; winters in Africa
SIZE	Up to 27cm long

Broad wings
with long
flight feathers

DIAMOND DOVE

Diamond doves live in dry parts of Australia. Like many other birds that live in dry places, they are nomadic, moving on whenever food gets hard to find. Diamond doves have blue-grey bodies, and are named after the diamond-like flecks of white on their wings. They feed on the ground, and fly to waterholes in the late afternoon before roosting for the night.

SCIENTIFIC NAME	*Geopelia cuneata*
DISTRIBUTION	Northern, western and central Australia
SIZE	Up to 21cm long

SPINIFEX PIGEON

This Australian pigeon lives in open country dotted with clumps of spinifex grass – a tough drought-resistant plant with spear-shaped leaves. Spinifex grass grows only after rain, but it produces large crops of seeds that can keep the

pigeon fed during dry weather. Spinifex pigeons are small with spiky, upright crests, and have brown markings that blend in with the ground. If they are disturbed, they often scuttle away around the spinifex instead of flying to safety.

SCIENTIFIC NAME	*Petrophassa plumifera*
DISTRIBUTION	Central and western Australia
SIZE	Up to 23cm long

SUPERB FRUIT-DOVE

Compared to most doves and pigeons, fruit-doves are richly coloured. The superb fruit-dove has a lime-green body, orange shoulders and a bright purple patch on its head. It lives in tropical and subtropical forests, and feeds mainly in the treetops, only occasionally coming to the ground. Fruit-doves eat small, oily fruits, usually swallowing them whole. They digest the flesh, but scatter the seeds in their droppings, helping trees to spread.

SCIENTIFIC NAME	*Ptilinopus superbus*
DISTRIBUTION	Northeastern Australia, New Guinea and adjacent islands
SIZE	Up to 24cm long

VICTORIA CROWNED PIGEON

This extraordinary and rare bird is one of the largest members of the pigeon family. The size of a chicken, it has lustrous turquoise plumage, and a fan-shaped crest of lacy feathers that stays up all the time. Crowned pigeons live in rainforests, and they feed on fallen fruit on the forest floor. Like most pigeons, they are a popular source of food, and hunting has severely reduced their numbers.

SCIENTIFIC NAME	*Goura victoria*
DISTRIBUTION	New Guinea
SIZE	Up to 84cm long

ABOVE *The collared dove (Streptopelia decaocto) lived originally in Asia.*

BELOW *Turtle doves feed mainly on small seeds in fields and open places.* BOTTOM *Australia is home to more than 24 kinds of pigeon and dove. The diamond dove, shown here, is one of the smallest.*

PARROTS

The parrot family includes some of the world's most colourful and distinctive birds. They have hooked beaks that turn down close to their faces, and strong feet for climbing and for picking up food. Most parrots eat fruit, seeds or nectar, and they feed in trees or on the ground. They fly in pairs or flocks, calling noisily as they speed along. Parrots usually nest in holes in trees, and lay a small number of white, almost round eggs. There are about 300 species of parrot, and most are found in the southern hemisphere. Deforestation and illegal hunting are making it hard for many species to survive, and some face extinction.

SULPHUR-CRESTED COCKATOO

Cockatoos are the only parrots with feathery, fan-like crests. They can raise or lower these crests to show their mood. The sulphur-crested cockatoo has a bright yellow crest and the rest of its plumage is white – an unusual colour for a parrot. It lives in a range of habitats, from forests to farmland, and roosts high up in eucalyptus trees. Sulphur-crested cockatoos are popular pets because they can imitate human speech.

SCIENTIFIC NAME
Cacatua galerita

DISTRIBUTION Originally from northern and eastern Australia, New Guinea; introduced into New Zealand

SIZE Up to 50cm long

GALAH

This attractive pink and grey cockatoo is one of Australia's best-known parrots. Flocks of galahs can be seen in parks and on beaches, but they are particularly common in wooded country and farmland, where they sometimes cause damage by eating grain. Even by parrot standards, galahs are noisy and energetic birds, particularly when hundreds of them speed through the air, twisting and turning with split-second coordination. Galahs usually nest in holes in trees but, unlike most parrots, they line the hole with leaves and twigs before laying their eggs.

SCIENTIFIC NAME *Cacatua roseicapilla*

DISTRIBUTION Australia, except Tasmania

SIZE Up to 38cm long

COCKATIEL

This popular cage-bird is Australia's smallest cockatoo, and the only one with a long, pointed tail. Cockatiels have grey and white bodies and yellow crests. The male's face is more brightly coloured than the female's. Wild cockatiels live in flocks, and feed mostly on the ground. They lay up to seven eggs in a tree-hole by water, and the parents share the work of incubation.

SCIENTIFIC NAME *Nymphicus hollandicus*

DISTRIBUTION Australia, except far north and coastal regions

SIZE Up to 33cm long

LEFT *Sulphur-crested cockatoos often live in city parks and gardens, screeching noisily as they fly through the trees.*
RIGHT *A pair of cockatiels sit on a branch. When they fly, cockatiels fold their crests flat against their heads.*

White plumage tinged with yellow under the tail

BUDGERIGAR

Few people need to be told what a budgerigar looks like because this small Australian parrot is one of the world's most popular cage-birds. Pet 'budgies' can have a variety of colours, including blue, yellow and white, but wild budgerigars are always yellow and green. Wild budgerigars live in Australia's interior, where the food supply depends on rainfall. If it is dry, flocks of budgerigars wander hundreds of kilometres looking for food. Budgerigars nest in dead trees or fallen logs, lining their nest-holes with wood chips. They lay up to eight eggs at a time.

Featherless patch around the eye

Two budgerigars on a perch

SCIENTIFIC NAME	*Melopsittacus undulatus*
DISTRIBUTION	Central Australia
SIZE	Up to 20cm long

RAINBOW LORIKEET

Instead of feeding on seeds or fruit, lorikeets eat mainly nectar and flower pollen. Their tongues have a brush-like tip, helping them to lap up their food. The rainbow lorikeet is one of the most widespread species, and is vividly coloured with a mixture of blue, yellow, red and green. Like other lorikeets, it sets off to find food at sunrise, screeching loudly as it clambers about high up in the trees. Rainbow lorikeets are easy to tame, and in some places they visit gardens to feed at flowers.

SCIENTIFIC NAME	*Trichoglossus haematodus*
DISTRIBUTION	New Guinea and adjacent islands, parts of Indonesia, northern and eastern Australia, Tasmania
SIZE	Up to 26cm long

ECLECTUS PARROT

Male and female parrots can look similar, but in this species they are easy to tell apart. The males are bright green but, unusually for a bird, the females are even more colourful, with bright red heads, blue chests and deep-red backs. Eclectus parrots live in forests, and they eat fruit, flowers and buds. Compared to other parrots, their flight is slow, but they have the typical parrot habit of calling as they fly along. They nest high up in trees, and usually lay just two eggs at a time.

SCIENTIFIC NAME	*Eclectus roratus*
DISTRIBUTION	New Guinea and adjacent islands, Cape York Peninsula (northeastern Australia)
SIZE	Up to 43cm long

GREY PARROT

This large African parrot is unusual in having mainly grey plumage, apart from its bright red tail. It lives in forests and mangrove swamps and, although it spends most of its life in the treetops, it sometimes lands in fields to feed on grain. Grey parrots fetch high prices as cage-birds because they are expert at copying human speech – some have been taught a vocabulary of more than 750 words. This makes them seem highly intelligent, though, as with all 'talking' birds, they repeat words without understanding their meaning. Grey parrots are bred in captivity, but birds are also collected in the wild and smuggled abroad for sale.

SCIENTIFIC NAME	*Psittacus erithacus*
DISTRIBUTION	Tropical western and central Africa
SIZE	Up to 33cm long

TOP *Like all parrots, budgerigars have four toes. Two point forwards and two point backwards, giving them a good grip.* ABOVE *Many large parrots, such as this African grey, have a patch of bare skin around their eyes. Compared to other birds, parrots have small eyes, although they are still good at spotting food.*

LEFT *Like all their relatives, blue and yellow macaws (Ara ararauna) are noisy birds, screeching loudly as they skim over the treetops.* **BELOW** *A scarlet macaw's beak is a multi-purpose tool, used for preening feathers and cracking open food.*

SCARLET MACAW

Macaws are the world's largest parrots. They live in Central and South America, and have long, tapering tails and powerful wings. They often travel in pairs, flying over forests and open woodland as they look for nuts and seeds growing on the trees below. There are about 15 species of these magnificent birds and the scarlet macaw is probably the most numerous, although all of them are under threat. It feeds high up in trees, and is a messy eater, dropping pieces of fruit on the ground. When macaws start to feed, agoutis (page 257) and other animals soon arrive to eat this fallen feast. Scarlet macaws usually raise two chicks a year, and it is about three months before the chicks leave the nest.

SCIENTIFIC NAME *Ara macao*
DISTRIBUTION Central America, northern South America
SIZE Up to 85cm long

HYACINTH MACAW

This South American macaw is the largest member of the parrot family. It is deep blue all over, except for a bright yellow patch around each eye and beneath its chin. It lives mainly among palm trees close to the banks of rivers. Even for a macaw, its beak is unusually large, and it uses it to pick palm nuts and crack open their tough shells. Hyacinth macaws are a protected species, but even so they are sometimes trapped and sold as pets. Less than 3,000 of these birds survive in the wild.

SCIENTIFIC NAME *Anodorhynchus hyacinthinus*
DISTRIBUTION Brazil, Bolivia
SIZE Up to 1m long

A pair of scarlet macaws on a branch

HAWK-HEADED PARROT OR RED-FAN PARROT

This parrot gets its name from its large beak and slender shape, which give it a hawk-like look. When it is excited or alarmed, it shows off a more unusual feature – a ruff of red feathers that lifts up around the back of its head like a fan. Despite its name, it is a harmless vegetarian, feeding on fruit, seeds and nuts. Hawk-headed parrots live in forests and wooded grassland, and nest in tree-holes made by woodpeckers.

SCIENTIFIC NAME *Deroptyus accipitrinus*
DISTRIBUTION Northern South America; from Colombia to Brazil
SIZE Up to 35cm long

They use their group nests as a roosting site, particularly during the winter when it can be very cold at night.

SCIENTIFIC NAME	*Myiopsitta monachus*
DISTRIBUTION	Originally from central South America from Bolivia to Argentina; introduced into North America, some Caribbean islands
SIZE	Up to 22cm long

BLUE-CROWNED HANGING PARROT

Smaller than a sparrow, this blue-headed bird is one of the world's tiniest parrots. It lives in dense forest, and gets its name from the way it hangs upside down to rest. It flies fast and climbs well. Hanging parrots eat nectar, flowers and fruit, and lap up their food with their tongues. They nest in tree-holes, and line their nests with leaves, which they carry in the feathers on their rumps.

SCIENTIFIC NAME	*Loriculus galgulus*
DISTRIBUTION	Malaysia, Indonesia
SIZE	Up to 12cm long

KEA

The kea is a large, heavily built parrot from the mountains of New Zealand. Unlike other parrots, it eats dead animals and insects, as well as fruits and seeds. It has dark green plumage, a large beak and strong feet for walking on the ground. Keas are inquisitive and will help themselves to picnics and leftover food. They will also tug at shoelaces and car windscreen wipers. They used to be shot for apparently attacking sheep, but they are now protected.

SCIENTIFIC NAME	*Nestor notabilis*
DISTRIBUTION	South Island of New Zealand
SIZE	Up to 48cm long

KAKAPO

The kakapo is the heaviest parrot, and the only one that cannot fly. About the size of a chicken, it has green plumage, and emerges after dark to feed on flowers, seeds and leaves. In the breeding season, male kakapos go to mating grounds, or leks, every night, where they call the females with a booming sound that can be heard more than a kilometre away. Kakapos are among the most endangered parrots in the world.

SCIENTIFIC NAME	*Strigops habroptilus*
DISTRIBUTION	Islands off the coast of New Zealand
SIZE	Up to 65cm long

LEFT *Hyacinth macaws do not start to breed until they are about seven years old, and in an average year each pair manages to raise just one chick. This explains why this species is so easily endangered when its chicks are collected as pets.*

BELOW *The rose-ringed parakeet has managed to adapt to life in towns and cities. In its native home, it lives in large flocks.*

ABOVE *There are only about 50 kakapos left in the wild. They live on islands off the New Zealand coast, where their progress is carefully monitored.*

ROSE-RINGED PARAKEET

Parakeets are small or medium-sized parrots with slim bodies and long tails. Like many parakeets, the rose-ringed parakeet is mainly green, but the male has a thin black and red ring around its neck. This parakeet is one of the few species that is found in Africa as well as Asia, and in recent years it has managed to set up home in North America and Europe as well. In North America, escaped rose-ringed parakeets live around the cities of Los Angeles and Miami, and in Europe, they survive as far north as London, England.

SCIENTIFIC NAME	*Psittacula krameri*
DISTRIBUTION	Originally from central and eastern Africa, India, Sri Lanka; introduced into parts of North America, Europe
SIZE	Up to 41cm long

MONK PARAKEET

This green and grey parakeet is very unpopular with South American farmers because it lives in large, noisy flocks and has a habit of raiding fields and orchards for food. While a flock is feeding, some birds act as lookouts, giving the alarm if they spot anything dangerous coming their way. Monk parakeets are the only parrots that make their nests in the branches of trees. They usually build their nests very close together, making a giant structure high off the ground.

OWLS

Owls hunt live animals, and most of them catch their prey at night. They have large, forward-facing eyes, well-developed ears and powerful feet with sharp claws. Many species have soft fringes on their wing feathers, helping them to fly almost silently, so they can hear squeaks or rustling on the ground. During the day they hide away. There are about 130 species of owl spread across most of the world.

GREAT HORNED OWL

This is North America's largest owl, and it is large enough to kill a fully grown skunk or goose. It has staring yellow eyes, feathery feet and two feathery tufts on its head. These tufts are easily mistaken for ears, but they are not used for hearing – the owl's true ears are hidden beneath short feathers on either side of its head. Great horned owls sometimes lay their eggs in holes in trees or rocky crevices, but they usually take over nests abandoned by birds of prey. They lay two or three eggs, which often hatch several days apart.

Adult great horned owl with prey

SCIENTIFIC NAME *Bubo virginianus*

DISTRIBUTION North America, Central America, South America; from the Arctic to Tierra del Fuego

SIZE Up to 55cm long

BARN OWL

The barn owl is one of the world's most widespread birds. It has a pale underside and a flat, heart-shaped face, which makes it easily recognisable as it flaps slowly over the ground. Barn owls live in a wide variety of habitats, from pasture to semi-desert. They feed almost entirely on small rodents, hovering a metre or two above the ground before dropping down to make a kill. They lay their eggs in holes in trees or in old buildings, but do not use any nesting material.

ABOVE
The barn owl's ears are so sensitive it can hunt in complete darkness, and pinpoint its prey by sound alone.

SCIENTIFIC NAME *Tyto alba*

DISTRIBUTION Worldwide, except the extreme north, central Asia, Far East

SIZE Up to 40cm long

TAWNY OWL

This adaptable owl normally lives in woodland, but is equally at home among trees in parks and leafy gardens. The male's call is a deep hoot,

All owls have large eyes and can see well, even in the dark

ABOVE AND LEFT *Tawny owls can be brown or grey. Like other owls, tawny owl chicks hatch out in sequence, a few days apart. If food is scarce, only the oldest and largest chicks survive.*

while the female's reply is a high-pitched 'kee-wick'. Tawny owls feed mainly on small mammals, but they are also fond of earthworms. Their hearing is so good that they can hunt their prey in complete darkness.

SCIENTIFIC NAME	*Strix aluco*
DISTRIBUTION	Europe, northern Africa, central Asia, Far East
SIZE	Up to 38cm long

SNOWY OWL
The snowy owl lives in the Arctic tundra, where daylight lasts round the clock in the summer. The owl's white plumage makes it almost invisible against the melting snow. Snowy owls feed on lemmings and hares, and on other birds. They nest on the ground, laying up to eight eggs every time they breed. If lemmings are scarce, snowy owls sometimes venture outside the Arctic during the winter.

SCIENTIFIC NAME	*Nyctea scandiaca*
DISTRIBUTION	High Arctic worldwide
SIZE	Up to 66cm long

ELF OWL
The elf owl is the smallest owl in the world. It lives in deserts and on wooded hillsides, and eats mainly grasshoppers, moths and other insects, often swooping down on them from its perch. It has a short tail, tiny feet and a typically owl-like shape. Elf owls nest and roost in holes made by woodpeckers. In woodlands, these holes are in trees, but in the desert they are in saguaros – giant cacti with cylindrical stems.

SCIENTIFIC NAME	*Micrathene whitneyi*
DISTRIBUTION	Southwestern USA, Mexico
SIZE	Up to 15cm long

BURROWING OWL
Burrowing owls live in open places, where there is no cover for rearing a family. They dig burrows for shelter, or take over ones made by other animals. They have long, slender legs, and use their feet and beaks to scratch at the ground. Burrowing owls hunt at night, but spend much of the day standing by the entrances to their homes. If they are disturbed, they make a call that sounds like a rattlesnake shaking its tail.

SCIENTIFIC NAME	*Athene cunicularia*
DISTRIBUTION	North America, Central America, South America
SIZE	Up to 25cm long

LEFT *Female snowy owls, such as this one, have white plumage with black marks, but the males are often completely white.*
BELOW *An elf owl sits in front of its nest-hole with a moth in its beak.*

BOOBOOK OWL
This dark brown owl gets its name from its high-pitched two-note call. It is fully nocturnal, and perches on branches and fences, flying out to catch its prey. Boobooks eat insects and other small animals, and sometimes catch their food around streetlights in towns.

SCIENTIFIC NAME	*Ninox novaehollandiae*
DISTRIBUTION	Australia, New Zealand, New Guinea and adjacent islands
SIZE	Up to 35cm long

BROWN FISH OWL
Several of the world's owls, including the brown fish owl, prey on frogs and fish. Most of these owls have bare legs and feet, and sharp scales on their toes to stop their prey from slipping away. This species hunts at dusk, swooping over the water's surface or wading into the shallows to find food.

SCIENTIFIC NAME	*Bubo zeylonensis*
DISTRIBUTION	India, Southeast Asia
SIZE	Up to 56cm long

ABOVE *The burrowing owl is easy to recognize because it stands like a sentry by its burrow. These birds nest in all kinds of open places, including golf courses and airports.*

NIGHTJARS AND FROGMOUTHS

Nightjars, also known as nighthawks, are nocturnal birds that catch insects on the wing. They have small beaks, but their mouths open up like funnels to scoop up their food in mid-air. During the day they often rest on the ground, but their camouflage is so good that they are hardly ever seen. Frogmouths are similar to nightjars, but they catch their food on the ground and usually roost in trees. There are about 70 species of nightjar and 12 species of frogmouth. Nightjars are found in warm areas all over the world, but frogmouths live only in Southeast Asia and Australia. The oilbird – a remarkable relative of these strange birds – is found only in South America. Because it is so unusual, scientists classify it in a family of its own.

Male

Female

ABOVE *Male and female European nightjars have slightly different patterns.*
BELOW *A tawny frogmouth sits on its nest with two recently hatched chicks. The nest is a flimsy platform of sticks.*

EUROPEAN NIGHTJAR

After dark, the male European nightjar makes a soft churring noise like a motorbike far away. He adds to this courtship song by clapping his wings. European nightjars feed over heaths and scrubland, roosting on the ground in the day. Their plumage is grey and brown and, with their wings and eyes closed, they look just like pieces of fallen wood.

SCIENTIFIC NAME *Caprimulgus europaeus*

DISTRIBUTION Breeds in Europe, central Asia; winters in Africa

SIZE Up to 28cm long

COMMON NIGHTHAWK

This widespread American bird starts hunting before sunset, which means that it is quite easily spotted. It has slim grey-brown wings, with a splash of white near the tips that shows up when it flies. During the breeding season, the male carries out courtship flights as the light fades, swooping down to the ground and making a booming sound with his wings. Nighthawks normally nest on the ground or on tree-stumps, but in some places, they nest on flat roofs as well. They lay two camouflaged eggs at a time.

SCIENTIFIC NAME *Chordeiles minor*

DISTRIBUTION Breeds in North America, Central America; winters in South America

SIZE Up to 24cm long

TAWNY FROGMOUTH

If this grey or red bird is approached on its daytime perch, it does its best to look like a piece of wood. It flattens its feathers, points its beak skywards and keeps absolutely still. It closes its eyes until they are almost shut, leaving a gap so it can see what is happening. The tawny frogmouth lives in forests and open woodland, and feeds mainly on insects, though it also eats lizards and mice. It hunts after dark, and often catches its food along roads.

SCIENTIFIC NAME *Podargus strigoides*

DISTRIBUTION Australia, Tasmania

SIZE Up to 47cm long

OILBIRD

Oilbirds feed on oily fruit from rainforest trees, and breed and roost on ledges deep inside caves. They make their nests out of their own droppings. When they return from their nightly feeding trips, they fly up to 800m underground. They find their way like bats (pages 240-241), using bursts of sound to judge distances. As well as being able to navigate in darkness, they can find their own chicks among the hundreds or even thousands around them.

SCIENTIFIC NAME *Steatornis caripensis*

DISTRIBUTION Panama, northern South America, Trinidad

SIZE Up to 48cm long

CUCKOOS AND THEIR RELATIVES

Cuckoos are best known for their habit of laying their eggs in the nests of other birds. By doing this, they avoid the hard work that goes into feeding and looking after their young. There are about 130 species of cuckoo, and most of them live in trees. Only about 50 species actually use other birds as foster parents – the rest raise their own young. Turacos are relatives of cuckoos that live in forests in Africa. There are about 20 species and, unlike cuckoos, almost all of them are beautifully coloured.

Adult European cuckoo

Juvenile European cuckoo

COMMON CUCKOO

Throughout Europe and northern Asia, this bird's call – a loud 'cu-koo' – is a sign that spring is well underway. It lays its eggs in the nests of warblers and other small birds, fluttering down when the parents are away. The cuckoo lays just one egg in each nest it visits, and its chick is often the first one to hatch. The chick pushes the other eggs out of the nest so that it can get all the food. Amazingly, the foster parents do not realize that they have been tricked, even though the cuckoo chick grows to be several times their own size.

SCIENTIFIC NAME *Cuculus canorus*

DISTRIBUTION Breeds in Europe, northern Asia; winters in Africa, southern Asia

SIZE Up to 33cm long

GREATER ROADRUNNER

The roadrunner is one of a small group of cuckoos that spend most of their time on the ground. It lives in semi-desert and scrub, and speeds after lizards and snakes on its long legs. It has a long tail and short, broad wings, and it uses these to help it swerve around rocks and bushes faster than most people can run. Roadrunners build nests in cacti or thorn bushes, and they lay up to six eggs at a time.

SCIENTIFIC NAME *Geococcyx californianus*

DISTRIBUTION Southern USA, northern Mexico

SIZE Up to 58cm long

GREAT BLUE TURACO

This bird is the largest turaco, with a body as large as a pheasant's. It feeds mainly on fruit and, although it is not a good flier, it is an expert at hopping or running along branches to get at its food. Like other turacos, it has silky plumage, and nests high up in trees. Turaco chicks have tiny claws on their wings, which they use to clamber about among the branches near their nests.

SCIENTIFIC NAME *Corythaeola cristata*

DISTRIBUTION Central and western Africa

SIZE Up to 75cm long

HOATZIN

The South American hoatzin is one of the world's most eccentric birds. It has a long neck and a spiky crest, and lives in dense forest near rivers and lakes. It feeds entirely on leaves – a bulky diet that gives it a strong smell and makes it difficult for it to fly. Like young turacos, hoatzin chicks have claws on their wings. If they are threatened, the chicks drop into the water below their nests, clambering back up again when the coast is clear.

SCIENTIFIC NAME *Opisthocomus hoatzin*

DISTRIBUTION Northern South America

SIZE Up to 65cm long

ABOVE AND ABOVE INSET
Young cuckoos soon grow too large for their foster parents' nests. In this case, the foster parents are reed warblers (page 216).

ABOVE *The roadrunner can sprint at nearly 25km/h – faster than most lizards and snakes. It kills them by beating them on the ground.*

SWIFTS AND HUMMINGBIRDS

Swifts spend more time in the air than any other flying animals –
catching insects, drinking and even sleeping on the wing. Their
wings are long and slender, and their feet are so small that they can
cling to rough surfaces but cannot perch. Hummingbirds are close
relatives of swifts, and also have tiny feet. These minute, jewel-like
birds feed on nectar, and they hover in front of flowers while they
feed. There are nearly 100 species of swift, and they are found all
over the world, often as summer visitors. There are about 340
species of hummingbird, found only in the Americas.

BELOW *This young
Eurasian swift has only
recently left its nest, but it
is already a good flier.*

EURASIAN SWIFT

During its lifetime, this sleek, black bird spends
more time in the air than any other species that
lives over land. Once it has left its nest, it spends
three or four years in the air, until the time comes
for it to breed. Swifts usually nest in roofs, and
have two or three young each year. They snatch
up insects as they fly, and migrate northwards in
the spring. In the summer, small flocks often
hurtle over rooftops and along city streets,
screaming as they speed through the air.

SCIENTIFIC NAME *Apus apus*

DISTRIBUTION Breeds in Europe,
Asia; winters mainly in Africa

SIZE Up to 18cm long

ABOVE
*The Alpine
swift* (Apus melba) *is
a common summer visitor
to southern Europe.*

*Small, densely
packed feathers*

*Tiny feet
cannot be used
for perching*

*Tail feathers fan
out when the
bird is braking*

CHIMNEY SWIFT

This small, brown swift originally roosted and
nested in hollow trees, but it now uses barns
and chimneys. In late summer, some chimneys
get crowded when flocks of migrating birds use
them as stop-overs on their way south. Like
most swifts, these birds make their nests from
feathers and dust snatched up in mid-air, and
they glue this together with their sticky saliva.
Because chimneys make ideal nesting sites,
they are more common than they once were.

SCIENTIFIC NAME *Chaetura pelagica*

DISTRIBUTION Breeds in eastern
Canada, eastern USA; winters
in Central America,
northern South America

SIZE Up to
13cm long

*Each wing
can beat
independently*

*Grooves in
front of the eyes
allow the bird
to see forwards*

RUBY-THROATED
HUMMINGBIRD

During the summer, this mainly green
hummingbird flies as far north as Canada,
feeding on nectar from flowers, and also on small
insects. Like all hummingbirds, it has a tube-
shaped beak, and laps its food up with its tongue.
It makes its nest out of leaves and lichen tied
together with spiders' silk, and lays two white
eggs at a time, each smaller than a pea. Despite
being so tiny, hummingbirds are quite fearless,
and chase away rivals in noisy mid-air fights.

SCIENTIFIC NAME *Archilochus colubris*

DISTRIBUTION Breeds in eastern North America;
winters in Florida (USA), Central America

SIZE Up to 9cm long

SWORD-BILLED HUMMINGBIRD

The beak of this hummingbird is
almost as long as its body – a record
for any bird. It uses it to collect nectar
from downward-hanging flowers, hovering
beneath them as it feeds. When it perches, the
sword-billed hummingbird holds its beak almost
vertical, which makes it easier to support. This
hummingbird lives high up in trees, and rarely
comes down to the ground.

SCIENTIFIC NAME	*Ensifera ensifera*
DISTRIBUTION	Andes Mountains (northern South America)
SIZE	Up to 25cm long

BEE HUMMINGBIRD

This rarely seen hummingbird is the tiniest bird
in the world. Without its feathers, it would be
smaller and lighter than many bumblebees,
though it chases away butterflies several times its
own size. Its eggs can be as small as 6mm long,
and it lays them in a nest smaller than an egg-cup.
Bee hummingbirds feed from a wide range of
flowers, and catch insects to feed to their young.

SCIENTIFIC NAME	*Calypte helenae*
DISTRIBUTION	Cuba
SIZE	About 6cm long

GIANT HUMMINGBIRD

Although it is only the size of a starling, this
plain brown bird is by far the largest member
of the hummingbird family. It is not as good at
hovering as its relatives, and often perches next
to flowers to feed. The giant hummingbird lives
in the mountains, where its size helps it to cope
with the night-time cold.

SCIENTIFIC NAME	*Patagona gigas*
DISTRIBUTION	Andes Mountains (South America)
SIZE	About 22cm long

TROGONS AND MOUSEBIRDS

Trogons are forest birds that live in the tropics. There are about
35 species scattered across the Americas, Africa and Asia, and they
include some of the most beautiful birds in the world. Despite their
flamboyant colours, they are remarkably difficult to see because they
spend a lot of their time perched motionless high in the treetops.
Mousebirds are not related to trogons, and look quite dowdy by
comparison. There are six species, all from Africa, and they get
their name from their
habit of scurrying
about in trees.

RESPLENDENT QUETZAL

This Central American
bird is the most showy
member of the trogon
family. The males have red
underparts and green heads
and backs, but their most
spectacular feature is a
metre-long train of lacy
green plumes that hangs
down over their tails.
Quetzals live in mountain
forests, where they feed
on oil-rich fruit. They nest
in holes in trees, and both
parents share the work of
incubating the eggs. The
female can fit inside the
nest, but the male has to
turn around after he has
climbed in, so his tail
plumes hang out of
the entrance.

SCIENTIFIC NAME	
Pharomachrus mocinno	
DISTRIBUTION	Central America, northern South America
SIZE	Up to 1.4m long, including tail plumes

BLUE-NAPED MOUSEBIRD

Mousebirds have long, slender tails, brown or grey
fur-like plumage, and unusual feet with outer toes
that can be swivelled so that they point forwards
or backwards. They feed on leaves, seeds and
insects, scuttling along branches or hanging
upside down to get at their food. The blue-naped
mousebird is one of the most widespread species.
It lives in small flocks that flutter noisily from
tree to tree, and its young begin to creep among
the branches soon after they hatch.

SCIENTIFIC NAME	*Colius macrourus*
DISTRIBUTION	Tropical Africa
SIZE	Up to 35cm long

BELOW *With a fish firmly grasped in its beak, this common kingfisher is on its way back to its perch to feed. Like other waterbirds, kingfishers swallow fish headfirst.*

Wings beat rapidly during flight

Blue-green back camouflages the kingfisher in the shade

Small, bright orange legs and feet

Common kingfisher watching for food

BELTED KINGFISHER

This is the only kingfisher in most of North America. The males are mainly blue-grey and white, but the females have a rust-coloured 'belt' across their undersides. Belted kingfishers usually watch for food from branches above the water. If one spots a fish, it dives to catch it, then carries it back to its perch and stuns it against a branch before swallowing it. Where rivers freeze in winter, belted kingfishers migrate south.

Belted kingfisher on a perch

SCIENTIFIC NAME *Megaceryle alcyon*

DISTRIBUTION Breeds throughout North America; winters in southern USA, Central America, Colombia

SIZE Up to 33cm long

COMMON KINGFISHER

With its turquoise and orange plumage, this bird looks as though it belongs in the tropics, but it is found as far north as Scandinavia. Its hunting technique is similar to the belted kingfisher's, although the common kingfisher's small size means that it catches much smaller fish. It uses its beak and claws to dig a nest-burrow in the riverbank, and is careful to make the burrow slope upwards, so rain or river water cannot get in. Kingfishers do not use nesting material, but their burrows soon become cluttered with the bones of fish.

SCIENTIFIC NAME *Alcedo atthis*

DISTRIBUTION Europe, northern Africa, central and southern Asia

SIZE Up to 16cm long

KINGFISHERS AND THEIR RELATIVES

This varied group of birds includes kingfishers, rollers, hoopoes, bee-eaters and hornbills. All of these birds have partially joined front toes, and many of them are brightly coloured. Kingfishers are found in every continent, but only about half of the 92 species actually feed on fish. The rest live away from water, snatching up lizards and other animals from the ground. Their relatives also live mainly by catching animals, although hornbills often eat fruit. Rollers, hoopoes, bee-eaters and hornbills are mainly tropical birds, though none of them live in the Americas.

Laughing kookaburra overpowering a snake

LAUGHING KOOKABURRA

This giant Australian kingfisher is famous for its call, which sounds like crazy laughter. It often lives in family groups and, if one bird starts to call, the others soon follow suit. Laughing kookaburras live in dry forests and they catch their prey on the ground. They eat insects, lizards and small birds, and they are also adept at catching snakes. Just like waterside kingfishers, they usually stun their prey before swallowing it, either by dropping it on the ground, or by battering it against a branch.

Kookaburras usually nest in hollow tree-trunks. Young birds often help their parents for several breeding seasons by bringing food to the nest.

SCIENTIFIC NAME	*Dacelo novaeguineae*
DISTRIBUTION	Eastern and southwestern Australia
SIZE	Up to 47cm long

EUROPEAN ROLLER

Rollers look quite like jays (page 229), but they are more closely related to kingfishers. Many of them, including the European roller, are brown and bright blue, and most feed on insects, catching them on the ground, or sometimes in the air. Rollers get their name from the male's aerobatic courtship display, in which he flies high into the air and then dives down, twisting as he falls. European rollers nest in unlined tree-holes, and they lay up to five white eggs at a time.

SCIENTIFIC NAME	*Coracias garrulus*
DISTRIBUTION	Breeds in Europe, Siberia; winters in Africa
SIZE	Up to 32cm long

HOOPOE

The hoopoe is a ground-feeding bird with a pink body, and black and white wings. It has a crest that it can flick up over its head, and a long, curved beak. It uses its beak to probe grass and animal dung for worms and grubs. Hoopoes nest in holes in trees and walls, and are famously unhygienic. The female incubates the eggs, and she and her nest give off a strong smell that may help to keep predators away.

SCIENTIFIC NAME	*Upupa epops*
DISTRIBUTION	Europe, southern Asia, Africa
SIZE	Up to 29cm long

CARMINE BEE-EATER

Bee-eaters specialize in eating bees. They snatch them in mid-air with their long, curved beaks, and carry them back to a perch. There they wipe the bees against the perch to squeeze out the poison from their stings, making them safe to eat. Most bee-eaters have vivid colours. This species is one of the brightest, with a red body and wings, and a turquoise head.

SCIENTIFIC NAME	*Merops nubicus*
DISTRIBUTION	Central Africa
SIZE	Up to 33cm long

GREAT INDIAN HORNBILL

Hornbills live in Africa and southern Asia, and feed on small animals and fruit. They get their name from their massive curved beaks that are often topped with a hard shield or casque. The great Indian hornbill is one of the largest species, with a wingspan of about 1.8m. Hornbills nest in tree-holes, and the female incubates the eggs. Once she is in the nest, the male seals the entrance with mud, leaving a small hole through which he can pass food. The female stays imprisoned for up to three months, until her nestlings are ready to venture out. This remarkable behaviour helps to protect the chicks from snakes and other predators.

SCIENTIFIC NAME	*Buceros bicornis*
DISTRIBUTION	India, Southeast Asia
SIZE	Up to 1.2m long

BELOW LEFT *The European roller watches for food from high lookout posts, such as telegraph poles and dead trees.*
BELOW CENTRE *A hoopoe uses its eyecatching crest to show its mood. Here, it is alert. When the crest is raised, it folds forwards and over the bird's head.*
BELOW RIGHT *Great Indian hornbills eat anything they can collect or overpower. This bird has caught a lizard, which it will swallow whole.*

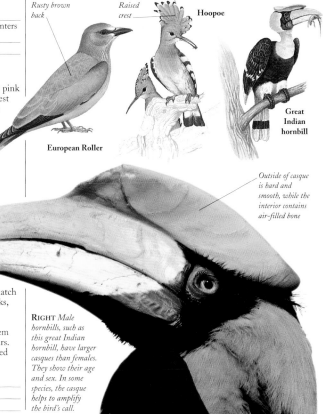

Rusty brown back

Raised crest

Hoopoe

European Roller

Great Indian hornbill

Outside of casque is hard and smooth, while the interior contains air-filled bone

RIGHT *Male hornbills, such as this great Indian hornbill, have larger casques than females. They show their age and sex. In some species, the casque helps to amplify the bird's call.*

WOODPECKERS AND TOUCANS

Woodpeckers and toucans live in trees, but they feed in quite different ways. Most woodpeckers hack away at wood with their beaks, so that they can reach insect grubs hidden inside. They are good climbers, and they cling to the bark with their sharp claws, bracing themselves with their stubby tails. Toucans feed mainly on fruit, and they perch on top of branches instead of climbing up them. Their beaks are enormous and vividly coloured, but also surprisingly light. Toucans use them like giant pairs of pincers, craning forwards to reach their food. There are about 200 species of woodpecker, and they live all over the world, except in Madagascar and Australia. The toucan family contains only about 35 species, all in Central or South America.

ABOVE
Watched by her mate, a female black woodpecker looks out from her nest-hole.
LEFT *Strong feet and a stiff tail give this green woodpecker a steady grip.*

RIGHT *An adult acorn woodpecker returns with food for its young. Its nest is surrounded by acorns that have been wedged into holes in the bark.*

GREEN WOODPECKER
Instead of feeding in trees, this green and yellow woodpecker gets most of its food on the ground. Ants are its favourite prey, and it collects them by pushing its tongue deep into their nests. All woodpeckers have long tongues, often with spiny tips. The green woodpecker's tongue is spiny and sticky, which helps it to collect its prey. Most woodpeckers signal to each other by drumming their beaks against trees, but this one uses its loud laughing cry instead.

SCIENTIFIC NAME	*Picus viridis*
DISTRIBUTION	Europe
SIZE	Up to 32cm long

BLACK WOODPECKER
This is one of the world's largest woodpeckers, and it has an exceptionally powerful peck. When searching for food, it can chisel its way through 15cm of solid wood, scattering wood chips the size of clothes-pegs. As with other woodpeckers, its brain is specially cushioned inside its skull. Without this protection, it would soon be damaged by the impact of the beak smashing into trees. Black woodpeckers feed mainly on insect grubs, but they also break open nests in tree-holes so they can eat the young birds inside.

SCIENTIFIC NAME	*Dryocopus martius*
DISTRIBUTION	Europe, Asia
SIZE	Up to 45cm long

ACORN WOODPECKER
Acorn woodpeckers live in family groups of up to 15 birds. They eat insects in summer, but they use acorns as a winter food. To make sure that they have enough acorns to stay well fed, they store them in holes pecked in dead trees called 'granary trees'. Each hole is large enough for only one acorn, and the woodpeckers drill thousands of holes all the way up the trunk. They hammer

the acorns very tightly into the wood, and then keep a close watch on their food stores, chasing other birds away before they can steal anything.

SCIENTIFIC NAME	*Melanerpes formicivorus*
DISTRIBUTION	Western North America, Central America
SIZE	Up to 23cm long

NORTHERN FLICKER

Flickers are ground-feeding woodpeckers that live throughout the Americas. Like the green woodpecker, they are fond of ants, and have sticky tongues. Their plumage is distinctive, and they have spotted undersides that show up when they fly. The northern flicker breeds in North America, and chisels nest-holes in trees, telegraph poles and sometimes in the walls of wooden houses. During the spring it makes a loud drumming sound by hammering on dead branches and roofs.

SCIENTIFIC NAME	*Colaptes auratus*
DISTRIBUTION	North America, Central America, Caribbean islands
SIZE	Up to 32cm long

TOCO TOUCAN

This extraordinary bird is the largest toucan, with a bright yellow beak and a blue ring around its eyes. Its beak is about as long as a banana, and contains lots of air-filled spaces that make it less heavy and cumbersome than it looks. Toco toucans hop along branches on their pale blue, scaly feet, feeding on fruit and small animals such as insects. Scientists are not sure why toucans' beaks are so huge. They are useful for reaching food, but they may also help the different species to recognize each other, because each one has its own beak colours.

SCIENTIFIC NAME	*Rhamphastos toco*
DISTRIBUTION	Tropical South America
SIZE	Up to 60cm long

KEEL-BILLED TOUCAN

The keel-billed toucan is slightly smaller than the toco toucan, but it has an even more showy beak, coloured brown, orange, green and blue. It lives in forests and in wooded areas near farms. Like other toucans, it flies by alternately flapping its wings and then closing them up by its sides. This makes it dip up and down in the air – something that woodpeckers also do when they fly from tree to tree. Toucan chicks take a

long time to develop. The keel-billed toucan's young take a month to start growing their feathers, and do not leave the nest-hole until they are nearly two months old.

SCIENTIFIC NAME	
Rhamphastos sulfuratus	
DISTRIBUTION	Central America, South America; from Mexico to Venezuela
SIZE	Up to 56cm long

GREEN ARACARI

Aracaris are medium-sized toucans with relatively small, slender beaks. There are about 11 species, and the green aracari is one of the brightest, with a green back and a bright yellow chest. Like its larger relatives, it nests in tree-holes, and lays between two and four eggs a year. Aracaris are the only toucans that use tree-holes as overnight roosts as well as places to breed. Several birds often use the same roost. In order to fit in, they make themselves more compact by turning their beaks over their backs.

SCIENTIFIC NAME	*Pteroglossus viridis*
DISTRIBUTION	Tropical South America
SIZE	Up to 30cm long

BLUE-THROATED BARBET

Barbets are small birds with strong beaks and thickset bodies, related to woodpeckers and toucans. There are about 80 species throughout the tropics, and many have long, repetitive calls. They get their name from the bristles, or barbs, around the bases of their beaks. The blue-throated barbet lives in forests and gardens, where it feeds on fruit and insects.

SCIENTIFIC NAME	*Megalaima asiatica*
DISTRIBUTION	India, Southeast Asia
SIZE	Up to 23cm long

Patch of bare skin around eyes

Yellow throat patch

Both halves of the beak have serrated edges

Two toes point forwards and two backwards

TOP *Like all large toucans, this keel-billed toucan has a black body, a bright throat patch and a giant-sized beak.*
ABOVE *Different species of toucan sometimes feed together. Here, two keel-billed toucans look on as a toco toucan carefully leans forwards to pick a berry.*

PERCHING BIRDS

More than 5,000 species of bird – over half the world's total – belong to a group called the passerine, or perching birds. Most of them are small, and all of them have slender, unwebbed toes that can fold around branches, twigs or wires. When these birds rest on a perch, their toes lock in position so they cannot fall off, even when they are asleep. There are more than 60 families of perching birds, and almost all of them nest in trees. Their nestlings are blind and helpless when they hatch, and are fed by their parents until they are fully fledged and able to find food for themselves. Perching birds are found worldwide, but few live on water. Primitive perching birds, which are featured on these two pages, are often poor singers, but songbirds (pages 212–229), include the best singers in the world.

RUFOUS OVENBIRD OR RUFOUS HORNERO

This small brown bird is unremarkable to look at, but it is famous for its extraordinary nests. It uses wet mud and straw as building materials, and makes a structure shaped like an old-fashioned clay oven, which becomes rock-hard as it slowly dries out. The nest's entrance leads into a spiral passageway, and this crosses over a low threshold before opening out into the nesting chamber itself. The nest is usually positioned on a branch or on top of a fence post, often where it is easy to see. Ovenbirds use their nests for just one breeding season, and make new ones each year.

SCIENTIFIC NAME	*Furnarius rufus*
DISTRIBUTION	Central South America
SIZE	Up to 18cm long

LOVELY COTINGA

This jewel-like bird lives in the forests of Central America, where it feeds on fruit and insects. The females are dark brown, but the males are truly lovely to look at, with sky-blue feathers all over their bodies, and a lilac patch on their throats and chests. There are about 90 species of cotinga, and almost all of them live in trees. They are common throughout warm parts of the Americas, but are not found anywhere else.

SCIENTIFIC NAME	*Cotinga amabilis*
DISTRIBUTION	Central America
SIZE	Up to 20cm long

THREE-WATTLED BELLBIRD

Bellbirds live in dense forest, and are often difficult to spot. However, there is no mistaking their call – a sudden explosion of sound that can be heard up to 800m away. The male three-

TOP *This Rufous ovenbird is standing in a half-built nest. It will finish the nest by constructing a roof to protect the chicks.*
ABOVE *A three-wattled bellbird prepares to call a mate from his display perch in a forest in Costa Rica.*

wattled bellbird has another striking feature – three black, worm-like wattles that hang down from the top and sides of its beak. Bellbirds belong to the cotinga family, and there are four species, each with their own colours and calls.

SCIENTIFIC NAME	*Procnias tricarunculata*
DISTRIBUTION	Central America
SIZE	Up to 30cm long

UMBRELLABIRD

This all-black cotinga is the largest species in its family, with a body the size of a crow. It gets its name from its flattened crest, which looks like an umbrella or hat, but it also has a feathery pouch hanging from its throat. The pouch is inflatable, and in males it can be more than 30cm long when it is fully extended. The male lets his pouch hang over a branch when he broadcasts his courtship call.

SCIENTIFIC NAME	*Cephalopterus ornatus*
DISTRIBUTION	Northern South America
SIZE	Up to 50cm long

GUIANAN COCK-OF-THE-ROCK

Many cotingas are brightly coloured, and the cock-of-the-rock is one of the most beautiful species of all. The female is black, but the male is an intense orange – a rare colour even in tropical birds. The male birds are made even more striking by their semi-circular orange crests, which fold out to reach the tips of their beaks. During the breeding season, the males gather at traditional courtship grounds, or leks, where they carry out noisy displays. The females watch the performance, and select the most impressive males as their mates.

SCIENTIFIC NAME	*Rupicola rupicola*
DISTRIBUTION	Northern South America
SIZE	Up to 32cm long

Slender display feathers on wings

RIGHT *Standing on a log, a male Guianan cock-of-the-rock shows off his spectacular plumage. Once a male has mated, he takes no part in building a nest or raising the young.*

Fully open crest almost hides the beak

Round eye becomes elliptical during displays

Black and white wing feathers

Strong feet for feeding on the forest floor

LEFT *An Eastern kingbird watches for flying insects from its perch on an overhead wire.*

EASTERN KINGBIRD

This common bird breeds across most of North America, apart from the far west. It belongs to a family called the tyrant flycatchers, and feeds on insects by swooping out from a perch to snap them up in mid-air. It lives in woodland clearings and around farms, and nests in trees or on fence posts. The kingbird fearlessly defends its nest, which is how the tyrant flycatcher family got its name.

SCIENTIFIC NAME *Tyrannus tyrannus*

DISTRIBUTION Breeds in North America; winters in Central America, South America

SIZE Up to 22cm long

EASTERN PHOEBE

Phoebes get their name from their song – a sharp-sounding 'fee-bee, fee-bee, fee-bee'. They belong to the tyrant flycatcher family, and fly out to catch insects from a perch. Eastern phoebes are brown and white, with small whiskers around their beaks. They often live near water, and originally nested on cliffs or banks. Today, many nest in buildings or under bridges.

SCIENTIFIC NAME *Sayornis phoebe*

DISTRIBUTION Breeds in eastern North America; winters in southeastern USA, Mexico

SIZE Up to 18cm long

SUPERB LYREBIRD

The lyrebird is a well-known Australian bird. It feeds on the ground, and has large legs and a plump body covered in grey and brown feathers. The female's tail is long and thin, but the male's has four curved feathers, and lacy plumes that spread open and tip forwards during the bird's courtship display. Lyrebirds live in forests and feed on insects and other small animals. They have powerful calls and are skilful mimics, copying many sounds from birdsong to machinery.

SCIENTIFIC NAME *Menura novaehollandiae*

DISTRIBUTION Southeastern Australia, Tasmania

SIZE Up to 1m long, including tail

SKYLARK

Larks are small brown and grey birds that feed and nest on the ground. Many of them are good singers, but the skylark outshines all the others. It sings while it climbs into the sky, and keeps singing from high up in the air. Skylarks tuck away their cup-shaped nests out of sight in grassy fields, and raise two or three families a year. They eat insects and seeds.

SCIENTIFIC NAME *Alauda arvensis*

DISTRIBUTION Europe, Asia, northern Africa

SIZE Up to 18cm long

ABOVE *Skylarks have been badly affected by changes in farming practices because they need undisturbed pasture for nesting. This kind of habitat can be hard to find on modern farms.*

BELOW AND BOTTOM
A swallow's tail feathers help to show how old it is. This swallow has short feathers, showing that it is less than a year old.

SWALLOW

The swallow is one of the world's best-known migrants. It feeds on insects, which it catches in mid-air. Its streamlined blue and white body is shaped for fast, long-distance flight, and its narrow wings and forked tail make it highly manoeuverable, so that it can twist and turn after its prey. Swallows make their nests from mud and grass, and they often fasten them to wooden beams and walls.

SCIENTIFIC NAME
Hirundo rustica

DISTRIBUTION Breeds in the northern hemisphere; winters in the southern hemisphere

SIZE Up to 19cm long

HOUSE MARTIN

This airborne insect-eater is a close relative of the swallow, and is sometimes mistaken for it. However, it has a short tail and a large white patch on its deep blue back. Also, its underside is completely white. House martins make their nests out of mud, with tiny entrance holes, and like nesting on buildings even more than swallows. House martins usually nest under overhanging eaves, where they are protected from the rain, but they also build nests under bridges and on rock faces and cliffs.

SCIENTIFIC NAME *Delichon urbica*

DISTRIBUTION Breeds in Europe, Asia; winters in Africa, India, Southeast Asia.

SIZE Up to 13cm long

Food in beak shows that this house martin is raising a family

Legs tucked up during flight

RIGHT AND FAR RIGHT
House martins often feed in the same areas as swallows, but they usually fly higher up. This prevents the two species competing for the same food.

Short tail feathers

PURPLE MARTIN

Every spring, millions of purple martins fly northwards to the USA and Canada to return to the places where they bred or hatched the previous year. Unlike most other martins and swallows, these birds vary in colour according to their sex. The males are shiny purple all over, but the females are grey underneath. Purple martins normally nest in tree-holes and on rocky ledges but, in the east particularly, they find purpose-built bird-houses an irresistible attraction. These houses usually have many compartments, and they can be home to lots of birds.

SCIENTIFIC NAME *Progne subis*

DISTRIBUTION Breeds in North America; winters in northern South America

SIZE Up to 19cm long

PIED WAGTAIL

Whether they are walking about or standing still, wagtails constantly bob their tails up and down. This tail-wagging probably helps them to keep their balance as they move around on the ground looking for insects to eat. There are eight species of wagtail, and all have slender bodies, narrow beaks and long legs and toes. Pied wagtails are black, grey and white. They live on open ground, around farms and in gardens, and often build their nests on creeper-covered walls.

SCIENTIFIC NAME *Motacilla alba*

DISTRIBUTION Europe, northern Africa, Asia

SIZE Up to 18cm long

ROCK PIPIT

Pipits are small brown birds that spend most of their lives on the ground. Most are found inland, but the rock pipit lives along the shore, where it feeds on small snails, sandhoppers and tiny flies that breed in rotting seaweed. The rock pipit nests in

Long, narrow wings provide speed and manoeuvrability

crevices in cliffs, and makes its cup-shaped nest out of grass. Like many songbirds, it often collects hair or wool caught on fences, and uses this to give its nest a warm lining.

SCIENTIFIC NAME *Anthus petrosus*

DISTRIBUTION Western Europe

SIZE Up to 17cm long

RED-EYED BULBUL

In Africa and southern Asia, bulbuls feed in open woodlands, parks and gardens, and in other places where there is a chance of finding insects and ripe fruit. There are more than 100 species of bulbul, and the red-eyed bulbul is a typical example, with a whistling call and busy, self-assured manner. It has a greyish-brown body and black head, and gets its name from the bright red rings around its eyes. Like most other bulbuls, it nests in low trees and bushes. The parents take turns to incubate the eggs and they both feed their young.

SCIENTIFIC NAME
Pycnonotus jocosus

DISTRIBUTION Southern Africa

SIZE Up to 21cm long

RED-BACKED SHRIKE

Although they are songbirds, shrikes behave more like miniature birds of prey. They attack insects, lizards, birds and small rodents, killing them with their hooked beaks. If they manage to kill more animals than they need, they store the surplus food by impaling it on thorns, or sometimes on the spikes of barbed-wire fences. The red-backed shrike is one of several species that migrate northwards to Europe every year. It has a grey head, a rusty-red back and a black stripe running across its eyes – rather like a bandit's mask. It nests in thorny bushes, and lays up to six eggs at a time.

SCIENTIFIC NAME *Lanius collurio*

DISTRIBUTION Breeds in Europe, western Asia; winters mainly in Africa

SIZE Up to 18 cm long

TOP *The pied wagtail feeds on the ground but it is an expert at catching insects that try to fly away. This one is collecting food for its nestlings.*
ABOVE *A red-eyed bulbul pants in the midday heat. Birds cannot lose heat by sweating because they do not have sweat glands. Instead, many of them pant when they get too hot.*

MOCKINGBIRD

The mockingbird is a tuneful singer, and the best bird mimic in the whole of North America. It imitates a bewildering variety of sounds, from ringing telephones to barking dogs, and has been known to copy the songs and calls of up to 30 different birds. Mockingbirds are not spectacular to look at – their plumage is light and dark grey – but they are successful and adaptable. They live in cities as well as the countryside, and feed mainly on seeds, fruit and small animals. Mockingbirds nest in trees, and chase off any other birds that venture too close.

Adult mockingbird on a branch

SCIENTIFIC NAME *Mimus polyglottus*

DISTRIBUTION North America

SIZE Up to 25cm long

NORTHERN WREN

Wrens are small, highly active birds that often have upright tails. There are more than 60 species, but the northern wren is the only one that is found outside the Americas. This tiny bird can fly well, but it spends most of its time hopping and flitting over the ground or through bushes, probing for insects and spiders with its needle-sharp beak. During the breeding season, male northern wrens flutter up onto treetops or telephone wires, where they sing amazingly loudly. Northern wrens build domed nests in thick vegetation, and they raise up to two families a year.

SCIENTIFIC NAME *Troglodytes troglodytes*

DISTRIBUTION North America, Europe, northern Africa, central Asia, Far East

SIZE Up to 8cm long

BELOW LEFT Because they are so small, northern wrens are vulnerable to winter cold. This one has survived through to spring and is gathering food.
BELOW The songthrush starts singing in January – an early sign that spring is not far away.

Upright stance is typical of the songthrush

DIPPER

The dipper looks like a giant white-breasted wren, but it has a remarkable lifestyle all of its own. It feeds on insect grubs and other small animals in fast-flowing rivers, and gets at its food by swimming and walking underwater. It always walks against the current, so that the force of the water presses down on its back, stopping it from bobbing back up to the surface. Dippers do not have webbed feet, but they have well-developed nictitating membranes – semi-transparent eyelids that wipe water off their eyes.

SCIENTIFIC NAME *Cinclus cinclus*

DISTRIBUTION Europe, North Africa, parts of central Asia

SIZE Up to 18cm long

BOHEMIAN WAXWING

This sleek, crested songbird normally lives in northern forests, where it feeds on insects in summer, and berries during the winter. Every few years, the berry crop fails and the hungry waxwings fly south, turning up in places where they are rarely seen. Scientists call these sudden movements irruptions. Bohemian waxwings are grey-brown, with black and yellow tips to their wings and tails. They have large appetites, and sometimes eat so much that they can hardly fly.

SCIENTIFIC NAME *Bombycilla garrulus*

DISTRIBUTION North America, Europe, northern Asia

SIZE Up to 18cm long

SONGTHRUSH

Thrushes make up one of the largest families of songbirds, with more than 300 species. Many species, including the songthrush, are talented singers. Although they nest in trees, most of them feed on the ground, where they eat fruit and small animals such as earthworms. The songthrush is also an expert at dealing with snails. When it finds one, it hits it against a large stone, breaking open its shell. Thrush stones are easy to spot because they are often littered with smashed shells.

SCIENTIFIC NAME *Turdus philomelos*

DISTRIBUTION Originally from Europe, northern Africa, Middle East, central Asia; introduced into Australia, New Zealand

SIZE Up to 23cm long

Wings are strong and flexible

Streamlined body feathers

BLACKBIRD
The blackbird was originally a forest bird, but in northern Europe it often feeds and nests in gardens. It pulls up earthworms on lawns, and also turns over fallen leaves, snapping up other small animals such as insects. Because they are ground-feeding birds, blackbirds have to keep a constant lookout for danger. If a blackbird spots a predator, such as a cat, it follows it at a safe distance, noisily sounding the alarm. Only male blackbirds are black; the females are dark brown. Males and females work together to make cup-shaped nests lined with mud and grass. They raise up to three families each year.

Flight feathers spread during take off

SCIENTIFIC NAME
Turdus merula

DISTRIBUTION
Originally from Europe, northern Africa, parts of Asia; introduced into Australia, New Zealand

SIZE Up to 24cm long

EURASIAN ROBIN
This common bird is well known for its bright red breast, and also for its friendly behaviour. In western Europe, robins often follow gardeners to eat worms turned up during digging, and they sometimes become so tame that they will take food from an open hand. Robins are not so neighbourly with each other. The males defend their territories vigorously, chasing away any rival males, but allowing females to enter. Once a male and female robin have mated, the female builds a domed nest lined with moss and animal hair. The nest is usually hidden away near the ground, but robins also nest in garages and garden sheds.

SCIENTIFIC NAME *Erithacus rubecula*

DISTRIBUTION Europe, northern Africa, Middle East, western Asia

SIZE Up to 14cm long

AMERICAN ROBIN
American and Eurasian robins both belong to the thrush family, and both have orange-red breasts. However, the American robin is a much larger bird, with a brown-grey back and a streaked black and white throat. American robins often live in parks and gardens, where they pull up earthworms from the ground. Like other large thrushes, they find worms by sight, but their habit of cocking their heads makes it look as though they are listening for them instead. American robins are tuneful singers. They nest in trees and buildings, and lay pale blue eggs.

SCIENTIFIC NAME *Turdus migratorius*

DISTRIBUTION North America

SIZE Up to 25cm long

ABOVE *A fast getaway helps the blackbird to survive in gardens where cats are on the prowl. Its piercing alarm call warns other birds to be on the alert.*
RIGHT *Like the blackbird, the American robin is a woodland bird that has successfully adapted to life in parks and gardens.*

Both males and females have bright red breasts

ABOVE *With an insect held tightly in its beak, a Eurasian robin comes in to land. Robins are very good at spotting the slightest movement, and they often swoop on worms or insect grubs from several metres away.*

Clawed feet can cling tightly to a perch

NIGHTINGALE

In Europe, the nightingale has a reputation for being one of the finest singers in the bird world. Its plain brown plumage and secretive habits make it difficult to see, but its rich, fluty song is impossible to mistake. Nightingales are unusual because they sing by night as well as by day, which is how they get their name. They feed on insects and fruit, and nest low down in tangled vegetation.

SCIENTIFIC NAME *Luscinia megarhynchos*

DISTRIBUTION Breeds in Europe, central Asia; winters mainly in Africa

SIZE Up to 17cm long

EASTERN BLUEBIRD

Bluebirds are not outstanding singers, but they are among the most colourful birds in the thrush family. There are three species in North America. The eastern bluebird has an orange-red chest and a deep blue head and back. Unlike most thrushes, bluebirds nest in holes, and eastern bluebirds often use those made by woodpeckers. During the last one hundred years, they have had to cope with stiff competition from introduced starlings, but nest-boxes are now helping them to survive.

SCIENTIFIC NAME *Sialia sialis*

DISTRIBUTION Eastern North America, Central America

SIZE Up to 18cm long

ABOVE LEFT *The nightingale lives mostly in woodlands.*
ABOVE RIGHT *Reed warblers are often tricked by cuckoos (page 203) into raising their young.*

REED WARBLER

Warblers are small, unobtrusive birds that feed largely on insects. There are more than 300 species scattered across Europe, Africa, Asia and Australia and, although some look almost identical, their distinctive songs help in telling them apart. The reed warbler lives in reedbeds, where it usually stays well out of sight. It makes a cup-shaped nest slung between three or four reed-stems, and raises two families a year. Its song sounds like a busy chatter, with lots of notes repeated three or four times in quick succession. Like most other warblers, it migrates to breed. American warblers (page 220) share similar lifestyles, but they belong to a separate family of birds.

SCIENTIFIC NAME *Acrocephalus scirpaceus*

DISTRIBUTION Breeds in Europe; winters mainly in Africa

SIZE Up to 13cm long

GOLDCREST

The goldcrest is one of the tiniest warblers, with a green and white body and a bright yellow stripe on its head. It lives mainly in coniferous forests, where it flits along branches and twigs, eating small insects and their eggs. It makes a cup-shaped nest out of moss and spiders' webs, and often hangs it near the end of a branch. The goldcrest has four equally small relatives that live in forests across the northern hemisphere. They are known collectively as kinglets.

SCIENTIFIC NAME
Regulus regulus

DISTRIBUTION Europe, northern Africa, central Asia, Far East

SIZE Up to 9cm long

Narrow beak for extracting insect grubs and eggs from bark

ABOVE *Weighing as little as five grams, the goldcrest is one of Europe's smallest birds. Despite its small size, it is a fearless fighter and will peck at anything that comes close to its nest.*

Short, slightly forked tail

Clawed feet well developed for perching

GREAT TIT

The great tit belongs to a family of small birds known as titmice. They are acrobatic, and often hang upside down in trees as they search for insects and seeds. Many of them store food for the winter, and they often visit bird-tables in cold weather. The great tit is the largest species, and it has a wide distribution. Its colour varies, but it usually has a black head and a bright yellow underside marked with a black stripe. Like other titmice, it nests in holes and often raises two families a year.

SCIENTIFIC NAME *Parus major*

DISTRIBUTION Europe, northern Africa, central and southern Asia

SIZE Up to 14cm long

Open beak is used as a threat

Blue tits can fit through a hole just 3cm across

BLACK-CAPPED CHICKADEE

The chickadee is one of about 12 different titmice that live in North America. It gets its name from its call, which sounds like 'chickadee-dee-dee'. It has a black head and grey back – a colour scheme shared by several other chickadees that have slightly different songs. Chickadees live in woodlands and in gardens with trees. During the spring, they feed their young on caterpillars and other insects, but in winter they feed on small nuts and seeds.

Black-capped chickadee

SCIENTIFIC NAME
Parus atricapillus

DISTRIBUTION North America

SIZE Up to 13cm long

AFRICAN PARADISE FLYCATCHER

Paradise flycatchers are not much larger than sparrows, but the males have long tail feathers that more than double their total body length. These elegant white or chestnut-coloured birds feed entirely on flying insects, and flutter from a perch to snatch them out of the air. There are several species, and they are found from Africa eastwards to Japan. All of them make

Small, compact wings

well-constructed cup-shaped nests, held together with spiders' silk.

SCIENTIFIC NAME *Tersiphone viridis*

DISTRIBUTION Africa

SIZE Males up to 40cm long, including tail feathers

SPLENDID WREN

The splendid wren is one of Australia's most colourful birds. The females are brown, but during the breeding season, the males are often an intense light blue. Splendid wrens have long upturned tails but they are not closely related to true wrens, which live in other parts of the world.

SCIENTIFIC NAME *Malurus cyaneus*

DISTRIBUTION Central and southern Australia

SIZE Up to 14cm long

ABOVE A great tit (top) and a blue tit (Parus caeruleus) (centre) argue over a nest-hole. For these birds, a good supply of nest-holes is almost as important as a good supply of food.

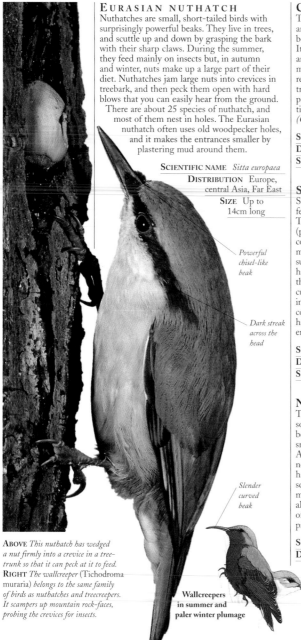

EURASIAN NUTHATCH

Nuthatches are small, short-tailed birds with surprisingly powerful beaks. They live in trees, and scuttle up and down by grasping the bark with their sharp claws. During the summer, they feed mainly on insects but, in autumn and winter, nuts make up a large part of their diet. Nuthatches jam large nuts into crevices in treebark, and then peck them open with hard blows that you can easily hear from the ground.

There are about 25 species of nuthatch, and most of them nest in holes. The Eurasian nuthatch often uses old woodpecker holes, and it makes the entrances smaller by plastering mud around them.

SCIENTIFIC NAME *Sitta europaea*

DISTRIBUTION Europe, central Asia, Far East

SIZE Up to 14cm long

Powerful chisel-like beak

Dark streak across the head

Slender curved beak

ABOVE *This nuthatch has wedged a nut firmly into a crevice in a tree-trunk so that it can peck at it to feed.*
RIGHT *The wallcreeper* (Tichodroma muraria) *belongs to the same family of birds as nuthatches and treecreepers. It scampers up mountain rock-faces, probing the crevices for insects.*

Wallcreepers in summer and paler winter plumage

COMMON TREECREEPER

This small brown-backed bird feeds on insects and spiders on trees, and uses its narrow, curved beak to pick them out of crevices in the bark. It starts looking for food at the base of a tree, and then works its way upwards with a jerky movement, using its tail as a prop. When it reaches the top, it flies to the bottom of another tree and starts again. Treecreepers nest behind pieces of loose bark, and lay up to six eggs at a time. In North America, the brown creeper *(Certhia americana)* lives in a very similar way.

SCIENTIFIC NAME *Certhia familiaris*

DISTRIBUTION Europe, central Asia, Far East

SIZE Up to 13cm long

SCARLET-CHESTED SUNBIRD

Sunbirds live in Africa, Asia and Australia, and feed on insects and sugary nectar from flowers. Their lifestyle is very like that of hummingbirds (pages 204–205), as are their brilliant metallic colours. However, sunbirds cannot hover, and must perch on flowers to feed. The scarlet-chested sunbird is a typical species from Africa – the male has a scarlet chest and shiny green head, while the female is mostly brown. It has a long, slightly curved beak – an ideal implement for reaching into flowers for food. Like most sunbirds, it constructs a remarkable purse-shaped nest which hangs from the end of a branch. The nest has an entrance hole near the top, covered by a porch.

SCIENTIFIC NAME *Nectarinia senegalensis*

DISTRIBUTION Tropical and southern Africa

SIZE Up to 15cm long

NOISY FRIARBIRD

This large Australian bird is one of the few songbirds to have an almost bald head. Its beak is large and slightly curved, with a small knob on the top, just above the base. Apart from these physical oddities, its most noticeable feature is its voice. It sounds harsh and aggressive, particularly when squabbling over food. Noisy friarbirds feed mainly on nectar and fruit, although they also eat insects. They live in a wide range of habitats, including forests, gardens and parks, and make their nests high in trees.

SCIENTIFIC NAME *Philemon corniculatus*

DISTRIBUTION Eastern Australia

SIZE Up to 37cm long

RIGHT *Treecreepers move in a spiral up tree-trunks. They use their stiff tail feathers to brace themselves as they feed.*

BLUE-FACED HONEYEATER

The blue-faced honeyeater is a close relative of the noisy friarbird, but its head is partly feathered. It gets its name from the patch of bright blue skin behind each eye. Blue-faced honeyeaters are bold and aggressive birds, and are not afraid of people. As well as eating nectar and fruit, they raid banana plantations, and eat syrup in fields of harvested sugar cane. They sometimes build their own nests, but they often take over nests made by other birds.

SCIENTIFIC NAME *Entomyzon cyanotis*

DISTRIBUTION Eastern and northern Australia, New Guinea

SIZE Up to 33cm long

ABOVE *The woodpecker finch is one of the few birds that uses tools to get at its food. In captivity, some other Galapagos Island finches have been seen to copy its behaviour.*

WOODPECKER FINCH

This bird is famous for the way it uses tools to get at its food. It eats insects and other small animals, and normally picks them out from wood or from crevices in bark. If an insect is hard to reach, the finch sometimes uses a cactus spine to lever out its prey. The woodpecker finch is one of 13 species of finch that live on the remote Galapagos Islands in the eastern Pacific. Biologists believe that these finches all evolved from one original species that reached the islands from the South American mainland thousands of years ago.

SCIENTIFIC NAME *Camarhynchus pallidus*

DISTRIBUTION Galapagos Islands

SIZE Up to 15cm long

NORTHERN CARDINAL

With its spiky crest and crimson plumage, the male northern cardinal is one of the most colourful birds in North America. Unlike most songbirds, both the males and females sing, and they keep up their song for most of the year. Cardinals live in woodlands and thickets, and also in gardens. They eat insects and seeds, and often visit bird-tables during the winter. During the last one hundred years, cardinals have spread steadily northwards – food provided in gardens during the winter may be helping them to thrive.

Adult male northern cardinal

SCIENTIFIC NAME *Cardinalis cardinalis*

DISTRIBUTION Originally from eastern North America, Central America; introduced into Hawaii

SIZE Up to 22cm long

WESTERN TANAGER

Tanagers are brightly coloured birds found only in the Americas. There are more than 200 species. Many live all year round in the tropics, but some, including the western tanager, migrate to breed. They feed mainly on insects, and hide in trees and bushes. Western tanagers nest in mountain forests. The female makes the nest and incubates the eggs. She is yellowish-green, but during the breeding season, the male is yellow with black wings and a red head.

SCIENTIFIC NAME *Piranga ludoviciana*

DISTRIBUTION Breeds in western North America; winters in Central America

SIZE Up to 20cm long

Extra-large claws cling to bark

Short, rounded wings

Tips of tail feathers are worn to sharp points

YELLOW WARBLER

This bright yellow insect-eater belongs to a family of birds called wood warblers, which contains about 100 species. Wood warblers live throughout the Americas, and about half of them, including the yellow warbler, migrate northwards every spring to breed. Wood warblers often join other species to form mixed flocks when they migrate, and they travel in straggling waves containing millions of birds. Like most of its relatives, the yellow warbler feeds on insects. It makes a small cup-shaped nest near the water's edge, and lays up to five eggs at a time.

SCIENTIFIC NAME *Dendroica petechia*

DISTRIBUTION Breeds in North America; winters in Central America, northern South America

SIZE Up to 13cm long

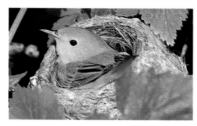

CENTRE LEFT *Tucked up in its nest, a yellow warbler incubates its clutch of eggs.*
LEFT *An Eastern meadowlark sings on a fence post. Like many other birds that breed in grassy fields, meadowlarks are threatened by farm machinery, which often destroys their nests.*

Spotted flanks

Black V-shaped band on breast

Strong feet for feeding on the ground

BLACK-AND-WHITE WARBLER

North American wood warblers can be difficult to identify because many of them look very similar. This species is easy to recognize because it is entirely black and white. It also scuttles up and down tree-trunks and along branches, picking insects out of crevices in the bark. This warbler is among the earliest to fly north in spring, because the insects on which it relies do not feed on leaves.

SCIENTIFIC NAME *Mniotilta varia*

DISTRIBUTION Breeds in North America, except the west; winters in Central America, northern South America

SIZE Up to 13cm long

COMMON GRACKLE

Grackles look quite like crows (page 228), but they are smaller with narrow beaks and slender legs, and often have a purple sheen. They belong to the American blackbird family – a group of birds that also includes meadowlarks, bobolinks, orioles, cowbirds and oropendolas. These birds live in a wide variety of habitats, and they are all good fliers, with long, pointed wings. Common grackles feed on farmland and in towns, and although they eat plenty of insects, they can

sometimes be a problem for farmers when they raid fields for grain. They breed in small groups, but in winter they gather together in immense, noisy roosts that can contain more than one million birds.

SCIENTIFIC NAME *Quisqualus quiscula*

DISTRIBUTION Eastern North America

SIZE Up to 32cm long

EASTERN MEADOWLARK

Meadowlarks are birds of open, grassy places. They nest on the ground, and use their needle-sharp beaks to probe the grass for worms and other animals. The eastern meadowlark has a streaked brown and white back, a yellow breast, and a whistle-like song. A similar species, called the western meadowlark *(Sturnella neglecta)*, looks almost identical, and the two birds' ranges overlap. They sound quite different, which helps to ensure that they breed only with their own kind. Both species fly south for the winter.

SCIENTIFIC NAME *Sturnella magna*

DISTRIBUTION North America, Central America, South America

SIZE Up to 25cm long

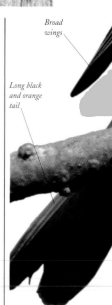

Broad wings

Long black and orange tail

BELOW *Northern orioles have two different plumage patterns. Male birds from the east of their range, like the one shown here, have all-black heads.*

White wing patch

ABOVE *This young male northern oriole has a coloured face, showing that it comes from western North America. As it gets older, its plumage will turn more orange. Most northern orioles spend the winter in the tropics, but a few stay behind, particularly in areas where people put out food.*

NORTHERN ORIOLE

With their bright orange and black plumage, male northern orioles are a common sight throughout North America during the spring and summer months. The females are not nearly as eyecatching as the males because their plumage is greenish-brown. Northern orioles live in woodland and open ground with trees, and they feed on fruit and insects. They lay their eggs in pouch-shaped nests that hang from the outer branches of trees.

SCIENTIFIC NAME	*Icterus galbula*
DISTRIBUTION	Breeds in North America; winters in Central America, northern South America
SIZE	Up to 22cm long

BROWN-HEADED COWBIRD

Cowbirds are the only birds in North America that always lay their eggs in other birds' nests. Unlike the common cuckoo (page 203), the brown-headed cowbird is not at all fussy when it comes to choosing foster parents. More than 200 species are known to raise its eggs. The cowbird leaves a single egg in each nest, and this usually hatches before the other bird's eggs, giving the cowbird chick a good chance of getting the most food. Some birds throw out the cowbird egg, but most raise the chick along with their own. Cowbirds eat insects, and they get their name because they often feed among cattle in fields.

SCIENTIFIC NAME	*Molothrus ater*
DISTRIBUTION	North America
SIZE	Up to 19cm long

CRESTED OROPENDOLA

This tropical rainforest bird is one of the largest members of the American blackbird family. It is mainly black, with a yellow and black tail, and has a flat forehead that seems to merge with its beak – a typical feature in this group of birds. Oropendolas make an amazing collection of sounds, but their most interesting feature is the way in which they nest. They breed together in very tall trees, and build hanging nests up to a metre long. There can be more than one hundred nests in a single tree and, from a distance, the hanging nests look like giant fruit dangling from the branches.

SCIENTIFIC NAME	*Psarocolius decumanus*
DISTRIBUTION	Central South America, tropical South America
SIZE	Up to 48cm long

BOBOLINK

The bobolink gets its name from the males' bubbling songs. Females have brown plumage, but during the breeding season the males are mainly black and white. Bobolinks feed on insects and seeds, and they nest on the ground. Like many other ground-nesters, they have been affected by modern farming methods because grass is often cut before spring is over. This makes it harder for them to raise their young.

SCIENTIFIC NAME	*Dolichonyx oryzivorus*
DISTRIBUTION	Breeds in North America; winters in South America
SIZE	Up to 18cm long

AMERICAN GOLDFINCH

Finches are small songbirds with short, strong beaks. They feed mainly on seeds, cracking open the husks to get at the nutritious food inside. There are hundreds of species of finch, and they are found all over the world, particularly in woodlands, farmland and grassy places. The American goldfinch is a typical farmland species that often feeds in weed-covered fields. It is most noticeable in late summer and autumn, when large flocks gather to feed on thistle and sunflower seeds. The Eurasian goldfinch *(Carduelis carduelis)* is a close relative. It is about the same size, but has a bright red face.

SCIENTIFIC NAME   *Carduelis tristis*

DISTRIBUTION   North America; from Canada to Mexico

SIZE   Up to 13cm long

ABOVE *This male American goldfinch is in his breeding plumage. When the summer ends, he will lose his black cap and his body will turn grey-brown.*

CHAFFINCH

This lively little finch is one of Europe's most common birds. It feeds mainly on the ground in fields, gardens and other open places, and it nests wherever there are bushes or trees. If it gets enough food, it can raise two families a year, and its young are ready to fly just 12 days after they hatch. Chaffinches collect insects when they are feeding their young, but in winter they live mainly on seeds. At this time of year, they often form mixed flocks with other small birds – a habit that helps them to spot danger.

SCIENTIFIC NAME   *Fringilla coelebs*

DISTRIBUTION   Europe, northern Africa, western Asia

SIZE   Up to 15cm long

Broad wings help the bird to take off quickly

LEFT *Like all finches, the chaffinch has short, broad wings that are ideal for quick bursts of flight when searching for food. This bird is female – males have brighter colours.*

Female

Male

Legs held against the body during flight

Male

GOULDIAN FINCH

Named after John Gould, a famous English ornithologist, this Australian finch is one of the most colourful finches in the world. It has a black, red or yellow face, bright green wings, a lilac breast, yellow undersides and a light blue base to its tail. Gouldian finches are found only in Australia's far north, and because changes in farming methods have made life harder for them, they are now quite rare. During the dry season they feed on seeds, but during the wet season, when they nest and raise their young, they feed mainly on flying insects.

SCIENTIFIC NAME   *Chloebia gouldiae*

DISTRIBUTION   Northern Australia

SIZE   Up to 13cm long

Female

Male

Male

Female

ABOVE LEFT *In Europe, greenfinches (Chloris chloris) often live on farms and in gardens.*

ABOVE *The hawfinch (Coccothraustes coccothraustes) has a heavy-duty beak that can crack open cherry stones.*

ABOVE *The serin (Serinus serinus) is a common finch in southern Europe. It lives in parks, farmland and gardens.*

ABOVE *The bullfinch (Pyrrhula pyrrhula) is not popular with fruit-growers because it eats fruit-tree buds in winter.*

RED CROSSBILL

Crossbills are very unusual finches that live in coniferous forests. They feed on seeds in cones, and they get at their food using their remarkable beaks, which have tips that cross over. This kind of beak is particularly useful for dealing with green, unripe cones. Crossbills hold down the cones with their feet, and then slice them open to reach the juicy seeds hidden inside. There are four species of crossbill, and they all specialize in tackling seeds from different trees. The red crossbill is the most widespread. It feeds mainly on spruce seeds, and spends most of its time high in trees. Only the male is red – the female is a drab olive-grey.

SCIENTIFIC NAME *Loxia curvirostra*

DISTRIBUTION Northern hemisphere, particularly in the far north

SIZE Up to 16cm long

HOUSE SPARROW

The house sparrow is one of the world's most successful birds. It originally lived only in southern Europe, northern Africa and the Middle East but, because it thrives wherever people live, it has managed to spread to almost all the inhabited parts of the world. It swept across North America after arriving in 1852, and it did almost as well in Australia when it was introduced about ten years later. House sparrows eat seeds, insects and leftover food. They rarely stray far from buildings, and they make nests from dry grass, often in holes in walls. They lay up to six eggs at a time, and raise up to three families a year.

SCIENTIFIC NAME *Passer domesticus*

DISTRIBUTION Worldwide

SIZE Up to 15cm long

VILLAGE WEAVER

Close relatives of the house sparrow, weaver birds live in Africa and southern Asia. They usually breed in groups, and are famous for their nest-building skills. The village weaver makes its nest from strips of grass, and hangs it high in a tree. The male weaves the grass into a hollow ball. He finishes it by adding a hanging entrance, and then flutters beneath it, enticing females to look inside. If a female likes the nest, she moves in and lays her eggs. Village weavers are the most common species of weaver bird in Africa, and a single tree can hold many nests.

SCIENTIFIC NAME *Ploceus cucullatus*

DISTRIBUTION Tropical and southern Africa

SIZE Up to 17cm long

RED-BILLED QUELEA

This small, pale brown African weaver is probably the most abundant bird in the world. Flocks of queleas sometimes contain more than one hundred thousand birds, and the total number of breeding adults may be as many as 1.5 billion. Queleas usually live in grassy places and scrub, but they can cause devastation when they settle in fields of crops.

SCIENTIFIC NAME *Quelea quelea*

DISTRIBUTION Tropical and southern Africa

SIZE Up to 13cm long

Male pine grosbeak

Female pine grosbeak

Parrot crossbill

ABOVE *The red crossbill has an unusual beak. The top half almost always crosses over to the right.*

FAR LEFT *Parrot crossbills (Loxia pytyopsittacus) get their name from their habit of gripping cones with their feet as they feed – like parrots.*

LEFT *The pine grosbeak (Pinicola enucleator) is a relative of the crossbills. At 20cm long, it is Europe's largest finch.*

RIGHT *House sparrows are highly adaptable birds. They have been found living high up inside skyscrapers and even down coal mines.*

NESTS

Animals make nests to shelter their young, and to protect themselves from predators or from the weather. Birds are the best-known nest-builders, but nests are made by other animals too. The largest nests, made by termites (page 55), can be up to 6m high.

Animals use a wide variety of building materials, including sticks, leaves, mud and saliva, but when they build their nests they always follow the same plan. This is because they work by instinct, following a pattern of behaviour that is different for each species. Although they do not need to learn how to build, they often improve with experience.

For male weaver birds, producing a good nest is essential. This is because these birds often use their nests to attract mates. If a nest does not impress any females, the male bird will often abandon it and build a new one.

Weaver bird at its nest

COMMON STARLING

This familiar bird lives in flocks, and feeds mainly on the ground, jabbing its beak into grass to find insects and earthworms. It also snaps up leftover food, and so it thrives in towns and cities. Starlings normally nest in tree-holes, but they often take over nest-boxes meant for other birds. Outside the breeding season, starlings often gather together to roost. In some cities, thousands of them pour in from the countryside on winter afternoons to settle on trees or under bridges for the night.

SCIENTIFIC NAME
Sturnus vulgaris

DISTRIBUTION Originally from Europe, northern Africa, Middle East, western Asia; introduced into North America, South Africa, Australia

SIZE Up to 20cm long

Adult has staring yellow eyes

Wings with pointed tips

Common starling

LEFT This common starling's spotted plumage shows that it is an adult. Young birds are greyish-brown all over.
BELOW LEFT The superb starling is a noisy and sociable bird that feeds in small flocks.

SUPERB STARLING

There are more than 100 species in the starling family, many of which are brightly coloured. The African superb starling is one of the showiest, with a glossy green back, orange undersides and pale yellow eyes. Superb starlings originally lived in wooded grassland, but today they often live in fields and gardens too. Like most starlings, they are not afraid of people, and they gather at campsites to feed on leftover scraps of food. Superb starlings nest in holes in trees or in thorn bushes.

SCIENTIFIC NAME *Spreo superbus*

DISTRIBUTION Eastern Africa

SIZE Up to 18cm long

RED-BILLED OXPECKER

Oxpeckers have an unusual way of finding food. Using their strong feet and sharp claws, they scamper over the skins of rhinos, giraffes and other grazing mammals, picking off ticks and other parasites. The oxpeckers' hosts seem to realize that they are useful visitors, because they do not brush them away. If an oxpecker is alarmed, it will often scuttle around its host until it is out of sight – like a squirrel hiding behind the trunk of a tree. There are two species of these intriguing birds. The red-billed oxpecker is mainly brown, with a bright red beak.

SCIENTIFIC NAME *Buphagus erythrorhynchus*

DISTRIBUTION Eastern and southern Africa

SIZE Up to 19cm long

Glossy plumage without speckles

Superb starling

Red-billed oxpeckers looking for food on a rhino

HILL MYNAH
Hill mynahs are popular cage-birds because they are good at imitating human speech. They are more talkative than parrots, and they can even become a problem because they make so much noise. They are mainly black, but they have yellow beaks, and a conspicuous patch of bare yellow skin around the sides and back of their heads. In the wild, hill mynahs eat fruit and insects, getting their food from trees.

SCIENTIFIC NAME	*Gracula religiosa*
DISTRIBUTION	Southeast Asia
SIZE	Up to 30cm long

GREAT RACQUET-TAILED DRONGO
Drongos are tree-dwelling birds that live in Africa, southern Asia and Australia. Most of them are black and glossy, and they feed mainly on insects, pouncing on them in mid-air and then carrying them back to a perch. They are well known for their aggressive behaviour, launching furious attacks on anything that comes near their nests. The racquet-tailed drongo is the largest and most flamboyant of these birds. It gets its name from its two extra-long tail feathers, which have narrow shafts and rounded ends, like a pair of tennis racquets.

SCIENTIFIC NAME	*Dicrurus paradisaeus*
DISTRIBUTION	India, Southeast Asia
SIZE	Up to 64cm long, including tail feathers

SADDLEBACK
This rare bird from New Zealand belongs to a family called the wattlebirds, which are named after the fleshy wattles on either side of their beaks. The saddleback's wattles are red, and its body is black and brown. Saddlebacks feed in trees, and once lived all over New Zealand. Today, they survive on only a handful of islands. The huia, a relative of the saddleback, died out in 1907. It was the only bird with a different beak shape for each sex – the male's was straight, and the female's was long and curved.

SCIENTIFIC NAME	*Creadion carunculatus*
DISTRIBUTION	Islands off the coast of New Zealand
SIZE	Up to 25cm long

MAGPIE-LARK
The magpie-lark is neither a magpie nor a lark. It belongs to a small family of songbirds found only in Australia and New Guinea. Magpie-larks have long legs and black and white plumage. They live in a wide variety of habitats, including towns, but usually stay near water, which is where they find most of their food. Pairs of magpie-larks often sing duets, taking turns to call. Both birds help to make a nest out of mud and grass, often on a branch overhanging water.

SCIENTIFIC NAME	*Grallina cyanoleuca*
DISTRIBUTION	Australia
SIZE	Up to 30cm long

AUSTRALIAN MAGPIE
Australian magpies are larger than magpie-larks, and they are famous for their musical calls. They feed on insects and other animals on the ground, and nest in groups of as many as six birds, headed by a single dominant male. Each of these groups has its own territory, and its members fight off other magpies that come within range.

SCIENTIFIC NAME	*Gymnorhina tibicen*
DISTRIBUTION	Originally from Australia, New Guinea; introduced into New Zealand
SIZE	Up to 40cm long

TOP AND CENTRE *Hill mynahs have strong beaks for collecting fruit and insects, and sturdy legs for perching as they reach out for food.*
ABOVE *A young magpie-lark stands on the edge of its nest. Magpie-larks often paddle their way through shallow water searching for insects and snails to eat.*

RAGGIANA BIRD OF PARADISE

Male birds are often more colourful than their mates, but with birds of paradise the difference is astounding. The females are drab, but the males have flamboyant plumage that they show off during their courtship displays. When Europeans first saw the birds' feathers nearly 500 years ago, they thought they came from paradise, which is how the birds got their name. Like most of its relatives, the Raggiana bird of paradise lives in the dense tropical forests of New Guinea. The male has a yellow head, a metallic green throat, and a bushy crimson tail. During the breeding season, rival males show off their plumage in the treetops, trying to attract the attention of passing females. After mating, the females build nests and look after the nestlings on their own.

SCIENTIFIC NAME *Paradisaea raggiana*

DISTRIBUTION New Guinea

SIZE Up to 33cm long

BLUE BIRD OF PARADISE

The blue bird of paradise lives in forest-covered mountains and eats fruit and insects. Males of this species have blue-black heads, turquoise wings and two long tail-streamers that look like pieces of wire. During their courtship displays, they hang upside down from branches, fluttering their open wings to show off their beautiful colours. They also make a variety of harsh noises that sound like machinery high up in the treetops. Little is known about how this bird breeds but, as with other birds of paradise, the males probably take no part in caring for the young.

SCIENTIFIC NAME *Paradisaea rudolphi*

DISTRIBUTION New Guinea

SIZE Up to 30cm long, excluding tail-streamers

BELOW LEFT *With his beak wide open, a male Raggiana bird of paradise shows off the lustrous plumage on his head and neck. Most male birds of paradise display to females on their own, but male Raggianas gather in small groups, where they compete to produce the best show. At the climax of a display, each male tips his body forwards and spreads a ruff of red plumes over his back.*

Strong beak for collecting fruit, buds and insects

Contrasting feathers at the base of the beak

Male blue bird of paradise

Male Raggiana bird of paradise

Metallic feathers on the throat collar

KING OF SAXONY BIRD OF PARADISE

This bird is one of several that European naturalists named after royal figures when they explored New Guinea's forests more than 100 years ago. Compared to some birds of paradise, the males look ordinary, but they have one remarkable feature – a pair of plumes on their heads that look like giant antennae. The plumes are up to 50cm long, and they have a row of blue flaps along one side. The males usually keep their plumes close to their backs, but during courtship displays they hold them almost upright.

SCIENTIFIC NAME	*Pteridophora alberti*
DISTRIBUTION	New Guinea
SIZE	Up to 22cm long

KING BIRD OF PARADISE

There are about 40 different birds of paradise, and this species is one of the smallest. The males are bright orange-red with white undersides, and they have two long tail-streamers with tips that are coiled up like springs. Like other birds of paradise, they feed on insects and fruit, and spend most of the time high above the ground.

SCIENTIFIC NAME	*Cicinnurus regius*
DISTRIBUTION	New Guinea
SIZE	Up to 17cm long

MAGNIFICENT RIFLEBIRD

This long-beaked bird of paradise gets its name from its call, which sounds like the whine of a rifle bullet. The females are brown and dove, but the males are much more spectacular, with shiny blue-green caps and throats, and blue-black wings. Instead of hanging upside down when they display, the males perch on top of high branches with their wings held out like a pair of fans. During the display, they shake their bodies and flick their heads from side to side.

SCIENTIFIC NAME	*Ptiloris magnificus*
DISTRIBUTION	New Guinea, northern Australia
SIZE	Up to 33cm long

SATIN BOWERBIRD

Bowerbirds are close relatives of the birds of paradise, but instead of using bright plumage to attract their mates, the males make structures called bowers. They build their bowers on the ground out of sticks. Some bowers are shaped like miniature circus rings or thatched huts, but the satin bowerbird makes an avenue-shaped bower with a pair of narrow walls. When it is complete, the male bird daubs it with 'paint' made from saliva and fruit, and decorates it with

TOP *A female satin bowerbird peers into a bower built by a male. This is the signal for the male to begin his courtship display.*

ABOVE *Perched on a high branch, a male king bird of paradise shows off his remarkable tail-streamers, which hang in the air behind him.*

blue objects of all kinds, from feathers to bottle tops. If a female comes close to the bower, the male picks up these objects during his display, as he tries to entice her to mate.

SCIENTIFIC NAME	*Ptilonorhynchus violaceus*
DISTRIBUTION	Eastern Australia
SIZE	Up to 32cm long

GARDENER BOWERBIRD

Males of this species make the largest and most complicated bowers of all. They find a sturdy sapling and build up sticks around it, using the tree as a central support. The finished bower has a steeply sloping roof up to 2m high, and it opens out into a 'garden' area that the male bird decorates with flowers and shells. Bowers this large can take weeks to build, and instead of making a new one each year, gardener bowerbirds often repair ones that they have used in previous breeding seasons.

SCIENTIFIC NAME	*Amblyornis inornatus*
DISTRIBUTION	New Guinea
SIZE	Up to 25cm long

Raven has strong, thick beak

Red-billed chough has long, curved beak

Powerful, all-purpose beak

TOP *The raven can be identified by its large size, and by the shaggy feathers beneath its throat.*
ABOVE *Unlike many of its relatives, the red-billed chough is a shy bird that steers clear of people.*
RIGHT *Carrion crows usually have jet-black plumage, though one variety called the hooded crow is black and grey.*

Thickset neck

Glossy black plumage

RAVEN

Ravens are the largest birds in the crow family, with wings that can measure nearly 1.5m from tip to tip. They have jet-black bodies, deep, croaking calls and beaks strong enough to break a finger. They live on hillsides and in open country, and they fly high up, like some birds of prey. Ravens feed mainly on dead remains, but they are also effective predators, killing rabbits and other birds. They often travel in pairs and, during the breeding season, they carry out acrobatic display flights, rolling and tumbling towards the ground.

SCIENTIFIC NAME *Corvus corax*
DISTRIBUTION North America, except the east, Europe, northern Asia
SIZE Up to 65cm long

CARRION CROW

There are about one hundred species in the crow family, and they include some of the world's most intelligent and adaptable birds. The carrion crow is one of the most widespread, living right across Europe and Asia. It is normally black all over, with a heavy beak and powerful wings. Carrion crows feed on a wide range of food, from seeds and baby birds to dead animals, or carrion, including those killed on roads. They often visit rubbish dumps, where they eat leftovers of all kinds. Carrion crows nest in the tops of trees, and they make a loud 'cawing' sound if anything comes too close.

SCIENTIFIC NAME *Corvus corone*
DISTRIBUTION Europe, Middle East, central Asia, Far East
SIZE Up to 48cm long

RED-BILLED CHOUGH

This bird is easy to tell apart from its all-black relatives, because it has a bright red beak and feet. Its beak is also an unusual shape – it is long and curved, with a sharp point. Choughs live on mountains and along seashore cliffs, and they use their beaks to probe for insects living in grass. They live in flocks, and are famous for their aerobatic skill, swooping and diving over rocky crags, even in the strongest winds.

SCIENTIFIC NAME *Pyrrhocorax pyrrhocorax*
DISTRIBUTION Western Europe, parts of southern Asia
SIZE Up to 40cm long

CLARK'S NUTCRACKER

This grey and black bird lives in the mountain pine forests of western North America, where winters are cold and long. It eats pine seeds, and survives the winter by building up a giant seed bank before the cold weather sets in. A nutcracker can collect up to 100 pine seeds at a time, and it buries them individually, storing up to 30,000 a year. During the summer, nutcrackers often visit picnic sites, where they take food that people put out for them.

SCIENTIFIC NAME *Nucifraga columbiana*
DISTRIBUTION Western North America
SIZE Up to 30cm long

BLUE JAY

This bright blue North American bird is a frequent visitor to parks and gardens, where it feeds on insects, nuts and seeds. Like other jays, it also eats eggs and nestlings, which means that it is not always welcome. Blue jays are noisy birds with bold habits. They feed in groups, and often bury nuts and seeds to help them to survive through the winter.

SCIENTIFIC NAME
Cyanocitta cristata

DISTRIBUTION   Eastern North America

SIZE   Up to 28cm long

Long tail spread out in flight

White flight feathers tipped with black

RIGHT *The black-billed magpie chatters loudly as it searches for food. Despite its size, it is often chased off by smaller birds.*

EURASIAN JAY

Jays are much more colourful than crows, and they spend more of their time in trees. The Eurasian jay has a pinkish-brown body, a black tail and a striking patch of pale blue on each of its wings. Jays eat many things, including insects, eggs and young birds, but in the winter they often survive on acorns. During the autumn, they bury acorns in the ground, and several months later, when other kinds of food are hard to find, they dig them up again. Although jays have good memories, some of the buried acorns get forgotten, and this helps oak trees to spread.

SCIENTIFIC NAME
Garrulus glandarius

DISTRIBUTION
Europe, Asia, Far East

SIZE   Up to 34cm long

Pale blue patch on wing

Body colours may vary depending on where the bird comes from

ABOVE *The Eurasian jay's screeching call makes it easy to pinpoint, even when it is hidden away high up in the trees. This common woodland bird is noisiest in the winter and early spring, but it becomes quieter when raising its young, to avoid attracting predators to its nest.*

BLACK-BILLED MAGPIE

Magpies have rounded wings and long, straight tails. Compared to other members of the crow family they are not powerful fliers, and they spend a lot of time in trees and on the ground. The black-billed magpie is a striking black and white bird, with a harsh, noisy call. It originally lived in woodland, but is now found on farmland and in towns too. It usually eats insects, seeds and dead remains, but sometimes steals the eggs and chicks of smaller birds.

SCIENTIFIC NAME   *Pica pica*

DISTRIBUTION   Western North America, Europe, northern Asia, Far East

SIZE   Up to 48cm long

AZURE-WINGED MAGPIE

This black, grey and blue magpie is a bird with a puzzling distribution. It is found mainly in China and neighbouring parts of the Far East, but some azure-winged magpies live in Spain and Portugal, thousands of kilometres to the west. Some ornithologists believe that the European birds were accidentally introduced by sailors returning from China centuries ago. Azure-winged magpies often hang from branches to feed.

SCIENTIFIC NAME
Cyanopica cyana

DISTRIBUTION   Spain, Portugal, Far East

SIZE   Up to 33cm long

Azure-winged magpie

MAMMALS

NUMBERING ABOUT 4,000 SPECIES, MAMMALS
ARE A VERY VARIED GROUP OF ANIMALS. THEY
ARE THE ONLY ANIMALS THAT HAVE HAIR
AND FEED THEIR YOUNG ON MILK.

EGG-LAYING MAMMALS

Of all the mammals alive today, egg-laying mammals, or monotremes, are the most primitive. There are three species of monotreme and they are found only in New Guinea and Australia. Monotremes have other features that make them unusual. The adults have beak-like mouths without teeth, and the females produce milk, but do not have teats. The milk comes from mammary glands scattered over the skin.

PLATYPUS

When the first stuffed platypus reached Europe, about two centuries ago, scientists were so amazed by it that they thought it was a hoax. This is hardly surprising, because the platypus looks like a cross between a mammal and a bird. It has soft, brown fur and four webbed feet, but it also has a rubbery beak. Platypuses live in lakes and rivers, and they use their beaks to probe the mud on the bottom for insect grubs, crustaceans and other small animals. During the breeding season, the female digs a long burrow, and lays two or three eggs. She curls around the eggs until they hatch, and then feeds her young on milk for up to five months. Male platypuses have poisonous spurs on their back legs that can inflict a painful wound.

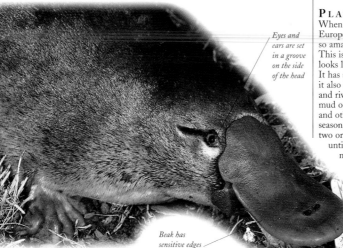

Eyes and ears are set in a groove on the side of the head

Beak has sensitive edges

SCIENTIFIC NAME
Ornithorhynchus anatinus

DISTRIBUTION   Eastern Australia, Tasmania

SIZE   Up to 65cm long, including tail

TOP *The platypus shuts its eyes underwater, and finds its food entirely by touch.*
ABOVE *The long-nosed spiny anteater feeds on earthworms as well as ants.*

The earliest mammals lived on land, but today's mammals also live in fresh water, sea water and the air. Land mammals have four legs, but swimming mammals often have flippers instead. Mammals that fly and glide, such as bats and flying squirrels, have flaps of stretchy skin that help them stay in the air. Many mammals have good eyesight and a keen sense of smell and, compared to other animals, they have highly developed brains. They are warm-blooded, which means they can remain active when it is cold. Most mammals give birth to live young, but a few lay eggs.

LONG-NOSED SPINY ANTEATER OR ECHIDNA

There are two species of spiny anteater, and this one is the larger. It has a round body covered with fur and spines, and a remarkable curved snout that is little wider than a pencil. Its legs are short, and its feet have powerful claws. Spiny anteaters are good diggers, and they use their claws to break open the nests of ants and termites, before sweeping them up with their long tongues. During the breeding season, the females lay between one and three eggs, which they incubate inside a temporary pouch. When the young hatch, they stay in the pouch for up to eight weeks, when their spines begin to develop.

SCIENTIFIC NAME   *Zaglossus bruijni*

DISTRIBUTION   New Guinea

SIZE   Up to 75cm long

MARSUPIALS

Marsupials are mammals that raise their young inside a pouch. They include kangaroos, wallabies and koalas, as well as some lesser-known animals that look like mice. A marsupial's young are very poorly developed when they are born, and they usually stay in the pouch until their bodies are fully formed. The pouch contains teats, so young marsupials can feed without having to go outside. Marsupials are found mainly in forests or on grasslands, and many of the smaller kinds are nocturnal. There are about 250 species. Most of them live in Australia or New Guinea, but more than 75, including the ones on this page, live in the Americas.

Ears can fold up close to the head

Large eyes for seeing in the dark

Small, sharply pointed teeth

VIRGINIA OPOSSUM

This large, rat-like animal is the largest marsupial in the Americas, and the only one that lives north of Mexico. It has a pointed snout, untidy fur and a long, bare tail. Virginia opossums are tree-dwelling animals. They feed after dark and eat almost anything – alive or dead. If they are cornered, they react by 'playing possum', or pretending to be dead. Females can give birth to more than 30 young at a time, but only a small number survive.

SCIENTIFIC NAME *Didelphis virginiana*

DISTRIBUTION Southern Canada, USA, Central America

SIZE Up to 1m long, including tail

RIGHT *When young Virginia opossums grow too large for their mother's pouch, they ride about on her back.*

MOUSE-OPOSSUM

This animal is one of nearly 50 species of mouse-like opossums that live in the forests of Central and South America. It spends most of its time in trees, and tracks down insects and other animals after dark using its keen eyesight and hearing. Female mouse-opossums have simple flap-like pouches, and their young have to cling to their mother's fur as she scuttles about.

SCIENTIFIC NAME *Marmosa murinum*

DISTRIBUTION Northern South America

SIZE Up to 45cm long, including tail

WATER OPOSSUM OR YAPOK

This is the only marsupial that lives partly in water. It has a long body with a rat-like tail, water-repellent fur and webbed back feet. Yapoks dive to catch their food of fish and other water animals. Females can shut their pouches with a ring of muscle when they dive, to prevent their young from drowning.

SCIENTIFIC NAME *Chironectes minimus*

DISTRIBUTION Central America, South America

SIZE Up to 80cm long, including tail

RIGHT *Unlike true mice, mouse-opossums live by hunting. Grasshoppers and crickets are among their favourite prey. They eat most of the insects' bodies, but throw away their legs.*

ABOVE *Eastern quolls can give birth to about 25 young - many more than they can feed. About six of the young manage to fasten themselves to the mother's teats, but the rest do not survive.*

KOALA

The koala is one of Australia's most famous animals. Although it is often called a koala bear, koalas and bears are very different. The koala is a marsupial, and it feeds entirely on the leaves of the gum tree, or eucalyptus, getting all its water from its food. Koalas have sharp claws, and they can grip even the smoothest barks, shinning upwards to reach their food. Female koalas have one offspring at a time. They have a backward-opening pouch so, most of the time, the opening is towards the ground. Although this sounds dangerous, the young koalas never fall out.

SCIENTIFIC NAME	*Phascolarctos cinereus*
DISTRIBUTION	Eastern Australia
SIZE	Up to 85cm long

EASTERN QUOLL

Quolls are the marsupial equivalents of small cats. There are six species, all from Australia or New Guinea, and most of them have lithe and slender bodies, large eyes and spotted fur. Quolls live in forests and open country, and climb well. They eat all kinds of small animals, including lizards and small birds, and are efficient hunters, although they are not good at defending themselves against the cats and dogs that have been introduced. The eastern quoll has almost disappeared from the Australian mainland, leaving Tasmania as its last stronghold.

SCIENTIFIC NAME	*Dasyurus viverrinus*
DISTRIBUTION	Southeastern Australia, Tasmania
SIZE	Up to 75cm long, including tail

COMMON WOMBAT

Wombats are heavily built marsupials that spend their lives on or under the ground. They are even more bear-like than koalas, with powerful front feet equipped with impressive claws. Wombats dig burrows up to 30m long, and they rest inside these during the day. At night, they come out to feed on grass and other plants. There are three species of wombat, and they are found only in Australia and Tasmania. The common wombat is the heaviest, weighing up to 35kg.

SCIENTIFIC NAME	*Vombatus ursinus*
DISTRIBUTION	Southeastern Australia, Tasmania
SIZE	Up to 1.2m long

MARSUPIAL MOLE

This animal is one of Australia's most elusive marsupials – partly because it lives in remote places, but mainly because it spends most of its life underground. It has silky, golden-yellow fur, long claws and a flat shield on its head with which it pushes sand aside as it burrows. It can dig down to depths of 2.5m. Marsupial moles feed on insects and the females have a backward-opening pouch.

SCIENTIFIC NAME	*Notoryctes typhlops*
DISTRIBUTION	Northern and central Australia
SIZE	Up to 20cm long, including tail

BRUSH-TAILED POSSUM

This squirrel-like animal is one of Australia's most common marsupials, and one of the few that is quite at home in towns and cities. Originally a tree-dweller, it often runs over roofs or into attics after dark, making so much noise that it keeps people awake. Brush-tailed possums feed on leaves, flowers and fruit. They spend the day holed up out of sight, so they are heard more often than they are seen.

SCIENTIFIC NAME	*Trichosurus vulpecula*
DISTRIBUTION	Originally from Australia, Tasmania; introduced into New Zealand
SIZE	Up to 90cm long, including tail

GREATER GLIDER

There are no flying marsupials, but some species are experts at gliding from tree to tree. They launch themselves from the treetops and glide up to 100m through the air on flaps of tightly stretched skin. When they land on another tree-trunk, the skin folds up and they scamper away. The greater glider is the largest of these airborne marsupials, with a body about the size of a cat's. Its skin-flaps reach from its elbows to its ankles,

and it balances with its long, flattened tail. Greater gliders feed on leaves, and rarely come to the ground.

SCIENTIFIC NAME	*Schoinobates volans*
DISTRIBUTION	Eastern Australia
SIZE	Up to 1m long, including tail

PYGMY GLIDER

This mouse-sized animal is the smallest gliding marsupial. It is nocturnal, but easy to spot by torchlight because it is grey on top and white underneath. Pygmy gliders feed on insects, flowers and eucalyptus gum. A female can hold up to four young in her pouch, and the young stay on board at all times – even when their mother launches into the air.

SCIENTIFIC NAME	*Acrobates pygmaeus*
DISTRIBUTION	Eastern Australia
SIZE	Up to 16cm long, including tail

The Tasmanian devil was once endangered

TASMANIAN DEVIL

The Tasmanian devil hunts slow-moving animals, including insects and snakes, but feeds mainly on dead animals such as birds, wombats and sheep. It can crush bones with its teeth, and will eat the whole carcase, including the fur and feathers. Tasmanian devils usually search for food on their own, but they gather in groups where there is lots to eat.

SCIENTIFIC NAME	*Sarcophilus harrisi*
DISTRIBUTION	Tasmania
SIZE	Up to 1.1m long, including tail

TOP *A young common wombat stays with its mother for at least a year.*
ABOVE *The marsupial mole has no eyes and finds its food by touch and smell. It has extra-long claws on two of its fingers, which it uses for digging.*
BELOW *Brush-tailed possums have become a problem in New Zealand, where they have been introduced, because they damage young trees.*

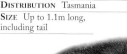

EASTERN GREY KANGAROO

Kangaroos are the world's largest marsupials, and also the fastest. Eastern grey kangaroos are up to 1.5m tall when they rest on their haunches, but they are even taller when they stand on their toes. They can run at up to 55km/h in short bursts, taking leaps the length of two average-sized cars. Kangaroos live in dry, open country. They feed mainly on grass, and breed whenever the food supply is good enough.

RIGHT Long-footed potoroos use their front feet to dig for roots and insect grubs, and to hold their food while they eat.

1

2

3

ABOVE A young grey kangaroo is helpless when it is born, and its first priority is to find its mother's pouch. **1** *Using its front legs, the newly born joey crawls through its mother's fur.* **2** *The joey enters the pouch and fastens itself to one of its mother's teats.* **3** *Within six months, the joey completely fills the pouch, and is large enough to feed outside.*

LEFT While its mother keeps a lookout for danger, a young grey kangaroo peers out from her pouch. Muscles in the wall of the pouch tighten when the mother hops, so the joey stays secure.

Female kangaroos give birth to one young, or joey, at a time. When a joey is born, it is less than 5cm long and only its front legs are fully formed. It crawls through its mother's fur and into her pouch, where it spends the next six months. It then leaves the pouch, but for several months it will climb back in if danger threatens.

SCIENTIFIC NAME	*Macropus giganteus*
DISTRIBUTION	Eastern Australia, Tasmania
SIZE	Up to 2.4m long, including tail

LONG-FOOTED POTOROO

Potoroos belong to the kangaroo family, but look more like giant rodents. They have soft, silky fur and pointed muzzles, but they also have the kangaroo 'trademark' – powerful back legs, and much smaller front legs. Potoroos live in grassland and scrub. Compared to their larger relatives, thay eat a wide range of food including grass, insects and fungi.

SCIENTIFIC NAME	*Potourous longipes*
DISTRIBUTION	Southeastern Australia
SIZE	Up to 2.8m long, including tail

MUSKY RAT-KANGAROO

This miniature kangaroo lives in Australia's rainforests, where it feeds on leaves, fruit and small animals. It is unusual for several reasons – one is that it often darts about on all fours, trailing its rat-like tail. It is also the only kangaroo that gives birth to twins. All other kangaroos have just one joey at a time. Musky rat-kangaroos sleep in nests that they build on the ground. Most mammals carry nesting material in their mouths or paws, but these kangaroos use their tails instead.

SCIENTIFIC NAME	*Hypsiprymnodon moschatus*
DISTRIBUTION	Northern Queensland (Australia)
SIZE	Up to 50cm long, including tail

YELLOW-FOOTED ROCK WALLABY

Rock wallabies are similar to kangaroos, but they are much more agile. They live in mountains and other rocky places, and have soft, non-slip pads on their feet. These give them such a good grip that they can climb vertical cliffs, and bound across ravines up to 4m wide. Unlike most kangaroos, their tails do not have a thickened base, and they use them for balance rather than as a prop. There are six species of rock wallaby. The yellow-footed rock wallaby is the largest, and it is also one of the most endangered because until recently it has been hunted for its fur.

SCIENTIFIC NAME	*Petrogale xanthopus*
DISTRIBUTION	Eastern Australia
SIZE	Up to 1.5m long, including tail

RUFOUS HARE-WALLABY OR MALA

This endangered marsupial is not much larger than a hare. It lives on dry plains studded with clumps of drought-resistant spinifex grass, and it feeds on seeds and leaves. During the day, it usually rests in any shade that it can find, although it dashes off like a hare if anything comes nearby. Two hundred years ago, rufous hare-wallabies were common across much of Australia, but today very few are left, and a programme is underway to save the species from extinction.

SCIENTIFIC NAME	*Lagorchestes hirsutus*
DISTRIBUTION	Western Australia
SIZE	Up to 95cm long, including tail

QUOKKA

The quokka was one of the first marsupials to be seen by Europeans when they explored the coast of western Australia in the late 1600s. They thought that it was a kind of rat, and called one of its main breeding areas 'Rat's Nest Island'. Quokkas

are actually much larger than rats, but they do have rodent-like faces and long, almost bare tails. They feed on plants, sometimes climbing into shrubs to get at leaves.

SCIENTIFIC NAME	*Setonix brachyurus*
DISTRIBUTION	Southwestern Australia
SIZE	Up to 95cm long, including tail

BENNETT'S TREE KANGAROO

Tree kangaroos live in tropical rainforests, and are very different from kangaroos that live on the ground. Their front and back legs are almost the same length, and their feet have soft pads and sharp, curved claws. Instead of tapering to a point, their tails are the same thickness all the way along, often with a fluffy tip. Tree kangaroos eat leaves and fruit, and they spend most of their time in their forest canopy. Bennett's tree kangaroo is one of two Australian species. Several others live in New Guinea – the most recently discovered was found in 1990.

SCIENTIFIC NAME	*Dendrolagus bennettianus*
DISTRIBUTION	Northern Queensland (Australia)
SIZE	Up to 1.7m long, including tail

Keen hearing to listen for danger

Shaggy hair with soft underfur

BELOW *Female yellow-footed rock wallabies cannot climb if they have a large joey in their pouch. They leave the joey in a safe place while they search for food.*

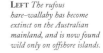

BELOW *Balancing with its tail, a Bennett's tree kangaroo gets ready to jump from a branch. Like other tree kangaroos, it feeds at night, and spends the day sleeping high up in the treetops.*

LEFT *The rufous hare-wallaby has become extinct on the Australian mainland, and is now found wild only on offshore islands.*

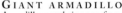

ANTEATERS, ARMADILLOS, SLOTHS, PANGOLINS AND AARDVARKS

Anteaters, armadillos and sloths are quite closely related. They all have small teeth, or none at all, and they are the only living mammals to have reinforced backbones, specially for digging. There are 30 species altogether, all of which live in the Americas. Some of them feed on ants and termites, while others eat leaves. Pangolins and aardvarks have no close relatives, so biologists classify them in groups of their own. They live in Asia and Africa, and also eat ants and termites.

GIANT ANTEATER

Although ants and termites are tiny, they are often extremely numerous. Several kinds of mammal specialize in eating them, and the giant anteater is one of the largest. Weighing up to 40kg, it has a bushy tail and powerful front legs armed with long claws. It has no teeth, but its extraordinary snout contains a long, and very sticky tongue. The giant anteater feeds on the ground, and rips open ant and termite nests with its claws. While the insects rush for cover, the anteater sweeps them up into its mouth with its tongue. It can eat up to 30,000 ants in a day. Female giant anteaters give birth to a single baby, which rides on its mother's back.

SCIENTIFIC NAME *Myrmecophaga tridactyla*

DISTRIBUTION Central America, South America

SIZE Up to 2m long, including tail

TREE ANTEATER OR TAMANDUA

This animal is much smaller than the giant anteater, and it lives in trees instead of on the ground. Its tail is slender and prehensile, and it uses it to hang on to branches while it feeds. If a tree anteater is threatened by a predator, it can prop itself up on its back legs and tail and defend itself with its front claws.

SCIENTIFIC NAME *Tamandua mexicana*

DISTRIBUTION Central America, tropical South America

SIZE Up to 1.1m long, including tail

TOP LEFT *Using its front claws, a nine-banded armadillo digs its way into an underground ant nest.*
TOP RIGHT *When an armadillo rolls up into a ball, its head and tail fit side by side to make the ball complete.*
ABOVE *Giant anteaters walk on the knuckles of their front feet to keep their long digging claws out of the way.*

ABOVE AND RIGHT
The tree anteater is choosy about its food, and avoids ants that have powerful bites or stings. It is a creature of habit, and it often follows the same route night after night, looking for ant and termite nests to raid.

GIANT ARMADILLO

Armadillos get their name from the armour-plating that covers most of their bodies. The armour is formed by hundreds of small, hard scales, and it works like a flexible shell. Some armadillos can roll up in a ball if they are under attack, but with a body weighing up to 60kg, the giant armadillo is too large to do this. Instead, it either runs for safety, or digs into the ground, using its armoured back to fend off attack. Giant armadillos live in forests, and feed on termites and other small animals. They shelter in burrows underground, and the females give birth to one or two young each year.

SCIENTIFIC NAME *Priodontes maximus*

DISTRIBUTION South America

SIZE Up to 1.5m long, including tail

NINE-BANDED ARMADILLO

There are 20 species of armadillo, but this is the only one that lives as far north as the USA. It usually has nine armoured bands across its back, although the number can range between six and eleven. It is a good digger, and it can partly roll up although, given the chance, it more often runs away. Nine-banded armadillos are remarkable animals because they always give birth to identical quadruplets. In each family, the young are either all male, or all female.

SCIENTIFIC NAME *Dasypus novemcinctus*

DISTRIBUTION North America, Central America, South America; from southeastern USA to Uruguay

SIZE Up to 90cm long, including tail

THREE-TOED SLOTH

Sloths feed in trees, and are the only mammals that spend almost their entire lives hanging upside down. There are five species, and all have long arms, hooked claws and fur that hangs downwards, helping rain to run off. Sloths feed on leaves, and are famous for moving very slowly. During the day, they stay completely still, and even after sunset often move only a few metres in a night. Strangely, sloths clamber to the ground to bury their droppings – it is not yet known exactly why. The three-toed sloth has one baby a year, which she carries on her chest for about five months.

SCIENTIFIC NAME *Bradypus tridactylus*
DISTRIBUTION Central America, South America
SIZE Up to 65cm long

TREE PANGOLIN

With their overlapping dark brown scales, pangolins look more like moving pine cones than mammals. Their scales cover most of their bodies, apart from their undersides and feet, and provide some protection from enemies. Pangolins feed on ants and termites and, like anteaters, they have long, sticky tongues but no teeth. The largest species live on the ground, but the tree pangolin has a long prehensile tail and is a good climber.

SCIENTIFIC NAME *Manis tricuspis*
DISTRIBUTION Tropical Africa
SIZE Up to 1.05m long, including tail

AARDVARK

In Dutch, aardvark means 'earth pig', which is a good description of this large African mammal. It has a pig-like snout and powerful claws, and spends the day in burrows underground. It surfaces at night, and uses its keen sense of smell to track down ants and termites. Aardvarks also have very good hearing, thanks to their large upright ears. When they go underground into their burrows, their ears are conveniently folded out of the way.

SCIENTIFIC NAME *Orycteropus afer*
DISTRIBUTION Tropical and southern Africa
SIZE Up to 2.2m long, including tail

ABOVE *The three-toed sloth gets its colour from microscopic plants that grow in its damp fur.*
BELOW AND LEFT *The aardvark has a sticky tongue about 30cm long.*

ABOVE AND LEFT
Pangolins sometimes protect themselves from attack by coiling up. They can also raise their scales so that the sharp edges point outwards.

Pangolins walk on the sides of their front feet

Overlapping scales have ridges and sharp edges

MOLES, HEDGEHOGS AND SHREWS

The mammals in this group are known as insectivores because they feed mainly on insects and other small animals. Most of them are small and nocturnal, and live on their own. They have poor eyesight, but a good sense of smell, and small, very effective teeth. There are nearly 400 species, and they live in all kinds of habitat, from deserts to fresh water. Moles and shrews are found across most of the world except Australia and New Zealand, but hedgehogs live only in Europe, Africa and Asia.

EUROPEAN MOLE

This furry black animal spends most of its life underground, and has very poor eyesight. Its movements are easy to track because it pushes piles of excavated soil, called molehills, up onto the surface. European moles dig with their spade-like front paws, and they make a network of tunnels for catching food. They patrol the tunnels at frequent intervals, eating any earthworms that have fallen in. They often bite the heads off the worms and store the bodies until they need them.

SCIENTIFIC NAME	*Talpa europaea*
DISTRIBUTION	Western and central Europe, parts of Asia
SIZE	Up to 20cm long, including tail

STAR-NOSED MOLE

Unlike the European mole, the star-nosed mole likes wet ground, and it feeds in ponds and streams. Its nose has a ring of 22 pink, fleshy tentacles, which it uses to feel for insect grubs and other animals underwater. Its large front feet work like paddles when it swims, and like spades when it tunnels through the ground.

SCIENTIFIC NAME	*Condylura cristata*
DISTRIBUTION	Northeastern North America
SIZE	Up to 20cm long, including tail

PYRENEAN DESMAN

Desmans are strange, mole-like animals that hunt in rivers and streams. They have webbed feet, waterproof fur and a long, flattened tail that works like a cross between a rudder and a propeller. They are almost as blind as moles, and find their prey by touch, feeling among underwater stones with their long,

Pyrenean desman at water's edge

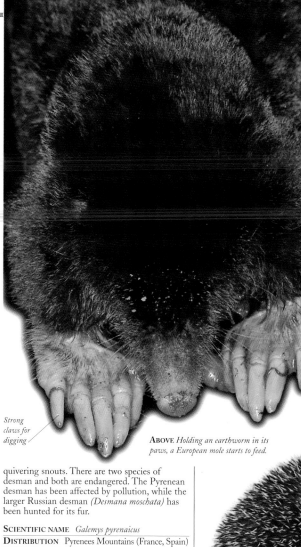

Strong claws for digging

ABOVE *Holding an earthworm in its paws, a European mole starts to feed.*

quivering snouts. There are two species of desman and both are endangered. The Pyrenean desman has been affected by pollution, while the larger Russian desman *(Desmana moschata)* has been hunted for its fur.

SCIENTIFIC NAME	*Galemys pyrenaicus*
DISTRIBUTION	Pyrenees Mountains (France, Spain)
SIZE	Up to 30cm long, including tail

WESTERN HEDGEHOG

Many insectivores run away at the first sign of danger, but the hedgehog reacts quite differently. Its back is covered with about 6,000 sharp spines, and if it is threatened, it rolls up into a ball and makes its spines stand on end. This behaviour protects it

against most predators. Hedgehogs live in many habitats, from sand-dunes to suburban gardens, hibernating for up to six months every year. They eat a wide range of small animals, mainly insects, spiders, slugs and earthworms.

SCIENTIFIC NAME	*Erinaceus europaeus*
DISTRIBUTION	Originally from Europe; introduced into New Zealand
SIZE	Up to 27cm long

ETRUSCAN SHREW

The Etruscan shrew is the world's smallest land mammal. Even when it is fully grown, it could sit in a teaspoon. It has a short life and reaches old age within a year. Shrews need to eat around the clock because tiny bodies are difficult to keep warm. Unless they have a constant supply of 'fuel', in the form of food, they run out of energy and die. They find their food by smell and touch, and overpower it with the help of a poisonous bite. Etruscan shrews are extremely aggressive, but they are also highly strung – they sometimes die simply because they are picked up.

SCIENTIFIC NAME	*Suncus etruscus*
DISTRIBUTION	Europe, Africa, Asia
SIZE	Up to 8cm long, including tail

FLYING LEMURS AND TREE SHREWS

Flying lemurs, also known as colugos, are the world's largest gliding mammals. They glide on flaps of skin that stretch down either side of their bodies, from their necks all the way down to their tails. There are two species. Both are nocturnal and live in the forests of Southeast Asia. Tree shrews come from the same part of the world, but they are climbers instead of gliders. There are 16 species and, unlike flying lemurs, most of them are active during the day.

PHILIPPINE FLYING LEMUR

When it is clinging to a branch, a flying lemur looks as if its body is covered by a spotty cloak. The cloak is actually the animal's flight membrane – an elastic sheet of skin that it uses to sail through the air. It has such a large flight membrane that it can glide through the air for more than 125m – a record for any mammal. Flying lemurs feed on leaves, flowers and fruit, and they use gliding as a quick way to travel between the trees. Females give birth to a single baby each time they breed, and they carry it until its weight makes it hard for them to glide.

SCIENTIFIC NAME	*Cynocephalus volans*
DISTRIBUTION	Philippines
SIZE	Up to 70cm long, including tail

COMMON TREE SHREW

Despite its name, this animal looks more like a squirrel than a shrew. It has large claws and a bushy tail, and it feeds on almost anything edible it can find, in trees or on the ground. Tree shrews are of particular interest to biologists, because they strongly resemble fossils of the world's earliest mammals. They give us an idea of what the first mammals looked like, and how they behaved.

Etruscan shrew

Pygmy shrew (Sorex minutus)

Water shrew (Neomys fodiens)

SCIENTIFIC NAME	*Tupaia glis*
DISTRIBUTION	Southern and Southeast Asia
SIZE	Up to 40cm long, including tail

ABOVE LEFT *Shrews live all over the world, except Australia, New Zealand and parts of South America. These three species are all found in Europe.*

LEFT *Hedgehogs are useful animals in gardens because they eat slugs and other insect pests. Despite having short legs, they can roam more than 1km in their nightly search for food.*

TOP *This flying lemur is getting ready to jump from a branch high above the forest floor. Flying lemurs are superb gliders, but they are almost helpless if they accidentally land on the ground.*

ABOVE *With its long snout, keen sense of smell and good eyesight, a common tree shrew can quickly track down food on the forest floor.*

BATS

There are nearly 1,000 species of bat, and they are found worldwide, except in places that are very cold. Bats are the only mammals that can truly fly instead of gliding. Their wings are made of skin stretched between long, slender fingers. They are nocturnal animals, and most of them feed either on fruit and flowers, or on flying insects. The fruit-eating species have large eyes and can see in the dark, but the insect-eaters have poor eyesight. They find their prey using a technique called echolocation.

Giant fruit bat in flight

GIANT FRUIT BAT OR FLYING FOX

With a wingspan of up to 1.5m, this is the world's largest bat. It has a long muzzle and a keen sense of smell, and it roosts upside down in treetops with its wings wrapped around its body. At dusk, flocks of fruit bats set off to feed. When they eat, they squash fruit in their jaws, drinking the juice but dropping the seeds and flesh to the ground. Female fruit bats give birth to one baby each time they breed, and they carry their young around for two months.

SCIENTIFIC NAME *Pteropus giganteus*

DISTRIBUTION Southern and Southeast Asia

SIZE Up to 40cm long

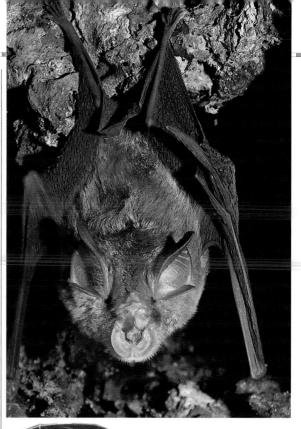

PIPISTRELLE

This common European bat is a typical insect-eating species, with a body that would fit inside a matchbox. It hunts by echolocation, using its large ears to pick up echoes from insects in the air. During the day, pipistrelles often roost in buildings. In the winter, they crowd together to hibernate in lofts and caves. Female pipistrelles normally have just one baby a year, which they leave in a nursery roost when they set off to feed.

SCIENTIFIC NAME *Pipistrellus pipistrellus*

DISTRIBUTION Europe, parts of Asia

SIZE Up to 7cm long, including tail

GREATER HORSESHOE BAT

The 70 species of horseshoe bat get their name from their strangely shaped noses, which have complicated folds of bare skin. They hunt by

TOP RIGHT *The Eastern horseshoe bat (Rhinolophus megaphyllus) lives in New Guinea and eastern Australia.*
ABOVE LEFT *The pipistrelle is the smallest European bat.*
LEFT *The greater horseshoe bat is guided by its sensitive hearing.*

echolocation, and use these folds to focus bursts of sound. Unlike most insect-eating bats, the greater horseshoe bat collects some of its food on the ground. It swoops down on insects, often carrying them to a perch to feed.

SCIENTIFIC NAME *Rhinolophus ferrumequinum*

DISTRIBUTION Europe, northern Africa, Asia

SIZE Up to 16.5cm long, including tail

KITTI'S HOG-NOSED BAT

This minute bat is probably the world's smallest mammal. It weighs about 2g, and its body is only about 3cm long. It has a tiny, pig-like snout and well-developed ears, but it does not have a tail. Kitti's hog-nosed bat was first seen by scientists in 1973. It lives in tropical forests, and spends the day roosting in caves. It feeds on insects.

SCIENTIFIC NAME *Craseonycteris thonglongyai*

DISTRIBUTION Thailand

SIZE Up to 3cm long

Kitti's hog-nosed bat on a finger

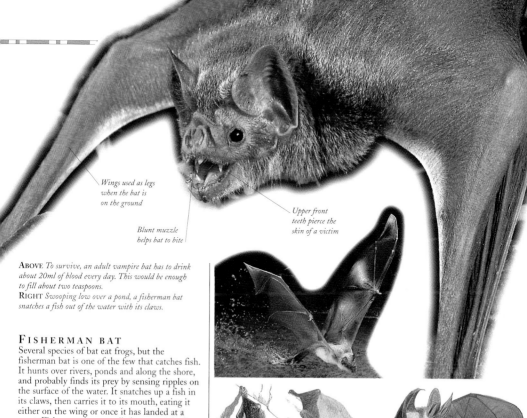

Wings used as legs
when the bat is
on the ground

Blunt muzzle
helps bat to bite

Upper front
teeth pierce the
skin of a victim

ABOVE *To survive, an adult vampire bat has to drink about 20ml of blood every day. This would be enough to fill about two teaspoons.*
RIGHT *Swooping low over a pond, a fisherman bat snatches a fish out of the water with its claws.*

FISHERMAN BAT

Several species of bat eat frogs, but the fisherman bat is one of the few that catches fish. It hunts over rivers, ponds and along the shore, and probably finds its prey by sensing ripples on the surface of the water. It snatches up a fish in its claws, then carries it to its mouth, eating it either on the wing or once it has landed at a roost. Fisherman bats usually hunt at night, but they have been spotted during the day catching fish that have been disturbed by birds.

SCIENTIFIC NAME	*Noctilio leporinus*
DISTRIBUTION	Central America, South America
SIZE	Up to 14cm long, including tail

VAMPIRE BAT

The vampire bat is notorious for its eating habits because it feeds on fresh blood – usually from horses and cattle, but sometimes from human beings. To get its food, it lands near its victim, and then scuttles towards it, using its wings as legs. After biting away any fur or feathers, it makes an incision in the skin, and then patiently sucks up its meal. Vampire bats do not drink much blood when they feed, but they are harmful because they can spread rabies, a potentially fatal disease that can infect humans.

SCIENTIFIC NAME	*Desmodus rotundus*
DISTRIBUTION	Central America, South America
SIZE	Up to 9cm long

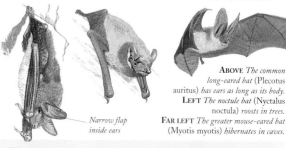

Narrow flap
inside ears

ABOVE *The common long-eared bat* (Plecotus auritus) *has ears as long as its body.*
LEFT *The noctule bat* (Nyctalus noctula) *roosts in trees.*
FAR LEFT *The greater mouse-eared bat* (Myotis myotis) *hibernates in caves.*

ECHOLOCATION

Echolocation allows some animals to hunt in total darkness by sending out bursts of high-pitched sound. If another animal is nearby, some of the sound bounces back from its body, and the hunter can then home in on its prey. Echoes also bounce back from other objects, helping the hunter to build up a picture of its surroundings. Insect-eating bats are the world experts in the use of echolocation, but other echolocating animals include dolphins, some whales and tiny shrews.

Long-eared bat
homing in on a moth

PRIMATES

Primates are mammals that are adapted for life in trees. They have long arms and legs, and flexible fingers and toes. Most of them have flat nails instead of claws, and they curl their fingers and toes around branches to get a good grip. Primates also have forward-pointing eyes – a feature that helps them to judge distances as they jump and climb high above the ground. There are about 230 species of these mammals, found mainly in warm parts of the world.

Because the world's tropical forests are fast disappearing, many primates are in serious danger of becoming extinct.

Ring-tailed lemurs run on all fours

RING-TAILED LEMUR

Like most of the animals on these two pages, lemurs are primitive primates, or prosimians. They live on the island of Madagascar, which has more prosimians than anywhere else. The ring-tailed lemur has a cat-like face and a grey and white body. Its most eyecatching feature is its bushy upright tail, which has bold grey and black rings. Ring-tailed lemurs are unusual because they are active during the day and feed on the ground. They eat leaves and fruit, and also sugary sap, which they get by biting through bark. They live in troops of up to 20 animals.

SCIENTIFIC NAME	*Lemur catta*
DISTRIBUTION	Madagascar
SIZE	Up to 1m long, including tail

GREY MOUSE-LEMUR

Mouse-lemurs are among the world's smallest primates. They look very much like mice, but have forward-facing eyes, tiny fingers and toes, and long tails with fluffy tips. They often weigh less than 50g – about 6,000 times less than the largest primate, the gorilla (page 248). Like many primitive primates, mouse-lemurs move about at night. They eat a wide range of food, including insects, fruit and leaves. They give birth to two or three young after a gestation period of about eight months – a long time for animals of their size.

SCIENTIFIC NAME	*Microcebus rufus*
DISTRIBUTION	Madagascar
SIZE	Up to 30cm long, including tail

TOP *Ring-tailed lemurs use the position of their tails to indicate their rank in the troop. These two are showing they are dominant males.*
ABOVE *A grey mouse-lemur wraps its fingers and toes around a twig as it sits in a tree.*

Indri in typical pose

INDRI

The indri looks like a grey and black teddy bear, with a very small tail and large, rounded ears. As well as being Madagascar's largest primate, it is also the loudest, with an extraordinary song that can be heard more than 2km away. Indris live in family groups, and they sing to claim a territory in the treetops. They feed during the day, eating leaves, buds and fruit.

SCIENTIFIC NAME	*Indri indri*
DISTRIBUTION	Madagascar
SIZE	Up to 75cm long, including tail

AYE-AYE

The aye-aye is about the size of a cat. It lives in Madagascan rainforests, feeding on fruit, birds' eggs and insects. The aye-aye's middle finger on both hands is much longer than the others. It uses these extra-long fingers to tap against tree-trunks and branches. If it hears movement beneath the bark, it probes inside with a finger and pulls out its prey.

SCIENTIFIC NAME	*Daubentonia madagascarensis*
DISTRIBUTION	Madagascar
SIZE	Up to 1.05m long, including tail

GREATER BUSHBABY

The bushbaby is one of 11 primitive primates that live on the mainland of Africa. It gets its name from its bushy tail and child-like cry, and looks a bit like a large squirrel. It feeds at night, using its keen senses to find fruit, insects and sweet sap that oozes from trees. Like most primates, bushbabies climb well because they have opposable thumbs. This means they can close them with their fingers around branches, increasing their grip.

Greater bushbaby gripping a branch

SCIENTIFIC NAME	*Otolemur crassicaudatus*
DISTRIBUTION	Eastern and southern Africa
SIZE	Up to 95cm long, including tail

SLENDER LORIS

Most primates are fast-moving animals, but the slender loris is the opposite. It creeps along branches on its spindly legs, and ambushes insects and other small animals in the dark. Instead of using its teeth to catch prey, the slender loris lunges forwards and grabs victims with its hands. Slender lorises have flat faces with large eyes, and hardly any tail. They spend the day asleep, and rarely come to the ground.

SCIENTIFIC NAME	*Loris tardigradus*
DISTRIBUTION	Southern India, Sri Lanka
SIZE	Up to 26cm long

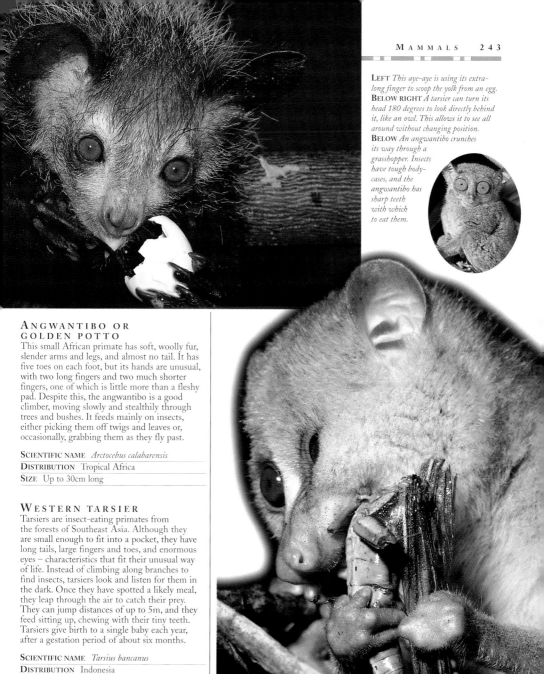

LEFT *This aye-aye is using its extra-long finger to scoop the yolk from an egg.* **BELOW RIGHT** *A tarsier can turn its head 180 degrees to look directly behind it, like an owl. This allows it to see all around without changing position.* **BELOW** *An angwantibo crunches its way through a grasshopper. Insects have tough body-cases, and the angwantibo has sharp teeth with which to eat them.*

ANGWANTIBO OR GOLDEN POTTO

This small African primate has soft, woolly fur, slender arms and legs, and almost no tail. It has five toes on each foot, but its hands are unusual, with two long fingers and two much shorter fingers, one of which is little more than a fleshy pad. Despite this, the angwantibo is a good climber, moving slowly and stealthily through trees and bushes. It feeds mainly on insects, either picking them off twigs and leaves or, occasionally, grabbing them as they fly past.

SCIENTIFIC NAME	*Arctocebus calabarensis*
DISTRIBUTION	Tropical Africa
SIZE	Up to 30cm long

WESTERN TARSIER

Tarsiers are insect-eating primates from the forests of Southeast Asia. Although they are small enough to fit into a pocket, they have long tails, large fingers and toes, and enormous eyes – characteristics that fit their unusual way of life. Instead of climbing along branches to find insects, tarsiers look and listen for them in the dark. Once they have spotted a likely meal, they leap through the air to catch their prey. They can jump distances of up to 5m, and they feed sitting up, chewing with their tiny teeth. Tarsiers give birth to a single baby each year, after a gestation period of about six months.

SCIENTIFIC NAME	*Tarsius bancanus*
DISTRIBUTION	Indonesia
SIZE	Up to 43cm long, including tail

RIGHT *The woolly monkey's thick coat is made up of long outer hairs with much denser underfur close to the body. When it rains, the outer hair gets wet, but the underfur stays dry.*

Flat face with short muzzle

ABOVE *Pygmy marmosets weigh up to 140g – about the same as a well-fed hamster. These tiny but highly active primates have sharp teeth, and they bite holes in tree bark to feed on the sticky sap.*

BELOW *The golden lion tamarin has fur that can glint in the sun like gold.*

PYGMY MARMOSET

Marmosets and tamarins are found only in Central and South America. Many of them look like small monkeys with extra-long tails, but, unlike true monkeys, they do not have grasping hands and feet. Instead of clinging to branches, they scamper along the top. The pygmy marmoset is the smallest species, and the tiniest primate anywhere in the Americas. It has grey-brown fur that camouflages it among the branches, and yellowish hands and feet. Like other marmosets, it feeds during the day, and eats insects, fruit, sugary nectar and sap.

SCIENTIFIC NAME	Cebuella pygmaea
DISTRIBUTION	Northern South America
SIZE	Up to 35cm long, including tail

GOLDEN LION TAMARIN

This rare animal is one of the world's most beautiful and endangered primates. It has a luxurious coat of orange-yellow fur, with a flowing mane and a long, silky tail. Golden lion tamarins come from forests on the Atlantic coast of Brazil – a habitat that has almost vanished in the last 25 years. To make matters worse, many golden lion tamarins have been caught and sold as pets. It is now illegal to catch or buy golden lion tamarins, and an international breeding programme is at work to save the species.

SCIENTIFIC NAME	Leontopithecus rosalia
DISTRIBUTION	Eastern Brazil
SIZE	Up to 55cm long, including tail

WOOLLY MONKEY

This black-furred monkey is one of more than 40 species that live in Central and South America. Unlike monkeys from Africa and Asia, these New World monkeys all have nostrils that open sideways. Many of them, including the woolly monkey, also have prehensile tails. Woolly monkeys live in large troops, and feed mainly on fruit and seeds. Their tails work like an extra leg, helping them to hang on to branches while they feed. Woolly monkeys have one baby each time they breed, and the mother carries her newborn infant on her chest or back.

SCIENTIFIC NAME	Lagothrix lagotricha
DISTRIBUTION	Northern South America
SIZE	Up to 1.4m long, including tail

BLACK SPIDER MONKEY

No other monkey can rival this species for sheer acrobatic skill. It can swing arm-over-arm through the treetops faster than a person can run, and it can also hang from branches by its tail, leaving its arms and legs dangling in the air. Like the woolly monkey, its tail has a bare patch near the tip, which gives it a good grip. Spider-monkeys feed mainly on fruit and nuts, and they live in troops up to 30 strong.

Prehensile tail is like an extra hand

Black spider monkey balanced on a branch

SCIENTIFIC NAME	*Ateles paniscus*
DISTRIBUTION	Northern South America
SIZE	Up to 1.4m long, including tail

RED HOWLER MONKEY

Howler monkeys get their name from their loud calls, which ring out over the treetops at dawn and late in the day. To produce the calls, they use a resonating chamber in their throats. This acts like a built-in amplifier, allowing the sound to be heard up to 3km away. There are six species of howler. They are the largest New World monkeys, and also the most sluggish. They survive almost entirely on leaves, so they never have to travel far to find their food. The red howler is a deep rusty colour, but other howlers are black, brown or grey.

Red howler monkeys howling

SCIENTIFIC NAME	*Alouatta seniculus*
DISTRIBUTION	Northern South America
SIZE	Up to 1.6m long, including tail

SQUIRREL MONKEY

This is one of the smallest New World monkeys, measuring as little as 30cm from the top of its head to the base of its tail. However, its total length more than doubles if its tail is included. Squirrel monkeys' tails are not prehensile, so they cannot hang on with them. Instead, they use them for balancing when they sit or climb. Like most monkeys, they have a wide-ranging diet, and they sometimes raid plantations for food. In undisturbed forest they form large troops, sometimes numbering up to 500 animals.

SCIENTIFIC NAME	*Saimiri sciureus*
DISTRIBUTION	Northern South America
SIZE	Up to 70cm long, including tail

UAKARI

This South American monkey is instantly recognizable because it is has a bald, bright red head and face. It is also the only monkey in the Americas that does not have a long tail. Uakaris live in parts of the Amazon rainforest that are flooded during the wet season. They are shy, unaggressive monkeys, and they feed mainly on seeds and nuts. They stay in the treetops, and hardly ever come to the ground.

SCIENTIFIC NAME	*Cacajao calvus*
DISTRIBUTION	Northern South America
SIZE	Up to 65cm long, including tail

DOUROUCOULI

Also known as the night monkey, this is one of the few nocturnal monkeys. It has a small body, a long tail and a round head with large eyes. Its eyesight is so good that it can run along branches and jump between trees even on dark, moonless nights. In typical monkey fashion, douroucoulis eat a wide range of food, including insects and fruit. They have stretchy pouches under their throats, which they inflate when they call.

SCIENTIFIC NAME	*Aotus trivirgatus*
DISTRIBUTION	Central America, northern South America
SIZE	Up to 77cm long, including tail

BELOW *Uakaris have white or red fur, and extra-strong jaws for cracking nuts open.*

Scarlet skin looks as if it is sunburned

JAPANESE MACAQUE

Nearly 100 species of monkey live in the Old World, which includes Europe, Africa and Asia. Unlike New World monkeys, which live in the Americas, these animals have nostrils that are close together, and their tails are never prehensile. The Japanese macaque is a typical Old World monkey in many ways, but its fur is unusually thick. It needs this warm coat because it lives in a cold climate, further north than any other primate in the world. Japanese macaques feed on the ground and in trees. During the winter, they sometimes lounge in hot springs to avoid the worst of the cold.

SCIENTIFIC NAME *Macaca fuscata*

DISTRIBUTION Japan

SIZE Up to 1.05m long, including tail

BARBARY MACAQUE

This macaque is the only monkey that lives in Europe. It is similar to the Japanese macaque, but does not have a tail. In prehistoric times, Barbary macaques were common in southwestern Europe, but today the only European macaques live in Gibraltar, where they are specially protected. Females normally give birth to one baby when they breed. At first, the young macaque clings to its mother's underside, but it later rides on her back.

SCIENTIFIC NAME *Macaca sylvanus*

DISTRIBUTION Gibraltar, northern Africa

SIZE Up to 75cm long

VERVET MONKEY OR GREEN GUENON

This lively and agile animal is one of about 25 closely related species that live in Africa. Most of these monkeys have slender bodies and long tails, and the easiest way to tell them apart is by the colours and patterns on their faces. The vervet usually has a black face surrounded by white fur, and a greenish-grey body. It lives mainly on plants, and is just as good at running as it is at

ABOVE Cradling its baby to keep it warm, a Japanese macaque braves the cold. Its fur insulates it from the snow and ice. During the winter, these monkeys have to survive on a meagre diet of bark, buds and roots.
LEFT This female vervet monkey is grooming her baby's fur. Grooming is important for monkeys that live in groups. They do it to keep clean and also to show friendship or submission to each other.

climbing trees. Vervets breed all year round, and the mothers suckle their young until they are about six months old.

SCIENTIFIC NAME *Cercopithecus aethiops*

DISTRIBUTION Eastern and southern Africa

SIZE Up to 1.5m long, including tail

OLIVE BABOON

Baboons are powerfully built African monkeys that spend most of their time on the ground. They have dog-like muzzles and sloping backs, and the males, which are about twice as large as the females, have fearsome teeth. Baboons eat almost anything, including young antelopes and other mammals. To protect themselves, they forage and sleep in large troops. If a predator threatens them, the males go on the attack while the females and young run up trees for safety.

SCIENTIFIC NAME	Papio anubis
DISTRIBUTION	Tropical Africa
SIZE	Up to 1.75m long, including tail

MANDRILL
Mandrills are closely related to baboons. They are the heaviest monkeys in the world, weighing as much as 55kg. Male mandrills are much larger than females, and they have brilliantly coloured faces, with red and blue muzzles. These monkeys live on the ground in dense rainforest and form troops of up to 20 animals, led by an adult male. Although they feed mostly on plants, they also kill anything that they can overpower.

SCIENTIFIC NAME	Mandrillus sphinx
DISTRIBUTION	Tropical western Africa
SIZE	Up to 1m long

LANGUR
In southern Asia, this black-faced monkey often lives near houses, where it is always on the lookout for food. It is a good runner and an agile climber, so it is able to escape quickly if it manages to snatch a meal. In the wild, langurs live in forests and rocky places, but they find most of their food on the ground. Langurs are regarded as sacred animals in India, and this has helped them to thrive.

SCIENTIFIC NAME	Presbytis entellus
DISTRIBUTION	India, Sri Lanka
SIZE	Up to 1.8m long, including tail

PROBOSCIS MONKEY
The male proboscis monkey is impossible to mistake because it has a pink face and a long swollen nose. Its nose normally hangs down in front of its mouth, but it straightens out when the monkey calls. Proboscis monkeys live in mangrove swamps, and feed on shoots and leaves. They normally climb about among the mangroves, but they are also good swimmers, and will cross deep channels to reach food or to escape from danger.

SCIENTIFIC NAME	Nasalis larvatus
DISTRIBUTION	Borneo
SIZE	Up to 1.5m long, including tail

Thick mane of grey fur

Long, fleshy nose of a mature male

LEFT *There are five species of baboon. This is a Hamadryas baboon (Papio hamadryas). Males of this species are twice as large as the females.*

Back feet are partly webbed

ABOVE *The male proboscis monkey's remarkable nose develops as it grows older. It probably helps males to attract females. In females and young males, the nose is small and upturned.*

EASTERN BLACK AND WHITE COLOBUS
Colobus monkeys live in African forests, and hardly ever go down to the ground. The eastern black and white colobus has a remarkably luxurious coat, with black fur over most of its body, apart from two long white fringes along its sides. Its tail is like a giant tassel, with an enormous tuft of white fur at the tip. Although they do not have thumbs, colobuses are superb climbers. They cling on with their fingers as they run or leap through the trees.

SCIENTIFIC NAME	Colobus guerzera
DISTRIBUTION	Tropical Africa
SIZE	Up to 1.6m long, including tail

ABOVE AND LEFT *As well as being brightly coloured, the male mandrill has deep grooves down either side of its muzzle. The colour varies with age.*

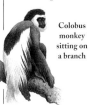

Colobus monkey sitting on a branch

MAKING TOOLS

For humans, using tools is part of everyday life, but in the animal world, it is much more rare. Some animals pick up objects and use them as tools, but very few shape tools for particular tasks. The chimpanzee is one animal that does this. Chimps often feed on ants and termites, but their fingers are too large to reach into the nests. Instead, they pick up sticks and chew them or strip off the bark. They then poke the sticks into the nests, and eat the insects that swarm over them. Chimps also use stones to crack open nuts, and even use leaves to pick up water so that they can drink or wash.

A young chimp learns how to use a stick by watching its mother

Lar gibbon swinging through the forest canopy

LAR GIBBON

Most primates are good climbers, but gibbons are the unrivalled experts at speeding through the treetops. They have short legs and long arms, and they use their hands like hooks as they swing from branch to branch. This way of moving is called brachiation. Gibbons are so good at it that they can reach a speed of about 15km/h, flinging themselves across gaps between the trees. There are eleven species of gibbon, and all of them live in the dense forests of the Far East and Southeast Asia. Like all its relatives, the lar gibbon does not have a tail.

SCIENTIFIC NAME	*Hylobates concolor*
DISTRIBUTION	Asia; from southeastern China to Cambodia
SIZE	Up to 65cm long

LEFT *A female gorilla holds her baby. Gorillas usually have just one baby at a time, and their young are born about three or four years apart. This baby is about two years old.*

SIAMANG

The siamang is the largest gibbon, weighing up to 13kg. It has long black fur and feeds mainly on fruit, as well as some flowers, buds and insects. Gibbons live in small family groups. They have loud hooting calls, and the siamang has one of the loudest. The males and females perform a duet that can be heard more than 1km away. Siamangs usually pair for life, and have one baby at a time.

SCIENTIFIC NAME	*Hylobates syndactylus*
DISTRIBUTION	Malaysia, Sumatra
SIZE	Up to 90cm long

GORILLA

Weighing up to 300kg, gorillas are the largest primates in the world. They belong to a group of primates called the great apes. There are only four species of great ape – the gorilla, two kinds of chimpanzee and the orang utan. They have large brains, and are good at picking up and holding things with their hands and feet. Unlike monkeys, they sometimes stand upright, and do not have tails. Gorillas live in forests, in groups of up to 20 animals, led by a large male. They feed on the ground and in trees, snapping off leaves and stems with their hands. The group moves on slowly during the day, stopping in the late afternoon. Each gorilla then makes itself a nest of branches and leaves, and settles down to sleep. Recently, the number of gorillas has fallen fast, as a result of hunting and deforestation.

SCIENTIFIC NAME	*Gorilla gorilla*
DISTRIBUTION	Western and central Africa
SIZE	Up to 1.8m high

CHIMPANZEE

Chimps are our closest living relatives, and after humans, probably the most intelligent animals. They live in large groups in grassland and open woodland, and communicate with facial expressions and more than 30 different calls. They feed mainly on plants, insects and other small animals, but they have been known to hunt much larger animals, including monkeys. In the wild, chimps start breeding between the ages of 13 and 16, and they can live to about 60 years old.

SCIENTIFIC NAME	*Pan troglodytes*
DISTRIBUTION	Western and eastern Africa
SIZE	Up to 1.5m high

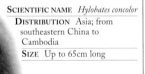

BONOBO OR PYGMY CHIMPANZEE

Bonobos are rarely seen outside their natural home, so they are not nearly as well known as chimpanzees. From a distance, they look quite similar to chimps, but their faces are often black, and they have smaller ears and longer legs. They also live in a different habitat from chimps – dense rainforest, instead of open woodland. Bonobos feed mainly on fruit and leaves, which they collect in trees.

SCIENTIFIC NAME	*Pan paniscus*
DISTRIBUTION	Central Africa
SIZE	Up to 1m high

RIGHT *Orang utans move slowly, but they are good climbers. They have slender legs, and their fingers and toes can keep a tight grip for a long time.*

ORANG UTAN

The orang utan is the second-largest great ape after the gorilla, and the only one with bright red fur. The males can weigh up to 90kg, and as they get older they develop fleshy pads on either side of their faces. Unlike gorillas, they spend most of their time in the trees, and often live alone. Because orang utans depend on forests for their survival, they are very vulnerable to habitat change. During the last ten years, their natural home has shrunk dramatically, because large areas of forest have been burned or cut down. Young orang utans are also sometimes taken from their mothers and sold as performing pets – a sad fate for such intelligent animals.

SCIENTIFIC NAME	*Pongo pygmaeus*
DISTRIBUTION	Sumatra, Borneo
SIZE	Up to 1.5m high

BROWN HARE

Hares look like large rabbits with extra-long ears. Unlike rabbits they are usually solitary animals, and they spend all of their lives above ground. Because they do not have burrows, hares depend on speed for safety, and they can run at up to 50km/h. Female brown hares have several families a year, and they give birth in a shallow hideaway called a form. Compared to baby rabbits, young hares, called leverets, are well developed when they are born, and they can run about within a few hours.

SCIENTIFIC NAME *Lepus europaeus*

DISTRIBUTION Originally from Africa, Europe, Asia; introduced into North America, South America, Australia, New Zealand

SIZE Up to 75cm long

LEFT *This snowshoe hare is alert to danger at all times. Its predators include the Arctic fox (page 266).*

SNOWSHOE HARE

Snowshoe hares live in the Arctic, and they change colour with the seasons. During the summer they are brown, but in winter they turn white to match the snow, except for a patch of black on the tips of their ears. Using fur-trappers' records, scientists have found that the number of snowshoe hares rises and falls in a ten-year cycle. The population rises dramatically when there is plenty of food, but as soon as the food supply begins to run out, their numbers slump.

SCIENTIFIC NAME *Lepus americanus*

DISTRIBUTION Northern North America

SIZE Up to 55cm long

AMERICAN PIKA

Pikas are close relatives of rabbits and hares, but they do not have long ears. Some species live in woodlands, but the American pika lives on mountain slopes among broken rocks, where there are plenty of places to hide. During the summer, pikas gather grass and pile it up in heaps. When snow covers the ground in winter, they use this stored grass as food.

SCIENTIFIC NAME *Ochotona princeps*

DISTRIBUTION North America

SIZE Up to 22cm long

RABBITS, HARES AND PIKAS

This group of plant-eating mammals contains about 65 species, scattered across many parts of the world. All of them live on the ground, where they nibble food with their sharp front teeth. They escape danger by running, and most of them have keen eyesight and hearing – adaptations that give them a head start on any predators. Rabbits and hares live in open country of all kinds, from grassland to desert, but pikas often live on rocky mountain slopes.

Mountain hare in winter coat

Mountain hare in summer coat

TOP *Brown hare leverets are ready to breed when they are six months old.*
ABOVE *Several species of hare turn white in winter. The mountain hare (Lepus timidus) lives in northern Europe and Asia.*

COMMON RABBIT

With its long ears and fluffy grey fur, the common rabbit is an appealing animal, but unfortunately it is also a farmland pest. It eats grass and crops, and it breeds so quickly that it can cause a lot of damage. Common rabbits usually live in burrows. They come out to feed in the evening, and stay above ground all night. If a rabbit senses danger, it strikes the ground with its back feet. When other rabbits hear this, they run for safety. Rabbits have been bred for food and for their fur for more than a thousand years. Today there are more than 60 varieties of domestic rabbit, many of which are kept as pets.

SCIENTIFIC NAME *Oryctolagus cuniculus*

DISTRIBUTION Originally from Europe, northern Africa; introduced into Australia, New Zealand

SIZE Up to 75cm long

RODENTS

With more than 1,800 species, rodents make up the largest group of mammals. They include squirrels, rats, porcupines and many other animals from all over the world. Rodents get their name from the Latin word *rodere* meaning 'to gnaw'. They have sharp front teeth, or incisors, which never stop growing and always stay sharp. Many rodents use them to gnaw through obstacles or to burrow, and beavers even use them to cut down trees. Compared to other mammals, rodents have a short life-span, but they reproduce rapidly.

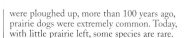

Red squirrel   Grey squirrel

LEFT *Squirrels use their bushy tails for balance as they scamper along branches.*

ABOVE *Chipmunks store any surplus food in their underground burrows.*
BELOW *Alpine marmots have keen eyesight, which helps them to spot predators, such as birds of prey.*
BOTTOM *A young black-tailed prairie dog samples a piece of grass.*

RED SQUIRREL

Squirrels are bushy-tailed rodents that are usually active by day. Some live on the ground, but most, including the red squirrel, live in trees. Tree-dwelling species have sharp claws for clinging on as they run along branches, or up and down trees. The red squirrel eats mainly seeds from pine cones. It is common in continental Europe, but in most of Britain it has been supplanted by the grey squirrel *(Sciurus carolinensis)*, a species introduced from North America.

SCIENTIFIC NAME	*Sciurus vulgaris*
DISTRIBUTION	Europe, northern Asia, Far East, Japan
SIZE	Up to 45cm long, including tail

EASTERN CHIPMUNK

Rodents are not always popular animals, but in North America the chipmunk is everybody's favourite. This small, stripy-sided animal lives in forests, and spends most of its time on the ground. Chipmunks are bold and inquisitive, and they show little fear of people. They normally forage for seeds and berries, but they also help themselves to pieces of fruit or bread that have been left over after picnics. Chipmunks breed in burrows, and raise about eight young each year.

SCIENTIFIC NAME	*Tamias striatus*
DISTRIBUTION	Eastern North America
SIZE	Up to 30cm long, including tail

BLACK-TAILED PRAIRIE DOG

This animal is not a dog at all, but a large ground-dwelling squirrel with a dog-like bark. It lives on grassy plains, and survives in this open habitat by digging burrows beneath the surface. A network of prairie dog burrows, called a township, has its own ventilation system and sleeping quarters, and can house thousands of animals. Before North America's prairies were ploughed up, more than 100 years ago, prairie dogs were extremely common. Today, with little prairie left, some species are rare.

SCIENTIFIC NAME	*Cynomys ludovicianus*
DISTRIBUTION	Central USA
SIZE	Up to 40cm long, including tail

ALPINE MARMOT

Marmots live in mountain pastures. During the long winters, they hibernate in deep burrows for up to nine months a year. Before hibernating, they build up their body fat, which acts like a food store, keeping them alive while they 'sleep'. There are at least ten species of marmot scattered across the northern hemisphere.

SCIENTIFIC NAME	*Marmota marmota*
DISTRIBUTION	Europe
SIZE	Up to 70cm long, including tail

DESERT KANGAROO-RAT

Kangaroo-rats are small rodents with large eyes, long tails and extra-long legs. They live in dry places in North America, and move around by jumping like kangaroos – up to 2m in one jump. They get most of the water they need from the plants they eat, and they also save water by coming out only at night, when the air is cooler and more moist than it is during the day. There are more than 20 species of these animals; the desert kangaroo-rat is one of ten species that live in southwestern USA.

SCIENTIFIC NAME	*Dipodomys deserti*
DISTRIBUTION	Southwestern USA, northern Mexico
SIZE	Up to 38cm long, including tail

AMERICAN BEAVER

Mammals are not great builders, but beavers are an exception to this rule. They cut down trees and dam streams, making lakes where they are safe from attack. Beaver dams can be more than 500m long, and they are so strong that they can easily bear a person's weight. Beavers are shaped for life in water, with webbed feet and paddle-shaped tails. They feed on bark and leaves, and store branches underwater as winter food. Their home is a giant mound of branches called a lodge, which they build in the centre of the lake. The entrances are underwater, so the beavers can come and go without being seen.

SCIENTIFIC NAME	*Castor canadensis*
DISTRIBUTION	North America
SIZE	Up to 1.6m long, including tail

SPRING HARE

Despite its name, this curious African rodent looks less like a hare than a squirrel with giant back legs. It normally moves on all fours, but if it is threatened it can hop more than 4m in a single bound – a feat that helps it to escape leopards, lions and other predators. Spring hares spend the day in large burrows, and come out at night. They eat plants and roots, digging them up with their front feet.

SCIENTIFIC NAME	*Pedetes capensis*
DISTRIBUTION	Eastern and southern Africa
SIZE	Up to 90cm long, including tail

GOLDEN HAMSTER

Hamsters are burrowing rodents that live in dry parts of Europe and central Asia. The golden hamster is just one of more than 12 species, but it is the best-known by far because it is often kept as a pet. Hamsters feed on seeds and insects. To survive when food is hard to find, they collect seeds in their cheek-pouches, and store them in their burrows. At the end of the summer, a golden hamster's larder may contain more than 10kg of food – enough to see it through the winter.

SCIENTIFIC NAME	*Mesocricetus auratus*
DISTRIBUTION	Syria
SIZE	Up to 20cm long, including tail

LEMMING

The lemming's fame is based on the myth that it commits mass suicide by throwing itself into the sea. In fact, this Arctic rodent is a very successful animal, although its fate is closely connected to its food supply. While there is plenty to eat, lemmings have lots of young, and their numbers rise sharply. As the population expands, food starts to run out, and hungry lemmings move off to find more. Many starve or accidentally drown, reducing the population to its original level. Lemmings live above ground, but tunnel their way beneath the snow in winter.

SCIENTIFIC NAME	*Lemmus lemmus*
DISTRIBUTION	Scandinavia
SIZE	Up to 17cm long, including tail

BANK VOLE

Voles look similar to mice, but they have blunt noses and short tails. They are active around the clock, though they are not often seen because they stay undercover, often in long grass. This does not protect them from foxes and owls, which hunt by sound as much as by sight. Bank voles nest on the ground, and raise up to four families a year.

SCIENTIFIC NAME	*Clethrionomys glareosus*
DISTRIBUTION	Europe, central Asia
SIZE	Up to 17cm long, including tail

MUSKRAT

The muskrat is a giant-sized relative of voles and lemmings, sometimes weighing more than 2kg. It is a good swimmer, and has webbed back feet and a flat tail that it uses as a rudder. Muskrats eat waterside plants, and occasionally small animals. They normally burrow into riverbanks, but if the ground is flat, they make a home by piling plants into a heap up to a metre high. Muskrats have thick, waterproof coats.

SCIENTIFIC NAME	*Ondatra zibethicus*
DISTRIBUTION	Originally from USA; introduced into Europe
SIZE	Up to 65cm long, including tail

GERBIL

Gerbils specialize at living in dry places. Like kangaroo-rats, they obtain nearly all their water from food, and they avoid the worst of the heat by staying underground during the day. Gerbils also have furry feet – another adaptation that helps to keep them cool. There are many species of gerbil. The ones most often kept as pets are Mongolian gerbils, or jirds *(Meriones unguiculatus).*

SCIENTIFIC NAME	*Meriones* and other genera
DISTRIBUTION	Southern Europe, Africa, Middle East, Asia
SIZE	Typical length 20cm, including tail

ABOVE *A bank vole feeds on some seeds.*

ABOVE *Field voles* (Microtus agrestis) *live in grassland and meadows. They eat leaves, sometimes causing damage to crops.*

ABOVE *The northern water vole* (Arvicola terrestris) *swims well, and often lives on riverbanks.*
BELOW *Like most rodents, muskrats can use their front feet to hold their food. Their back feet are webbed, which helps them to swim.*
BOTTOM *A female Egyptian gerbil* (Gerbillus *sp.) watches over her family.*

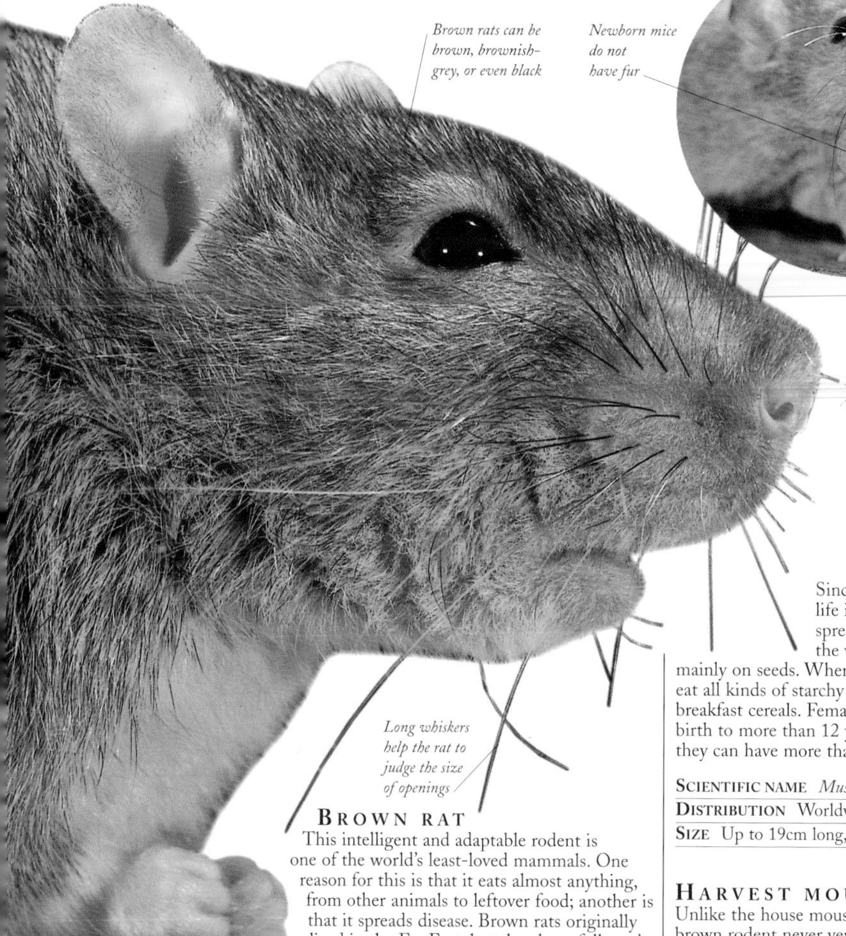

Brown rats can be brown, brownish-grey, or even black

Newborn mice do not have fur

TOP *Carrying a baby in her mouth, a female house mouse moves to a new nest.*
ABOVE *Mice are naturally inquisitive, which helps them to find food.*

Since then it has taken up life in houses and farms, and spread all over the world. In the wild, house mice feed mainly on seeds. When they live indoors, they eat all kinds of starchy food, from grain to breakfast cereals. Female house mice can give birth to more than 12 young at a time, and they can have more than ten families a year.

SCIENTIFIC NAME *Mus musculus*

DISTRIBUTION Worldwide

SIZE Up to 19cm long, including tail

Long whiskers help the rat to judge the size of openings

BROWN RAT

This intelligent and adaptable rodent is one of the world's least-loved mammals. One reason for this is that it eats almost anything, from other animals to leftover food; another is that it spreads disease. Brown rats originally lived in the Far East, but they have followed people all over the world. Compared to mice they are large and aggressive, and will attack if they are cornered. Getting rid of rats is not easy because they learn to steer clear of traps, and are wary of poisoned food.

SCIENTIFIC NAME *Rattus norvegicus*

DISTRIBUTION Worldwide

SIZE Up to 60cm long, including tail

TOP AND ABOVE *The brown rat can find its way around in complete darkness using its nose and sensitive whiskers.*

HOUSE MOUSE

This familiar rodent is one of the most successful mammals in the world. It originally comes from central Asia, where it lives in open grasslands.

HARVEST MOUSE

Unlike the house mouse, this tiny, light brown rodent never ventures indoors. It lives in hedgerows and fields, where it feeds on seeds and small insects. Harvest mice build round nests by weaving together strips of grass. Each nest is about the size of a tennis ball, and is slung between several grass stems about 10cm above the ground. The nest keeps the young mice warm, and also protects them from predators. Harvest mice have up to eight young each time they breed, and when there is a plentiful food supply, they may have up to six or seven families in a year.

SCIENTIFIC NAME *Micromys minutus*

DISTRIBUTION Europe, Asia, Far East

SIZE Up to 15cm long, including tail

WHITE-FOOTED MOUSE

This mouse is one of the most common rodents in eastern North America. It lives in forests and woodland of all kinds, from Canada to the steamy jungle of southeastern Mexico. It feeds mainly on seeds and insects, and like the house mouse, it is not often seen indoors. One of its closest relatives, the deer mouse *(Peromyscus maniculatus)* is found throughout North America, right up to the Arctic.

SCIENTIFIC NAME *Peromyscus leucopus*

DISTRIBUTION Eastern and central USA, southeastern Mexico

SIZE Up to 20cm long, including tail

FAT DORMOUSE

Dormice have grey fur and large, fluffy tails, which makes them look like squirrels. They get their name from the Latin word *dormire* meaning 'to sleep', because they hibernate for several months each year. There are about 20 species of dormouse, and they are found in Africa, Europe and Asia. The fat dormouse is one of the largest species. Like most of its relatives, it lives in woodlands, and is a good climber. It comes out after dark to feed on fruit and nuts.

SCIENTIFIC NAME *Glis glis*

DISTRIBUTION Europe, Asia

SIZE Up to 32cm long, including tail

ROUGH-LEGGED JERBOA

Jerboas live in dry places in Africa and Asia. Like desert kangaroo-rats (page 252), they bounce along on their back legs instead of running on all fours. A jerboa's back legs are more than four times larger than its front legs, allowing it to cover 3m or more in a single jump. Jerboas live in burrows, and they come out after dark. During the day, the rough-legged jerboa seals off the entrance to its burrow, helping it to stay cool inside during hot weather.

SCIENTIFIC NAME *Dipus sagitta*

DISTRIBUTION Central Asia, Far East

SIZE Up to 34 cm long, including tail

NAKED MOLE-RAT

These African animals are the strangest rodents in the world. They have pink, almost bald bodies, tiny eyes and large gnawing teeth. They feed on roots, and spend their lives in burrows underground. Naked mole-rats live in colonies of up to 100 animals, controlled by a single female, or queen. The queen gives birth to all the colony's young, while the other adults burrow for food. If the queen dies, one of the female workers takes her place and begins to produce young of her own.

SCIENTIFIC NAME *Heterocephalus glaber*

DISTRIBUTION Eastern Africa

SIZE Up to 13cm long, including tail

LEFT TOP *The number of harvest mice has fallen due to changes in farming practices. Modern machines destroy their nests.*
LEFT BELOW *A white-footed mouse searches for food.*

TOP *The fat dormouse puts on weight in autumn before it hibernates.*
ABOVE *Naked mole-rats from neighbouring nests confront each other in an underground fight for space.*

HIBERNATION

Many mammals, reptiles, amphibians and insects survive cold winters by hibernating. A hibernating animal looks as if it is asleep, but sleep and hibernation are quite different. When an animal sleeps, its body stays warm and its heart beats normally. When it hibernates, its temperature drops until it is just a few degrees above its surroundings, and its heart beats so slowly that it sometimes seems to have stopped. Some hibernating animals can move if they are touched, but others keep so still that they look dead. Animals in hibernation cannot eat, and they survive on stores of body fat. When the weather warms up in spring, their temperature rises, their hearts speed up and they gradually wake up and become active.

A hibernating common dormouse (*Muscardinus avellanarius*)

CRESTED PORCUPINE

As well as being Africa's largest rodent, this animal is by far the best-armed. Its back and sides are covered with hollow spines, called quills, which can be up to 35cm long. It has shorter quills on its tail, and these rattle when they are shaken. If it is threatened, the porcupine raises its quills and rattles its tail before charging backwards at its enemy. Its quills are easily dislodged, and they can stick in skin with very painful results. Crested porcupines feed on the ground at night, eating roots and fallen fruit.

Crested porcupine with its quills half raised

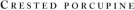

SCIENTIFIC NAME *Hystrix cristata*

DISTRIBUTION Northern and tropical Africa, parts of southern Europe

SIZE Up to 80cm long, including tail

CAVY

This small South American rodent is the original ancestor of the guinea pig, one of the world's most popular pets. It lives on grasslands and mountain slopes, feeding on grass and leaves, and sheltering in burrows and rocky crevices. Compared to other small rodents, cavies give birth to well-developed young that can fend for themselves when they are only a few days old. Cavies were first domesticated more than 3,000 years ago. They were originally kept for food, and this still continues in South America.

SCIENTIFIC NAME *Cavia tschudii*

DISTRIBUTION Central Andes Mountains (South America)

SIZE Up to 40cm long

MARA

The mara looks like a cross between a hare and a deer, with a long head and neck, and feet that end in hoof-like claws. It usually rests like a hare, sitting on its haunches, but at the first sign of trouble it races off in a peculiar bounding run, reaching speeds of up to 45km/h. Maras are vegetarians, and feed during the day. They have just two young each time they breed – a tiny number compared to many other rodents.

SCIENTIFIC NAME *Dolichotis patagona*

DISTRIBUTION Argentina

SIZE Up to 75cm long

LEFT *A female mara watches for danger while she suckles her young. Maras can have two or three families a year.*

ABOVE *An American porcupine climbs down a tree. Although these porcupines spend most of their lives above ground, they are short-sighted, and they clamber about instead of jumping. Surprisingly, they are good swimmers because their air-filled quills work like floats.*

AMERICAN PORCUPINE

Unlike porcupines that live in other parts of the world, American porcupines are good at climbing trees. They feed on buds and bark, often climbing high above the ground to find them. Their quills are only 7cm long, but they have more than 30,000 of them. They are mixed up among long hairs, and have barbed tips to make them stick in skin. If these porcupines are threatened, they use their tails as weapons, lashing them from side to side.

SCIENTIFIC NAME *Erithizon dorsatum*

DISTRIBUTION North America, Mexico

SIZE Up to 95cm long, including tail

CHINCHILLA

Many rodents have soft fur, but the chinchilla is in a class of its own. This grey, rabbit-sized animal lives high up in the Andes Mountains. Its coat protects it from the night-time cold. It has large ears and a bushy tail, and lives in crevices among rocks, emerging during the day to feed on plants. Its fur is so luxurious that some people will pay almost anything to wear it. Millions of chinchillas are now raised in captivity, but after years of hunting, the species is rare in the wild.

SCIENTIFIC NAME
Chinchilla laniger

DISTRIBUTION Central Andes Mountains (South America)

SIZE Up to 52cm long, including tail

Large, rabbit-like ears

Hairs are in densely packed clusters

AGOUTI

Like many South American rodents, the agouti has few defences apart from its speed. Its back legs are about twice as long as its front legs, and it reacts to danger by first freezing, then running for safety. There are 11 species of agouti, and they are common throughout the American tropics. Many live in forests, where they follow troops of monkeys, picking up fruit and seeds that the monkeys have dropped on the ground.

SCIENTIFIC NAME *Dasyprocta* species

DISTRIBUTION Central America, South America

SIZE Up to 60cm long, including tail

CAPYBARA

The capybara is the world's largest rodent, weighing up to 75kg. It looks like a giant guinea pig, with a large head, blunt nose and hardly any tail. Capybaras feed in herds in grassy places by rivers and lakes, and they never stray far from water. If one of them senses danger, it gives a short bark, and all the others around it gallop into the water for safety. Capybaras are good swimmers and have partly webbed feet. They can dive and stay underwater for up to five minutes, and they can swim with only their ears, eyes and nostrils showing above the surface.

SCIENTIFIC NAME *Hydrochoerus hydrochaeris*

DISTRIBUTION Tropical South America

SIZE Up to 1.3m long

PLAINS VISCACHA

South American rodents are famous for their curious shapes, and the plains viscacha is no exception. It has a large stripy head, a heavy body, large legs and a stumpy tail. Plains viscachas live in groups of up to 50 animals, and are great burrowers. They inherit their burrows from their parents and, as a result, the burrows can cover a large area, and may be many centuries old. Viscachas feed on plants, but they pick up all kinds of objects, from stones to camping equipment, and take them underground.

SCIENTIFIC NAME *Lagostomus maximus*

DISTRIBUTION Paraguay, Argentina

SIZE Up to 85cm long, including tail

ABOVE *This family of chinchillas have grown up in captivity. Captive chinchillas can live for more than 20 years.*

ABOVE *Capybaras live in herds up to 20 animals strong. They are headed by a large, powerful male.*

WHALES, DOLPHINS AND PORPOISES

Whales, dolphins and porpoises belong to a group of animals called cetaceans. While they look very much like giant fish, they are really mammals that spend their entire lives in water. Unlike fish, they breathe air, and their tails consist of a pair of horizontal rubbery flukes, or lobes, instead of a vertical fin. There are about 80 species of these animals, and they feed in two quite different ways. Baleen whales, which are shown on these two pages, do not have teeth. They eat by filtering fish or plankton through baleen plates. The whales on pages 260-261, together with dolphins and porpoises, have teeth, and they pursue their prey through the water. Apart from some dolphins, all the species in this group live in the sea.

BLUE WHALE

The blue whale is the largest animal that has ever lived. Some weigh more than 150 tonnes – twice as much as the heaviest dinosaurs. Blue whales have huge mouths, with several hundred baleen plates hanging from their upper jaws. When they take in water and close their mouths, the plates sieve krill and other small animals from the water. Females begin to breed when they are about ten years old. They give birth once every two or three years. In the early 1900s, there were about 200,000 blue whales. After one hundred years of whaling, there are now only about 12,000 left.

SCIENTIFIC NAME *Balaenoptera musculus*

DISTRIBUTION Worldwide, mainly in cold seas

SIZE Up to 30m long

TOP *The blue whale and its relatives are known as rorquals. These whales have deep grooves running down their throats. When they feed, the grooves open out to let their mouths expand. Rorquals feed only during the summer, and may swallow up to four tonnes of krill or fish every day.*

ABOVE *After the blue whale, the fin whale (Balaenoptera physalus) is the second largest animal on Earth, growing more than 25m long. It can dive to more than 200m, and often feeds by swimming on its right-hand side.*

RIGHT *Bursting upwards through the water's surface, a humpback whale shows its baleen plates. The plates are hard, but have frayed edges that trap the whale's food.*

MINKE WHALE

The minke whale belongs to the same family as the blue whale, but it is much smaller and more common. It has a grey back, and a white or pale grey underside. Minke whales feed on krill and other small animals in cold seas, but they eat fish in warmer waters. Minkes are the only baleen whales still hunted commercially. Like other whales, minkes sometimes leap head first out of the water, hitting the surface again with a huge splash. The reasons for this behaviour, called breaching, are not yet known.

SCIENTIFIC NAME *Balaenoptera acutorostrata*

DISTRIBUTION Worldwide

SIZE Up to 10m long

HUMPBACK WHALE

The humpback's enormous front flippers make it look quite different from other baleen whales. The flippers are up to 5m long, and the whale beats them like a pair of wings. Humpbacks have notched black and white tails, and the markings on them vary from one whale to another. Like blue whales, humpbacks migrate great distances between tropical waters, where they breed, and cold waters, where they feed. Humpbacks eat fish, and they often stay close to the coast.

SCIENTIFIC NAME *Megaptera novaeangliae*

DISTRIBUTION Worldwide

SIZE Up to 19m long

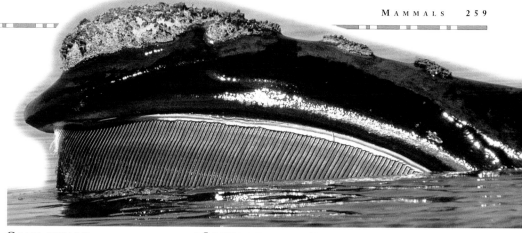

GREY WHALE

This whale is famous for its long migrations. Its main breeding area is off the coast of Mexico, but it spends the summer on the edge of the Arctic Ocean, about 10,000km away. It is easy to identify because it has mottled grey skin, and its head is encrusted with barnacles (page 39). Unlike most large whales, grey whales feed on the seabed, stirring up the bottom with their mouths. After sucking up the muddy water, they filter out any crustaceans and worms.

SCIENTIFIC NAME *Eschrichtius robustus*

DISTRIBUTION Northern Pacific Ocean; extinct in Atlantic Ocean

SIZE Up to 15m long

Humpback whale swimming and breaching

SOUTHERN RIGHT WHALE

Right whales got their names because they swim slowly and float when they are dead. As a result, whalers considered them to be the 'right' whales to hunt. There are two species – one in the northern hemisphere and one in the southern. Over the centuries, so many have been killed that the northern right whale *(Eubalaena glacialis)* is almost extinct, and only the southern right whale looks certain to survive.

Both species have blunt heads with enormous rows of baleen plates, and fat, blue-black bodies with white markings on their undersides. They feed on plankton, and give birth once every three or four years.

SCIENTIFIC NAME *Eubalaena australis*

DISTRIBUTION Southern hemisphere, in temperate and polar waters

SIZE Up to 18m long

Pale ring close to tail flukes

BOWHEAD WHALE

The bowhead is a close relative of right whales, and has a similar shape and the same enormous head. Like right whales, it was hunted to the verge of extinction. After several decades of being protected, there are still only about 10,000 of them. These whales spend their lives in the cold waters around the Arctic, usually close to the edge of floating sea ice.

SCIENTIFIC NAME *Balaena mystaceus*

DISTRIBUTION Arctic Ocean

SIZE Up to 20m long

TOP *A southern right whale feeds off the coast of South America. The white growths on its head are areas of hard skin covered with barnacles and parasitic lice. All right whales have these, though it is not known why.*

ABOVE *Right whales have steeply arched mouths, and their eyes are set low down, nearer their undersides than their backs.*

ABOVE *The bowhead whale stays warm because of a layer of insulating fat, or blubber, that can be more than 60cm thick. Unlike right whales, it does not have any growths on its head.*

SPERM WHALE

With an enormous head and formidable teeth, the 50-tonne sperm whale is the largest hunting animal in the seas. Instead of straining plankton out of the water, as baleen whales do, it dives after giant squid, sometimes reaching depths of at least 2km. It often holds its breath for nearly two hours. The sperm whale can hunt in total darkness, and it finds its prey by echolocation (page 241). Its head contains a waxy substance, called spermaceti, which probably helps to focus beams of sound, as well as control the whale's buoyancy. Sperm whales usually live in deep parts of the oceans, keeping clear of shallow coasts. They are easy to recognize when they surface, because they have a single nostril, or blowhole, on the left-hand side of their heads. When they breathe out, this produces a slanting cloud of vapour, or 'spout'.

SCIENTIFIC NAME	*Physeter macrocephalus*
DISTRIBUTION	Worldwide
SIZE	Up to 18m long

warbles and clicks. Female belugas start to breed at about seven years old and have one calf every three years.

SCIENTIFIC NAME	*Delphinapterus leucas*
DISTRIBUTION	Arctic Ocean, northern Pacific Ocean, North Atlantic Ocean
SIZE	Up to 5m long

NARWHAL

The male narwhal is the only whale that is armed with a tusk. The tusk is a modified tooth that grows forwards through the animal's upper jaw, and can be up to 3m long. At one time, scientists thought that narwhals used their tusks to feed or to deter predators, but it seems more likely that they use them to fight rival males. Very occasionally, female narwhals develop a

Narwhal

tusk, but this is usually less than a metre long. Narwhals feed on fish and squid. They are close relatives of belugas, but they live further north than any other whale, and often swim underneath the sea ice.

SCIENTIFIC NAME	*Monodon monoceros*
DISTRIBUTION	Arctic Ocean
SIZE	Up to 5m long

TRUE'S BEAKED WHALE

Compared to other marine mammals, beaked whales are mysterious animals. There are nearly 20 species, but some are known only from dead remains washed up on the shore. True's beaked whale is a medium-sized species, with a grey and cream body, small flippers and a narrow, protruding 'beak'. Its two teeth stick out when its mouth is closed, but they are too small to be used for eating. Like its many relatives, this whale is a good diver, and feeds mainly on squid.

SCIENTIFIC NAME	*Mesoplodon mirus*
DISTRIBUTION	Worldwide
SIZE	Up to 5m long

BELUGA OR WHITE WHALE

This small whale is the only species in the world with creamy white skin. It has small flippers, a rounded head and a beak-like mouth packed with up to 40 teeth. It lives in the cold seas of the far north, feeding on crustaceans and fish. Belugas spend a lot of their time at the surface or in shallow water, and are sociable and very noisy animals. They find their prey partly by echolocation, and partly by sight. They also use sound to keep in touch with each other, and produce a range of squeaks,

Beluga whale

ABOVE LEFT *The beluga's rounded forehead changes shape when it makes sounds, bulging outwards, then shrinking.*

LONG-FINNED PILOT WHALE

Pilot whales belong to the dolphin family, and get their name from their habit of swimming in front of ships as if they were guiding them. They are mainly black, with curved flippers and bulbous heads. They live in groups, or pods, of up to 40 animals, and feed mostly after dark, on fish and squid. Like other toothed whales, pilot whales navigate and find food by using sound. This system works well in deep water, but pilot whale pods sometimes lose their way in shallow water and become stranded on the shore. Mass strandings can also occur with other whales – the exact reason for this is not known.

SCIENTIFIC NAME   *Globicephala melas*

DISTRIBUTION   North Atlantic Ocean, cold seas in southern hemisphere

SIZE   Up to 6m long

TOP *The long-finned pilot whale has unusually long and slender front flippers, with a backswept curve.*
ABOVE *True's beaked whale has only two teeth, right at the end of its lower jaw.*

KILLER WHALE OR ORCA

Weighing up to nine tonnes, the black and white killer whale is the largest member of the dolphin family. It is also one of the most intelligent, and has a complex social life based on extended family groups. Killer whales communicate by sound, and they often travel in formation, sometimes bobbing out of the water to scan the surrounding sea. Despite their name, killer whales have never been known to attack humans, although they are fearsome predators of other animals. They eat fish and squid, but when they hunt as a group they can tackle much larger prey, including walruses and other whales. They are among the most widespread mammals on Earth, living in coastal waters as well as in the open sea.

SCIENTIFIC NAME   *Orcinus orca*

DISTRIBUTION   Worldwide

SIZE   Up to 9.5m long

ABOVE *Killer whales often attack seals, especially pups, because they are easier to catch than adults. The whales sometimes throw themselves onto beaches to catch pups near the water's edge.*

LEFT *With its head pointing downwards, a sperm whale sets off on a dive. This whale is surrounded by remoras (page 125), which are hitching a ride to find food.*

TOP *The Atlantic white-sided dolphin* (Lagenorhynchus acutus) *lives in large schools that may be up to 1,000 strong.* **ABOVE** *The rough-toothed dolphin* (Steno bredanensis) *lives in warm waters worldwide.* **BELOW** *Common dolphins can dive for more than five minutes, but spend most of their time close to the surface.*

COMMON DOLPHIN

Dolphins belong to the same group of mammals as whales, but their smaller size and streamlined shape makes them look even more like fish. They are fast-moving, acrobatic and playful animals, capable of swimming at up to 40km/h, and of bursting right out of the water. The common dolphin is one of the most widespread species, with a complicated pattern of white, yellow, black and grey. Like most other ocean-going dolphins, it feeds on fish, and has beak-like jaws which contain more than 200 small teeth. Dolphins are famous for their intelligence and their close family life. When a dolphin gives birth, other females gather round to help the baby dolphin swim up to the surface to breathe air.

SCIENTIFIC NAME	*Delphinus delphis*
DISTRIBUTION	Warm waters worldwide
SIZE	Up to 2.4m long

ABOVE *Boutos are slow swimmers. But they are experts at finding fish to eat in the murky water of the Amazon.*

BOTTLENOSE DOLPHIN

There are more than 30 species of dolphin, but this all-grey species is by far the best-known. This is because it is sometimes kept in captivity, where its sociable nature and intelligence make it a star performer. In the wild, bottlenose dolphins

live in schools of up to 12 animals. Like other dolphins, they use echolocation to find fish, and often cooperate to round up their prey. They frequently ride on the bow-waves of boats, and will sometimes approach swimmers, allowing themselves to be patted or stroked.

SCIENTIFIC NAME	*Tursiops truncatus*
DISTRIBUTION	Worldwide, except in polar waters
SIZE	Up to 3.9m long

INDUS RIVER DOLPHIN

This rare, grey-brown animal is one of a handful of dolphins that live in fresh water. A closely related species lives in the River Ganges, in India. It has very slender jaws armed with needle-sharp teeth, and broad flippers that look like paddles. Its eyes are so small that it is almost blind, and it finds its food entirely by echolocation. At one time, these dolphins were found all along the River Indus, but several dams and barrages have been built on the river, stopping the dolphins from swimming up and down. Altogether, there are probably fewer than 500 of these endangered animals left.

SCIENTIFIC NAME	*Platanista minor*
DISTRIBUTION	River Indus (Pakistan)
SIZE	Up to 2.5m long

BOUTO

The bouto is the world's largest river dolphin, and one of the few that is still fairly common. It lives in the Rivers Amazon and Orinoco – a vast network of waterways in the heart of South America. Like the Indus river dolphin, it has very narrow jaws, but its colour varies from grey to bright pink. Boutos feed on fish, crayfish and other small animals, and they find their prey by sight and touch as well as by echolocation. During the dry season, they gather in schools of up to 12 animals, but for the rest of the year they usually live in pairs.

SCIENTIFIC NAME	*Inia geoffrensis*
DISTRIBUTION	Rivers Amazon and Orinoco (South America)
SIZE	Up to 2.5m long

DALL'S PORPOISE

Unlike dolphins, porpoises have short snouts and barrel-shaped bodies. There are six species, and Dall's porpoise is the largest, weighing up to 200kg. Although it is not much longer than an adult human, this black and white porpoise is one of the world's fastest sea-going mammals, reaching speeds of up to 55km/h. Dall's porpoises live in schools of up to 20 animals, although many more may gather where there is

ABOVE *Harbour porpoises start to breed when they are about five years old, and usually have one calf a year. Unlike the teeth of true dolphins, which are pointed, porpoises' teeth have two flat sides and a sharp edge.*

plenty of food. They can dive to depths of at least 500m to catch fish and squid and, although their eyesight is good, they probably use echolocation to help them when they hunt.

SCIENTIFIC NAME	*Phocoenoides dalli*
DISTRIBUTION	Northern Pacific Ocean
SIZE	Up to 2.2m long

HARBOUR PORPOISE OR COMMON PORPOISE

This grey and white animal spends most of its life close to the coast, or in shallow seas offshore. It sometimes swims into estuaries and harbours, which is how it gets its name. Although harbour porpoises are widespread, they are not often seen because they rarely jump out of the water and keep well clear of moving boats. Like dolphins, porpoises have been harmed by modern fishing techniques. When they become tangled up in nets, they die because they cannot swim up to the surface to breathe.

SCIENTIFIC NAME	*Phocoena phocoena*
DISTRIBUTION	Northern waters worldwide
SIZE	Up to 1.9m long

VAQUITA

This highly endangered animal is one of the smallest cetaceans – the group of mammals that also includes dolphins and whales. When it is newborn, it is only about 60cm long, and when it is fully grown it rarely exceeds 1.5m. It lives close to the shore in the Gulf of California – a long arm of the Pacific Ocean in northwestern Mexico. Vaquitas are grey with stumpy bodies, and they feed mainly on fish. At present, only a few hundred of these porpoises survive in the wild. Without careful protection, they will almost certainly become extinct.

SCIENTIFIC NAME	*Phocoena sinus*
DISTRIBUTION	Gulf of California
SIZE	Up to 1.5m long

LEFT *This bottlenose dolphin is swimming over a coral reef in the Caribbean Sea. In some parts of the world, bottlenose dolphins are so tame that they come close to the shore to beg people for fish.*

DOGS AND FOXES

With their keen senses, long legs and sharp
teeth, dogs and foxes are well equipped for
hunting. They belong to a group of meat-
eating mammals called carnivores (page 266),
that feed mostly on living prey. Wild dogs
and their relatives usually catch their prey by
running it down in a chase, but foxes often
hunt by stealth, pouncing before their target
can run or fly away. Most of these animals
hunt alone, but some, notably the grey wolf,
catch their food in packs. There are about
36 species of wild dogs and foxes. The best-
known member of the family is the domestic
dog, which is descended from the wolf.

GREY WOLF

This is the largest member of the dog family. It
used to live in most of the northern hemisphere,
but after centuries of persecution, it is now found
mainly in remote areas, particularly dense forests.
Grey wolves live in packs that consist of a pair
of adults with several generations of their young.
They cooperate when they hunt, and this allows
them to kill animals several times their own size.
Although they share their food, wolves have
a strict order of seniority, and junior wolves
have to give way to larger, older animals.

SCIENTIFIC NAME *Canis lupus*

DISTRIBUTION Eastern Europe, Asia, parts of
North America

SIZE Up to 1.8m long, including tail

**Ready to
attack**

**Friendly
expression**

LEFT *Grey
wolves use facial
expressions to
communicate
with members
of their pack.*

COYOTE

The coyote usually finds food on its own. It eats
all kinds of food, including snakes, insects, fruit
and dead remains, but it also has a reputation for
attacking farm animals. Over the years, hundreds
of thousands of coyotes have been poisoned or
shot, but the species has managed to survive. In
the spring, females give birth to litters of about
six pups in a burrow. The father brings them
food while they stay safely underground.

SCIENTIFIC NAME *Canis latrans*

DISTRIBUTION North America, Mexico

SIZE Up to 1.3m long, including tail

GOLDEN JACKAL

Jackals look similar to coyotes. Like most members of the dog family, they survive by a mixture of hunting and scavenging, and use their keen hearing and sense of smell to track down food after dark. Golden jackals live in dry places, sometimes close to farms and villages. Although they attack livestock, they also perform a useful service for farmers by killing poisonous snakes.

SCIENTIFIC NAME
Canis aureus

DISTRIBUTION Southeastern Europe, northern Africa, Middle East, southern Asia

SIZE Up to 1.3m long, including tail

Golden jackal

DINGO

Australia does not have any native dogs, but it does have the dingo – an animal introduced by settlers thousands of years ago. Some dingos escaped and managed to establish themselves in the wild, and today their descendants roam across the outback. Unlike domesticated dogs, dingos cannot bark. They have extra-large paws, and ears that are always upright. Dingos can be a problem because they often attack sheep. To prevent this happening, the farming country of southeastern Australia is cordoned off by a dingo-proof fence more than 5,000km long.

SCIENTIFIC NAME *Canis familiaris dingo*

DISTRIBUTION Australia

SIZE Up to 1.8m long, including tail

AFRICAN WILD DOG

With its blotchy fur and rounded ears, this animal is one of the most distinctive members of the dog family. It is small and lightly built, but because it hunts in packs, it can kill animals as large as wildebeest (page 299). African wild dogs hunt in open grassland, and literally drag their prey to its knees. Once the animal has collapsed, there is no escape, and the pack immediately starts to feed.

LEFT *Grey wolves use speed and endurance to outpace their prey. They can run faster than 50km/h for nearly half an hour – long enough to exhaust large animals such as moose.*

ABOVE *African wild dogs are messy killers, but they are not aggressive towards each other. When these pups are old enough, the adults will give them the first turn at feeding after a successful hunt.*

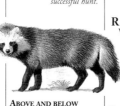

ABOVE AND BELOW *Raccoon-dogs' diets include seeds and insects, as well as frogs, birds and small mammals.*

African wild dogs were once common, but numbers have fallen, probably due to disease and changes in their habitat. Today, only about 2,000 are left.

SCIENTIFIC NAME *Lycaon pictus*

DISTRIBUTION Tropical Africa

SIZE Up to 1.2m long, including tail

BUSH DOG

This rare brown dog lives in forests and grassland. Its legs and tail are short and stumpy and, unlike most dogs, it is active during the day. It feeds on large rodents, and is a good swimmer. Bush dogs live in packs of up to ten animals.

SCIENTIFIC NAME *Speothos venaticus*

DISTRIBUTION Northern South America

SIZE Up to 90cm long, including tail

RACCOON-DOG

With its small ears and black eye patches, this dog looks very like a raccoon (page 270). It has smaller teeth than other dogs, and is the only dog that hibernates. It is native to the Far East, but was taken to Russia more than 50 years ago for its fur. Since then, it has spread across Europe as far as France.

SCIENTIFIC NAME *Nyctereutes procyonoides*

DISTRIBUTION Originally from the Far East, including Japan; introduced into Europe

SIZE Up to 75cm long, including tail

Pups will be ready to breed when they are one year old

TOP AND ABOVE *The Arctic fox's winter coat is the warmest in the animal world. In summer, the fox loses its long fur, which makes it look much slimmer.*
RIGHT *By playing at fighting, these two red fox cubs are learning skills that will help them to hunt as adults.*

Short, blunt claws

Front legs are used for pouncing on prey

Coat stays the same colour all year round

Tail usually has a white tip

ARCTIC FOX
There are ten species of fox. They belong to the same family as dogs, but they are more lightly built and, instead of chasing animals, they often pounce on them like a cat. The Arctic fox can survive temperatures of -50°C, thanks to its thick coat and warm fur on the undersides of its paws. Its fur is brown in summer, but in autumn and winter it turns white. Arctic foxes eat live animals, and dead remains, and they travel across the frozen Arctic Sea to find food left by polar bears. They make dens on the tundra, but if they are caught in a blizzard, they dig burrows in the snow.

SCIENTIFIC NAME	*Alopex lagopus*
DISTRIBUTION	Arctic
SIZE	Up to 1m long, including tail

RED FOX
The red fox is the largest and also the most widespread fox. It is nocturnal and hunts alone or in family groups rather than in packs. Red

CARNIVORES

Carnivore skull

A carnivore is any meat-eating animal. But the same word is also used in a narrower way to mean mammals that specialize in eating flesh. Mammalian carnivores include dogs, foxes, bears and cats, as well as many smaller hunters, such as raccoons, badgers, otters and skunks. Despite their differences, mammalian carnivores have many features in common. They all have keen senses, and teeth that are designed to deal with meat. At the front of their mouths they have pointed canine teeth, which are shaped to stab and grip. Towards the back, many of them have long carnassial teeth, which work like scissors to slice through the toughest flesh. Because these animals can eat their food in pieces instead of swallowing it whole, they can sometimes tackle prey that is larger than themselves. Some mammalian carnivores hunt by day, but most are active at night, when their victims find it harder to escape. There are about 240 species of these mammals and they live all over the world from the tropics to the Arctic ice.

foxes raise their cubs in underground dens. Their natural habitat includes forests and open grassland, but in some places they have successfully established themselves in suburban gardens, and even in busy city centres.

SCIENTIFIC NAME *Vulpes vulpes*

DISTRIBUTION Originally from North America, Europe, Asia; introduced into Australia

SIZE Up to 1.4m long, including tail

SWIFT FOX OR PRAIRIE FOX

This small, sandy-coloured American fox feeds mainly on rodents. Like other foxes, it sometimes kills more than it is able to eat at a single meal, and it buries the surplus food so that it can return to it later. Swift foxes are harmless to livestock, but in recent years they have been harmed by poisoned food left for coyotes.

SCIENTIFIC NAME *Vulpes velox*

DISTRIBUTION Southern Canada, western North America

SIZE Up to 80cm long, including tail

FENNEC FOX

This nocturnal desert animal is the smallest member of the dog family, and its ears are enormous compared to the size of its body. It feeds on rodents and other small animals, using its keen hearing to pinpoint its prey. Its ears also help to keep it cool because body heat is lost from all over their large surface. Fennec foxes are sandy coloured – an adaptation that camouflages them if they venture out during the day.

SCIENTIFIC NAME *Fennecus zerda*

DISTRIBUTION Northern Africa, Middle East

SIZE Up to 60cm long, including tail

GREY FOX

Grey foxes live in forests and desert scrub, and also on the outskirts of towns. They usually raise their cubs in a den, either on top of or underneath the ground, though in some places they breed in trees. If they are threatened, grey foxes sometimes hide under boulders, but more often they climb trees to escape danger. They grip the tree-trunks with the strong claws on their back feet, and cling on with their front legs. In order to get down to the ground again, they have to move tail-first.

SCIENTIFIC NAME *Urocyon cinereoargenteus*

DISTRIBUTION North America, Central America, northern South America

SIZE Up to 1.15m long, including tail

CRAB-EATING FOX

Despite its name, this fox eats much more than just crabs. Rodents and insects make up part of its diet, as do birds' eggs and freshwater turtles. The crab-eating fox has even been known to raid plantations for bananas and other fruit, making it unpopular with farmers. These greyish-brown animals have bushy tails and live in grassland and open woodland. Because they live in a warm place, they can breed at any time of the year.

SCIENTIFIC NAME
Cerdocyon thous

DISTRIBUTION
South America

SIZE Up to 1m long, including tail

TOP *The fennec fox's outsized ears are extremely sensitive.*

ABOVE *Grey foxes are sometimes eaten by coyotes, especially in winter when other food is scarce.*

LEFT *A crab-eating fox hunts in grassland in Brazil.*

BEARS

With their heavy bodies and powerful jaws, bears include the largest meat-eating animals that live on land. A male polar bear can weigh more than 600kg, and can be as tall as 1.6m at the shoulder when standing on all fours. Bears move with a lumbering walk on their massive paws, but are capable of sudden bursts of speed. They have a varied diet and, despite their fearsome teeth, many of them eat fruit, roots and insects as well as meat. There are seven species of bear, although some scientists also classify the giant panda (page 270) as a bear, bringing the total to eight.

POLAR BEAR

This well-known animal is the world's largest bear. Females can weigh more than 300kg, but the males may be double this weight. During the summer, polar bears often eat berries and rodents but, in winter, they wander over the frozen sea, attacking seals as they surface to breathe. Polar bears are superb swimmers, and have been seen in open water hundreds of kilometres from land. They have furry paws that give them a non-slip grip, and dense fur that keeps their skin dry. The males are usually active all year round, but the females hibernate during the winter in ice dens. They give birth to their cubs there and emerge with their youngsters in spring.

SCIENTIFIC NAME
Thalarctos maritimus

DISTRIBUTION	Arctic
SIZE	Up to 2.5m long

BROWN BEAR OR GRIZZLY BEAR

The brown bear has a reputation for being a dangerous and unpredictable predator. On its back legs, it can stand more than 3m high, and it is strong enough to drag away a horse. Brown bears live mainly in forests. They are not good climbers, but over short distances they can run at high speed. They eat almost anything, including fruit, deer and migrating fish, and they can catch and kill other bears. In places with cold winters, brown bears hibernate in dens underground. In late winter, the females give birth to two to four cubs, which stay with their mother for at least a year.

ABOVE A brown bear stands up on its hind legs. Bears stand like this when they feel threatened, or when they are trying to catch a scent in the air.

SCIENTIFIC NAME *Ursus arctos*

DISTRIBUTION	North America, northern Asia; scattered groups in eastern Europe
SIZE	Up to 2.8m long

ABOVE Female polar bears have to guard their cubs carefully because adult males may attack them.
BELOW For a polar bear, winter is the best time for hunting.
1 *It waits by a seal's breathing hole for a seal to surface.* **2** *It drags the seal from the water onto the ice.*

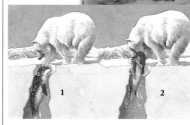

1   2

ASIATIC BLACK BEAR

This animal looks similar to the American black bear, but it has a broader face, and a V-shaped patch of white fur on its chest. It is a good climber, and clambers up trees to reach fruit, and collect honey from the nests of wild bees. It also eats insects and other small animals, and sometimes attacks farm livestock. In some parts of Asia, black bears are at risk of dying out because their natural habitat is being destroyed by deforestation. Hunters, who can sell their body parts for use in traditional medicines, pose a further threat to this species.

SCIENTIFIC NAME *Ursus thibetanus*

DISTRIBUTION	Central and Southeast Asia, Far East
SIZE	Up to 1.8m long

of animals. They spend much of their lives in trees, sleeping in the day in nests made of leafy branches.

SCIENTIFIC NAME
Helarctos malayanus

DISTRIBUTION
Southeast Asia

SIZE Up to 1.4m long

ABOVE *The spectacled bear is named after the white rings around its eyes.*

SPECTACLED BEAR

This is the only bear that lives in South America. Apart from its white 'spectacles', its fur is mostly black or brown. Despite weighing 100kg or more, spectacled bears are good climbers. They build platforms in trees which they stand on to collect their food of fruit and young leaves. Because they live in a warm climate, they do not need to hibernate.

SCIENTIFIC NAME *Tremarctos ornatus*

DISTRIBUTION Tropical South America

SIZE Up to 1.8m long

SLOTH BEAR

For a bear, this shaggy Asian animal has a very unusual diet. It feeds mainly on termites, which it sucks up like a vacuum cleaner. It closes its nostrils while it feeds, making sure that it does not breathe in the termites and choke. This way of eating is very noisy, and can be heard more than 150m away. Sloth bears have powerful feet and long claws. They are not normally dangerous to people, but like all their relatives, they have bad eyesight and poor hearing, and can attack if they are caught by surprise.

SCIENTIFIC NAME *Ursus ursinus*

DISTRIBUTION Southern Asia; from Nepal to Sri Lanka

SIZE Up to 1.9m long

AMERICAN BLACK BEAR

The American black bear is much smaller than the brown bear, and much more widespread. It is often found in national parks, where it raids campsites for food. It usually hunts at night, using its sense of smell. It hibernates during the winter but, like the brown bear, its winter sleep is light, and its body temperature drops only a few degrees. If anything disturbs it in its den, it can wake up quite quickly. American black bears tend to steer clear of people, but can be dangerous if they are disturbed while protecting their cubs.

SCIENTIFIC NAME *Ursus americanus*

DISTRIBUTION North America, northern Mexico

SIZE Up to 1.8m long

ABOVE *This American black bear cub will stay with its mother for about a year. It will be able to breed by the age of four.*

SUN BEAR

This is the smallest bear, and one of the most intelligent. Its fur is black and short, so that it looks as if it has been given a trim. Sun bears live in tropical forests, feeding on fruit and a variety

PANDAS AND RACCOONS

Compared to other carnivores, pandas and raccoons do not show a special liking for meat. Many of them catch birds, insects and other small animals, but they are just as fond of eggs, seeds and fruit. The giant panda is highly unusual because it rarely eats meat at all. Pandas and raccoons are good climbers, and most of them become active at night, using their eyes and keen sense of smell to find food. There are 20 species in this family of mammals. Apart from pandas, which are native to Asia, they all live in the Americas.

GIANT PANDA

Few endangered animals are as well-known as the giant panda. It is almost entirely vegetarian, whereas all its relatives are carnivorous. It feeds on the shoots of bamboo plants, and it eats sitting down, gripping its food in its front paws with the

ABOVE AND LEFT *Raccoons remain active throughout the year, but they hole up in a den if the weather turns very cold. They give birth to three or four young in early spring.*

help of special pads that work like thumbs. Giant pandas have become rare, partly through hunting, but mainly because their natural habitat – the bamboo forests of central China – is slowly being destroyed. Giant pandas survive quite well in captivity, but it is very difficult to encourage them to breed. Baby pandas are about 8cm long when they are born, and they feed on their mother's milk for at least nine months.

ABOVE *The giant panda is one of the world's most remarkable mammals. Some scientists classify it as a relative of the red panda and raccoon, but others think that it is an unusual kind of bear.*

SCIENTIFIC NAME	*Ailuropoda melanoleuca*
DISTRIBUTION	Central China
SIZE	Up to 1.6m long, including tail

LESSER PANDA OR RED PANDA

This animal looks quite unlike its larger and more famous relative, the giant panda. It has bright rusty-red fur, slender legs and a long, bushy tail. Red pandas are nocturnal, and they live in mountain forests. Although they are good climbers, they feed mainly on the ground, eating shoots, roots and small animals.

BELOW *The lesser panda is good at coping with the cold, and it lives in areas up to 4,000m high. When it is asleep, it curls its tail around its body to keep itself warm.*

SCIENTIFIC NAME	*Ailurus fulgens*
DISTRIBUTION	Southern Asia, China
SIZE	Up to 1.1m long, including tail

RACCOON

Like the red fox (pages 266–267), the raccoon is a woodland animal, though it has learned how to live in built-up areas. In its natural habitat, it eats all kinds of food, from frogs to fruit, but in towns and suburbs it raids rubbish bins and eats the remains of animals that have been run over. Raccoons are nocturnal, have a keen sense of smell, and are good climbers. They have long fur and black patches around their eyes, which makes them look as if they are wearing a mask. Compared to most mammalian carnivores, they are very adept with their paws, using them to pick up and hold their food.

SCIENTIFIC NAME	*Procyon lotor*
DISTRIBUTION	North America, Central America
SIZE	Up to 1m long, including tail

COATI

Coatis belong to the same family as raccoons and red pandas, but they are active by day instead of by night. They are also sociable animals, living in groups up to 20 strong. Coatis have long snouts, and long, banded tails that they hold upright when they are on the ground. They snuffle among low-growing plants and fallen leaves in woods and forests, searching for small animals, fruits and seeds. Adult coatis have few enemies, but the young are attacked by jaguars and snakes.

SCIENTIFIC NAME	*Nasua nasua*
DISTRIBUTION	North America, Central America, South America; from Arizona to Argentina
SIZE	Up to 1.25m long, including tail

MUSTELIDS

The mustlelid family contains nearly 70 species of carnivorous mammals, including martens, weasels, badgers and skunks. Most mustelids are long-bodied animals with short legs, and they hunt mainly by using the senses of sight and smell. Although they are not large, they can be ferocious and remarkably strong, killing animals larger than themselves, and sometimes chasing away other predators from their kills. Mustelids live across most of the world, except Australia, New Zealand and Antarctica.

ABOVE *Like many mustelids, the American marten has thick fur that keeps it warm in winter.*
BELOW *The least weasel is the smallest carnivorous mammal in the world.*

AMERICAN MARTEN

Martens are skilful climbers with reddish-brown fur and short, stocky legs. Although they get some of their food on the ground, they also hunt in trees. The American marten lives in coniferous forests, and is expert at catching squirrels, which it chases through the treetops.

SCIENTIFIC NAME	*Martes americana*
DISTRIBUTION	Canada, Alaska, western USA
SIZE	Up to 65cm long, including tail

SABLE

Many mustelids have thick, soft fur, but the sable's is the most luxurious of all. The sable lives in the coniferous forests of northern Asia, and develops an extra-long winter coat to keep it warm in the penetrating cold. It lives on the ground, and feeds on nuts and berries, as well as small animals. For hundreds of years, sable fur has commanded very high prices, and hundreds of thousands of these animals have been trapped in the wild. Today, sables are also farmed commercially for their fur.

SCIENTIFIC NAME	*Martes zibellina*
DISTRIBUTION	Siberia, Korea, Japan
SIZE	Up to 64cm long, including tail

LEAST WEASEL

This tiny hunter has a slender body that is not much thicker than a finger. It lives in a variety of habitats, and hunts day and night for animals such as mice. Because it is so small, it can chase mice into their burrows, something that few other predators can do. Its young grow quickly, and can kill prey when they are eight weeks old, using their small, but very sharp, canine teeth.

SCIENTIFIC NAME	*Mustela nivalis*
DISTRIBUTION	Originally from North America, Europe, northern Africa, Asia; introduced into New Zealand
SIZE	Up to 30cm long, including tail

STOAT

The stoat looks like a larger version of the least weasel. In summer it is mainly brown, but in northern regions its fur often turns white in the winter. Stoats live wherever there is cover. They feed on rodents and birds, and they can kill fully grown rabbits several times their own size. Stoats breed in hollow trees and burrows.

SCIENTIFIC NAME	*Mustela erminea*
DISTRIBUTION	Originally from North America, Europe, Asia; introduced into New Zealand
SIZE	Up to 40cm long, including tail

Stoat's winter coat is white except for black tip of tail

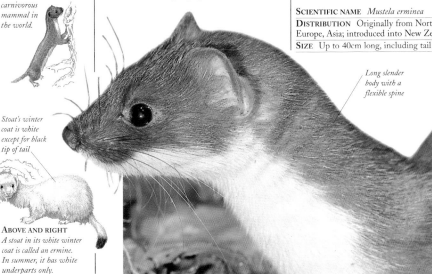

Long slender body with a flexible spine

ABOVE AND RIGHT
A stoat in its white winter coat is called an ermine. In summer, it has white underparts only.

TOP AND ABOVE
Eurasian badgers often follow the same route each night, when they are hunting for food. They may also collect leaves and dry grass to line their underground chambers.
RIGHT *Ratels are good climbers, clinging on with their sharp claws. This ratel is foraging for insects on a dead tree.*

EURASIAN BADGER

With its stripy face and pointed nose, the badger is a familiar animal throughout Europe, though as it is nocturnal, few people get a chance to see one. Badger burrows, called setts, are easy to spot. They are usually in woodland, and often have many entrances (the record is nearly 200), each flanked by a pile of excavated earth and turned-out bedding. Setts are handed down from one generation to another, and large ones may be more than a century old. Badgers are creatures of habit, and they emerge after dusk to forage along well-worn paths. They eat anything they can find, but earthworms and insects often feature in their diet. Although they do not hibernate, they become dormant, or sleepy, in winter. The females give birth to up to five cubs before spring.

SCIENTIFIC NAME *Meles meles*

DISTRIBUTION Europe, northern Asia, Far East

SIZE Up to 1m long, including tail

Ratels can produce an evil-smelling fluid from their undertail glands

ABOVE *Looking like a cross between a dog and a bear, the wolverine is the largest mustelid that hunts on land. It is so ferocious that it can drive even bears from their kills.*

WOLVERINE OR GLUTTON

This powerfully built animal is famous for its strength and for its large appetite. It lives in northern forests and tundra, and is a formidable hunter. Its legs are so powerful that it can chase reindeer across frozen snow. During the summer, when the ground is boggy, it feeds mainly on fruit and dead remains and may wander up to 45km a day to find food.

SCIENTIFIC NAME *Gulo gulo*

DISTRIBUTION Scandinavia, Siberia, North America

SIZE Up to 1.1m long, including tail

RATEL OR HONEY BADGER

This low-slung animal has unusual colouring, with black sides and underparts, and white fur along its head and back. Its eating habitats are stranger still, because it specializes in breaking open bees' nests to reach the honey inside. In Africa, ratels are often led to bees' nests by a bird called the honeyguide. In return for showing the ratel where to get a meal, the honeyguide eats the leftovers of the nest, including the wax. Ratels have long claws on their front feet, and their thick fur protects them from being stung. Their skin is very tough, and it is also unusually loose. This allows them to twist around and bite anything that attacks them.

SCIENTIFIC NAME *Mellivora capensis*

DISTRIBUTION Africa, Middle East, southern Asia

SIZE Up to 1m long, including tail

SPOTTED SKUNK

Many carnivores have glands that produce strong scents, but in skunks the scent is so powerful that it makes a very effective weapon. If a spotted skunk is threatened by another animal, it raises its bushy tail and stamps on the ground. If this warning signal does not deter its enemy, it turns around and produces a jet of spray from glands just beneath its tail. The spray makes it difficult for the attacker to breathe, and it is so strong that it can be smelled more than 1km away downwind. Skunks live in open country and woodland, and eat both plants and small animals.

Spotted skunks fending off a lynx

SCIENTIFIC NAME	*Spilogale putorius*
DISTRIBUTION	USA, Mexico
SIZE	Up to 55cm long, including tail

BELOW *This giant otter is feeding on a piranha that it has just caught. Its sharp front claws give it a good grip.*

EURASIAN OTTER

Otters are carnivores that hunt their prey in water. There are more than 12 species, and all of them have lithe bodies, thick waterproof underfur, tapering tails and webbed feet. The Eurasian otter lives in rivers and lakes, and also on rocky coasts. It feeds mainly on fish and frogs, but it also catches land animals such as rabbits. It is largely nocturnal, and it hides away and rears its young in a den in the riverbank called a holt. During the last one hundred years, otters in Europe have been badly affected by water pollution, but where rivers have been cleaned up, their numbers have started to climb again.

Eurasian otter trying to pick up a scent

SCIENTIFIC NAME	*Lutra lutra*
DISTRIBUTION	Europe, northern Africa, Asia, Far East
SIZE	Up to 1.3m long, including tail

GIANT OTTER

This South American animal is the world's longest otter, although it is not as heavy as the sea otter. It lives in rivers and swamps in thick forest, and feeds mainly on fish. Unlike smaller freshwater otters, which have cylindrical tails, its tail is flattened towards its tip. Giant otters have become rare because they are hunted for their fur. They are easy for hunters to track down because they feed by day and make loud calls.

SCIENTIFIC NAME	*Pteronura brasiliensis*
DISTRIBUTION	Tropical South America
SIZE	Up to 2.4m long, including tail

SEA OTTER

Otters often feed on the shore, but this species is the only one that spends its entire life at sea. It stays close to the coast, usually in beds of giant kelp – the world's fastest-growing seaweed. Sea otters feed on fish and crabs, but they specialize in eating molluscs. To eat clams, they float on their backs and smash open the shells with a stone. Unlike most sea mammals, sea otters do not have blubber to keep them warm. Instead, their fur is amazingly fine and dense, and it traps a layer of air so their skin never gets wet. Female sea otters have just one pup at time. The mother floats on her back, nursing her pup on her chest.

SCIENTIFIC NAME	*Enhydra lutra*
DISTRIBUTION	Northeastern Pacific Ocean; inshore from Aleutian Islands to California
SIZE	Up to 1.5m long, including tail

GENETS, CIVETS AND MONGOOSES

This family of mammals contains about 70 species of carnivore, all from Europe, Africa or Asia. They are slender-bodied predators with short legs and long tails, and their thick fur is often boldly marked. They live in forests or grassland, and many of them are graceful and agile climbers, pouncing on other animals in trees or among rocks. Mongooses will hunt by day, but genets and civets are nocturnal and, although they live near people, they are rarely seen. All of these animals are good at defending themselves. They have scent glands at the base of their tails, and some use these to squirt out a horrible-smelling liquid at anything that comes too close.

BELOW For the common genet, small birds make tasty snacks. Genets can creep stealthily through trees and bushes to catch their prey unawares.

Large ears pick up faint sounds

COMMON GENET

Common genet on a branch

With its long tail and spotty coat, the common genet looks very much like a cat. Unlike a real cat (pages 276-279), it has a pointed muzzle, and its claws only partly retract when they are not being used. Common genets live in woodland, scrub and rocky ground, and they hunt during the night. They feed mainly on rodents, mice in particular, but they also specialize in hunting roosting birds. Most birds are reluctant to fly after dark, making this a good time to attack them.

SCIENTIFIC NAME *Genetta genetta*

DISTRIBUTION Southwestern Europe, Africa, Middle East

SIZE Up to 1.1m long, including tail

AFRICAN CIVET

This grey and black animal has a dog-like muzzle and a long, bushy tail. It lives in forests and grassland, and feeds after dark. It can catch and kill young antelope, but its usual foods are small lizards and rodents, and fruit. Like all its relatives, the civet has a keen sense of smell, and it marks its territory with scent.

SCIENTIFIC NAME *Viverra civetta*

DISTRIBUTION Africa south of the Sahara Desert

SIZE Up to 1.3m long, including tail

BANDED MONGOOSE

Mongooses eat a variety of food, but they are famed for the way they attack snakes. They rely on speed to catch a snake before it strikes, gripping it just behind the head. Their thick fur gives them some protection, and they also have partial immunity to snakebite. There are more than 25 species of mongoose. The banded mongoose from Africa has light and dark bands running across its back. It lives in family groups of up to 30 animals, and feeds during the day.

Banded mongoose attacking a cobra

SCIENTIFIC NAME *Mungos mungo*

DISTRIBUTION Africa south of the Sahara Desert

SIZE Up to 75cm long, including tail

BINTURONG

This black, shaggy-furred animal is one of the few carnivorous mammals that has a prehensile tail. It lives in Asia's tropical forests, and uses its tail as it climbs about to find food. Compared to most carnivores it moves slowly, though it still manages to catch insects and roosting birds. Binturongs swim well, despite their long fur.

SCIENTIFIC NAME	*Arctitis binturong*
DISTRIBUTION	Southeast Asia
SIZE	Up to 1.8m long, including tail

MEERKAT

For meerkats, living together is the key to survival. These African animals live in dry, open country and shelter in burrows underground. They feed during the day on insects and other small animals. When they are above ground they are vulnerable to attack, so while some of the group feed, others act as lookouts, propping themselves up on their back legs and tails. A typical meerkat community contains between 20 and 30 animals belonging to several separate families.

Meerkats looking for food

SCIENTIFIC NAME	*Suricata suricatta*
DISTRIBUTION	Southern Africa
SIZE	Up to 60cm long, including tail

FOSSA

The fossa is Madagascar's largest carnivore. It has a sleek, reddish-brown body, and a very long, slender tail. Fossas are nocturnal. They live in forests, and hunt on the ground and in trees. Like many mammals in Madagascar, they have been badly affected by deforestation.

SCIENTIFIC NAME	*Cryptoprocta ferox*
DISTRIBUTION	Madagascar
SIZE	Up to 1.6m long, including tail

HYENAS AND AARDWOLVES

Hyenas look like dogs, but they belong to a different family of mammals. There are four species, and three of them are among the most versatile carnivores in the world. Hyenas often hunt live prey, but they also specialize in eating dead remains. They have amazingly strong jaws and teeth, and can tear apart and eat every scrap of a carcass, including the bones. The fourth member of this family, called the aardwolf, has a very different way of life, feeding entirely on insects. Hyenas and aardwolves are found in Africa and warm parts of Asia, and they are mainly nocturnal.

Short hind legs

ABOVE RIGHT *Spotted hyenas can swallow pieces of bone up to 9cm long, and they can digest even their prey's teeth. They eat all kinds of dead remains, including those that are several months old.*

BELOW *Aardwolves are easy to tell from meat-eating hyenas because they have long manes down their backs, and they live alone instead of in packs.*

LEFT *Fossas look very much like cats. They are superb climbers and sometimes chase lemurs through the trees.*

SPOTTED HYENA

Weighing up to 80kg, this is the largest, most powerful hyena. It lives in Africa's open plains in packs up to one hundred strong, preying on animals such as zebras. A spotted hyena can eat nearly 15kg of food at one meal. Spotted hyenas have shaggy fur and sloping backs, and can run at up to 60km/h. They breed in underground dens, and the females give birth and suckle their cubs in a central nursery area.

SCIENTIFIC NAME	*Crocuta crocuta*
DISTRIBUTION	Africa south of the Sahara Desert
SIZE	Up to 1.9m long, including tail

AARDWOLF

Instead of eating meat, the aardwolf feeds mainly on termites, which it laps up with its sticky tongue. Compared to hyenas, it has weak jaws and small teeth, but its hearing is very good, which helps it to track down food. Aardwolves feed after dark, using their paws to dig insects out of the ground. During the day, they hide in underground burrows, often those that have been abandoned by aardvarks (page 237).

SCIENTIFIC NAME	*Proteles cristatus*
DISTRIBUTION	Eastern and southern Africa
SIZE	Up to 1.1m long, including tail

CATS

With their lithe bodies, keen hearing and superb eyesight, cats are the stealthiest hunting mammals. Compared to other carnivores, most of them are dedicated meat-eaters, ignoring all other foods in favour of living prey. They usually kill with a single bite, though they catch their prey using their sharp claws. Except for the cheetah, all cats can retract their claws inside a protective sheath when they are not in use. There are about 38 species in the cat family. Many are now rare, either because they are killed for their fur and body parts, or because their habitat is being destroyed.

TOP RIGHT *As well as using their paws to catch fish, fishing cats sometimes wade into the water to catch fish in their mouths.*
TOP LEFT *A Eurasian wild cat flattens its ears and exposes its teeth to stop enemies from coming near.*
ABOVE *The serval is sometimes hunted by people, but one of its most dangerous enemies is a larger member of the cat family – the leopard.*
(page 279).

EURASIAN WILD CAT

The world's largest cats are heavyweight predators, but other species, including this one, are not much larger than the domestic cats that people keep as pets. The Eurasian wild cat is solidly built, with thick fur and a bushy tail. It lives in rocky places and forests, and feeds on rodents, rabbits and occasionally young deer. Because it hunts mainly by night and is wary of people, it is seldom seen. The African wild cat *(Felis libyca)* is similar, but less shy. It is thought to be the ancestor of all domestic cats.

SCIENTIFIC NAME	*Felis sylvestris*
DISTRIBUTION	Europe, Middle East, central and southern Asia
SIZE	Up to 1.1m long, including tail

AFRICAN GOLDEN CAT

This cat lives in the dense forests of tropical Africa. It is about twice the size of a domestic cat, and has golden-brown fur. Some golden cats are spotted all over, but others have hardly any spots at all. Like most cats, it is solitary and nocturnal, and hunts in trees and on the ground.

SCIENTIFIC NAME	*Felis aurata*
DISTRIBUTION	Western and central Africa
SIZE	Up to 1.4m long, including tail

FISHING CAT

Apart from the jaguar (page 278), most cats keep well away from water and try not to get wet. But the fishing cat spends most of its life by rivers and streams, and often wades or swims. Fishing cats eat frogs and snakes, but fish make up most of their diet. They wait at the water's edge for a fish to swim within range, then they flick the fish onto land with their partly webbed front paws.

SCIENTIFIC NAME	*Felis viverrina*
DISTRIBUTION	India, Sri Lanka, Southeast Asia
SIZE	Up to 1.1m long, including tail

SERVAL

With its long legs, large ears and short tail, the serval is one of Africa's most distinctive cats. It lives in scrub and grassland, and uses its keen hearing to pinpoint prey in the undergrowth, before pouncing and catching animals with its front paws. The serval has such sensitive hearing that it is able to find mole-rats by listening for the faint sounds that they make as they tunnel underground.

SCIENTIFIC NAME	*Felis serval*
DISTRIBUTION	Africa
SIZE	Up to 1.3m long, including tail

CARACAL

The caracal has long legs, an unspotted coat and tufts of black fur at the tips of its ears. It lives in dry, open country and hunts mainly at night. An expert at catching birds, the caracal has such fast reactions that it can knock low-flying birds out of the air.

Caracal leaping after a flying bird

SCIENTIFIC NAME	*Lynx caracal*
DISTRIBUTION	Africa, Middle East, southwestern Asia
SIZE	Up to 1.2m long, including tail

LYNX

Lynx look quite different from other cats because they have very short tails and tufted ears. Experts disagree about how many species there are. Some think there is only one, but many believe that there are three – one in North America, another in Europe and Asia, and a third one in Spain and Portugal. Wherever they are found, lynx live mainly in forests and other places where there is lots of cover. They eat a wide variety of birds and small mammals, but in North America they particularly depend on snowshoe hares (page 250). North American lynx have large, round paws, which helps them to walk on snow.

SCIENTIFIC NAME *Lynx lynx*

DISTRIBUTION North America, Europe, northern and central Asia

SIZE Up to 1.5m long, including tail

BOBCAT

This North American cat looks like a lynx, but it is smaller, and lives further south. Its ear-tufts are also shorter, and sometimes difficult to spot. Bobcats live in a wide range of habitats, and they feed mainly on rodents, rabbits and hares. During the winter they sometimes attack deer, and they may also eat animal remains, though only if they have died very recently. Bobcats make dens in rocky crevices and hollow trees, and females produce a litter of up to six kittens every year.

Bobcat on a rock

SCIENTIFIC NAME *Lynx rufus*

DISTRIBUTION North America; from southern Canada to Mexico

SIZE Up to 1.2m long, including tail

OCELOT

Ocelots live in a wide variety of habitats, and feed mainly on the ground. They eat deer, monkeys, rodents and sometimes snakes. Female ocelots usually give birth to two kittens at a time. The father helps his partner by bringing food to the den. Spotted cats are often hunted for their fur, but few have suffered as much as the ocelot. Its markings are so attractive that its fur fetches an extremely high price, and at one time more than 10,000 ocelot skins were sold every year. The trade is now banned, but hunting still goes on.

SCIENTIFIC NAME *Felis pardalis*

DISTRIBUTION North America, Central America, South America; from Arizona to Argentina

SIZE Up to 1.7m long, including tail

TOP *Despite its cuddly looks, the ocelot is an effective killer. Like other cats, it sharpens its claws on trees, and retracts them when they are not needed.*
RIGHT *Lynx have disappeared from many parts of Europe, though they have been reintroduced into some countries, including France.*

Single dominant male watching over his pride

PUMA OR COUGAR

This widespread American predator has a variety of alternative names. It is often known as the mountain lion, although it does not have much in common with a lion. Unlike a lion, the puma purrs instead of roaring, and hunts on its own. Deer are among its favourite prey. If it catches more than it can eat, it often hides the remains under branches, returning later to finish feeding. Female pumas have up to six kittens a year. The kittens are spotty when they are born, but lose their spots during their first few months of life.

SCIENTIFIC NAME *Felis concolor*

DISTRIBUTION Western North America, Central America, South America

SIZE Up to 2.6m long, including tail

CHEETAH

Instead of hunting by stealth, the cheetah relies on speed. It is the fastest land animal on Earth and can reach speeds of about 95km/h in just three or four seconds – an acceleration rate that beats most cars. Cheetahs can do this because they have slender bodies, long legs and springy backbones. Unlike other cats, they do not have retractable claws on their front feet, and they bring down their prey by knocking it to the ground. Cheetahs feed mainly on antelopes and other grazing mammals, and they live in grassland and semi-desert.

SCIENTIFIC NAME *Acinonyx jubatus*

DISTRIBUTION Africa south of the Sahara Desert, parts of Middle East

SIZE Up to 2.3m long, including tail

ABOVE *Lions in a pride often relax together. The females form the core of the pride, although the males are in charge. When a male lion gets old and weak, he is driven away by a younger male, who takes over command.*

Puma preparing to pounce on its prey

RIGHT *This tiger lives in India, where there are more tigers than anywhere else. Its stripes break up its outline in the dappled shade in the forest, helping to camouflage it from its prey.*

A cheetah chasing a young antelope

LION

Although it is often called the king of the jungle, the lion lives in plains and woodlands, not in dense forest. It is the world's second largest cat, after the tiger, and one of the few that hunts in groups. A typical lion group, or pride, consists of about 15 animals. Two or three are adult males, and the rest are females and their young. The females carry out most of the hunting but, after a successful kill, the males soon arrive to take their share. Lions can bring down animals as large as buffaloes but, when food is short, they will eat anything they can find, including tortoises, lizards and dead remains. Thousands of years ago, lions roamed right across Africa, southern Europe and Asia. Today, most lions live in Africa, with just a few hundred in northwestern India.

SCIENTIFIC NAME *Panthera leo*

DISTRIBUTION Africa, Gir Forest (Northwestern India)

SIZE Up to 3m long, including tail

JAGUAR

Although it is slightly shorter than the leopard, the jaguar is more heavily built and can weigh up to 150kg. It has beautiful spotted fur and, during the 1950s and 1960s, it was hunted on a massive scale. Jaguars live mainly in forests and swamps. Unlike most cats, they are good swimmers, and seem to enjoy going into water. They often hunt along riverbanks, attacking otters, turtles and even large snakes. Jaguars are capable of killing people, but attacks are rare, and the cats normally give humans a wide berth.

SCIENTIFIC NAME *Panthera onca*

DISTRIBUTION Central America, South America; from Mexico to Argentina

SIZE Up to 2.6m long, including tail

LEOPARD

This lithe and beautiful spotted animal is one of the most adaptable of the big cats. It lives in a remarkable variety of habitats, from tree-studded grasslands and deserts to mountain slopes. It feeds mainly at night, and attacks from close quarters instead of chasing its prey. Leopards are good climbers, and they often haul their kills into trees to prevent scavengers from stealing them. They are strong enough to lift animals heavier than themselves.

SCIENTIFIC NAME *Panthera pardus*

DISTRIBUTION Africa, Middle East, central and southern Asia

SIZE Up to 3m long, including tail

Female leopard carrying a cub

SNOW LEOPARD

Less is known about the snow leopard than about most big cats because it lives in remote mountains at altitudes of up to 6,000m. Its fur is grey, soft and exceptionally thick, and it has an extra-long tail that it wraps around its body to keep warm. Snow leopards hunt during the day, attacking all kinds of wild animals, as well as livestock. They are sometimes killed by farmers, and are also hunted for their fur. No one knows exactly how many of these magnificent cats there are left in the wild, but the total number may be as few as 5,000.

SCIENTIFIC NAME *Panthera uncia*

DISTRIBUTION Central Asia

SIZE Up to 2.3m long, including tail

TIGER

The cat family includes many well-known hunters, but the tiger is the largest and most powerful of them all. The record weight for an adult male is more than one-third of a tonne. Like leopards, tigers feed mainly at night. Despite their enormous size, they can stalk their prey in almost total silence, before pouncing at close range. They grip their victims with their front claws, then kill them with a bite to the throat. Tigers can be dangerous to people and have been responsible for many deaths, especially in places where humans are disrupting the tiger's natural habitat. In recent years, the world's tiger population has collapsed, mainly because of illegal hunting. Today, there are probably fewer than 7,000 tigers left in the wild.

SCIENTIFIC NAME *Panthera tigris*

DISTRIBUTION Southern and Southeast Asia, eastern Siberia

SIZE Up to 3.75m long, including tail

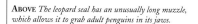

SEALS, SEALIONS AND MANATEES

Seals and sealions are carnivorous mammals that spend most of their lives in water. They can stay at sea for weeks at a time, though they give birth on land. They have flippers instead of legs, and are expert swimmers and divers, feeding mainly on fish. Manatees belong to a group of mammals called sirenians. They are vegetarians, and spend their entire lives in water. There are about 34 species of seal, sealion and their relatives, and four kinds of sirenian. Seals can survive in polar waters, but sirenians are found only in warm places.

ABOVE *The leopard seal has an unusually long muzzle, which allows it to grab adult penguins in its jaws.*

The winner gathers together a band of females, and fathers all their pups. Elephant seals get their name from their size, and also from the male's bulbous, trunk-like nose.

SCIENTIFIC NAME	*Mirounga leonina*
DISTRIBUTION	Cold water regions in and near the Southern Ocean
SIZE	Up to 4.9m long

GREY SEAL

On land, the grey seal is a cumbersome animal that lumbers along with its body on the ground. In water, it is very different – a fast and graceful swimmer that can dive to depths of more than 75m. Like all true seals, it uses only its rear flippers to swim, spreading them out and then closing them together, like someone clapping their hands. Grey seals usually have their pups between September and March, giving birth on isolated rocks and beaches. Their pups have soft white fur when they are born, but they soon grow a new coat of grey fur, and follow their mothers into the sea.

Adult grey seal with speckled coat

Young grey seal with silky, white coat

SCIENTIFIC NAME	*Halichoerus grypus*
DISTRIBUTION	North Atlantic Ocean
SIZE	Up to 3.3m long

LEOPARD SEAL

This slender seal is one of the Southern Ocean's largest and most ferocious predators, with sharp teeth and powerful jaws. It will feed on fish, krill and even other seals, but specializes in preying on penguins. It lurks in the sea near penguin colonies, and grabs the penguins as they enter the water. The seal shakes the bird from side to side to kill it, and then either eats it piece by piece, or swallows it whole.

SCIENTIFIC NAME	*Hydrurga leptonyx*
DISTRIBUTION	Southern Ocean
SIZE	Up to 3.5m long

SOUTHERN ELEPHANT SEAL

Male seals are often much larger than females but, in the southern elephant seal, the difference in size is greater than in any other species. The males can weigh a colossal 3,500kg – more than four times as much as the females. Male elephant seals use their tremendous weight to battle with their rivals for a mate during the breeding season. Facing each other head on, they rear up and strike out with their teeth.

BELOW *With his nose inflated, a male southern elephant seal roars at his rivals on a breeding beach.*

CALIFORNIA SEALION

Sealions look similar to seals, but they are much better at moving on land. Their front flippers are strong enough to hold their bodies off the ground, and their back flippers can turn forwards to work like feet. Instead of shuffling along like true seals, they can almost gallop. There are five species of sealion. The shiny, black California sealion is the best known because it is easy to tame and train. In the wild, California sealions live on rocky coasts and feed on fish and squid.

SCIENTIFIC NAME	*Zalophus californianus*
DISTRIBUTION	California (USA), Galapagos Islands
SIZE	Up to 2.2m long

ANTARCTIC FUR SEAL

Most seals have a coat of short, rough fur. Fur seals are different because they have a thick layer of soft underfur as well. Their underfur is waterproof and it helps to keep them warm. There are nine species of fur seal, and they are found mainly in the southern hemisphere. The Antarctic fur seal, which is one of the most common, lives furthest south of all, and breeds on islands at the very edge of Antarctica. At one time, these seals were hunted for their fur, and were brought to the brink of extinction. They are now protected, and have made a spectacular recovery.

SCIENTIFIC NAME	*Arctocephalus gazella*
DISTRIBUTION	Southern Ocean
SIZE	Up to 1.9m long

WALRUS

After elephant seals, the walrus is the second largest sea mammal that comes ashore to breed. It feeds in the cold waters of the far north. The males have two large, downward-pointing tusks. At one time, it was thought that male walruses used their tusks

Male walrus showing fang-like tusks

TOP *A female common, or harbour, seal (Phoca vitulina) lies beside her pup on the shore of the North Atlantic Ocean.* **ABOVE** *Mediterranean monk seals (Monachus monachus) are some of the world's rarest sea mammals.*

BELOW *An American manatee takes a playful bite at one of its partner's flippers. Manatees have large mouths and can weigh as much as half a tonne. They are harmless vegetarians.*

to feed, but most experts now think that the tusks act as status symbols when the walruses compete for the chance to mate. Walruses feed mainly on molluscs, sucking them up whole and then spitting out the empty shells.

SCIENTIFIC NAME	*Odobenus rosmarus*
DISTRIBUTION	Arctic Ocean and surrounding seas
SIZE	Up to 3.5m long

AMERICAN MANATEE

Although this endangered animal looks like a giant seal from a distance, it differs from seals in several ways. It has a paddle-like tail instead of hind flippers, and its mouth and jaws are designed for grazing underwater plants, not for catching fish. Manatees live in rivers and coastal lagoons, and never venture on land. They often spend the day dozing near the surface of the water, and feed at night. They are difficult to spot, and in places where there are lots of boats, sleeping manatees are often injured when they collide with them.

SCIENTIFIC NAME	*Trichecus manatus*
DISTRIBUTION	Gulf of Mexico, Caribbean Sea; from Florida to Guyana
SIZE	Up to 4m long

ELEPHANTS

Both of the two species of elephant – Asiatic and African – are instantly recognizable by their gigantic size and their trunks. An elephant's trunk is a long, flexible nose, with nostrils right at the tip. It is used for breathing, and for other tasks like sucking up water to take a shower, stripping leaves off branches or gently nudging a calf out of harm's way. Elephants are vegetarians, and have a small number of large, flat-topped teeth at the back of their jaws. They eat plant food of all kinds, and even smash down trees to reach foliage high off the ground. They are intelligent and sociable, and are among the longest-living animals in the wild, often surviving into their 70s.

TUSKS

One-third of tusk is in skull

Tusks are specialized teeth. They grow out of an animal's mouth, and can point upwards, downwards or occasionally straight ahead. Tusks grow throughout their owner's life, often developing a curved or spiral shape. Elephants have the largest and most versatile tusks in the animal world. They use them to dig for water, to strip bark off trees and to fend off rivals and predators. Some other tusk-bearing animals, such as male walruses and narwhals, use their tusks during contests in the breeding season, just as elephants do. The contestants rarely hurt each other but, when tusks are turned on other animals, the results can be deadly.

Cross-section of an elephant head showing tusk formation

ABOVE *This Asiatic elephant is giving itself a shower in a river. Elephants are good swimmers and they bathe regularly when they have the chance. In shallow water, they often roll over on their sides.*

ASIATIC ELEPHANT

The Asiatic elephant is the smaller of the two species of elephant. It is a slightly different shape from the African elephant, with an arched back, smaller ears and just one finger-like tip to its trunk. Asiatic elephants live mainly in forests, where they feed on grass and leaves. Like African elephants, they use their trunks as tools, pulling up plants or ripping branches off trees. Males sometimes have large tusks, but the females either have small tusks, or none at all. Asiatic elephants have been tamed and used as working animals for at least 4,000 years. They are still caught and trained, although the number of Asiatic elephants living in the wild has fallen during recent years.

SCIENTIFIC NAME *Elephas maximus*

DISTRIBUTION India, Sri Lanka, Southeast Asia

SIZE Up to 4m long, excluding trunk

AFRICAN ELEPHANT

Standing up to 3.7m high at the shoulder, the African elephant is the world's largest land animal. Adult males, or bulls, can weigh up to six tonnes, which is roughly 80 times as much as an average, fully grown man. To survive, they need to eat up to 300kg of food, and drink more than 100 litres of water, a day. Unlike Asiatic elephants, African elephants have sloping backs and rounded ears. Their trunks have two tips, which they use like fingers to pick up things. The males and females both have tusks, but the males' are much larger, often growing to 3m long. African elephants live in forests, grassland and semi-desert, in herds that normally include several adult females and their young. Elephant calves feed on their mothers' milk for at least 18 months, and do not start to breed until they are 11 or more years old. At one time, elephants were common in many parts of Africa, but ivory hunting has destroyed many herds. The sale of ivory is now strictly controlled, but illegal elephant hunting still continues.

SCIENTIFIC NAME *Loxodonta africana*

DISTRIBUTION Africa south of the Sahara Desert

SIZE Up to 4.5m long, excluding trunk

HYRAXES

With their compact bodies and stubby legs, hyraxes look quite like rodents. However, they differ from rodents in many ways and, strange though it may seem, biologists think that their closest living relatives may be either hoofed mammals or elephants. Hyraxes are good climbers, and live in rocky places or in forests. Instead of claws, they have stubby toes that end in flattened nails, and bare soles that help to give them a good grip. They are vegetarians, feeding either by day or night, depending on where they live. There are seven species of hyrax, and they are found in Africa and southwestern Asia.

ROCK HYRAX

This agile and inquisitive animal is common on Africa's plains, where it lives among piles of boulders called kopjes. It feeds during the day and eats grass and the leaves of shrubs, sometimes climbing along branches to get at the newest growth. It lives in groups of about 50 animals, which often huddle together at night for warmth. Rock hyraxes have many enemies, such as eagles, leopards and snakes, but they can be tame enough to take food scraps from people.

ABOVE *Rock hyraxes need shelter to survive because they do not cope well with extremes of either heat or cold. This rock hyrax is warming itself up by sunbathing on a ledge.*

SCIENTIFIC NAME *Procavia capensis*

DISTRIBUTION Arabian Peninsula, eastern and southern Africa

SIZE Up to 45cm long

Tusks can be used as dangerous weapons

LEFT *With its ears spread wide, a bull African elephant strides across the ground. This behaviour means that the elephant has sensed possible danger and may be about to charge.*

TREE HYRAX

The tree hyrax is nocturnal, and is heard much more often than it is seen. It has a blood-curdling call that echoes through forests after dark. It often feeds several metres off the ground, tearing off its plant food by gripping it with its back teeth. Like rock hyraxes, tree hyraxes are mainly brown, but they have a tuft of white hair on their backs, which they raise when they are alarmed.

SCIENTIFIC NAME *Dendrohyrax arboreus*

DISTRIBUTION Eastern and southern Africa

SIZE Up to 60cm long

RIGHT *Tree hyraxes can eat one-third of their body weight a day.*

HORSES, RHINOCEROSES AND TAPIRS

There are four species in the horse family, five species of rhinoceros and four species of tapir. They are solidly built grazing or browsing animals, with long legs ending in hoofed toes. Horses live in open country, while tapirs live in forests. The largest kinds of rhino live in open grasslands, while the smallest ones are forest animals. Some species in the horse family are still quite common, but rhinos and tapirs have been badly affected by hunting and by deforestation.

PRZEWALSKI'S WILD HORSE

Many 'wild' horses are descendants of horses that have escaped from captivity. Przewalski's wild horse is different because it is a completely wild animal. It has brown fur, an upright black mane and a black tail. The future of this species looks uncertain. It is endangered by hunting, and also threatened by domesticated horses, which have taken over most of its habitat. Almost all Przewalski's wild horses are now kept in zoos, but some are being released into the wild.

SCIENTIFIC NAME *Equus ferus*

DISTRIBUTION Mongolia, China

SIZE Up to 2m long, excluding tail

ABOVE *African asses use their outsize ears to listen for signs of danger.*

BELOW *There are only about 1,000 Przewalski's wild horses in the world.*

AFRICAN ASS

This grey-brown animal is the ancestor of the domestic donkey. It looks similar to a donkey, but it has a lighter build and stripes on its legs. African asses live in hot, dry places, in herds of up to 50 animals. They rely on speed for self-defence, although they can also give a powerful kick. Wild African asses are now quite rare, but escaped donkeys, known as burros, live in many parts of the world.

SCIENTIFIC NAME *Equus africanus*

DISTRIBUTION Northern Africa

SIZE Up to 2m long, excluding tail

COMMON ZEBRA OR PLAINS ZEBRA

Bold black and white stripes make this one of Africa's most familiar animals. It lives in open grassland in scattered herds that contain hundreds of animals. Like other wild horses, it depends on speed for survival, and can run at up to 40km/h. There are three species of zebra – the common zebra is easy to identify because it is the only one with a striped underside.

SCIENTIFIC NAME *Equus burchelli*

DISTRIBUTION Eastern and southern Africa

SIZE Up to 2.4m long, excluding tail

LEFT *It is not certain why zebras have stripes. They may act as markers, helping the zebras to recognize each other and keep together. These individuals are all common zebras.*

White rhino
(Ceratotherium simum)

Sumatran rhino
(Dicerorhinus sumatrensis)

Black rhino
(Diceros bicornis)

Javan rhino
(Rhinoceros sondaicus)

ABOVE *Rhinos live in Africa and warm parts of Asia. They differ in size, in the number of horns they have, and in the shape and texture of their skin.*

WHITE RHINOCEROS

After elephants, white rhinos are the largest land animals in the world. They eat grass, and have broad mouths and two horns. Males can weigh up to 3.6 tonnes, which is about four times as heavy as a family-size car. They have bad eyesight, but good hearing and a keen sense of smell. White rhinos are peaceful animals, and usually run away from people instead of launching an attack. Sadly, this is not enough to save them from poachers, who hunt rhinos to sell their horns. Today, there are probably fewer than 7,000 white rhinos left.

SCIENTIFIC NAME	*Ceratotherium simum*
DISTRIBUTION	Tropical and southern Africa
SIZE	Up to 4.2m long, excluding tail

BLACK RHINOCEROS

Unlike the white rhino, the black rhino feeds on trees and shrubs. It has a flexible, pointed upper lip, and it uses this to collect its food. It is more aggressive than the white rhino and, instead of running away from danger, it often charges towards it. This rhino is probably the world's fastest-disappearing large mammal. In the early 1960s, there were about 100,000 black rhinos but, after four decades of poaching, their numbers have dropped to about 2,000. Anti-poaching patrols have been set up and, without these, the species would almost certainly die out.

SCIENTIFIC NAME	*Diceros bicornis*
DISTRIBUTION	Tropical and southern Africa
SIZE	Up to 3.7m long, excluding tail

INDIAN RHINOCEROS

This rhino has extraordinarily thick, grey skin that looks like armour-plating. It hangs down in heavy folds, and is studded with small bumps. The rhino has a single stubby horn and lives in grassy swamps, where it feeds on leaves, branches and fruit. Like Africa's rhinos, this animal is targeted by poachers, and it is protected by armed guards in national parks.

SCIENTIFIC NAME	*Rhinoceros unicornis*
DISTRIBUTION	Nepal, northern India
SIZE	Up to 3.8m long, excluding tail

ASIATIC OR MALAYAN TAPIR

Tapirs are found in two widely separated parts of the world – Southeast Asia and South America. They have pig-like bodies, long heads and fleshy snouts. The Asiatic tapir is the only black and white species, and its snout is so long that it allows the tapir to feel for food in the same way as elephants do with their trunks. Asiatic tapirs feed after dark, and usually stay close to water. Their young have white stripes and spots, which help to camouflage them on the forest floor.

SCIENTIFIC NAME	*Tapirus indicus*
DISTRIBUTION	Southeast Asia
SIZE	Up to 2.5m long, excluding tail

ABOVE *Indian rhinos can weigh two tonnes, and are dangerous if they charge.*

ABOVE *Asiatic tapirs live in dense rainforest – a habitat that is fast disappearing.*

HOOFED MAMMALS

A hoof is a toe that is designed for carrying an animal's weight. It has a reinforced tip made of keratin, the same substance found in claws and fingernails. Hoofs are compact but tough, providing good grip on the ground and allowing an animal to run at speed. Biologists divide hoofed mammals into two groups. The largest group includes pigs, camels, deer, giraffes and antelopes (pages 286-303). These animals are sometimes known as 'cloven-hoofed' because their hoofs are split in two down the middle. The other group includes horses, rhinos and tapirs. These animals have an uneven number of toes, from as few as one to as many as five.

Horse's hoof is a single toe

PIGS, PECCARIES AND HIPPOPOTAMUSES

Pigs and peccaries are intelligent and adaptable animals. There
are 11 species altogether. Wild pigs are found in Europe, Africa
and Asia, while peccaries live in the Americas. They live in
forests or open grassland, and feed by digging up the ground
with their flattened snouts. Unlike other hoofed mammals,
they are not strict vegetarians, and they often eat small
animals and dead remains. There are two species of hippo,
and both are found in Africa. Hippopotamuses eat plants,
and spend most of the day lounging in water or mud.

WILD BOAR

This forest animal is the ancestor of the
domestic pig, but it looks very different
from the pigs that are now raised on
farms. It is covered with bristly fur,
and has small ears and powerful legs.
The males have two pairs of short
tusks, which they use to fight off
enemies if they are attacked. Wild boars
live alone or in small herds, and they usually feed
at night. The females give birth to litters of up to
ten stripy piglets inside nests made of leaves.

**Wild boar in
winter coat**

SCIENTIFIC NAME	*Sus scrofa*
DISTRIBUTION	Europe, northern Africa, Asia
SIZE	Up to 1.7m long, excluding tail

BUSH PIG

Most wild pigs are grey, but this species is
brightly coloured. It has a black and white head,
red fur over its sides and legs, and a white mane
running along its back. Bush pigs live in forests
and swampy places, and they feed both by day
and by night. In some parts of Africa, they
cause serious problems by raiding crops.

SCIENTIFIC NAME	*Potamochoerus porcus*
DISTRIBUTION	Africa south of the Sahara Desert, Madagascar
SIZE	Up to 1.5m long, excluding tail

WARTHOG

With its straggly fur and knobbly
face, the warthog is probably
the most unusual member
of the pig family. It is,
however, one of
the toughest.

RIGHT *The babirusa
sharpens its lower tusks
by rubbing them
against trees. Its
upper tusks can
be more than
25cm long, but
are usually blunt.*

BELOW
*Warthogs
wallow in
mud to cool
off. This keeps
their skin in
good condition.*

Its strength and alertness mean that it can survive in open grassland, even though it is easily spotted by predators. Warthogs feed mainly on grass, and they often drop down on their knees to eat. If they spot danger, they run to shelter in burrows or among rocks although, if they have to, they will stand and fight with their tusks. During the breeding season, male warthogs use their tusks to battle head-on. These battles are not as dangerous as they look, because the animals' thick, warty skin protects them from serious injury.

SCIENTIFIC NAME	*Phacochoerus aethiopicus*
DISTRIBUTION	Tropical and southern Africa
SIZE	Up to 1.4m long, excluding tail

BABIRUSA

This rare wild pig from Southeast Asia has highly unusual tusks. In males, the bottom pair grows up from the corners of the mouth, but the top pair grows through the animal's snout. As the tusks get longer, they start to curve back towards its eyes. The babirusa lives near rivers in forests, and feeds during the day.

SCIENTIFIC NAME	*Babyrousa babyrussa*
DISTRIBUTION	Philippines
SIZE	Up to 1.1m long, excluding tail

COLLARED PECCARY

Peccaries are small, pig-like animals with bristly fur and slender legs. They live in large roving herds, and eat a wide range of food, from insects and seeds to the stems of prickly pears. Compared to some pigs, their tusks are short, but they are still good at fighting off attack. Collared peccaries get their name from the band of white fur around their necks. They are the most widespread species, and the only peccaries that live as far north as the USA. Despite being hunted for food, they still manage to survive in the wild.

SCIENTIFIC NAME	*Tayassu tajacu*
DISTRIBUTION	North America, Central America, South America; from Arizona to Argentina
SIZE	Up to 90cm long, excluding tail

COMMON HIPPOPOTAMUS

The common hippo is one of Africa's largest mammals. It has a barrel-shaped body that can weigh more than three tonnes. Its huge jaws hold a pair of tusks up to 50cm long. These are strong enough to smash through the side of a boat. Despite this weaponry, the hippo is a vegetarian, lounging in water or

ABOVE *Hippos float well, but swim slowly. When they dive, they often walk along the riverbed.*

Hippo foot showing four webbed toes

Hippo has large tusks in lower jaw

BELOW *A pygmy hippo's skin looks oily because it is covered by a slippery fluid that keeps it moist.*

mud by day, and emerging at night to feed. Hippos have webbed feet, and nostrils that they can close up. They can stay underwater for more than 15 minutes. Their skin is unusually thin, but it is protected by an oily red fluid that is a natural sunscreen. On land, hippos will wander as far as 5km to feed, and they eat an average of 40kg of food each night. Females give birth on land, and usually have a single calf each year.

SCIENTIFIC NAME	*Hippopotamus amphibius*
DISTRIBUTION	Africa south of the Sahara Desert
SIZE	Up to 4m long, excluding tail

PYGMY HIPPOPOTAMUS

Unlike the common hippo, this rare animal lives in Africa's tropical forests. It looks like a miniature version of its larger relative, but its mouth is narrower and its body sleeker. Pygmy hippos feed on leaves and fallen fruit, and are active at night. They run into water to escape danger, but otherwise spend most of their lives on land.

SCIENTIFIC NAME	*Hexaprotodon liberiensis*
DISTRIBUTION	Tropical western Africa
SIZE	Up to 1.7m long, excluding tail

CAMELS AND THEIR RELATIVES

The animals in this family live in two different parts of the world. Camels themselves live in Africa and Asia, while guanacos and vicunas live in South America. They all have long necks, divided upper lips, and only two toes on each foot. Camels live in places that can be dry and hot by day, but often chillingly cold at night, while guanacos and vicunas live in high mountains, where the air is very thin. There were originally four wild species in this family but, at different times, all of them have been domesticated.

Long eyelashes keep sand out of eyes

Slit-shaped nostrils

DROMEDARY

In northern Africa and the Middle East, this one-humped camel is used by many people to carry themselves and their belongings. It was domesticated more than 5,000 years ago, and the original wild species has since died out. Dromedaries are well equipped for life in dry places. They have cushioned feet, which spread their weight over the ground, and they are able to close their nostrils when sand is blowing in the wind. They can drink more than 50 litres of water at a time, and their humps contain fat reserves, which act as on-board food stores.

SCIENTIFIC NAME   *Camelus dromedarius*

DISTRIBUTION   Originally from northern Africa, Middle East; introduced into Australia

SIZE   Up to 3.4m long, excluding tail

BELOW *Like all camels, dromedaries walk by moving both left feet together, and then both right feet. When they lie down, they tuck their legs underneath their bodies.*

Hump stores fat, not water

Dense fur helps to stop sunshine from warming the skin

Long legs with rounded feet

BACTRIAN CAMEL

Unlike the dromedary, the Bactrian camel is brown rather than yellow, and it has two humps. It lives in the deserts of central Asia, where winter temperatures fall far below freezing. To survive these conditions, it grows an extra-thick coat in the autumn, and sheds it the following spring. A few hundred of these camels still survive in the wild, mainly in Mongolia and China, but most Bactrian camels are domesticated. The gap between their two humps makes a comfortable seat for riding.

SCIENTIFIC NAME *Camelus bactrianus*

DISTRIBUTION Central Asia

SIZE Up to 3m long, excluding tail

VICUNA

Compared to camels, the vicuna is a dainty animal. It has a slender body and a deer-like head, but it is much tougher than it looks. It manages to survive on barren mountain slopes up to 5,000m high. At this altitude, the air contains much less oxygen than lower down, but the vicuna still manages to run as fast as 50km/h. Vicunas live in small herds, and they feed on grass and other plants. In the past, they have been extensively hunted, and they are now rare in the wild.

SCIENTIFIC NAME *Vicugna vicugna*

DISTRIBUTION Central Andes Mountains (South America)

SIZE Up to 1.6m long, excluding tail

GUANACO

The guanaco looks similar to the vicuna, but it is larger and has darker fur. It lives in the Andes Mountains and on South America's grassy plains in family groups of up to 12 animals. It is a fast runner and a good swimmer, and it shares an unusual characteristic with camels – when it lies down, it drops on its front knees and tucks its legs under its body. Female guanacos usually have one calf a year. Within hours of being born, the calf can run almost as fast as its mother.

SCIENTIFIC NAME *Lama guanicoe*

DISTRIBUTION South America; from Peru to Tierra del Fuego

SIZE Up to 1.7m long, excluding tail

LLAMA

The llama is a domesticated form of the guanaco, with a larger body and more powerful legs. Its thick fur can be brown, black or white. Before horses and donkeys were introduced into South America, it was the only animal that could be used for carrying food and goods. It was also used as a source of food, leather and fur that could be made into ropes. Like the guanaco, the llama is sure-footed, which makes it ideal for journeys along narrow mountain paths. It is not strong enough to carry people.

SCIENTIFIC NAME *Lama glama*

DISTRIBUTION Andes Mountains (South America)

SIZE Up to 2.2m long, excluding tail

ALPACA

Like the llama, the alpaca is also a domesticated descendant of the guanaco. Instead of being used as a pack animal, it is raised for its fine wool. Some alpacas have wool that is so long it almost touches the ground. Unlike llamas, which can survive by browsing shrubs, alpacas need grass, so they are kept in pastures.

SCIENTIFIC NAME *Lama pacos*

DISTRIBUTION Andes Mountains (South America)

SIZE Up to 1.4m long, excluding tail

RIGHT *The guanaco is the tallest wild mammal in South America, standing at up to 1.9m high.*

ABOVE *This Bactrian camel has its winter coat. In spring, the winter fur peels away in long patches, making the animal look untidy for a short time.*

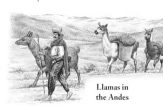

Llamas in the Andes

Alpacas grazing in high altitude pasture

Deer

With their slender legs and long necks, deer are among the world's most graceful plant-eating mammals. They have plain or spotted coats, two-toed hoofs, and are the only mammals that grow antlers. Antlers are made of bone, and are shed each year. They develop only in adult males, called stags, and are used during the breeding season, when the deer compete for a chance to breed. There are about 45 species of true deer, and four species of mouse deer. They live in forests and open grassland in most parts of the world except Australia.

Male Chinese muntjac

1   2   3   4

ABOVE Like most male deer, a red deer stag grows a new set of antlers every year. **1** *The antlers start to form from two bumps on the top of the skull.* **2** *At first, the antlers are covered with 'velvet' – a soft, furry skin.* **3** *As the antlers grow, they begin to form branches.* **4** *Finally, the velvet becomes loose and the deer rubs it away. The antlers are now complete.*

LESSER MOUSE DEER OR CHEVROTAIN

Mouse deer are tiny, secretive animals that live in tropical forests and swamps. They have slender, hump-backed bodies with pencil-thin legs, and are not much larger than a hare (page 250). Mouse deer do not have antlers, but they do have tiny, downward-pointing tusks. Despite their name, they are probably more closely related to wild pigs than to other deer. The lesser mouse deer is the smallest species, and the tiniest hoofed mammal. The females, or does, are larger than the males, but they are still only knee-high.

SCIENTIFIC NAME *Tragulus javanicus*
DISTRIBUTION Southeast Asia
SIZE Up to 48cm long, excluding tail

FOREST MUSK DEER

There are five species of musk deer, and they are unusual in several ways. The males have long downward-pointing tusks instead of antlers. They also have a pouch on their undersides, which produces a strong-smelling substance called musk. They use this to scent-mark the boundaries of their territories. The forest musk deer lives in mountains and usually feeds alone, eating grass, moss and buds. All species of musk deer are threatened by the demand for musk, which is used to make perfumes. Because it is difficult to collect, it fetches an enormous price.

SCIENTIFIC NAME *Moschus chrysogaster*
DISTRIBUTION Central Asia; from Afghanistan to China
SIZE Up to 1m long, excluding tail

RIGHT Two male fallow deer lock antlers as they fight for a female. Although these fights look dangerous, they rarely result in injury because the loser usually runs away.

CHINESE MUNTJAC

This small Far Eastern deer lives in woodlands and forests, and it often feeds at night, when it is safer from attack. The males' antlers are among the smallest of any deer, measuring only about 15cm long. Chinese muntjacs make a loud barking sound when they are alarmed, and they can keep this up for more than an hour.

SCIENTIFIC NAME *Muntiacus reevesi*
DISTRIBUTION Originally from China, Taiwan; introduced into northwestern Europe
SIZE Up to 1m long, excluding tail

FALLOW DEER

With its spotted coat and broad, flat-tipped antlers, this is the most handsome deer in Europe. It lives wild in woodlands, forests and farmland, and is normally shy, though where it is kept in parks it feeds out in the open. Female fallow deer live in scattered herds, but adult males usually live alone. In autumn, at the start of the breeding season, rival males battle for supremacy, locking antlers in a test of strength. The females give birth to one fawn in early summer. The fawns can stand soon after they are born, but they spend most of the time safely out of sight until they are several weeks old.

SCIENTIFIC NAME *Dama dama*
DISTRIBUTION Western and central Europe
SIZE Up to 1.7m long, excluding tail

CHITAL

Standing up to 1m high at the shoulder, the chital is India's most widespread deer. It has a reddish-brown coat dappled with white spots, and the males have long, branching antlers. Chitals live in open woodland and grassy plains, in herds up to 200 strong. Thousands of chitals were once killed by tigers each year but, because tigers are now rare, few die in this way today.

SCIENTIFIC NAME *Axis axis*

DISTRIBUTION Originally from Southern Asia, from Nepal to Sri Lanka; introduced into many other parts of the world

SIZE Up to 1.6m long, excluding tail

RED DEER OR WAPITI

This is one of the world's most widespread deer. It lives in forests, woodland and open hillsides, feeding on leaves, buds and bark. Red deer stags are larger than the hinds. In prime breeding condition they have shaggy manes and antlers up to 1.5m long. In autumn, they roar at their rivals, challenging them for the right to breed. They lock antlers, pushing and twisting to throw each other off balance. Calves are born in late spring and have dappled fur for camouflage.

SCIENTIFIC NAME *Cervus elaphus*

DISTRIBUTION Originally from North America, Europe, northern Africa, northern Asia, Far East; introduced into New Zealand

SIZE Up to 2.6m long, excluding tail

ABOVE *A herd of chital drink at a lake. Their spots help to camouflage them on a sunlit forest floor.*

Male red deer, or stag

SAMBAR

A close relative of the red deer, this species has a dark brown coat, and unusually thick antlers with two or three branches. It lives in woodland, often on mountain slopes, and usually feeds after dark. Male sambars can weigh as much as a quarter of a tonne, and their antlers grow up to 1m long.

SCIENTIFIC NAME *Cervus unicolor*

DISTRIBUTION Originally from southern and Southeast Asia; introduced into USA, Australia, New Zealand

SIZE Up to 2.4m long, excluding tail

RIGHT *While her fawn nudges her for attention, a female sambar listens intently for sounds that may signal that a predator is nearby.*

ELK OR MOOSE

This is the world's largest deer. Males can weigh more than half a tonne, and have flattened antlers with a spread of up to 1.8m. The females are smaller but the same shape, with long heads, drooping upper lips and a flap of skin hanging beneath their throats. Elks live in woodland and open country. In winter they eat twigs and bark, and in summer they wade into rivers and lakes to eat water plants. Adults live alone, but the calves stay with their mothers for a year.

Male elk

SCIENTIFIC NAME	*Alces alces*
DISTRIBUTION	Far north worldwide
SIZE	Up to 3m long, excluding tail

Velvet falls away in strips

RIGHT *This reindeer's antlers have finished growing, and their velvet is falling off. This happens in late summer – a difficult time for reindeer, because the peeling skin attracts flies.*

RIGHT *A female roe deer sets off to find food.*
BELOW *Père David's deer* (Elaphurus davidianus) *lives in China, but is also kept in parks and zoos.*

Widely spaced branches

Antlers are largest in males

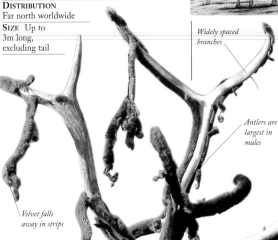

ROE DEER

Although it is a shy animal, this small European deer has been remarkably successful at surviving alongside people. It normally lives in woodland, but also feeds in fields, leaping over walls and fences to find its food. It usually lives alone and feeds at night – a habit that allows it to avoid being seen by people. Male roe deer have short, spiky antlers. In the summer, males and females are plain sandy brown, but they turn darker when they grow their winter coats.

SCIENTIFIC NAME	*Capreolus capreolus*
DISTRIBUTION	Europe
SIZE	Up to 1.3m long, excluding tail

REINDEER OR CARIBOU

This deer is the only species in which both males and females have antlers. Its hoofs work like snowshoes, preventing it from sinking into the snow. This helps it to survive in the far north, where snow can lie for up to six months each year. In Scandinavia, reindeer herds can be several hundred animals strong, but in North America they sometimes number more than 500,000. During the summer, these herds wander over the open tundra, but in autumn they head south towards forests, travelling up to 100km a day. Reindeer feed on leaves and twigs, but they specialize in eating lichen – a moss-like plant that grows on trees and rocks. In Europe and Siberia, they were domesticated more than 3,000 years ago, and are still kept for meat and milk.

SCIENTIFIC NAME	*Rangifer tarandus*
DISTRIBUTION	Far north worldwide
SIZE	Up to 2.2m long, excluding tail

PAMPAS DEER

Before farming began in the grassy plains, or pampas, of South America, this deer was a very common animal. Today, with most of its original habitat grazed by cattle, it is struggling to survive. The pampas deer has spotted fawns, but it is brown or grey when it is fully grown. The males have narrow antlers with two or three branches. Like other deer, this animal has a good sense of smell, and males mark their territory by scent. They have scent glands on their hoofs, which leave a 'signature' wherever they go.

SCIENTIFIC NAME	*Ozotoceros bezoarcticus*
DISTRIBUTION	South America; from Brazil to central Argentina
SIZE	Up to 1.4m long, excluding tail

WHITETAIL DEER

No other deer can match this species in coping with different types of forest habitat. The whitetail deer manages to survive in forests in the cold Canadian subarctic, on the dry mountainsides in Mexico and in the steamy heat of Central and South America. One reason for this wide range is that it feeds on many different kinds of food, including leaves, bark and fallen fruit. The whitetail deer's coat is reddish in the summer and grey in the winter, but it gets its name from a patch of white fur on the underside of its tail. When it is threatened, it runs for cover, holding its tail up. The flash of white acts as a danger signal for other deer.

SCIENTIFIC NAME	*Odocoileus virginianus*
DISTRIBUTION	Originally from North America, Central America, South America, from Canada to Brazil; introduced into Finland
SIZE	Up to 2.1m long, excluding tail

SOUTHERN PUDU

Pudus are the smallest true deer in the world. There are only two kinds, and both of them live in the forested foothills of the Andes Mountains. The southern pudu is the smallest species, weighing as little as 7kg when it is fully grown. It has a sleek rodent-like body, short legs, a tiny tail and miniature antlers that look like a pair of spikes. Southern pudus are endangered by hunting, and also by the steady destruction of their forest home.

SCIENTIFIC NAME	*Pudu puda*
DISTRIBUTION	Chile, Argentina
SIZE	Up to 70cm long

Whitetail deer stag and doe with fawn

BELOW *Like most of its relatives, the pampas deer has scent glands just in front of its eyes and also on its hoofs.*

ANTLERS AND HORNS

Antlers and horns can look similar, but they are made from different substances and grow in different ways. Antlers are made of solid bone, and are shed and regrown each year. They develop from two knobs on the top of a deer's skull, and grow at their tips, like a plant sprouting from the ground. Antlers usually branch, and the number of branches often increases when a new set grows. Horns are made of keratin, like claws, nails and hair. They grow from the bottom upwards, and usually last throughout an animal's life. Horns are hollow and less heavy than they look. They are often curved, but never branch.

An elk with huge, flattened antlers

GIRAFFES AND OKAPIS

This family of mammals contains just two species, both found in Africa. Despite their different shapes, the giraffe and okapi share many features, including long legs, a long neck and an extremely long, flexible tongue. They eat the leaves of trees, and their front legs are longer than their back ones, which helps to increase their reach. Giraffes and okapis have short, stubby, skin-covered horns.

GIRAFFE

This is the world's tallest living animal. The average height for a male is about 5m, but the tallest giraffes on record have measured nearly 6m. A giraffe's neck makes up about half its height, and allows it to reach leaves far above the ground. Giraffes live in open woodland, and gather food with their tongues. Their height helps them to watch for danger, but if they are attacked they can kick with deadly results. Giraffes have to splay their front legs in order to drink.

Tough lips for protection against thorns

SCIENTIFIC NAME *Giraffa camelopardalis*

DISTRIBUTION Africa south of the Sahara Desert

SIZE Up to 5.5m high

Neck is lowered when the giraffe is drinking or when it sleeps standing up

Front legs are used for kicking enemies

ABOVE *The okapi is a daytime feeder. Its stripes break up its outline, making it harder to see.*

OKAPI

Until 1901, the okapi was unknown outside central Africa. It remained undiscovered for so long because it lives in dense rainforest and is seldom seen. From the shoulders downward, it looks like a long-legged horse, with a brown coat and horizontal white stripes on its back legs and flanks. It has an extra-long neck, and its black tongue is long enough to lick its eyes. Okapis live alone, except when caring for their calves.

SCIENTIFIC NAME *Okapia johnstoni*

DISTRIBUTION Central Africa

SIZE Up to 1.8m long

PRONGHORNS

The pronghorn is a grazing mammal that is classified in a family of its own. With its hoofs and short, hooked horns, it looks like a cross between a deer and an antelope. Unlike antelopes and their relatives, it sheds and regrows its horns every year.

PRONGHORN

The natural habitat of the pronghorn is open prairie and scrub, where speed is essential for survival. It is the fastest hoofed mammal in the world, cruising at 50km/h, but reaching above 80km/h in short bursts. It takes long bounds on its slender legs, and has an unusual habit of shaking itself when it comes to a halt. Pronghorns have distinctive brown and white markings, and their horns are almost black. The horns curve backwards at the tip and, in males, they also have a forward-pointing prong. Before Europeans arrived in North America, more than 30 million pronghorns roamed the prairies. By the 1920s, hunting and farming had reduced their numbers to only about 20,000. Today, the pronghorn is protected, and the total population is nearly one million.

Male pronghorn with curving horns

SCIENTIFIC NAME *Antilocapra americana*

DISTRIBUTION Western USA; adjoining parts of Canada and Mexico

SIZE Up to 1.5m long, excluding tail

LEFT *Giraffes have a number of different coat patterns, which vary from place to place. This is a reticulated giraffe, which has a net-like pattern of fairly straight, pale lines.*

ANTELOPES, CATTLE AND THEIR RELATIVES

With about 140 species, these animals make up the largest family of hoofed mammals. In the wild, their natural range covers most of the world, except for South America, Australia and New Zealand. Their domesticated relatives, which include cattle, sheep and goats, can be found almost everywhere. Many species are grazers, which means that they feed on grass, but others are browsers and eat the leaves of shrubs and trees. Like most hoofed mammals, these animals have complicated digestive systems to enable them to break down their food. They have keen senses, and often live in herds, which increases their chances of spotting danger and avoiding attack.

ABOVE *For mammals like this nilgai, keen senses and fast reactions are essential for survival. Nilgais feed mostly at dawn and in the late afternoon, and are always ready to run if danger strikes. They can reach speeds of 50km/h – fast enough to escape predators as quick as the leopard, but only if they have a head start.*

COMMON ELAND

This African animal is the world's largest antelope, with a maximum weight of just less than a tonne. From a distance, it looks like a pale brown cow or bull, but it has longer legs than farm cattle, and a longer neck with a narrower head. It also has straight horns with a spiral twist – a feature that is shared by many smaller antelopes. Elands are browsers, and they feed in open country scattered with trees. As well as eating leaves, they dig up roots with their hoofs. Common elands are easy to tame, and are sometimes farmed for their meat and for their milk.

SCIENTIFIC NAME	*Taurotragus oryx*
DISTRIBUTION	Tropical Africa
SIZE	Up to 3.5m long, excluding tail

NILGAI OR BLUEBUCK

This is the largest antelope in Asia. The males can weigh more than 250kg but, as with most antelopes, the females are smaller. Nilgai have sloping shoulders and small heads, and only the male has horns. They live in thorny scrub and rocky places, and move about in small herds. They feed by grazing and browsing, and sometimes cause problems for farmers by raiding crops – especially sugar cane. Female nilgais usually give birth to twins at the beginning of the monsoon season, when food is easy to find.

SCIENTIFIC NAME	*Boselaphus tragocamelus*
DISTRIBUTION	India, Pakistan
SIZE	Up to 2.1m long, excluding tail

GREATER KUDU

Of all Africa's antelopes, the greater kudu has the most magnificent horns. They measure up to 1m from base to tip but, because they are spiral-shaped, they are actually much longer than this. For kudus, they are a mixed blessing because hunters kill the antelopes to take their horns as trophies. Greater kudus live in woodland, and feed both day and night.

SCIENTIFIC NAME	*Tragelaphus strepsiceros*
DISTRIBUTION	Eastern, central and southern Africa
SIZE	Up to 2.4m long, excluding tail

AFRICAN BUFFALO

This buffalo is one of Africa's heaviest and most dangerous hoofed animals. Both sexes have large, curved horns and, in bulls, these meet at the base to form a shield called a boss. A bull buffalo can tip over a car, and wound or even kill an adult lion with its horns. African buffaloes live in grassland and in forests. Grassland buffaloes are grey; forest animals are smaller and reddish. African buffaloes feed at dusk and at night, using their keen senses to detect danger.

SCIENTIFIC NAME	*Syncerus caffer*
DISTRIBUTION	Tropical and southern Africa
SIZE	Up to 3.4m long, excluding tail

ABOVE
African buffaloes often play host to oxpeckers (page 224) – birds that feed on parasites on their skin.

WATER BUFFALO

This blackish-grey Asian buffalo has the largest horns of any living animal. The longest pair on record measured more than 4m from tip to tip. Water buffaloes live in swamps and grassy places, and are fairly peaceful animals. They were first domesticated about 5,000 years ago, and few of the animals alive today are truly wild.

SCIENTIFIC NAME	*Bubalus arnee*
DISTRIBUTION	Originally from southern and Southeast Asia; introduced into other parts of the world including Australia, South America
SIZE	Up to 3m long, excluding tail

RUMINANTS

Grass and leaves are easy to find, but they are hard to digest. Some mammals cope with this kind of food by having a four-chambered stomach and by chewing their food twice. These animals are called ruminants, and they include antelopes, cattle and their relatives, as well as deer, and the giraffe, okapi and pronghorn. When ruminants swallow, the food travels into two stomach chambers, where it is mixed with saliva. Micro-organisms feed on substances in the food, breaking it down and making it much easier to digest. The animal then regurgitates the food and chews it again – a process called chewing the cud. Once it has been swallowed for a second time, the food travels through the other two stomach chambers, and is digested.

LOWLAND ANOA OR DWARF BUFFALO

This is the smallest buffalo in the world, and one of the most endangered. Even when it is fully grown, the lowland anoa is often less than 1m high at the shoulder, which makes it shorter than many species of deer. Lowland anoas live in tropical forests and lowland swamps. They have black coats and conical, backswept horns.

SCIENTIFIC NAME	*Bubalus depressicornis*
DISTRIBUTION	Sulawesi (Indonesia)
SIZE	Up to 1.8m long, excluding tail

BELOW *Wallowing in a mud pool, a water buffalo shows off its spectacular horns. Horns of this size appear heavy and cumbersome, but because they are hollow they are less heavy than they look. Like all horns, they keep growing throughout the buffalo's lifetime.*

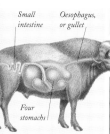

Small intestine | Oesophagus, or gullet

Four stomachs

African buffalo showing four-chambered stomach

Domesticated yak carrying baggage

American bison fighting during the breeding season

RIGHT *The European bison has a blunt, heavily built head, just like its American relative. The European species nearly died out a century ago, but it survived because some animals were kept in zoos. Today, there are about 3,000 European bison and they are carefully protected.*

VU QUANG OX OR SAO LA

This secretive forest animal hit the headlines in 1992, when scientists discovered it in a remote part of Vietnam. It has dagger-shaped horns, like those of the gemsbok (page 299), and a dark brown coat. The Vu Quang ox almost certainly lives in herds, and may be quite widespread. Because so few have been seen, little else is known about it.

SCIENTIFIC NAME *Pseudoryx nghetinhensis*

DISTRIBUTION Vietnam, possibly Laos

SIZE Up to 1.5m long, excluding tail

YAK

With its long, shaggy coat and short, sturdy legs, the yak is well equipped for mountain life. It lives in the Himalayan Mountains, and can survive above 6,000m, which is higher than any other large mammal. Although it looks clumsy, it is a good climber – even at altitudes that would leave most animals gasping for breath because of the lack of oxygen. Yaks were first domesticated more than 2,000 years ago, and domesticated animals now far outnumber any that live wild. They are smaller than wild yaks, and are kept for meat, milk and wool.

SCIENTIFIC NAME *Bos mutus*

DISTRIBUTION Tibet

SIZE Up to 3.2m long, excluding tail

AMERICAN BISON

Until the mid-1800s, when European settlers arrived in America's great plains, this was one of the world's most numerous grazing mammals. But, in the 50 years that followed, so many bison were shot that the species came close to extinction. Fortunately, a few hundred were spared, allowing bison to survive to this day. Compared to other wild cattle, the American bison looks front-heavy, with massive humped shoulders and an outsize head. Its head and forequarters are covered in shaggy, dark brown fur, which makes it look larger than it really is. American bison are highly sociable animals and, in the past, they formed vast herds more than 100,000 strong. Today's surviving herds are much smaller, and are confined mainly to national parks.

SCIENTIFIC NAME *Bison bison*

DISTRIBUTION North America

SIZE Up to 3.5m long, excluding tail

EUROPEAN BISON

The European bison is a forest animal, with a slightly smaller build and shorter fur than its American relative. It eats leaves in summer, and bark and twigs in winter. Bison were once found throughout Europe but, today, herds survive only in eastern Europe, where their original forest habitat is still intact.

SCIENTIFIC NAME *Bison bonasus*

DISTRIBUTION Poland, Belarus

SIZE Up to 3.5m long, excluding tail

COMMON REEDBUCK

Reedbucks are African antelopes that live in swamps and wet grassland. They have sandy-coloured coats, and the males have short, ridged horns that point forwards at the tips. There are three species of these animals, and the common reedbuck is the largest, standing up to 95cm high at the shoulder. Like its two relatives, it is a graceful animal, and runs with high, bounding leaps. When reedbucks are alarmed, they make a whistling sound through their noses to warn the herd. If they catch the scent of a leopard or lion after dark, they can keep up this sound for more than half an hour.

SCIENTIFIC NAME	*Redunca arundinum*
DISTRIBUTION	Central and southern Africa
SIZE	Up to 1.4m long, excluding tail

WATERBUCK

This sturdily built African antelope stands up to 1.3m high at the shoulder, and can weigh more than 200kg. It has a coarse grey or reddish-brown coat, smeared with an oily substance that gives it a musky smell. The males have long, curved horns, with a slight bend that makes them look like a pair of tweezers. Waterbucks live up to their name by staying near water all the time. They feed mainly on grass. In the breeding season, the males defend their territories against rivals, sometimes injuring each other with their horns.

SCIENTIFIC NAME	*Kobus ellipsiprymnus*
DISTRIBUTION	Africa south of the Sahara Desert
SIZE	Up to 2.2m long, excluding tail

KOB

A close relative of the waterbuck, the kob is smaller, with shorter fur. Its overall colour is usually light brown, with pale undersides. It also has white rings around its eyes. The males have graceful, backswept horns. Kobs live on grassland close to rivers and waterholes, and they feed by grazing. Like many antelopes, they bounce high into the air if they are threatened. This behaviour, called stotting, may be a way of making predators believe that they they can move quickly and are not worth chasing.

SCIENTIFIC NAME	*Kobus kob*
DISTRIBUTION	Tropical Africa
SIZE	Up to 1.8m long, excluding tail

RIGHT *Sword-shaped horns and bold markings make the gemsbok easy to recognize. Compared to most other antelopes, this handsome animal is good at defending itself – it has even been known to stab lions fatally with its horns.*

BELOW *Waterbucks are usually safe in the open, but their liking for water brings danger. They are often caught by crocodiles, which lurk near the water's edge.*

Horns have sharp tips

Muscular neck

Herd of common wildebeest on the move

COMMON WILDEBEEST OR GNU

The common wildebeest is an ungainly looking animal, with close-set eyes, an untidy beard and mane and spindly legs. Despite its clumsy appearance, it is one of Africa's most successful grazers, forming some of the largest herds on Earth. In Tanzania's Serengeti National Park, more than a million wildebeest migrate in step with the seasons, moving to find fresh grass. The females give birth at the start of the rainy season, and their calves can run soon after being born.

SCIENTIFIC NAME	*Connochaetes taurinus*
DISTRIBUTION	Eastern and southern Africa
SIZE	Up to 2.4m long, excluding tail

GEMSBOK

This striking animal belongs to a group of mammals called horse antelopes, which get their name from their sturdy, horse-like build. There are six species, and they all have long horns. Some have curved horns, but the gemsbok's are almost straight. They can be more than 1m long, with pointed tips, and are deadly weapons. Gemsboks survive well in dry places where water is hard to find. Instead of drinking, they get water from their food. They live in herds of up to 50 animals, and breed throughout the year.

SCIENTIFIC NAME	*Oryx gazella*
DISTRIBUTION	Eastern and southwestern Africa
SIZE	Up to 1.6m long, excluding tail

IMPALA

This sleek, graceful animal is one of Africa's most agile antelopes, capable of leaping more than 10m in a single bound. It eats grass, leaves and seeds, and lives in open woodland and tree-studded savanna. Instead of staying in the open like most grazing antelopes, impalas run for cover if they are threatened. Only male impalas have horns, but both sexes have a dark vertical stripe on their hindquarters, and a tuft of black hair on their back legs.

SCIENTIFIC NAME	*Aepyceros melampus*
DISTRIBUTION	Eastern and southern Africa
SIZE	Up to 1.5m long, including tail

HARTEBEEST

The hartebeest is a medium-sized antelope that lives on open grassland. It has sloping shoulders and short fur, and the males and females both have small, sharply bent horns, which grow from a bulge on the top of their heads. During the breeding season, the males use their horns to fight, but instead of standing up, rivals get down on their knees and then push against each other in a test of strength. A century ago, the hartebeest was the most widespread African antelope, living as far north as Morocco and Egypt. After decades of hunting, it is now found only further south.

SCIENTIFIC NAME	*Alcelaphus buselaphus*
DISTRIBUTION	Africa south of the Sahara Desert
SIZE	Up to 2.4m long, excluding tail

LEFT *This group of hartebeest is resting during the midday heat. They manage to survive without water by eating fruit and digging up roots.*

BELOW Kirk's dik-diks get their name from the alarm call that they make when they run from danger. The call warns other dik-diks to be alert, and also lets other animals know that predators may be about.
BOTTOM These two klipspringers are using their scent glands to mark a bush. The scent will linger for several days and alert other klipspringers that they live in the area.

ROYAL ANTELOPE

After the lesser mouse deer (page 290), the royal antelope is one of the smallest hoofed mammals in the world. When fully grown, it measures only about 25cm high at the shoulder, and weighs roughly as much as a large chicken. The males have the tiniest horns of any hoofed mammal, at about only 2.5cm long. Royal antelopes live in dense forest, where they feed on leaves, flowers and fruit. Solitary animals, they spend most of their time on their own, and bound away like rabbits if they are disturbed.

SCIENTIFIC NAME	*Neotragus pygmaeus*
DISTRIBUTION	Tropical western Africa
SIZE	Up to 50cm long, excluding tail

KIRK'S DIK-DIK

This miniature antelope lives in dry African scrub – a habitat that teems with predators. Although it looks very vulnerable, it is well able to look after itself. Its large eyes and ears are always alert for danger and, if it is alarmed, it runs away with zigzagging leaps, which makes it harder to catch. Dik-diks have furry crests on their heads and unusual noses that look like short snouts. The females normally give birth to one young at a time, but they can breed twice a year.

SCIENTIFIC NAME	*Madoqua kirki*
DISTRIBUTION	Kenya, Tanzania, Namibia, Angola
SIZE	Up to 70cm long, excluding tail

ORIBI

This long-necked animal is the largest of the dwarf antelopes – a group that includes royal antelopes, dik-diks and klipspringers. It is the only one of these antelopes that feeds mainly on grass, and it lives in places where the grass is short, so that it can keep a lookout for danger. The oribi feeds in groups of up to six animals. It is reddish-brown, with white underparts and a black tail. It also has a bare black spot beneath each ear. This contains glands that release scent into the air.

SCIENTIFIC NAME	*Ourebia ourebi*
DISTRIBUTION	Africa south of the Sahara Desert
SIZE	Up to 1.4m long, excluding tail

KLIPSPRINGER

For an antelope, the klipspringer lives in a very unusual habitat – rocky outcrops and cliffs. It stands on the tips of its small rubbery hoofs, which give it an extremely good grip. It jumps from rock to rock, and can stand on ledges just a

Scent gland in front of eye

Small, pointed hoofs

few centimetres wide. Klipspringers live in small groups, and feed on shrubs growing among the rocks. They have rough, greyish-brown fur, and the males have short spiky horns.

SCIENTIFIC NAME
Oreotragus oreotragus

DISTRIBUTION Eastern and southwestern Africa; isolated groups in northern Nigeria

SIZE Up to 90cm long, excluding tail

THOMSON'S GAZELLE

Gazelles are medium-sized antelopes with sleek, lithe bodies and slender legs. Most of them, including Thomson's gazelle, have golden-brown upperparts, white undersides and horns with an S-shaped bend. Their horns have knobbly rings, and they are grown by females as well as males. Thomson's gazelles feed in open grassland, and they live in straggling herds that can contain several thousand animals. To survive in the open, they have to be vigilant around the clock. Although they often lie down, they sleep for no more than an hour a day, in short bursts of five minutes or less. Thomson's gazelles start breeding when they are two years old. The females usually have two young each year, roughly six months apart.

SCIENTIFIC NAME *Gazella thomsoni*

DISTRIBUTION Eastern Africa

SIZE Up to 1.1m long, excluding tail

SPRINGBOK

During the 19th century, springboks formed some of the largest herds on Earth. Some herds contained at least 10 million animals, and were as much as 150km long. Today, this brightly coloured antelope is not as common as it was, but it has been reintroduced into many parks and game reserves. Springboks get their name from their amazing jumping ability. They can leap up to 3.5m, and seem to bounce up again when they hit the ground. Their most unusual feature is a fold of skin running along their backs. When they are excited or alarmed, the fold turns out to show a crest of white hairs.

SCIENTIFIC NAME *Antidorcas marsupialis*

DISTRIBUTION Southern and southwestern Africa

SIZE Up to 1.4m long, excluding tail

BELOW Thompson's gazelles live in open grassland, where they have the best chance of spotting predators before they attack. In some parts of eastern Africa, these antelopes form herds thousands of animals strong.

Springbok leaping high into the air, or stotting, before fleeing from danger

GERENUK

This African gazelle has an exceptionally long neck, and it feeds on the leaves of trees and shrubs by standing on its back legs. It uses its front legs to keep itself steady, and also to pull branches within reach. Although the gerenuk measures only 1m tall at the shoulder, it can reach 2m high for food.

SCIENTIFIC NAME *Litocranius walleri*

DISTRIBUTION Eastern Africa

SIZE Up to 1.6m long, excluding tail

BLACKBUCK

This Asian antelope is one of the few species in which the males and females look quite different. Female and young blackbucks are yellowish-brown with white undersides, but adult males are dark brown or black on top, and white underneath. The males have spiral-shaped horns that can grow up to 60cm long. Blackbucks are grazers, and they live on open, grassy ground.

SCIENTIFIC NAME *Antilope cervicapra*

DISTRIBUTION India, Pakistan

SIZE Up to 1.2m long, excluding tail

SAIGA

Like all the animals on these two pages, the saiga belongs to a group of hoofed mammals called goat-antelopes. These animals are all very hardy, and many of them live in places where winters can be very cold. The saiga comes from the open plains of central Asia, and is a strange-looking animal with sandy-coloured fur, downward-pointing nostrils and a swollen muzzle. This may help it in winter, by warming frosty air before it reaches the lungs.

SCIENTIFIC NAME *Saiga tatarica*

DISTRIBUTION Central Asia

SIZE Up to 1.7m long, excluding tail

Cretan wild goat

CHAMOIS

As a mountaineer, the chamois is in a class of its own. It can run up almost sheer rock faces on its non-slip hoofs, jumping from ledge to ledge. It runs downhill with equal skill, dropping up to 6m in a single leap. Even young chamois can make death-defying leaps when they are just a few days old. Chamois are compact, elegant animals with short horns that bend backwards to form a hook. They live high above the treeline during the summer, but during the winter they come lower down to feed in forests.

Chamois on rocky ledge

SCIENTIFIC NAME *Rupicapra rupicapra*

DISTRIBUTION Originally from southern and central Europe, western Asia; introduced into New Zealand

SIZE Up to 1.3m long, excluding tail

Appenine wild goat

American mountain goat

ABOVE *There are eight species of wild goat, and most of them live in mountains and rocky places. The Cretan and Appenine wild goats (Capra aegagrus) are both closely related to the domesticated goats kept on farms. The American mountain goat lives at high altitudes and has a thick coat.*

AMERICAN MOUNTAIN GOAT

Compared to the chamois, this goat is slow-moving, but it is expert at surviving in difficult conditions. It lives on rocks near the snowline, feeding on grasses and low-growing plants. American mountain goats have long coats of white hair that extend down their legs like trousers. This long hair shrugs off rain and snow, and a layer of wool underneath keeps the animal warm. American mountain goats have small horns, and live in herds of up to ten animals.

SCIENTIFIC NAME *Oreamnos americanus*

DISTRIBUTION North America; from Alaska to the Pacific northwest

SIZE Up to 1.6m long, excluding tail

MUSK OX

Although it looks like a buffalo, the musk ox is much more closely related to the chamois and the mountain goat. It lives in the Arctic tundra, and has a shaggy coat of long brown hair that reaches almost to the ground during the winter months. Its hoofs are extra-large, which helps to stop it sinking into the snow, and both sexes have large, down-curved horns that meet in the middle of their heads. Musk oxen live in herds of up to 100 animals, and keep on the move constantly. If they are threatened, for example by wolves, the adults bunch together and form a ring, with their calves hidden inside.

SCIENTIFIC NAME *Ovibos moschatus*

DISTRIBUTION Northern Canada, Greenland

SIZE Up to 2.3m long, excluding tail

ALPINE IBEX

This sure-footed wild goat lives in the European Alps. It spends most of its life far above the treeline, where it eats mainly grass. Both sexes have large, backswept horns, but they are particularly spectacular in the males, reaching up to 1.4m long. Alpine ibexes have long been hunted, and also face danger from avalanches during the spring thaw. More than a century ago, the species was reduced to just one herd, containing about 60 animals. Since then, Alpine ibexes have been given protection, and their numbers have recovered to about 10,000.

SCIENTIFIC NAME *Capra ibex*

DISTRIBUTION Italy, France, Middle East, central Asia

SIZE Up to 1.5m long, excluding tail

LEFT *An Alpine ibex prepares to jump from a ledge. This exceptionally hardy animal lives at altitudes of up to 2,000m.*

RIGHT *This American bighorn sheep is calling to rival males. If one is close, fighting will break out.*

Impressive
horns spiral
around as
they grow

Short,
thick
summer
coat

MOUFLON

Most experts think that this wild sheep,
originally from southwestern Asia, is either
the direct ancestor of today's domesticated sheep,
or one of their closest living relatives. Compared
to farmed sheep, mouflons are sturdy animals.
They have coarse, blackish-brown hair, but in
the winter they also have a layer of softer wool
underneath. The males have large horns that
curve backwards towards their shoulders, and
they fight fiercely during the breeding season,
clashing head on. Mouflons live in mountains,
in herds of up to 20 animals, and they feed
on a wide range of plant food.

SCIENTIFIC NAME *Ovis orientalis*

DISTRIBUTION Southwestern Asia, Europe

SIZE Up to 1.3m long, excluding tail

Curved
horns

Mouflon male, or ram   **Mouflon female, or ewe**

AMERICAN BIGHORN SHEEP

Only two kinds of wild sheep live in North
America, and this species is easily the most
widespread. It lives on rocky
hillsides, from southwestern
Canada to Baja California
in Mexico – a range of more
than 3,000km. Bighorn sheep
are greyish-brown in colour,
with white hindquarters. The
females have small horns that
are almost straight, but the
males' horns are curved, and
much larger. For males, horns
are weapons and status symbols –
in old males, they often curve
around so far that they turn
a full circle.

**Male bighorn
sheep
clashing
head-on**

SCIENTIFIC NAME *Ovis canadensis*

DISTRIBUTION Western North America; from
Canada to northern Mexico

SIZE Up to 1.6m long, excluding tail

GLOSSARY

The following four pages explain most of the technical terms that are used in this book. In this glossary you can find words that refer to animal body parts, life-cycles and behaviour, and also to some of the processes that affect animals as a whole. Where a definition includes words in capital letters, it means that these words have entries of their own. If you want to find out about particular animals, or animal groups, refer to the index on pages 308–319.

Red fox *(Vulpes vulpes)*

ABDOMEN
The part of an animal's body that contains ORGANS used for digesting food, getting rid of waste, and reproducing. In insects, arachnids and crustaceans, the abdomen is at the rear of the body.

ALGA (plural: ALGAE)
Plant-like ORGANISMS that often live in water. Most algae are microscopic, but seaweeds, which are the largest algae, can be many metres long.

AMPHIBIOUS
Describes a creature that lives on land as well as in water.

ANTENNA (plural: ANTENNAE)
A long slender structure on an animal's head that is used for obtaining information by touching or smelling. Antennae are sometimes called feelers.

ARTHROPOD
An animal that has a hard EXOSKELETON, and legs that bend at joints. Arthropods include insects, spiders and crustaceans.

BALEEN
The fibrous substance that large whales use to sieve food from the water. Baleen hangs down like a curtain from a whale's upper jaw.

BARBEL
A fleshy feeler on the head of a fish. As well as sensing things by touch, barbels also sense things by taste.

BIOLUMINESCENCE
The production of light by living things. It is common in fish and insects, and in simple animals that live in the sea.

BLOWHOLE
A hole on a dolphin or whale's head, used for breathing. It closes when the animal dives, to stop water getting into the lungs.

BLUBBER
A thick layer of fat that helps some sea animals to keep warm. Whales, seals, polar bears and penguins have blubber.

BROWSER
A plant-eating animal that feeds on leaves and shoots from trees and bushes, instead of on grass. Deer are typical browsers.

BYSSUS
A collection of tough threads that some bivalve molluscs use to fasten themselves in place.

CAMOUFLAGE
A pattern or colour scheme that helps an animal to blend in with its surroundings. Animals use camouflage to ambush their PREY, or to avoid being eaten.

CANINE TEETH
Long, pointed teeth that meat-eating mammals have at the front of their mouths. The animals use their canine teeth to stab and grip food.

CARAPACE
A hard case or shield on an animal's back that protects its body. Crabs, tortoises and turtles are examples of animals with a carapace.

CARNASSIAL TEETH
Long, sharp-edged teeth that meat-eating mammals have towards the back of their jaw. Animals use their carnassial teeth to slice through food.

CARNIVORE
Any animal that eats meat. Carnivore can also refer to a mammal that specializes in hunting other animals.

CARTILAGE
A rubbery substance found in the skeletons of VERTEBRATES. Cartilage helps bones to slide over each other where they meet at joints. It also forms some parts of the body, such as noses and ears. In cartilaginous fish, the whole skeleton is made of cartilage instead of bone.

CASQUE
A hard 'helmet' on a bird's head, or on the top of its beak.

CELL
A microscopic unit of living matter. Cells contain all the equipment an animal or plant needs to stay alive, although they often specialize in particular tasks. Most animals have millions of cells in their bodies, but the simplest living things have just one.

CHRYSALIS
A hard case that protects a caterpillar while it turns into a butterfly or moth. A chrysalis often has a shiny surface.

CILIUM (plural: CILIA)
A microscopic hair-like thread on the surface of a CELL. Living things use cilia to swim, to creep about or to make things move.

CLUTCH
A collection of eggs laid at one time by a female animal, such as a bird or a reptile.

COCOON
A silk case spun by an insect or a spider, which it uses to protect itself or its eggs.

COLD-BLOODED
Describes an animal whose body stays at the same temperature as its surroundings. Cold-blooded animals are active when it is warm, but when the temperature drops they slow down or come to a halt.

COLONY
A group of animals living together as a single unit. Some colony-forming animals are permanently joined together.

COMPOUND EYE
An eye that is divided up into many separate compartments, which work together to produce a picture. Crustaceans and insects have compound eyes.

COURTSHIP
The behaviour that an animal uses to attract a partner to mate. Male animals use courtship behaviour to show that they are fit and healthy and will make suitable partners.

DEFORESTATION
The deliberate destruction of forests by people, either to supply timber, or to create open ground that can be farmed.

DIGESTION
The breakdown of food so that it can be absorbed and used by the body. Animals digest their food by chewing or grinding it up, so that powerful chemicals inside their bodies can turn it into simpler substances.

DISTRIBUTION
All the places in the world where an animal lives.

DOMESTICATED ANIMAL
An animal that is kept by people, instead of living wild. Some domesticated animals are kept as pets; others provide us with food or muscle-power.

DOWN FEATHERS
The fluffy feathers that a bird has next to its skin. Down feathers trap a layer of air, and this keeps the bird warm.

ECHOLOCATION
A way in which some animals sense objects and food by producing bursts of high-pitched sound. The echoes from the sounds bounce back towards the animal, which can then tell what is nearby. Animals that use echolocation include bats, whales and dolphins.

EGG
A CELL that can develop into a new animal. Nearly all animals reproduce by making eggs, but their eggs develop differently. In most animals, the eggs are laid, and they develop outside the mother. In mammals and some other animals, they develop inside the mother's body.

ELYTRON (plural: **ELYTRA**)
The hardened forewing of a beetle. Beetles have two elytra. They fit over the ABDOMEN like a case, protecting the hindwings while the beetle crawls about.

EVOLUTION
A very slow process of change that enables living things to adapt to the world around them. Instead of happening in a single lifetime, evolution happens over many generations. During evolution, new SPECIES develop, replacing those that have become extinct.

EXOSKELETON
A skeleton that is around the outside of an animal's body, instead of inside it. Exoskeletons provide protection, and also something solid for an animal's muscles to pull against.

EXTINCTION
The permanent disappearance of a SPECIES. Extinction can be caused by a number of things, including competition from other species, natural disasters and hunting by people.

EYE-SPOT
A very simple eye, or a patch of colour that looks like an eye.

FANG
A tooth or other mouthpart that is designed to stab. Some fangs inject poison, helping animals to overpower their PREY.

FERAL ANIMAL
A domesticated animal that has escaped from human control and taken up life in the wild.

FERTILIZATION
The process that enables a male and female cell to join together, to form a single EGG.

FILTER-FEEDER
An animal that gets its food by sieving it from water.

FLIGHT FEATHERS
The large feathers that form the surface of a bird's wings and tail, enabling it to fly.

FLUKE
A whale or dolphin's tail. Unlike a fish's tail, it beats up and down instead of from side to side.

GESTATION PERIOD
In mammals, the time that it takes a young animal to develop inside its mother's body, from the moment of FERTILIZATION, to the time when it is born.

GILL
A body part that water-dwelling animals use to collect OXYGEN from the water. Gills may either stick out from the body, or they may be hidden away inside.

GLAND
A body part that produces particular substances, such as venom or MUCUS.

GRAZER
A plant-eating animal that feeds mainly on grass, rather than on the leaves and shoots of trees and bushes.

GRUB
A young insect that has either very short legs, or no legs at all. (See LARVA)

HABITAT
The surroundings that a particular SPECIES needs to survive. Habitats include forests, grasslands, deserts and coral reefs. Most species live in just one habitat, but some can survive in several.

HAEMOGLOBIN
A red chemical that carries OXYGEN in an animal's blood.

HALTERE
In flies, a small ORGAN, shaped like a drumstick, that takes the place of the hindwings. Halteres help flies to balance in the air.

HIBERNATION
A deep winter sleep. Animals hibernate so that they can survive a time of year when food is hard to find.

HOST
An animal that a PARASITE uses as its home and food.

INCUBATION
The act of sitting on eggs to keep them warm. Birds have to incubate their eggs because they do not develop properly if they are cold.

Holly blue (male)

Holly blue (female)
(Celastrina argiolus)

Clouded yellow
(Colia crocea)

Painted lady
(Cynthia cardui)

Peacock
(Inachis io)

Red admiral
(Vanessa atalanta)

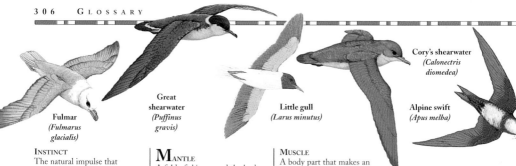

Fulmar
*(Fulmarus
glacialis)*

Great
shearwater
*(Puffinus
gravis)*

Little gull
(Larus minutus)

Cory's shearwater
*(Calonectris
diomedea)*

Alpine swift
(Apus melba)

INSTINCT
The natural impulse that
animals have, by which they can
follow a pattern of behaviour
without having to learn it first.

INSULATION
Something that slows down the
flow of heat. Animals use fur,
feathers and fat as insulation,
helping to keep them warm.
(See BLUBBER, DOWN FEATHERS)

INTRODUCED SPECIES
A SPECIES that people have
taken from one part of the
world and released into another.
In some parts of the world,
introduced animals have had
a bad effect on local wildlife.

INVERTEBRATE
Any animal that does not have
a backbone.

KERATIN
A strong but flexible substance
found in body parts that get a
lot of wear and tear. These body
parts include hair, fur, hooves,
horns and birds' beaks.

LARVA (plural: LARVAE)
A young animal that looks
completely different from its
parents, and which changes
shape as it grows up. In many
animals, the larva concentrates
on feeding, while the adult
concentrates on reproduction.

LEK
A place where male animals
gather during the breeding
season to attract females.
The males often fight to
be in the centre of the lek.

LIFE-CYCLE
All the steps in the life of an
animal, including the way it
starts life, the way it develops,
and the way it breeds.

MANTLE
A fold of skin around the body
of a mollusc. In most molluscs
it produces hard substances
that form a shell.

MEMBRANE
A thin film or a sheet of skin.

METAMORPHOSIS
The change in body shape as
an animal grows up. It can be
either gradual, when a tadpole
turns into a frog for example,
or sudden, when a caterpillar
turns into a butterfly.

MIGRATION
A long journey that animals
make to breed or to find food.
Most animals migrate along set
routes, guided by INSTINCT.

MIMIC
An animal, especially among
insects, that imitates something
else, often to avoid being eaten.
Some mimics look like twigs
or stones, but others imitate
poisonous animals.

MOLAR TEETH
Teeth that mammals have at the
back of the jaw, where their bite
is strongest. Molar teeth are
used to crush and chew food.

MOULTING
The shedding of an outer
covering, such as fur, feathers
or skin. Animals that have
EXOSKELETONS have to moult as
they grow, because the skeletons
do not grow with them.

MUCUS
A frothy or slimy liquid
produced by an animal. Animals
use mucus in many different
ways. Slugs and snails use it
to slide along, some insects
use it to hide from predators,
while treefrogs often use it
to make their nests.

MUSCLE
A body part that makes an
animal move. Muscles work
by contracting – they can
pull but they cannot push.

MUSK
An oily and strong-smelling
substance produced by
mammals such as deer.

NACRE
The smooth, shiny substance
that makes up the inner surface
of a mollusc's shell. Also known
as 'mother of pearl'.

NECTAR
A sweet, sugary liquid produced
by flowers. Plants make nectar
to attract animals. In return for
nectar, animal visitors spread
their POLLEN.

NEMATOCYST
In cnidarians, a specialized
CELL that can flick out a
poison-tipped thread.

NOCTURNAL
An animal that is active mainly
or entirely after dark.

NOMADIC
An animal that does not have
any fixed home. Nomadic
animals usually keep on the
move, travelling to wherever
there is food.

NOTOCHORD
In chordates, a reinforcing rod
that runs down the body.

NYMPH
A young insect that resembles
its parents, but which does not
have fully formed wings or
reproductive ORGANS.

OPERCULUM
A moveable flap that seals an
opening in an animal's body.

ORGAN
A part of the body that carries
out particular tasks, such as
digesting food or sensing sound.

ORGANISM
Any living thing.

OXYGEN
The chemical that all animals
need in order to get energy
from their food. Oxygen is in
the air, and dissolved oxygen
is in fresh water and the sea.

PARASITE
An animal that feeds on or
inside another living animal.
Unlike a PREDATOR, a parasite
is usually smaller than the
animal that it attacks, and often
has a complicated LIFE-CYCLE.

PECTORAL FINS
A pair of fins on the underside
of a fish, usually close to its head.

PELVIC FINS
A pair of fins on the underside
of a fish, usually close to its tail.

PLANKTON
Microscopic living things that
drift near the surface of lakes
and oceans. Plankton includes
ALGAE, which collect energy
from sunshine, and also tiny
animals, which eat algae or
each other.

POLLEN
A dust-like substance that
flowers make to produce
seeds. Many plants use
animals to spread their pollen
from one flower to another.

POLYP
An animal that has a tube-
shaped body, with a ring of
TENTACLES around its mouth.

PREDATOR
Any animal that lives
by hunting others.

PREHENSILE
Something that can wrap
around things to hold onto
them, or to pick them up.
Elephants have prehensile
trunks, and some monkeys
have prehensile tails.

PREY
The animals that a PREDATOR
hunts for food.

PROBOSCIS
A nose, or a collection of long
mouthparts. An elephant's
trunk is a proboscis, and so
is a butterfly's tongue.

PROTOZOAN
A simple, animal-like
ORGANISM that is made up of
just one CELL. Protozoans live
mainly in water, or in damp
HABITATS, such as soil.

PSEUDOPOD
An outgrowth from a CELL
that works like a temporary
foot. Many protozoans use
pseudopods to move, and so do
some cells in an animal's body.

PUPA (plural: **PUPAE**)
A resting stage during the
LIFE-CYCLE of an insect. Inside
the pupa, the young insect's
body is broken down, and an
adult one is assembled in its
place. A pupa usually has a
hard outer case, and is often
hidden inside a COCOON.

RUMEN
The large stomach chamber that
many plant-eating mammals use
to break down their food.

RUMINANT
A plant-eating mammal that has
hooves and a four-chambered
stomach. Deer, antelope and
cattle are all ruminants.

SCALES
Hard flaps that cover an
animal's body. Scales usually
help to protect animals from
attack but, in some butterflies
and moths, they help to keep
the body warm.

SCAVENGER
An animal that lives on
leftovers, including dead
remains that have been
left by PREDATORS.

SEGMENTS
Similar body parts that are
arranged in a line. Segments are
easy to see in earthworms and in
the ABDOMENS of many insects.

SILK
Stretchy natural fibres that
insects and spiders make from
a special liquid. These animals
use silk to catch food, to help
them move about or to protect
themselves or their eggs.

SIPHON
An open-ended tube in an
animal's body that sucks
in or squirts out water.

SOARING
Gliding by rising upwards
on currents of warm air.

SPECIES
A single type of living thing.
The members of a species can
all breed with each other, but
they normally do not breed
with anything else.

SPERM
CELLS produced by male
animals for reproduction. Sperm
cells usually have tiny 'tails', and
they can swim towards female
cells to fertilize them.

SPINNERET
In insects and spiders, a nozzle
that produces silk.

SWIMBLADDER
A gas-filled bag inside a fish.
The bag works like an adjustable
float, and it helps to stop the
fish from sinking through the
water, or rising to the surface.

SYMBIOSIS
A partnership that involves
two different SPECIES of animal
living together. By teaming up,
each partner has a better chance
of survival. Both partners may
be animals, or one may be an
animal and one a plant.

TALONS
The sharp claws that birds of
prey use to attack other animals.

TENTACLES
Long, fleshy 'feelers' that some
animals use to catch their food.

TERRITORY
A space that is claimed by an
animal, usually so that it can
breed. Most territories are set
up by males. Females can enter,
but rival males are chased away.

THORAX
The middle part of an animal's
body. In insects, the thorax
is the part that has legs
and wings attached to it.

TRACHEA
A tube that allows air
to flow into the body.
In mammals, it is also
known as a windpipe.

VENOMOUS
Describes an animal that is able
to produce venom, or poison.

VERTEBRA (plural: **VERTEBRAE**)
One of several bones that link
together to form the backbone.
Vertebrae fit together at joints,
allowing the backbone to bend.

VERTEBRATE
Any animal that has a backbone.

VOCAL SAC
An inflatable pouch of skin that
helps an animal to make sound.

WARM-BLOODED
Describes an animal that stays
at a steady warm temperature.
Warm-blooded animals are well
insulated, and can stay active
even when it is freezing.

WARNING COLOURS
Bright colours that warn that an
animal is poisonous or dangerous
in another way. Black and
yellow is a common pattern
of warning colours.

Leopard
*(Panthera
pardus)*

INDEX

ACKNOWLEDGEMENTS

The publishers would like to thank the following for their contributions to this book:

Photographs

(*t* = top; *c* = centre; *b* = bottom; *l* = left; *r* = right)

Front cover: Colour library images. Page 1 *c* Warren Photographic; 3 *c* OSF; 4 *cl* Warren Photographic, *cl* Warren Photographic; 5 *cl* Warren Photographic, *br* NHPA, *tr* Kingfisher; 6 *tr* Warren Photographic, *c* Warren Photographic; 7 *cr* Warren Photographic, *br* Warren Photographic; 12 *c* NHPA, *cl* Warren Photographic; 13 *cr* Warren Photographic, *tl* Warren Photographic; 14 *cl* NHPA; 14–15 t Warren Photographic; 15 *crt* OSF, *crb* Warren Photographic; 16 *cl* OSF, *br* Warren Photographic; 17 *tr* OSF, *cr* OSF, *br* Warren Photographic; 18 *bl* Warren Photographic, *tr* Warren Photographic; 18–19 t Warren Photographic; 19 *b* Warren Photographic; 20 *br* Warren Photographic; 20–21 t Warren Photographic; 21 *bl* Warren Photographic, *tc* Warren Photographic; 22 *b* OSF, *cl* Warren Photographic; 23 *bc* NHPA, *tr* Warren Photographic; 24 *tl* NHPA; 25 *b* NHPA, *cl* Warren Photographic; 26–27 *c* OSF; 27 *cr* OSF, *c* Warren Photographic; 28 *tl* Warren Photographic; 29 *l* NHPA; 30–31 *c* NHPA; 31 *br* NHPA; 32 *bl* Warren Photographic, *cl* Warren Photographic; 32–33 *t* NHPA; 34 *cl* NHPA; 34 *tl* Warren Photographic; 35 *bc* Warren Photographic, *tl* Warren Photographic; 36 *cl* OSF, *bl* Warren Photographic; 36–37 *t* Warren Photographic; 37 *cr* OSF; 38 *bc* Warren Photographic, *bl* Warren Photographic; 38–39 *t* OSF; 39 *br* Warren Photographic; 40 *c* Warren Photographic; 40–41 *b* Warren Photographic; 41 *trt* Warren Photographic, 41 *trb* Warren Photographic; 42 *t* NHPA; 43 *br* Warren Photographic, *l* Warren Photographic; 44 *tl* Warren Photographic, *cl* Warren Photographic; 44–45 *b* OSF; 45 *cr* Warren Photographic; 46 *cl* Warren Photographic; 47 *rt* NHPA; 48 *cl* Warren Photographic; 49 *cr* Warren Photographic, *b* OSF; 50 *bl* Warren Photographic, *tr* Warren Photographic; 51 *br* Warren Photographic; 52 *bc* Warren Photographic, *bl* Warren Photographic; 53 *c* Warren Photographic; 54 *cl* Warren Photographic, *b* Warren Photographic; 55 *tr* Warren Photographic; 56 *bl* Warren Photographic, *cl* Warren Photographic; 57 *t* Warren Photographic; 58 *cl* Warren Photographic, *tr* Warren Photographic; 59 *bc* Warren Photographic, *c* Warren Photographic; 60 *cl* Warren Photographic; 60–61 *t* Warren Photographic; 61 *tr* Warren Photographic; 62 *b* Warren Photographic; 63 *r* Warren Photographic; 64 *tl* Warren Photographic, *tr* OSF; 65 *br* Warren Photographic; 66 *tl* Warren Photographic; 67 *c* Warren Photographic, *tr* Warren Photographic; 68 *cr* Warren Photographic; 69 *tl* Warren Photographic, *b* Warren Photographic; 70 *cl* Warren Photographic, *t* Warren Photographic; 71 *b* Warren Photographic, *cl* Warren Photographic; 72 *cl* Warren Photographic, *tr* Warren Photographic; 73 *tr* Warren Photographic; 74 *l* Warren Photographic; 75 *t* Warren Photographic; 76 *bl* Warren Photographic; 76–77 *c* Warren Photographic; 78 *cl* Warren Photographic; 79 *cr* Warren Photographic, *b* Warren Photographic; 80 *b* Warren Photographic; 81 *bl* Warren Photographic, *tl* Warren Photographic; 82 *r* Warren Photographic; 83 *l* Warren Photographic; 84 *b* Warren Photographic; 85 *tc* Warren Photographic; 86 *bl* Warren Photographic; 86–87 *t* Warren Photographic; 87 *cr* Warren Photographic; 88 *tl* Warren Photographic; 89 *bl* Warren Photographic, *t* Warren Photographic; 91 *bc* Warren Photographic, *l* NHPA; 92–93 *t* Warren Photographic; 93 *c* Warren Photographic; 94 *cr* STILL Pictures; 94–95 *t* STILL Pictures; 95 *bl* OSF, *br* OSF; 96 *t* NHPA; 97 *b* STILL Pictures; 98 *br* STILL Pictures; 98–99 *t* NHPA; 100 *c* OSF; 101 *t* STILL Pictures, *cl* OSF; 102–103 *t* Warren Photographic, *c* NHPA; 103 *b* NHPA; 104 *b* NHPA; 105 *t* NHPA; 106 *t* Warren Photographic; 107 *b* Warren Photographic, *bc* Warren Photographic; 108 *c* STILL Pictures; 109 *br* Warren Photographic; 110 *bl* Warren Photographic; 110–111 *t* Warren Photographic; 111 *tr* Warren Photographic; 112 *cr* OSF, *cl* OSF; 113 *b* Warren Photographic; 114 *r* Warren Photographic; 115 *b* Warren Photographic, *cr* Warren Photographic; 116 *tr* Warren Photographic, *b* Warren Photographic; 118 *bl* NHPA; 118–119 *c* NHPA; 119 *tr* NHPA; 120 *cl* OSF, *bc* NHPA; 121 *t* Warren Photographic; 122 *bl* OSF; 123 *t* Warren Photographic; 124 *b* OSF; 125 *tr* STILL Pictures, *cl* NHPA; 127 *c* Warren Photographic; 128 *cl* Warren Photographic, *tc* Warren Photographic; 129 *l* Warren Photographic; 130 *bl* NHPA; *r* STILL Pictures; 132 *t* OSF; 133 *cr* Warren Photographic, *br* NHPA; 134–135 *b* Warren Photographic; 135 *t* Warren Photographic, *c* Warren Photographic; 136 *c* Warren Photographic, *b* Warren Photographic; 137 *tr* Warren Photographic; 138 *bc* OSF; 138–139 *t* Warren Photographic; 139 *br* Warren Photographic; 140 *cr* Warren Photographic, *t* Warren Photographic; 141 *bl* Warren Photographic; 142 *tr* Warren Photographic; 142–143 *b* Warren Photographic; 143 *tr* Warren Photographic; 144–145 *t* Warren Photographic, *b* Warren Photographic; 146 *b* Warren Photographic; 147 *tr* Warren Photographic, *br* NHPA; 148–149 *c* Warren Photographic; 149 *tr* Warren Photographic, *cr* NHPA; 150 *b* Warren Photographic; 151 *tr* OSF; 152 *tl* OSF, *br* OSF; 153 *br* Warren Photographic, *b* NHPA; 154 *c* Warren Photographic, *tr* Warren Photographic; 155 *t* Warren Photographic, *bl* Warren Photographic, *cl* Warren Photographic; 156 *bc* OSF; 156–157 *t* NHPA; 157 *c* NHPA; 158 *tr* Warren Photographic, *cl* Warren Photographic; 159 *l* Warren Photographic; 160 *br* Warren Photographic; 161 *b* Warren Photographic; 162 *bc* OSF; 163 *c* OSF, *tr* OSF; 164 *bl* NHPA; 165 *tr* Warren Photographic, *br* Warren Photographic; 166 *tr* Warren Photographic, *bl* NHPA; 167 *bc* Warren Photographic, *b* STILL Pictures; 168 *bc* Warren Photographic; 168–169 *c* Warren Photographic; 169 *tc* Warren Photographic; 170 *l* Warren Photographic; 171 *br* OSF; 172 *tl* Warren Photographic; 173 *b* Warren Photographic; 174 *b* OSF; 175 *tr* STILL Pictures; 176 *l* NHPA, *t* Warren Photographic; 177 *l* Warren Photographic; 178 *cl* NHPA; 179 *b* Warren Photographic, *tc* NHPA; 180 *cr* NHPA, *l* OSF; 181 *tr* STILL Pictures; 182 *l* OSF; 183 *tl* OSF; 184–185 *t* Warren Photographic; 185 *t* Warren Photographic; 186 *bl* NHPA; 187 *tr* NHPA, *l* NHPA; 188 *cl* Warren Photographic; 188–189 *t* Warren Photographic; 189 *tr* NHPA; 190 *bl* Warren Photographic, *tr* Warren Photographic; 191 *c* Warren Photographic; 191 *tr* Warren Photographic; 192 *bl* Warren Photographic, *tr* Warren Photographic; 192–193 *b* Warren Photographic; 194 *cr* Warren Photographic, *t* Warren Photographic; 195 *br* Warren Photographic; 196 *l* Warren Photographic, *tr* Warren Photographic; 197 *tc* Warren Photographic; 198 *bl* Warren Photographic; 199 *tl* Warren Photographic; 200 *b* Warren Photographic; 201 *tc* Warren Photographic; 202 *bl* NHPA; 203 *tc* Warren Photographic; 204 *c* Warren Photographic; 205 *cr* STILL Pictures; 206 *l* Warren Photographic; 207 *br* OSF; 208 *l* Warren Photographic; 209 *tr* Warren Photographic; 210 *cl* OSF, *bl* OSF; 211 *l* NHPA, *tr* OSF; 212 *l* Warren Photographic; 213 *cr* Warren Photographic; 214 *c* Warren Photographic; 215 *br* Warren Photographic; 216 *b* Warren Photographic; 217 *r* Warren Photographic; 218 *l* Warren Photographic; 219 *bl* Warren Photographic; 220 *tr* NHPA, *cl* NHPA; 221 *l* OSF; 222 *c* Warren Photographic; 223 *cr* Warren Photographic; 224 *tc* Warren Photographic; 225 *tr* Warren Photographic, *br* NHPA; 226 *bl* NHPA; 227 *tr* NHPA, *bc* NHPA; 228 *bl* Warren Photographic; 229 *tr* Warren Photographic, *bl* Warren Photographic; 230 *cl* NHPA; 231 *tr* OSF, *br* Warren Photographic; 232 *t* Floyd Sayers, *cl* NHPA; 233 *cr* NHPA, *br* NHPA; 234 *tr* NHPA, *l* Ardea; 235 *bc* OSF, *tr* NHPA; 236 *br* OSF; 237 *b* OSF; 238 *cr* Warren Photographic; 239 *bl* Warren Photographic, *cr* Warren Photographic, *br* NHPA; 240 *tr* NHPA; 241 *c* NHPA, *t* NHPA; 242 *cl* OSF; 243 *br* OSF, *tl* OSF, *tr* NHPA; 244 *bl* Warren Photographic, *tr* NHPA, *cl* NHPA; 245 *br* NHPA; 246 *tr* STILL Pictures, *bl* Warren Photographic; 247 *tc* Floyd Sayers, *c* NHPA; 248 *bl* Planet Earth Pictures; 249 *cl* Planet Earth Pictures, *r* Planet Earth Pictures; 250 *cr* Warren Photographic; 251 *br* OSF, *cr* OSF; 252 *t* Warren Photographic; 253 *cr* OSF, *br* Warren Photographic; 254 *l* Warren Photographic, *tr* Warren Photographic; 255 *cr* OSF, *br* Warren Photographic, *cl* Warren Photographic; 256 *br* OSF, *cl* OSF; 257 *br* OSF, *t* Warren Photographic; 258–259 *b* Planet Earth Pictures; 259 *t* Planet Earth Pictures; 260 *cl* OSF; 260–261 *c* OSF; 262 *cl* Planet Earth Pictures, *bl* Ardea; 263 *l* Planet Earth Pictures; 264 *r* Ardea; 265 *tc* OSF, *br* NHPA; 266 *tr* Warren Photographic, *cl* Warren Photographic; 267 *tr* Warren Photographic, *cr* NHPA, *br* NHPA; 268 *cl* Ardea; 268–269 *t* Ardea; 269 *tr* NHPA, *bl* Ardea; 270 *tl* OSF, *tr* Warren Photographic; 271 *tl* OSF, *br* Warren Photographic; 272 *tr* Warren Photographic, *tc* NHPA; 273 *bl* OSF, 274 *l* Warren Photographic; 275 *bl* OSF, *tr* OSF; 276 *tr* STILL Pictures, *tl* Warren Photographic, *cl* NHPA; 277 *tl* OSF, *br* Warren Photographic; 278 *t* Gallo Images (SA); 279 *l* OSF; 280 *tr* STILL Pictures, *bl* OSF; 281 *b* STILL Pictures; 282 *bl* NHPA; 282–283 *c* Ardea; 283 *c* Warren Photographic, *br* Warren Photographic; 284 *b* Warren Photographic; 285 *cr* STILL Pictures, *cr* OSF; 286 *bl* Warren Photographic, *r* NHPA; 287 *cr* Warren Photographic, *br* Warren Photographic; 288 *c* OSF; 289 *br* Warren Photographic, *tr* NHPA; 290–291 *t* Warren Photographic; 291 *tr* NHPA, *cr* NHPA; 292 *bl* Warren Photographic, *tr* Warren Photographic; 293 *cr* NHPA; 294 *bl* Warren Photographic, *tr* NHPA; 295 *t* NHPA; 296 *b* STILL Pictures; 297 *r* Warren Photographic; 298 *c* Warren Photographic; 298–299 *t* Warren Photographic, *b* Warren Photographic; 300 *cl* Warren Photographic, *b* NHPA; 301 *cr* Warren Photographic; 302 *bl* Warren Photographic; 303 *l* NHPA; 304 *tl* Warren Photographic; 307 *br* Warren Photographic.